Thomas Hardy
Selected Poems

Longman Annotated Texts

General Editors:

Charlotte Brewer, Hertford College, Oxford
H.R. Woudhuysen, University College London
Daniel Karlin, University College London

Published Titles:

Michael Mason, *Lyrical Ballads*

Alexandra Barratt, *Women's Writing in Middle English*

Tim Armstrong, *Thomas Hardy: Selected Poems*

Thomas Hardy
Selected Poems

Edited by
Tim Armstrong

LONGMAN
London and New York

Longman Group UK Limited,
Longman House, Burnt Mill,
Harlow, Essex CM20 2JE, England
and Associated Companies throughout the world.

Published in the United States of America
by Longman Publishing, New York

© Longman Group UK Limited 1993

All rights reserved; no part of this publication may be
reproduced, stored in a retrieval system, or transmitted
in any form or by any means, electronic, mechanical,
photocopying, recording, or otherwise without either the
prior written permission of the Publishers or a licence
permitting restricted copying in the United Kingdom issued
by the Copyright Licensing Agency Ltd,
90 Tottenham Court Road, London W1P 9HE.

First published 1993

ISBN 0 582 040515 CSD
ISBN 0 582 040612 PPR

British Library Cataloguing-in-Publication Data

A catalogue record for this book is
available from the British Library

Library of Congress Cataloging-in-Publication Data

Hardy, Thomas, 1840–1928.
  [Poems. Selections]
  Thomas Hardy – selected poems / edited by Tim Armstrong.
    p. cm. – (Longman annotated texts)
  Includes bibliographical references and index.
  ISBN 0-582-04051-5. – ISBN 0-582-04061-2 (pbk.)
  I. Armstrong, Tim, 1956– . II. Title. III. Series.
PR4741.A75 1993
821'.8 – dc20   92-44541
                                                                 CIP

Set by 8FF in 10/12pt Ehrhardt
Produced by Longman Singapore Publishers (Pte) Ltd.
Printed in Singapore

Contents

Acknowledgements	xii
List of abbreviations	xiii
Chronology	xv
Introduction	1
Hardy's 'second' career	1
Turning to poetry	1
Poetry as posthumous vision	4
Necessity and free will	7
Typology and the pattern of a life	10
Sequences and patterns	14
God and history	16
Hardy and the dead	19
The 'Poems of 1912–13'	22
Restoration and the past	26
Wessex	28
Hardy's style	30
The Gothic art-principle	31
Words	32
Prosody	35
Hardy and literary tradition	40
Selecting Hardy	42
A note on the annotations	44
A Note on the Text	45

The Poems 47

From *Wessex Poems and Other Verses* (1898) 49

1. The Temporary the All 50
2. Hap 52
3. Neutral Tones 53
4. The Peasant's Confession 55
5. A Sign-Seeker 60
6. Friends Beyond 63
7. Thoughts of Phena 65
8. Nature's Questioning 67
9. In a Eweleaze near Weatherbury 69
10. 'I look into my glass' 70

From *Poems of the Past and the Present* (1901) 72

11. V.R. 1819–1901 73
12. Drummer Hodge 74
13. The Souls of the Slain 76
14. Rome: Building a New Street in the Ancient Quarter 80
15. Rome: At the Pyramid of Cestius near the Graves of Shelley and Keats 81
16. A Commonplace Day 82
17. To an Unborn Pauper Child 84
18. Her Reproach 86
19. His Immortality 87
20. Winter in Durnover Field 88
21. The Darkling Thrush 88
22. The Respectable Burgher on 'The Higher Criticism' 91
23. The Self-Unseeing 93
24. In Tenebris I 94
25. In Tenebris II 96
26. In Tenebris III 98
27. Tess's Lament 100
28. Sapphic Fragment 102
29. 'ΑΓΝΩΣΤΩι ΘΕΩι 103

From *Time's Laughingstocks and Other Verses* (1909) 105

30. The Revisitation 106
31. A Trampwoman's Tragedy 112
32. In the Mind's Eye 117
33. He Abjures Love 117
34. Let Me Enjoy 119
35. Julie-Jane 120

36	The Dead Quire	121
37	Night in the Old Home	126
38	After the Last Breath	127
39	One We Knew	128
40	George Meredith, 1828–1909	130
41	Yell'ham Wood's Story	131
42	A Young Man's Epigram on Existence	132

From *Satires of Circumstance, Lyrics and Reveries* (1914) 133

43	In Front of the Landscape	134
44	Channel Firing	137
45	The Convergence of the Twain	138
46	'When I set out for Lyonnesse'	141
47	Wessex Heights	143
48	A Singer Asleep	145
49	Self-Unconscious	148
50	Under the Waterfall	150

'Poems of 1912–13' 151

51	The Going	153
52	Your Last Drive	155
53	The Walk	156
54	Rain on a Grave	157
55	'I found her out there'	158
56	Without Ceremony	160
57	Lament	161
58	The Haunter	163
59	The Voice	164
60	His Visitor	166
61	A Circular	167
62	A Dream or No	167
63	After a Journey	169
64	A Death-Day Recalled	171
65	Beeny Cliff	172
66	At Castle Boterel	173
67	Places	175
68	The Phantom Horsewoman	177
69	The Spell of the Rose	178
70	St Launce's Revisited	180
71	Where the Picnic Was	181
72	The Obliterate Tomb	183

73	The Workbox	187
74	Exeunt Omnes	188
75	A Poet	190
76	In the Cemetery	191

From *Moments of Vision and Miscellaneous Verses* (1917) — 192

77	Moments of Vision	193
78	The Voice of Things	194
79	Apostrophe to an Old Psalm Tune	195
80	At the Word 'Farewell'	196
81	Heredity	197
82	Near Lanivet, 1872	198
83	Copying Architecture in an Old Minster	199
84	To Shakespeare	201
85	Quid Hic Agis?	203
86	On a Midsummer Eve	206
87	The Blinded Bird	206
88	The Statue of Liberty	207
89	The Change	209
90	Lines to a Movement in Mozart's E-Flat Symphony	211
91	The Pedigree	212
92	His Heart: A Woman's Dream	215
93	The Oxen	216
94	The Photograph	217
95	The Last Signal	218
96	The Figure in the Scene	219
97	Overlooking the River Stour	220
98	The Musical Box	222
99	Old Furniture	223
100	The Five Students	225
101	The Wind's Prophecy	226
102	During Wind and Rain	228
103	A Backward Spring	230
104	He Revisits His First School	231
105	'I thought, my Heart'	232
106	The Shadow on the Stone	233
107	'For Life I had never cared greatly'	234
108	The Pity of It	236
109	In Time of 'The Breaking of Nations'	237
110	A New Year's Eve in War Time	239
111	'I looked up from my writing'	241
112	Afterwards	242

Contents

From *Late Lyrics and Earlier* (1922)   244

113	Weathers	253
114	'According to the Mighty Working'	254
115	The Contretemps	255
116	'And There Was a Great Calm'	257
117	The Selfsame Song	259
118	At Lulworth Cove a Century Back	260
119	The Collector Cleans His Picture	261
120	On the Tune Called the Old-Hundred-and-Fourth	263
121	Voices from Things Growing in a Churchyard	264
122	After a Romantic Day	266
123	In the Small Hours	267
124	Last Words to a Dumb Friend	268
125	A Drizzling Easter Morning	269
126	'I was the midmost'	270
127	The Inscription	271
128	The Whitewashed Wall	274
129	After Reading Psalms XXXIX, XL, etc.	276
130	Surview	277

From *Human Shows, Far Phantasies, Songs and Trifles* (1925)   279

131	Waiting Both	280
132	A Bird-Scene at a Rural Dwelling	280
133	In a Former Resort after Many Years	281
134	A Cathedral Facade at Midnight	282
135	The Monument-Maker	283
136	The Later Autumn	284
137	An East-End Curate	285
138	Sine Prole	286
139	A Sheep Fair	287
140	Snow in the Suburbs	289
141	A Light Snow-Fall after Frost	290
142	Music in a Snowy Street	291
143	In Sherborne Abbey	292
144	The Mock Wife	294
145	'Not only I'	296
146	Her Haunting-Ground	297
147	Days to Recollect	298
148	This Summer and Last	299
149	'Nothing matters much'	300
150	Before My Friend Arrived	301

151	The Bird-Catcher's Boy	301
152	Song to an Old Burden	304
153	'Why do I?'	305

From *Winter Words in Various Moods and Metres* (1928) — 307

154	The New Dawn's Business	309
155	Proud Songsters	310
156	The Prophetess	311
157	A Wish for Unconsciousness	312
158	The Love-Letters	312
159	Throwing a Tree	313
160	Lying Awake	314
161	Childhood Among the Ferns	315
162	A Poet's Thought	316
163	'I watched a blackbird'	317
164	A Nightmare, and the Next Thing	318
165	So Various	319
166	An Evening in Galilee	321
167	We Field-women	323
168	He Never Expected Much	324
169	Standing by the Mantelpiece	325
170	Our Old Friend Dualism	326
171	Drinking Song	327
172	The Aged Newspaper Soliloquizes	331
173	Christmas: 1924	331
174	The Boy's Dream	332
175	Family Portraits	333
176	Christmas in the Elgin Room	335
177	'We are getting to the end'	337
178	He Resolves to Say No More	338

From Hardy's Uncollected Poems — 340

179	Thoughts from Sophocles	340
180	The Eve of Waterloo	342
181	Prologue	344
182	Epilogue	345
183	On One Who Thought No Other Could Write Such English as Himself	346

Selections from Hardy's Autobiography 347

Appendix I: Two Early Versions of Poems by
Hardy   361

Appendix II: Page References in Hardy's
Autobiography   365

Bibliography   367
Index of titles   376
Index of first lines   381

Acknowledgements

For permission to quote from manuscripts I would like to thank the Trustees of the Hardy estate; the Trustees of the Thomas Hardy Memorial Collection; the Dorset County Museum; Birmingham City Museums and Art Gallery; the Bodleian Library, Oxford; the British Library; Fitzwilliam Museum, Cambridge; Magdalene College, Cambridge; Queen's College, Oxford; Yale University. I am grateful to the editor of *Victorian Poetry* for permission to adapt some material from an article which appeared there.

This volume would not be possible without the work of previous annotators of Hardy's verse and related writings: Richard Little Purdy, J.O. Bailey, F.B. Pinion, Samuel Hynes, Michael Millgate, Elizabeth Hickson, Dennis Taylor. I am similarly indebted to the many other critics whose work is referred to here. I would also like to thank the following for specific information and assistance: Matthew Campbell, F.B. Pinion, Barbara Rosenbaum, Dennis Taylor, Sue Wiseman.

List of abbreviations

The following abbreviations are used throughout:

Björk   *The Literary Notebooks of Thomas Hardy*, ed. Lennart A. Björk, 2 vols (London: Macmillan, 1986). Quoted by entry rather than page number.

CL   *The Collected Letters of Thomas Hardy*, ed. Richard Purdy and Michael Millgate, 7 vols (Oxford: Clarendon Press, 1978–88).

CPW   *The Complete Poetical Works of Thomas Hardy*, ed. Samuel Hynes, 3 vols (Oxford: Clarendon Press, 1982–5). The most authoritative modern edition of Hardy's poems.

EL   *The Early Life of Thomas Hardy*, by Florence Emily Hardy (London: Macmillan, 1928). Vol. I of Hardy's disguised autobiography (see Appendix II for collation with other editions).

LY   *The Later Years of Thomas Hardy*, by Florence Emily Hardy (London: Macmillan, 1930). Vol. II of Hardy's disguised autobiography (see Appendix II).

PN   *The Personal Notebooks of Thomas Hardy*, ed. Richard H. Taylor (London: Macmillan, 1978).

PW   *Thomas Hardy's Personal Writings*, ed. Harold Orel (Lawrence: University of Kansas Press, 1966).

SR   *Some Recollections*, by Emma Hardy, ed. Evelyn Hardy and Robert Gittings (London: Macmillan, 1961).

In addition, the following conventions are used in refering to individual editions of Hardy's works in annotations:

WP   *Wessex Poems*. Dates added refer to first edition (1898), and second edition (1903).

PP   *Poems of the Past and the Present*. Dates added refer to first edition (1901), second impression (1902), second (uniform) edition (1903).

TL	*Time's Laughingstocks*. Dates added refer to first edition (1909), second impression (1910).
SC	*Satires of Circumstance*. Dates added refer to first edition (1914), second impression (1915).
SP	*Selected Poems*, chosen by Thomas Hardy (1916).
MV	*Moments of Vision*. Dates added refer to first edition (1917), Uniform Edition (1919).
WE	Wessex Edition (1912–31). Dates added refer to Verse Vol. I (1912), Verse Vol. III (1913), Verse Vol. IV (1919), Verse Vol. V (1926).
CP	*Collected Poems*. Dates added refer to editions of 1919, 1923, 1928.
LL	*Late Lyrics and Earlier* (1922).
HS	*Human Shows* (1925).
WW	*Winter Words* (1928).

All page references to Hardy's novels are to the New Wessex Edition. Hardy's autobiography is cited from the two-volume original publication, but Appendix II collates page numbers in this edition with the one-volume edition, *The Life of Thomas Hardy, 1840–1928* (London, 1962), and with the recent 'restored' version, *The Life and Work of Thomas Hardy*, ed. Michael Millgate (London, 1985). References to the Bible are to the Authorized Version, but the text of the Psalms used is that of Coverdale's translation in the *Book of Common Prayer* (i.e. the version sung in church, which Hardy usually remembered).

Chronology

1840	Thomas Hardy born at Higher Bockhampton, Dorset (2 June), his father a builder and small-holder.
1848–56	Attends village school in Lower Bockhampton. After a year moves to a school in Dorchester. Teaches at Sunday school.
1856–61	Articled to John Hicks, a Dorchester architect. Meets William Barnes, Dorset poet, and Horace Moule, son of the vicar of Fordington. Studies Latin and Greek in spare time.
1857	Death of Mary Head Hardy, his paternal grandmother, the source of many family stories.
1862–7	Moves to London and works for the architect Arthur Blomfield. Reads widely in English poetry, writes verse. Probably a disappointed love affair in this period, alluded to in some poems.
1863	Wins prize for his essay 'The Application of Coloured Bricks and Terra Cotta to Modern Architecture'.
1865	Essay 'How I Built Myself a House' published in *Chambers's Journal*.
1867	Poor health forces him to return to Dorset. Works for Hicks again, and later for G.R. Crickmay in Weymouth. Begins his first novel, 'The Poor Man and the Lady' (unpublished, later destroyed).
1868–9	Submits novel to Macmillans and to Chapman and Hall, receives sufficient encouragement from the latter's reader (George Meredith) to begin *Desperate Remedies*. It has been suggested that Hardy had some kind of liaison with his cousin Tryphena Sparks in this period.
1870	Sent to St Juniot, Cornwall, to supervise church restoration (March). Meets and falls in love with

	Emma Lavinia Gifford (b. 1840).
1871	*Desperate Remedies* published. Moves between London, Weymouth, Cornwall.
1872	*Under the Greenwood Tree* published; *A Pair of Blue Eyes* appears serially in *Tinsley's Magazine*.
1873	Horace Moule kills himself in Cambridge.
1874	*Far From the Madding Crowd* published in the *Cornhill Magazine*, to great acclaim. Hardy marries Emma Gifford (September). They settle in Surbiton, outside London, but move again twice in the next year.
1876	They move to Yeovil, then to Riverside Villa, Sturminster Newton for two years (later remembered as the 'idyll'). *The Hand of Ethelberta* published.
1878	Move to London again. *The Return of the Native* published.
1880	*The Trumpet-Major* published. The Hardys visit Europe. Hardy falls seriously ill later that year.
1881	Move to Wimbourne, Dorset. *A Laodicean* published.
1882	*Two in a Tower* published.
1883	Move to Dorchester. Work begins on 'Max Gate', the house Hardy designed for himself (completed 1885).
1886	*The Mayor of Casterbridge* published. Hardy begins to plan *The Dynasts*, his epic-drama of the Napoleonic Wars.
1887	*The Woodlanders* published. Visit to Italy.
1888	*Wessex Tales* published. Visit to Paris.
1891	*A Group of Noble Dames* published. *Tess of the D'Urbervilles* published serially, somewhat bowdlerized, and then in book form. Its success assures Hardy's financial security. In this period, their marriage deteriorates. Emma keeps a notebook detailing her feelings about him.
1892	Hardy's father dies. *The Well-Beloved* published serially.
1893	Hardy meets (Mrs) Florence Henniker on a visit to Ireland, and becomes infatuated with her. He spends increasingly long periods in London.
1894	*Life's Little Ironies* published. In London again, April–August.
1895	*Jude the Obscure* published, to a hostile reception. Hardy decides to abandon novel-writing, but continues to write poetry.
1896	Visit to Flanders and Waterloo. The Hardys take up cycling.
1897	*The Well-Beloved* published in book form. Visit to Switzerland.

1898	First volume of poetry, *Wessex Poems*, appears to mixed reviews.
1899	Outbreak of Boer War. Hardy begins a series of war poems.
1901	*Poems of the Past and the Present* published.
1904	First volume of *The Dynasts* published. Hardy's mother dies (3 April).
1905	Hardy meets Florence Emily Dugdale (b. 1879), later advising her on her writing and having her undertake research for him.
1906	*The Dynasts*, Part II published.
1908	*The Dynasts*, Part III published. Hardy's edition of William Barnes's poetry published.
1909	Meredith dies (18 May) and Hardy succeeds him as President of the Society of Authors. *Time's Laughingstocks* published.
1910	Hardy made an O.M. (Order of Merit), having declined a knighthood.
1912	The Wessex Edition of Hardy's novels (and poems to date) published. Emma Hardy dies (27 November). Hardy discovers her notebooks, and begins to write his elegiac sequence the 'Poems of 1912–13'.
1913	Revisits the scenes of his courtship in Cornwall (March).
1914	Marries Florence Dugdale (10 February). Outbreak of First World War. *Satires of Circumstance*, including the 'Poems of 1912–13', published.
1915	His sister Mary dies (24 November).
1916	*Selected Poems* published, chosen by Hardy. Last visit to Cornwall.
1917	*Moments of Vision* published. Begins his disguised autobiography.
1919	The first *Collected Poems* published. Wessex Edition continues.
1920	Honorary degree from Oxford. A *de luxe* edition of his works, the Mellstock Edition, published. Reads Einstein.
1922	*Late Lyrics and Earlier* published.
1923	*The Famous Tragedy of the Queen of Cornwall* published.
1924	*Tess of the D'Urbervilles* adapted for the stage by 'The Hardy Players' in Dorchester. Hardy is captivated by Gertrude Bugler as 'Tess'.
1925	*Human Shows, Far Fantasies, Songs, and Trifles* published.
1927	Revises and rearranges *Selected Poems* (it appears

	posthumously as *Chosen Poems*).
1928	Hardy dies (11 January). His heart is buried in Dorset, and his ashes in Westminster Abbey. *Winter Words* appears posthumously. The first volume of his autobiography, *The Early Life of Thomas Hardy*, is published as the work of Florence Hardy.
1930	*The Later Years of Thomas Hardy*, again mostly written by Hardy, is published under Florence's name.
1937	Florence Hardy dies.
1940	Kate Hardy, the last of the family, dies a few months after the hundredth anniversary of Thomas Hardy's birthday.

Introduction

Hardy's 'second' career
Turning to poetry

Hardy's career as a poet is unique. After writing poetry in the 1860s, in the way that any young man with literary ambitions might, he established himself as a major Victorian novelist. When his novel-writing came to an end in 1895, he began a second career as a poet. The bulk of his poetry was thus produced between his fifty-fifth birthday and his death at the age of 87 (the exceptions are a number of poems first drafted in the 1860s: around sixty poems can be dated before 1890, including seven in this selection, though a number of other undated poems undoubtedly use early material). Though the late careers of poets like Victor Hugo and Wallace Stevens provide a comparison, few poets have written so well in late life. One set of questions presented by Hardy's poetic career is thus: To what extent is he a 'Victorian' poet? What was the impact of a career that was undertaken after an established career as a novelist? How did he sustain his writing? What were Hardy's own explanations of his continued productivity?

The reasons for Hardy's abandonment of the novel are complex. The motive he often gave was the hostile receptions of *Tess of the D'Urbervilles* and *Jude the Obscure*. Public controversy was matched by private hostility as he became estranged from his increasingly evangelical wife, Emma, who felt betrayed by the latter novel's bitter reflections on marriage and religion. He may also, Michael Mason suggests, have found public praise of these radical novels as hard to accept as blame, since he did not wish to become an apostle of free-thought (Mason 1988). As well as these external forces, the internal dynamics of the late novels involve a collapse of those structures which inform the Victorian novel: in *Jude the Obscure* family, succession, stable rural environment, and the possibilities of a future vanish (Said 1975: 137–9). Given that the novels had become the testaments of a failure of hope, he could not easily have written on.

Whatever the reasons for Hardy's abandonment of the novel, the mid–1890s were a period for crisis for him, as the 'In Tenebris' sequence and other poems of the period suggest. In the disguised third-person autobiography which he later wrote, he commented that 'His personal ambition in a worldly sense, which had always been weak, dwindled to nothing, and for some years after 1895 or 1896 he requested that no record of his life should be made. His verses he kept on writing from pleasure in them' (*LY* 84). Poetry, here, is seen as a private voice, dissociated from the 'worldly' ambitions of the novelist; the poems form a ghostly supplement to his public life, free from its problems of self-presentation – as Hardy implies in 'Wessex Heights' (47), contrasting the prose struggles of the 'lowlands' with the aloofness of the 'heights'. Yet once he was established as a poet Hardy refused to accept the idea that his poetic career was in any sense secondary. Poetry was, he later claimed, his *original* impulse, to which he was returning (*LY* 185). His attitude to his late career is thus complex, and relates to the status of poetry as both a kind of 'after-writing' (suggested by the poems which borrow from the novels), and a temporarily suppressed original impulse, even the core of his work.

Clearly the idea that Hardy was always a poet was, as Paul Zeitlow puts it, 'a myth of retrospective self-justification' (Zeitlow 1974: 42). In publishing poetry he was attempting to enter a new field, and inevitably encountered suggestions that he should have stuck to his old trade. There is ample evidence of how seriously he took his second career: his bitter disappointment at reviews of his poetry; his use of poems on public events to raise his profile (the Boer War, the turn of the century, the death of the Queen, even the *Titanic* disaster); his research into prosody in the British Museum, with the aim of extending his technical range. We can trace a gradual increase in his self-confidence as he published volume after volume: in 1898, 1901, 1909, 1914, 1917, 1922, 1925, and (posthumously) 1928. The 'General Preface' to his works, which he wrote in 1911, is a good marker here: it imagines poetry as part of 'a fairly comprehensive cycle': 'I had wished that those in dramatic, ballad, and narrative form should include most of the cardinal situations which occur in social and public life, and those in lyric form a round of emotional experiences of some completeness' (*PW* 49–50). By this stage he is clearly thinking of a whole poetic corpus, not something done purely 'for pleasure'.

Hardy's increasing self-confidence as a poet had a number of sources apart from the actual publication and increasingly respectful reviews of his individual volumes. One was the publication of his

Napoleonic epic *The Dynasts* in three volumes in 1904, 1906, and 1908. *The Dynasts*, for all its lukewarm reception, established Hardy as a kind of national laureate (selections were dramatized as a morale-boosting play during the war); a status confirmed by the Order of Merit conferred on him by the king in 1910. It was also in this period that Hardy became fully established as the resident genius (and copyright-holder) of 'Wessex', the name of the ancient kingdom which became the designated space of his novels. His awareness of his own status is peculiarly reflected in the two-volume autobiography which he began around 1917 and which – in one of the oddest acts of literary ventriloquism ever seen – was to be published posthumously as his second wife Florence's work. Though the imposture was doomed to failure, the *Life* (to use the convenient title of the one-volume edition) seems to have been important to Hardy in its 'fixing' of his public image, its establishment of a version of himself for posterity.

In a related way, Hardy also needed a psychological justification for his new career, an explanation for why a poet would continue to write. His notebook entries in the period after the turn of the century show a fascination with the late careers of other artists: Sophocles, Rembrandt, Wagner, Turner, Ibsen, and 'that amazing old man – Verdi', with his 'phoenix-like' second career (Björk entries 2309–10). He was seeking models. In 1906 he wrote after a concert:

> I prefer late Wagner, as I prefer late Turner, to early ... the idiosyncrasies of each master being more strongly shown in these strains. When a man not contented with the grounds of his success goes on and on, and tries to achieve the impossible, then he gets profoundly interesting to me. To-day it was early Wagner for the most part: fine music, but not so particularly his – no spectacle of the inside of a brain at work like the inside of a hive. (*LY* 117)

Here the implication is that the interest of old age lies in a pursuit of the individual, of 'idiosyncrasy', in continued ambition, and in the 'spectacle' of the working brain. The latter metaphor is particularly important because Hardy uses it in *The Dynasts* to describe the Will, figured as a giant brain gradually coming to consciousness. The process of awareness itself is the focus of attention – as in a number of other passages which Hardy excerpted into his notebooks in this period, including references to Henry James on the brain as a refracting medium (Björk entry 2462), on how Victor Hugo's 'supreme enjoyment was the exercise of his own brain' (Björk entry 2252). Such passages reflect Hardy's developing sense of a liberated subjectivity in his own writings, involving a 'lyric' self which was not subject to the same scrutiny as the supposedly 'realistic' novelist (see Wilson 1976; Armstrong 1988a).

Another important aspect of this acceptance of himself as the proper subject of his poems is suggested by a notebook entry copied from *The Nation* in late 1908:

> An artist's *self* – The most difficult thing in the world for any artist to achieve ... is to express himself, to strike out a style of writing which shall be as natural to him as the character of handwriting is to ordinary men. It is a truism to say that individuality is the last quality to be developed in a man. (Björk entry 2348)

For Hardy, his own 'individuality' was similarly latent, emerging fully in his late flowering as a poet, and particularly in the lyrics in which he meditates on the course of his own life. As we shall see, 'latency' is an idea which permeates Hardy's late career, from his interest in the theories of writers like Henri Bergson (whose *Creative Evolution* postulated a universe only slowly becoming aware of itself) to the plots of many of his most important poems. It also explains why he could continue to write: 'Among those who accomplished late, the poet spark must always have been latent; but its outspringing may have been frozen and delayed for half a lifetime' (*LY* 184). In the same way, the materials of his poetry are buried beneath the surface of consciousness and revealed by time: 'I have a faculty ... for burying an emotion in my heart or brain for forty years, and exhuming it at the end of that time as fresh as when interred' (*LY* 178). Poetry belatedly becomes the plot of his life, at the same time as the plot of his life becomes a story of belated recognition.

Poetry as posthumous vision

Hardy's late sense of poetic freedom seems to have been intensified by the fact that from the point of view of the outside world Hardy the grand old man was already a part of posterity, invisible behind the trees surrounding his house, Max Gate, his autobiography written, his portraits painted, and his manuscripts donated to national collections. He might have been already dead, and indeed being 'already' dead had existed as a possibility in Hardy's poetry from its inception, as part of a posture of protective self-effacement. In a conversation recorded in 1901 Hardy called this the stance of a 'ghost-seer' (Archer 1904: 37). In a diary entry in 1888 he describes the source of his 'detachment':

> For my part, if there is any way of getting a melancholy satisfaction out of life it lies in dying, so to speak, before one is out of the flesh; by

which I mean putting on the manners of ghosts, wandering in their haunts, and taking their views of surrounding things. To think of life as passing away is a sadness; to think of it as past is at least tolerable. (*EL* 275)

This sense of ghostliness is partly a product of that self-protective invisibility which sustains Hardy's career after the public controversy of the last novels, and the move to verse. In 'He Revisits His First School' (104) he cries:

> I should not have shown in the flesh,
> I ought to have gone as a ghost;
> It was awkward, unseemly almost,
> Standing solidly there as when fresh ...

Being disembodied, an observing eye, involves a self-protective minimalism which insists on 'neutral tones', a muted vision which guards the self. 'He Never Expected Much' he says in one title (168), and so could not be disappointed. Margaret Mahar (1978: 316) comments that:

> If *Jude the Obscure* was written from the perspective of the end, much of this poetry is written from a further perspective, beyond the end. That is not eternity but a time rather like Emily Dickinson's midnight, that moment when a fly buzzes, and both life and death are held at bay.

Hardy – who copied Emily Dickinson's '"I died for beauty"' into his notebook – often writes from this 'suspended' perspective, particularly in his great series of night and dawn meditations. In '"I looked up from my writing"' (111) he literally sees death (in the form of the moon) going about his business; in 'The New Dawn's Business' (154) he is passed over by death since he is, implicitly, already in that state; and in the final poem of *Moments of Vision* he writes about his own death from beyond the grave.

Hardy's sense of ghostliness is related to the actual structure of his career, as well as his natural self-protectiveness. After the death of his wife, Emma, in 1912 (and of a number of family members in the same period), he habitually saw himself as a ghost in a more literal sense: a remnant of a dying family and of dead passions, a 'dead man held on end', as he puts it in 'The Going' (51), buffeted by Fate, his emotional life behind him. Importantly, the earlier self-protective attitude and the later outcome are related. What had earlier been a protective distance from life helps create a tragic plot of failed communication with Emma, and, in 'The Going', Hardy's minimalism becomes the subject of self-accusation:

Here, a brief comment becomes an entire mode of vision, for the poet awaiting his own death.

Necessity and free will

Hardy's sense of the fragility of his self is closely related to his vision of the universe as alien, driven by Necessity, with human life dwarfed by its forces. In part this is a view which Hardy absorbed from nineteenth-century science, with its positivism, emphasis on a mechanical nature, and an implicit dualism which saw the self opposed to the forces of 'outer nature'. Here, for example, is a passage from John Morley which Hardy excerpted approvingly into his notebooks in the 1870s:

> *All phenomena are necessary.* No creature in the universe, in its circumstances and according to its given prophecy, can act otherwise than as it does act. Fire burns whatever combustible matter comes within the sphere of its action. Man necessarily desires what either is, or seems to be, conductive to his comfort and wellbeing. There is no independent energy, no isolated cause, no detached activity, in a universe where all things are incessantly acting on one another, and which is itself only one eternal round of movement, imparted and undergone, according to necessary laws.
>
> (*Fortnightly Review* 22: 268–9; Björk entries 1065–6)

In such a universe, free will is only an illusion, the product of humankind's restricted knowledge. Indeed, Hardy often saw human consciousness as an epiphenomenon – an accidental development in evolutionary terms, which leaves the self stranded and exposed in a world which has not developed to a point where it is suitable for thought. The 'coming universal wish not to live' in *Jude the Obsure* is a product of this painful over-extension, as is the wish for unconsciousness or death expressed in poems like 'To an Unborn Pauper Child' (17), the 'In Tenebris' series (24–6) and 'Thoughts from Sophocles' (179).

Hardy's relation to the 'problem' of free will is a complex one. His own 'solution' when pressed on the issue was placed within the context of his invention, in 'The Dynasts', of the idea of a Will of the Universe which represents necessity. It is within consciousness that what we call 'freedom' lies:

> The will of man is ... neither wholly free nor wholly unfree. When swayed by the Universal Will (which he mostly must be as a subservient part of it) he is not individually free; but whenever it happens that all the rest of the Great Will is in equilibrium the minute portion called one person's will is free, just as a performer's fingers are free to go on

playing the pianoforte of themselves when he talks or thinks of something else and the head does not rule them. (*LY* 125)

There are thus moments of freedom, or perhaps understanding, within the context of what Hardy often calls the 'web' of fate, which rules human life and history; but such moments only exist where the forces of fate are in equilibrium. As we shall see, they are also usually moments of retrospection.

The outcome of a view of the world like that sketched above is apparent throughout Hardy's poetry. In many poems, like 'The Wind's Prophecy' (101), nature is a vast, hostile machine; in others the corpse-like wasteland portrayed in 'The Darkling Thrush' (21), bereft of meaning except that which human beings project onto it. Again and again Hardy's poems deal with the isolated figures in a landscape – the subject of romantic lyrics like Wordsworth's 'The Solitary Reaper' – often in outline against the sky. In a hostile universe, the nature of individual perceptions which are 'projected' by the individual are what determine its subjective qualities. An 1865 diary entry states that 'the poetry of a scene varies with the minds of the perceivers. Indeed, it does not lie in the scene at all' (*EL* 66). The outcome of such an epistemology is a series of poems in which the mind's ability to project emotions onto a landscape is foregrounded, whether in direct and self-conscious inscription, as in Hardy's most ecstatic elegies, like 'At Castle Boterel' (66), or in something like the 'tide of visions' which overwhelms the poet in 'In Front of the Landscape' (43) – denizens of that 'dream-world of phantoms and spectres, the inexplicable swarm and equivocal generation of motions in our own brains' which Coleridge describes in the *Biographia Literaria* (ch. 8) as the inevitable outcome of any Idealist system.

Hardy's most intense poems, and those most centrally in the tradition of what M.H. Abrams calls the 'Greater Romantic Lyric', typically involve either a visionary pilgrimage across a barren landscape – 'The Wind's Prophecy' (101), '"For Life I had never cared greatly"' (107), or a retrospective which takes in a whole life, tracing its determined patterns – 'Quid Hic Agis?' (85), 'During Wind and Rain' (102). A number of poems involve both these features: 'The Five Students' (100) combines the metaphor of life's journey and a visionary retrospective. In a pair of poems, which seem to me at the very core of Hardy's achievement, 'The Pedigree' (91) and 'Family Portraits' (175), the poet watches a 'masque' in which all the central elements of his vision and vocabulary combine in an overwhelming scene which seems to offer the key to his life, and to the processes which have determined it. Heredity is a particular focus of Hardy's sense of entrapment in a Darwinian universe in which the individual is produced by a 'line' of progenitors, whose habits and characteristics he or she repeats. He saw himself as the product of a dying family whose history culminates in his own experience, as poems like 'Heredity' (81) suggest.

In 'The Pedigree' Hardy scans by moonlight the 'sire-sown tree' of his ancestry, with its twisted branches, until he sees a face form, and then a mirroring of that face as a series of faces, regressing before him to the point of origin, 'past surmise and reason's reach'. The outcome is a crisis of self-perception which is repeated at a number of points in Hardy's poetry: the poet faces the question of whether he is a 'mimicker' ('continuator' in the first edition) or is able to assert his own identity. Typically, Hardy here *says* that he is a 'counterfeit' (perhaps remembering the obsolete meaning of that word, 'made to a pattern'), but he *thinks* 'I am I, / And what I do I do myself alone'. Resistance is held within the mind of the poet, just as in Hardy's explanation of free will and necessity the individual is enmeshed in fate, but has in consciousness a measure of freedom. A similar question is posed in 'Family Portraits', published in Hardy's last volume, with what seems a more pessimistic answer. Again there is something akin to what Freud calls the primal scene: the poem presents a masque in which ancestral figures show 'some drama, obscure . . . Whose course begot me', so that again the poet becomes a 'continuator'. The scene will, he says, teach him the secret of his own being, and help him prevent the 'hurt' which is the human lot. But the poet cannot enter this situation: his cry of 'Why wake up all this?' pulls him out of the frame, leaving him to puzzle on the meaning of the drama he has see, still a slave to the Necessity which governs the universe.

In a difficult but useful comment on 'The Pedigree', Mary Jacobus elucidates the self-divison which she sees as producing Hardy's peculiar angle of vision – and helps explain why being 'a dead man held on end' might be productive for Hardy:

> Ultimately, the critical moment in Hardy's writing, that of imagined self-dissolution, permits the threatened or enfeebled consciousness to transfer its own displaced omniscience to the disembodied vision which he calls 'magian', rather than surrendering the fantasy altogether. Or, to put it another way, instead of limiting the grotesque and reconstituting it as irony, Hardy is able in his poetry to move beyond it to something nearer the supernatural. (Jacobus 1982: 275)

Jacobus sees Hardy as replacing the 'I' of authorial authority, which he cannot sustain, with the 'eye' of the disembodied and posthumous viewer who has the vision which the 'person' Hardy has abandoned, seeing all too well his own limitations, weakness, and enslavement to Necessity. In both the poems examined above, Hardy achieves a remarkable self-analysis, akin to that of Wordsworth's confrontation of time, repetition, and loss in 'Tintern Abbey', or Keats's version of his primal scene as a poet in 'Hyperion'; but what is involved is less the Romantic recovery of self than an achieved posthumousness which converts weakness into knowledge, the unfreedom of life into the freedom of suspended consciousness. Life is lived in a state of blindness, but an 'after-life' may be more productive of vision.

Typology and the pattern of a life

One aspect of Hardy's 'ghostliness' is his peculiarly modern sense of the nature of writing. Hardy, perhaps more than any other British writer, is aware of writing as an activity which is intimately bound up with death and the creation of a kind of double of the world – something we associate more closely with European modernism (Rilke, Proust, Kafka, Blanchot, Derrida) than with an English regionalist seemingly anchored in reality. He constantly reminds us that writing is *not* life, that language is predicated on loss, that words fail to fulfil the intentions of those that speak them, or become traps and snares as they 'freeze' lived experience into inappropriate patterns, so that the act of writing itself seems deathly – an 'inditing', to use one of his favourite double-edged words, both a setting-down and an accusation. As J. Hillis Miller puts it, 'For Hardy, it is not minds that generate signs, but minds that are generated, shaped, and coerced, done and undone, by signs' (Miller 1985: 306).

This experience of the interaction of writing and time is often expressed as a form of the system of meanings known as typology – a word seldom used to express Hardy's sense of repetition, but particularly useful because of its relevance to the aesthetics of those Victorians who participated in the Gothic revival (see Landow 1980). Strictly speaking, typology is the technique of biblical interpretation which sees passages in the Old Testament as 'foreshadowing' the life of Christ in the New Testament, as for example Abraham's intended sacrifice of Isaac acting as the 'type' of God's sacrifice of his son (the 'antitype'). This has often been broadened into a more general mode of mapping an earlier text onto a later one, whether the usage was Christian (as in Protestant spiritual autobiography) or more secular, as in Ruskin's vision of the nineteenth-century Gothic as a repetition of the fourteenth century.

Typology is not for Hardy, of course, what it is for someone who believes the Christian scriptures, since the empowering principle behind history – God's providential plan – has been lost. Despite Hardy's deployment of the idea of the 'Immanent Will', he could not help registering the fact that without God typology becomes a cruel irony, or just 'hap', chance. But it does survive as a textual relationship, as a trace of that gap left by the disappearance of god but the persistence of the shape of religion and its texts within human understanding. It becomes a method of interpretation (whether of self-understanding or historical awareness), a structure for the investigation of continuities in experience, and the way in which memory (or the historian) works by mapping earlier experience onto later. It thus registers the human desire for pattern, which both abstracts itself from events and intersects with them across time.

Like most Victorians, Hardy would have been automatically familiar with the typological tradition in hymns, sermons, and art. Holman Hunt's painting 'The Shadow of Death' (completed 1870–73) is one of the most famous examples: the yawning figure of the young carpenter Christ throws a shadow on the wall, prefiguring his Crucifixion. Hardy uses the same image in 'Near Lanivet, 1872' (82), where a woman leans against a handpost:

> She leant back, being so weary, against its stem,
>   And laid her arms on its own,
> Each open palm stretched out to each end of them,
>   Her sad face sideways thrown.
>
> Her white-clothed form at this dim-lit cease of day
>   Made her look as one crucified ...

Both the woman and the narrator understand this ominous sign. And since Hardy tells us that the poem was based on an actual incident involving him and Emma, it is also the plot of his own self-understanding, mapped across his life.

Central to the typological tradition is the doctrine of reserve: the idea that the truth is, for a time, hidden (latent) before being revealed. In a pervasive pattern in Hardy's poetry, he hears a text repeatedly, but only slowly comes to awareness of its importance, so that his inattention becomes part of its meaning at some late point. The result is that he realizes that the story of his life has, in a sense, been written for him. This applies to poems like 'The Mocking Bird' (in which the meaning of a song only becomes apparent when it is too late), and even to 'Standing by the Mantelpiece' (169), in which the gesture at the beginning of the poem is repeated at the end:

> And let the candle-wax thus mould a shape
> Whose meaning now, if hid before, you know ...

Phillip Davis extends this awareness to Hardy's sense of the relationship between his prose and his poetry: the plot of the novels, with their self-delusive characters, becomes the plot of his life; the tragic outcome of his courtship-novel *A Pair of Blue Eyes* or the delusion of Pierston, the hero of *The Well-Beloved*, anticipating his own fate (as it anticipates the plot of his poem 'The Revisitation' (30)). Hardy's sense of belated recognition focuses, in particular, on Emma Hardy's death and his sudden perception of the utter centrality of his love for her to his life. Dennis Taylor calls this awareness 'Hardy's Apocalypse' – Emma's death combined with the shock of the First World War producing a sense that things lying dormant for decades had come to fruition in a terrible climax (Taylor 1981: 88–138). In poem after poem, in *Moments of Vision* (1917) in particular, Hardy traces his life's course and examines its meanings, as in '"Why did I sketch?"' (not included in this selection), with its return to a 'thoughtless day' over forty years earlier:

> Why did I sketch an upland green.
> And put the figure in
> Of one on the spot with me? –
> For now that one has ceased to be seen
> The picture waxes akin
> To a wordless irony.

Hardy's ironies are, despite the latter phrase, deeply implicated in his words, or the words of others – even if words unspoken, since words (like pictures) attempt to 'hold' experience in place. In a late poem he wishes to have 'in a word, no cross to bear' (157), as if suggesting a release from that crucifixion implicit in 'Near Lanivet, 1872' (82).

Hardy's self-defining typology and its use to describe his life's patterns finds a particularly compelling focus in a passage from 1 Kings 19, which describes the prophet Elijah taking refuge in the wilderness near Mount Horeb. The text had deep personal associations: he annotated it frequently in his Bible, and attended church regularly on the 11th Sunday after Trinity ('Still Small Voice Sunday', as he called it) to hear it read as the lesson for that day. It describes how Elijah spent 30 days in the wilderness (a foreshadowing of Christ's time there):

> And behold, the Lord passed by, and a great and strong wind rent the mountains, and brake in pieces the rocks before the Lord; but the Lord was not in the wind: and after the wind an earthquake; but the Lord was not in the earthquake:

And after the earthquake a fire; but the Lord was not in the fire: and after the fire a still small voice ... [which] said, What does thou here, Elijah? (1 Kings 19: 11–13)

Hardy seems to have associated this passage with the aftermath of passion (perhaps specifically with a love-affair of the 1860s). The 'still small' voice which comes after the 'earthquake and fire' speaks for the self in a hostile world – like the voice in the fire in 'Surview' (130), which weaves the story of his life through a series of biblical texts. The text quoted above is taken up in 'Quid Hic Agis?' ('What does thou here?'), Hardy's central typological meditation (85). The 'passage from Kings / Harvest-time brings' is heard in church on three occasions across the years. At first the speaker barely notices it, as Elfride listened distractedly to Knight reading the same passage in *A Pair of Blue Eyes*:

> I did not apprehend
> As I sat to the end
> And watched for her smile
> Across the sunned aisle,
> That this tale of a seer
> Which came once a year
> Might, when sands were heaping,
> Be like a sweat creeping,
> Or in any degree
> Bear on her and on me!

On the second occasion, the narrator reads the lesson himself, but again does not see 'What drought might be / With her, with me'. It is only much later when his beloved is dead and war has come that he registers the fact that the lesson is the truth of his own life, and like Elijah feels 'the shake / Of wind and earthquake, / And consuming fire'.

Built into that structure is a time-equation, a sense that only in re-reading are true meanings released – just as Hardy, in the 'Poems of 1912–13', returns to the text of his courtship novel *A Pair of Blue Eyes* in order to measure his loss. It is this which helps answer those critics who see only sameness in Hardy's poetry – a repetition of fixed themes and topics. That repetition is certainly there; but crucially, it is repetition-within-a-series, or repetition-with-a-difference – a difference whose meaning is always measured in the poems. Just as Hardy sees the regressing 'file' of his progenitors in 'The Pedigree' (91), his poems form sequences which are time-bound, each text mapping onto the next (as 1 Kings 19 maps onto his life) in ever-tangling relationships. One cannot move backward through a series; the origins – or 'fuglemen', as he calls them in 'The Pedigree' – are lost in time. In an analogous way, a reader moves through Hardy's poetic corpus with a deeping sense of prediction, loss, and tragic coherence which is intimately related to a sense of existence in time.

Sequences and patterns

To say that there is a strong sense of chronology in Hardy's tracing of his life's pattern is not to deny the consistency that has led many critics to suggest that Hardy 'lacks development'. Early reviewers of his poetry noticed the recurrence of those topics which help characterize his 'idiosyncratic mode of regard' – Vita Sackville-West greeted *Winter Words* with the comment that 'carpenters are still making coffins; bastards are still born and furtively disposed of; lovers still fail to coincide; the old romance is still evoked and regretted' (*The Nation and Athenaeum*, 13 October 1928). It is possible to characterize his work in terms of recurrent patterns of imagery: the web, the gothic tracery, images relating to drawing, the use of music, the moon, and so on. Similarly his poems can be described in terms of common plots and structures: the plot of 'crossed fidelities' (as R.P. Blackmur called it) which is the subject of so many ballads, or the seasonal lament in which the passing seasons organize the poem, or the journey-poem, or the reverie. Hardy's characteristic topics can often be traced across sequences which span his entire career.

Some of these sequences are formal in origin: the beginning and end-pieces in the later volumes are connected, for example – not least because after the farewell at the end of each volume, possibly to be his last, Hardy had to 'stage' his reappearance in the next. Mary Jacobus writes of the end-pieces: 'These funereal anticipations share a common structure – a self-duplication or doubling that involves an encounter, or, more usually, a dialogue, between Hardy and his ghostly other' (1982: 259). A number of the late opening-groups involve a poem on the poet's 'rebirth' followed by a poem in which he is presented as a detached eye watching a bird-scene which signals a seasonal renewal. In his final opening poem, 'The New Dawn's Business' (154), he places himself in his typical posthumous position, writing of Death 'when men willing are found here / He takes those loth instead'.

As well as beginning and end-pieces, Hardy's ordering of his volumes includes sequences on related subjects, in some of which the poems are placed together – the series of bird-poems culminating in 'The Darkling Thrush' (21) in *Poems of the Past and the Present*; in *Moments of Vision* the three consecutive poems on his Sturminster Newton 'idyll' (see 97), and the three great time-and-journey poems 'The Five Students', 'The Wind's Prophecy', and 'During Wind and Rain' (100–2); the series of six winter-poems beginning with 'Snow in the Suburbs' (140) in *Human Shows*. There are other thematic sequences which are dispersed across his whole career – including poems on trees and leaves, end-of-year meditations, graveyard poems, architectural poems, as well as more general categories which have been isolated for study, such as war-poems and poems on biblical topics or religion.

Hardy's bird-poems provide a good example of such a sequence. As well as providing variations on a topos which runs through the whole of English literature (as exemplified in Peggy Kaufman's *Penguin Book of Bird Poetry*), they involve a profound meditation on the nature of poetry as 'song'. Song is a powerful folk-medium passed on from generation to generation ('The Selfsame Song' (117)); but also carries a negative potential, deceiving as the sound of the mocking-bird is, and like all art encaging the feelings which it seeks to express (as numerous poems on caged birds suggest). As a natural or 'wild' utterance – the 'ecstatic outpourings' of 'The Darkling Thrush' (21) – it implies unself-conscious or unburdened feelings; yet the status of that phrase as an echo of Keats's nightingale tells us that birdsong also represents loss, an echo of some original utterance forever passed away. This meditation spans Hardy's career as a poet, from 'Postponement', the sixth poem of *Wessex Poems*, and 'Shelley's Skylark', the invocation of a tradition near the beginning of *Poems of the Past and the Present*, through to 'The Bird-Catcher's Boy' (151) in *Human Shows*, and '"We are getting to the end"' (177), his penultimate poem.

In particular, bird-poems are closely related to the seasonal cycle in Hardy, the cycle of mourning, in which the same sacramental time (the 'Kalendar') is recovered, remembered, redescribed; the same questions asked (in what could be called re-petition). Thus, in a series of linked seasonal poems, Hardy begins by echoing Keats in the 'Ode to a Nightingale', who writes of 'the selfsame song that found a path / Though the sad heart of Ruth'. At the beginning of the series in 'A Backward Spring' (103), with the faintest of echoes, Hardy simply describes spring budding on 'the selfsame bough', the bud wondering whether to bloom and remembering winter. In 'The Selfsame Song' (117) the echo is made explicit: this may be the same song,

> – But it's not the selfsame bird –
> No: perished to dust is he. . . .
> As also are those who heard
>   That song with me.

Keats too is dead, who listens 'darkling' and writes of 'the self-same song', remembering in turn the Wordsworth who had written of the Cuckoo, 'the same whom in my schoolboy days / I listened to'. Hardy, at the end of the Romantic tradition, uses it to measure his own loss and the passing of time within a cycle which cruelly revives memories. At times he may be serene about what he calls 'such enactments' ('A Bird-Scene at a Rural Dwelling' (132)), but the perpetuation of song always involves a recognition of the passing of time, as in 'Proud Songsters' (155), where he remembers that just as the bird of the earlier poem is 'perished to dust', the 'brand-new birds' a year ago were 'only particles of grain, / And earth, and air, and rain'. If monuments represent poetry in its commemorative aspect, 'fixing' intention in a rigid frame, then bird-song represents poetry as a figure of voice, of the utterance in its moment. In 'To the Cuckoo' Wordsworth exclaims 'shall I call thee Bird / Or but a wandering Voice?', and the same status is accorded to Hardy's birds, their song rising up unannounced to remind, console, echo, or mourn.

Hardy was quite conscious of the associations of his echoes. He wrote, for example, a series of poems on falling leaves and mutability. The reference to 'sick leaves' in the first chorus of 'During Wind and Rain' (102) reflects Hardy's own note in his edition of Milton (in the DCM): beside the description of Satan's legions as 'Thick as autumnal leaves that strow the brooks / In Vallombrosa' (I, 302–3), Hardy refers us to the Virgilian source in Aeneas's journey to the underworld: 'cf. Virg. Aen, VI, 309 – Multa in Sylvis autumni etc.'; in Dryden's translation the ghosts 'Thick as the leaves in autumn strew the woods: / . . . so thick, the shivering army stands'. In his use of such echoes – to a range of writers from Virgil and Shakespeare to Tennyson and Elizabeth Barrett Browning – Hardy registers what Harold Bloom would call his own sense of 'belatedness', of writing within a poetic sequence, in the shadow of other texts which can uncannily seem to anticipate his own.

God and history

Hardy's relation to Christianity and its texts is a particularly intense one, typical of those late Victorians for whom the 'death of God' left a palpable absence – a God-shaped hole – which could not simply be a matter of indifference. Poems like 'The Respectable Burgher on the Higher Criticism' (22), 'God's Funeral', and the late 'Drinking Song' (171) chronicle the depredations of rationalist criticism and Darwinian science on accepted belief, and reprise Hardy's own loss of faith around 1865 (on Hardy's religious background, see Timothy Hands's *Thomas Hardy: Distracted Preacher?* (1989)). Yet Hardy was, he always insisted, 'Churchy' – he attended services all his life, retained a strong interest in church music, read the Bible regularly, and used religious ideas widely in his novels. In his poetry, poems on religious themes range from tales taken from the Bible and apocrypha to direct speculations about (or even interrogations of) God. As late as the 'Apology' to *Late Lyrics and Earlier* (1922) he expressed hopes for a reformed and rational Christianity.

It was the period in which he was writing his epic *The Dynasts*, and searching for a sense of causation behind human events, that Hardy was particularly concerned with the question of an alternative to the 'tribal god, man-shaped, fiery-faced and tyrranous' of orthodox religion (*LY* 176). Hardy's relation to History is a large subject (see Wright 1967; Miller 1990: 107–34). But clearly, it is bound up with the question of necessity and free-will discussed above, and his reading in the philosophy of history (Mill, Leslie Stephen, Comte, Darwin) reflects his search for an ordering principle. He used a variety of names for the abstracted and usually unconscious principle which he sometimes posited as lying behind creation, including the 'Immanent Will', the 'Willer', the 'All-One', the 'Spinner of the Years', the 'Mover', etc. (see poems 8, 11, 45). The Notebooks include many passages struggling for a definition of this Agnostic godhead, including the following summary of *c.* 1887 from Hartmann's *Philosophy of the Unconscious*:

> *The principle of the Uncons*⁵ ... wh. has formed the core of all great philosophies, the Substance of Spinoza, the Absolute Ego of Fichte, Schelling's Absolute Subject-Object, the Absolute Idea of Plato & Hegel, Schopenhauer's Will, &c.'
>
> (Björk entry 1444: cf. entries 1869, 2253)

In *The Dynasts* Hardy postulates an Unconscious Will of the Universe which 'is growing aware of Itself' (*LY* 125), connecting this to a theory of 'a limited God of goodness' (*LY* 73), who is in the main only dimly aware of creation. Hardy explores such ideas in poems like 'Nature's Questioning' (8), and uses the figure of the Willer or Mover in poems like 'The Convergence of the Twain' (45) and '"And There Was a Great Calm"' (116) to explain why the universe is governed by an iron Necessity.

But the First World War was a blow to the limited optimism attached to the God of gradual coming-to-consciousness or evolutionary meliorism. Hardy must have been reminded of the irony of postulating a cosmic observer who was all too like himself: watching, but only aware of the meaning of things when it was too late. After 1915, he was more defensive: writing in 1920 'I have called this Power all sorts of names – never supposing they would be taken for more than fancies' (*LY* 217). His use of a multiplicity of names for 'God' is thus ultimately a way of re-emphasizing the heuristic, speculative nature of all such naming, and the irresoluble unknowability of what lies beyond appearances. Indeed, Hardy's attitude is ultimately closer to that pole which Comte (whom he studied in detail in the 1880s) calls the 'Fetishistic', as opposed to the 'Theistic' (see Björk entry 754n). The 'Theist' postulates an abstract force behind events; the 'Fetishist' sees nature and events as alive with individual meanings, not governed by a Will but by their inbuilt impulsions. In poems like 'The Convergence of the Twain' (45) the debate between these two explanations can be seen working itself out.

Hardy was also careful to register the way in which historical meanings and theories were dependent on human attempts to impose patterns on the flux of events. He often depicted his poems as a flight from the 'sociological' paradigm of the novel – effectively a flight from immediacy into the space of 'lyric' utterance, or into memory; perhaps even, as Margaret Mahar argues, a flight from the 'closed' structures of the novels to the 'open' structures of poetry. Yet his poems do often intersect with their times, and attempt to subsume them within a larger vision of history, just as *The Dynasts* incorporates the Napoleonic Wars. His topical poems, for example, mark particular historical moments as important – the *Titanic* disaster, the Armistice, and so on. The play of what Hardy calls the 'topical' (or immediate) and the 'accidental' (or patterned) can be seen in his comments on '"According to the Mighty Working"' (114), a poem written in 1917, but published in 1919 in response to John Middleton Murray's request for something appropriate to the moment for publication in the *Athenaeum*. In a letter to Arthur McDowall he wrote:

> It must have been more of an accident than design I imagine that the lines suited the present date, for I told the editor I had nothing 'topical'. That is always the difficulty when one is asked for verses for a periodical: it is easy enough to send *something* that one has lying about, possibly on the moon, stars, trees, grass, or shadowy kine; but the reader of the paper says on seeing it – 'Why, what I want is the author's last word upon the world's events; not this stuff!' (*CL* V, 306–7).

What the poet has at hand is poems on nature (moon, stars, trees, grass). Yet even a poem which uses these universals, or draws its terms from the Bible, as '"According to the Mighty Working"' does, can come to seem like a comment on events when it enters the public domain. For all his comments to McDowall, the poem *was* topical, as Hardy later suggested in the *Life*, since in being written for the end of the Great War and suggesting that 'Peace' was an illusion it anticipated the beginnings of other troubles, and in particular the Zionist agitation over the Palestinian protectorate of the post-war period:

> In February he signed a declaration of sympathy with the Jews in support of a movement for the 'reconstitution of Palestine as a National Home for the Jewish People', and during the spring he received letters from Quiller-Couch, Crichton-Browne, and other friends on near and dear relatives they had lost in the war; about the same time there appeared a relevant poem by Hardy in the *Athenaeum* which was much liked, entitled in words from the Burial Service, 'According to the Mighty Working'. (*LY* 190)

In another poem in this period, 'Jezreel', Hardy is even more explicit in his commentary on the Palestinian question, mapping Allenby's 1918 attack on the town onto that described in 2 Kings 9.

What is offered here is (once again) a kind of typology, but Hardy acknowledges that the context of the poem's entry into the world itself creates meaning; the supposedly 'timeless' world of the Book interacts with historical time. Such moments occur throughout Hardy's verse, from his description of the *Titanic* disaster to his late poem 'The Aged Newspaper Soliloquizes' (172), in which he imagines himself as a public chronicle. The magnificent 'In Time of "The Breaking of Nations"' (109) is typical: it contrasts a seemingly timeless 'story' of love with the contingency of 'annals', but does so within an evolving historical vision which encompasses specific events – reawakening a memory of Waterloo in order to suggest a specific connection between the Napoleonic Wars, the Franco-Prussian War, and the context of the Great War. In such poems, the parallel between the Immanent Will and the brain of the poet comes alive, as consciousness interacts with the march of events to enable a sense that a pattern has emerged, and Hardy becomes a visionary historian.

Hardy and the dead

The dead comprise Hardy's single most important topic, particularly if we include related topics like poems set in graveyards (69 in all, according to Elizabeth Hickson), and poems about memories of the dead which are not explicitly elegiac. He wrote elegies for family, for friends, for Queen Victoria, for the dead of two wars, for the *Titanic*, for pets, but above all for his wife Emma, whose death in 1912 inspired his elegiac sequence the 'Poems of 1912–13' and many later poems. As J. Hillis Miller has remarked, 'his writing . . . is a resurrection and safeguarding of the dead', a sustained encounter not only with the past, but with what it is like to be someone who remembers, who carries the burden of the dead (Miller 1970: 29).

Hardy recognized his own tendency to melancholy – as he remarked of his work after Emma's death, he 'was "in flower" in these days, and, like Gray's, his flower was sad-coloured' (*LY* 156). This is not to say, as is sometimes too simply suggested, that he could love best those (women) who were dead. Rather we see in Hardy an extraordinarily strong attachment to the dead and to the past, and an eroticized relation to the dead subjects of his own romance which sees him returning to them again and again. Sigmund Freud, in his essay on 'Mourning and Melancholia', argues that the melancholic is the extremist of mourning who refuses to surrender those portions of the dead which are taken up into the psyche, producing a kind of narcissism. Hardy's melancholy is less narcissism (though it is self-absorbed enough) than a mixture of two contradictory impulses. On the one hand, there is a sense of the emotional energy bound up with the dead, producing the problematic co-incidence of *eros* and *thanatos* (or 'distance and desire', as J. Hillis Miller puts it). On the other hand, there is a sense of moral responsibility brought about by the fact that the self carries traces of the dead within it, like fossils in the geological record. 'In a Former Resort after Many Years' (133) provides a picture of the 'man of memories':

> Do they know me, whose former mind
> Was like an open plain where no foot falls,
>   But now is as a gallery, portrait-lined,
>   And scored with necrologic scrawls,
> Where feeble voices rise, once full-defined,
>   From underground in curious calls?

The voices here are 'curious' perhaps in a sense close to the root meaning of the Latin *curare*: Hardy must 'care' for the dead, who are helpless. Their presence is scored inside his mind (a 'necrology' is a list of the dead), like the transcriptions of sound on a gramophone record.

But this poem also raises the question of what such writing is, or does. What is the relationship between the 'official' portrait and the wall-writing (graffiti)? Do the dead write Hardy – as 'Family Portraits' (175) implies – or does he write them? Who is in control? Certainly they are so much a part of himself that to destroy any remnant of them is painful. In 'The Photograph' (94) he burns a relic, probably of his cousin Tryphena Sparks, with whom he may have been in love at one point, and is distressed at the return of repressed feelings:

> the deed that had nigh drawn tears
> Was done in a casual clearance of life's arrears;
> But I felt as if I had put her to death that night! . . .

A number of Hardy's poems are not so much elegies as meditations on the process of elegy itself, and the mind of the memorialist, as titles like 'Memory and I', '"Ah, are you digging on my grave?"', 'The Obliterate Tomb' (72), 'The Marble Tablet', and 'The Monument-Maker' (135) suggest.

The internalization of the dead explains some of the dynamics of Hardy's late verse – the libidinous pleasure attached to the memory of dead women, for example, and what Philip Larkin calls 'an undercurrent of sensual cruelty in his writing' (1966: 177). This is reflected in his undeniable fondness for stories of executions of women, visible in poems like 'The Mock Wife' (144) and 'On the Portrait of a Woman about to be Hanged' (which Robert Gittings traces to memories of a hanging in 1856). There is an erotic sense of free-play in some of Hardy's late poems on the dead, as well as a relish at his own survival – in 'Days to Recollect' (147) he seems to tease Emma for her unconsciousness: 'Say you remember / That sad November!' Because Hardy is the guardian of the dead, he can use them as he wishes (within limits which are sketched below): in 'The Chosen' the narrator combines all the dead women he knew in one, while in 'Louie', on his childhood sweetheart Louisa Harding, he declares 'I am forgetting Louie the buoyant; / Why not raise her phantom, too?' There is an almost fetishistic manipulation of their identities on the part of the male poet whose lyric subjectivity the dead have entered, which reflects the often scopic treatment of the heroines of his novels, particularly Tess – though it could be argued that in poems like 'Tess's Lament' (27), 'We Field-women' (167), and some of the elegies for Emma he moves towards the imagining of a feminine subjectivity which is less clearly present in the novels, while in other poems including 'One We Knew' (39) he acknowledges his debts to his mother and grandmothers for the folk-memory which informs his poetry. (On gender in the novels, see Boumelha 1982, Wright 1989, Higonnet 1993). Hardy's shifting and frequently contradictory complex of responses, whether custodial or manipulative, reflective or passionate, and the play of interactions with the dead, is evoked most powerfully in the central sequence of elegies which he wrote for his wife.

The 'Poems of 1912–13'

The 'Poems of 1912–13', included in their entirety in this selection, is a sequence of 21 poems written in the period after the death of Emma Hardy in November 1912. Emma's death was a shock to her husband, partly because of the diaries which he discovered in her room, detailing her resentments and bitterness at his behaviour; but more fundamentally because her death re-awakened him to the intense feelings he had experienced early in their courtship and marriage, a time already lost in the years of estrangement. The tragedy of her death became a double tragedy, involving not only loss but a mutual betrayal for which the poet could only blame himself. In March 1913 he travelled to Cornwall, revisiting the scenes of his courtship, and re-reading, it seems, his own courtship novel *A Pair of Blue Eyes*. The sequence he wrote was thus a retracing of lost ground, in both the temporal and topographical sense.

As Peter Sacks has shown, elegies and elegiac sequences have a trajectory which matches what Freud calls 'the work of mourning', beginning with a denial of and reaction against the shock, a repetition of it which aims at mastering the loss, detachment, and an eventual assertion of continuity as death is subsumed within a natural cycle, while the dead person is taken up into memory. (Other elements are also involved, including a measure of aggression against the dead.) Hardy's sequence is unusual in generic terms, not least because it is one of the few major sets of elegies for a wife, taking as its initial model Coventry Patmore's *The Unknown Eros* (1877). Nevertheless, many of the elements which Sacks identifies are present, as his own analysis shows – a constant return to the scene of death in the opening poems, a resort to images of pastoral continuity, and an eventual distancing of the poet from his losses, partly achieved through the creation of a satisfactory image of the dead, a symbolic replacement.

What is different in Hardy's sequence is the poet's sense of the over-plotted nature of the story he tells – something which begins for the reader with the epigraph, pulling us back to Virgil's tales of betrayal and death. Sacks is useful again here, writing about the way elegy deals with the interruption to 'natural' life which death brings, through a displacement which abstracts and 'blames' Time for the poet's predicament:

> In the elegy, the poet's preceding relationship with the deceased (often associated with the mother, or Nature, or a naively regarded Muse) is conventionally disrupted and forced into a triadic structure including the third term, death (frequently associated with the father, or Time of the

more harshly perceived necessity of linguistic mediation itself). The dead, like the forbidden object of a primary desire, must be separated from the poet, partly by a veil of words. (Sacks 1985: 8–9)

Within this scheme (which simplifies in the interests of clarity) the problem for Hardy was that he stood dangerously close to the processes involved. Had he not already plotted the story of his love and its lost opportunities in the tragic ending of *A Pair of Blue Eyes*? Had he not already replaced the real Emma with an ideal image of herself, held in memory (while he sought the company of Florence Henniker and others)? Hardy's word for this replacement of the beloved with an image is 'sublimation' – a term which suggests alchemy and a transmutation into something more ethereal, ghostly. He uses it in *A Pair of Blue Eyes*, ch. 20, where he comments 'Not till they parted, and she had become sublimated in his memory, could he be seen to have attentively regarded her' (p. 200); and again in *The Hand of Ethelberta*, ch. 40:

> What he [Christopher] had learnt was that a woman who has once made a permanent impression on a man cannot altogether deny him her image by denying him her company, and that by sedulously cultivating the aquaintance of this Creature of Contemplation she becomes to him almost a living soul. Hence a sublimated Ethelberta accompanied him everywhere. . . .

Implicit here is the idea that the kind of internalized image produced by 'sublimation' depends on removal, absence – as if Hardy had, by making Emma into the heroine of *A Pair of Blue Eyes*, anticipated (and in part formed) the shape of his tragedy. Hardy's elegies thus position the poet closer to the figure of Death or Necessity than most elegies; they are guilt-ridden, refuse consolation, and their author sees himself as 'a dead man held on end', victim of a plot which he cannot unwrite because it is his own. It is also, as Elizabeth Bronfen argues, a plot inscribed more generally within a culture which forms its ideas of masculine creativity on the symbolic (and therefore negated, dead) bodies of idealized women; a fact constantly registered in Hardy's novels (Bronfen 1993).

Throughout the 'Poems of 1912–13' there is a complex interplay of two sets of topics: those relating to voice, and those relating to vision and writing. In the first poem, he chastises her for not speaking before she dies: 'Never to bid good-bye / Or lip me the softest call' (51). In the second, he says that he failed to 'read the writing upon your face' (52). The same alternation between a desired but absent voice and a need to 'trace' or read the presence of Emma's ghost in the landscape governs much of the sequence, and typically Hardy does not discover the presence signalled by 'voice', but rather, at best, a vision of his dead wife as she once was which he can sustain only momentarily. An alteration in the opening line of 'After a Journey' (63) is symptomatic: 'Hereto I come to interview a ghost' became 'Hereto I come to view a voiceless ghost', removing the possibility of speech.

Of course, Emma *does* speak in the sequence; Hardy brings her to life and speaks in her voice in 'The Haunter' (58) and 'His Visitor' (60). But these poems are curiously ex-centric in relation to the sequence as a whole: they occur in the first half, set in Dorset, and the ghost which is imagined is a recent one, fussing about domestic changes. Emma's imagined ghost does not address Hardy, her soliloquy is directed at the *reader*. Moreover, these two poems in Emma's voice bracket 'The Voice' (59), which seems in its allusions, style, and content to problematize the idea that Hardy hears the voice of 'the woman' at all: 'Can it be you that I hear?' Voice fades into the poem's whispering wind-effects, 'listlessness . . . wistlessness', and the breakdown of metre which signals the quester's uncertainty. A question which the sequence raises is thus: what is the status of our imagining of the dead (the trope known as 'prosopopoeia')? Much of the debate on the 'Poems of 1912–13' has centred on this question, on the metaphysical status of Hardy's re-imagining of Emma.

The core of the sequence is the series of poems in which Hardy moves away from Dorset to Cornwall, returning to the scenes of his courtship. 'After a Journey' (63), 'Beeny Cliff' (65), and 'At Castle Boterel' (66) all deal with the immanence of memory, and the production of an image of Emma very different from the worried ghost in the first half of the sequence; an image drawn from the romance-world of courtship. Sacks sees this as part of the 'work of mourning', with the dispossessed poet achieving recovery through his assertion of Emma's continued presence in memory and in the poet's representations (though as we have seen, in some ways her existence as an ideal representation is precisely the *problem* for Hardy). Donald Davie, in his provocative analysis of the sequence, is much more absolute about that recovery: he sees Hardy as achieving an affirmation in which 'love triumphs over time', asserting Emma's absolute presence in the landscape of memory (1972: 149). That, for Davie, is the most important truth about the sequence: Hardy's realization that in the 'purple light' of romance, what 'At Castle Boterel' calls 'a time of such quality' has a permanent existence. Indeed, he sees Hardy as betraying that insight in transferring three poems from earlier in the volume to the end of the sequence in the *Collected Poems* of 1919: he argues that 'by adding on "The Spell of the Rose" and "St Launce's Revisited" and "Where the Picnic Was", [Hardy] psychologises his own metaphysical insights', returning to his normal scepticism in poems which cruelly assert that Emma has 'vanished / Under earth'.

Davie's is perhaps too Platonic a view of Hardy's moments of vision, which are always tentative. Hardy's tracing of Emma is qualified by an awareness of the irrecoverability of the love which is lost, and of its double lostness: dead, and before that swallowed in the bitterness of time and alienation, so that Emma's death and the earlier death of love become equivalent. 'After a Journey', in many ways the central poem of the sequence, states that unequivocally (again, notice the tension between voice – saying – and reading, tracking, or scanning):

> Yes: I have re-entered your olden haunts at last;
>   Through the years, through the dead scenes I have tracked you;
> What have you now found to say of our past –
>   Scanned across the dark space wherein I have lacked you?
> Summer gave us sweets, but autumn wrought division?
>   Things were not lastly as firstly well
>   With us twain, you tell?
> But all's closed now, despite Time's derision.

'After a Journey' is a bitter poem, showing Hardy following a 'thin ghost' from the past rather than any fuller presence. Rather than what Davie calls an 'unprecedented serenity' at the end of the poem, there is a harsh rhyme ('lours/flowers') and a declaration which, it seems to me, can only be read ironically and hopelessly against the background of loss:

> I am just the same as when
> Our days were a joy, and our paths through flowers.

I am the same, but you are not. The 'Trust me ... though Life lours' introducing this declaration might imply a recognition that trust may be betrayed.

In the volumes which follow *Satires of Circumstance*, Hardy's mourning for Emma changes character, becoming more distant from its object. At times he is surprised by the resurgence of feeling, at other times he actively seeks to sustain it (as in 'The Shadow on the Stone' (106)). In later poems he often has to actively seek her, reading her papers ('Read by Moonlight') or reinscribing her presence in the landscape. Inevitably, the elegiac impulse fails at times, either becoming mechanical or not producing anything. In 'They Would Not Come' he records 'no vision' in Cornwall, and in 'Her Haunting Ground' (146) he asks:

> Can it be so? It must be so,
> That visions have not ceased to be
> In this the chiefest sanctuary
> Of her whose form we used to know.

Hardy's late poems on dead family and friends seem similarly uninvolved: either marking anniversaries or commenting impassively ('"Nothing matters much"' (149)), or turning a brief moral ('The Love-Letters' (158)). At other times, as I have already suggested, he adopts an almost playful air with the dead, as if having been taken up into memory outside the tragic pattern of his relationship with Emma they can become part of a happier internalized romance.

Restoration and the past

If architecture provides a frame for Hardy's aesthetic theories, it also informs his thinking about his subject-matter, memory, and the dead. As an architectural assistant he was deeply involved in the Victorian debate about the preservation of Gothic churches – supervising the restoration of churches in the the late 1860s and early 1870s, as well as a late effort at West Knighton church in the 1890s, and commenting publicly on the issue in his 1906 essay 'Memories of Church Restoration'. What was at stake in this debate was the issue of the preservation of the original fabric of churches versus their restoration and structural improvement, often according to some abstract idea of the ideal Gothic style. The result could be barbarous, as Hardy admitted (and as the title of the modern guidebook *Churches the Victorians Forgot* testifies). Yet a real conflict was involved: on the one hand, a church could crumble into ruins if not restored; on the other hand, the past was bound up in the decaying fabric which brutal restoration could destroy for ever.

One answer, which Hardy addresses in his essay, is a fidelity to the original which reproduces its forms and shapes, what he called the 'aesthetic phantom without solidity' which is the Gothic design. Yet, as D. Drew Cox argues in his discussion of Hardy as architect, he cannot accept this position, recognizing that even in a sensitive restoration something is lost: the quirkiness of the artist, and above all the associations of the stones themselves:

> I think the damage done to this sentiment of association by replacement, by the rupture of continuity, is mainly what makes the enormous loss this country has sustained from its seventy years of church restoration so tragic and deplorable. The protection of an ancient building against renewal in fresh materials is, in fact, even more of a social – I may say a humane – duty than an aesthetic one. It is the preservation of memories, fellowships, fraternities. Life, after all, is more than art. . . . (*PW* 215)

In his speech a few years later at the ceremony in which he was given the freedom of Dorchester, Hardy takes up the same subject, meditating on the contrast between the Dorchester of his boyhood and the present town – a technique which might be borrowed from A.N. Pugin's famous 'Contrasts' series of drawings (1840), which showed the city of 1440 and the same scene 400 years later, the church spires overlaid with warehouses and boiler chimneys (the superimposition of two scenes is a favourite device in Hardy's poetry). Here, it is the associations alone which the poet celebrates:

> Our power to preserve is largely an illusion. Where is the Dorchester of my early recollection – I mean the human Dorchester – the kernel – of which the houses were but the shell? ... I see the streets and turnings not far different from those of my school-boy time; but the faces that used to be seen at the doors, the inhabitants, where are they? I turn up the Weymouth Road, cross the railway-bridge, enter an iron gate to 'a slope of green access', and there they are! There is the Dorchester that I knew best; there are the names on white stones one after the other, names that recall the voices, cheerful and sad, anxious and indifferent, that are missing from the dwellings and pavements. (*LY* 146)

A similar set of problems are involved in a poetry which, like Hardy's, attempts to preserve the past, to register its presence, and to superimpose past and present in order to measure the passing of time. Cox sees the architectural debate as fully resolved in Hardy's poetry: poetry is the place where Hardy could be 'both creator and preserver' (1972: 63). But the situation was not so simple. Constantly Hardy recognizes that individual lives carry their own radiation, like the stones of a church – something often designated by the word 'sheen' and its cognates: Emma in Cornwall 'shed her life's sheen here' in 'A Dream or No' (62); 'I see the hand of the generations / That owned each shiny familar thing' in 'Old Furniture' (99); the 'sudden shine' which is Barnes's last signal ('The Last Signal' (95)), the 'luminous line' of the family in 'The Obliterate Tomb' (72). In forging his memories into prose and poetry Hardy was altering, replacing the lived experience with an 'aesthetic phantom', and in so doing he was liable to compromise the fabric of the lives he remembers. This could involve deliberate distortion (as in the account of family history in his autobiography), but it could also simply include a recognition that the past is lost, and can only be reconstructed as a phantom of itself. The materials of the poet are deeply imbued with the presence of death, with the voices which are in fact 'missing from the dwellings and pavements'. Hardy was in many cases 'The Single Witness' (to borrow the title of a late poem about suppressing evidence) to what he had seen, and the rearrangement and concomitant destruction of materials was an integral part of his late career – in the disguised autobiography and the Max Gate bonfires into which he threw diaries and other papers.

Perhaps that is why in a number of poems the dead seem to speak back from within memory, criticizing the poet's portrait of them or somehow interfering with him. 'In Front of the Landscape' (43) presents the dead who are 'Rigid in hate, / Smitten by years-long wryness born of misprison'; they must (in a loaded word) be 'translated' into the forms of art. In 'The Monument-Maker' (135) the title-figure and his work are mocked by the ghost of his dead lover. In 'The Obliterate Tomb' (72) the architectural paradigm is fully-developed: a 'man of memories' promises himself that he will restore a set of graves in order to make amends for an old family feud, but is disturbed by a mysterious stranger who claims to be a relative of the dead, and to have the right to restore their graves himself. Even when the stranger vanishes, the narrator cannot bring himself to fulfil his vow: he dies, and the tombstones are used to repave the churchyard path. Since we know that this poem partly reflects the fate of the graves of Emma's family, the Giffords, the plot is also Hardy's in his role as commemorator, exploring what it means to use the dead, and to be the repository of their histories. His elegiac art is guilt-ridden and self-divided, balancing the privacy of memory against the public forms which it takes; use against faithfulness. In 1920 he wrote to the Rev. G.H. Moule on the architectural issue, ' "Reparation" is far better than "Restoration" ' (*CL* VI, 3) – the ambiguous 'reparation' suggesting both repairs and repayment, penance and healing.

Wessex

Hardy's larger dilemma as the mediator and purveyor of local memory under the guise of 'Wessex' is also a part of the problem of commemoration. 'Wessex' is one name for the locus of the intersection of past and present – a space which represented a realization of Hardy's memory, experiences, and sense of history – which is also, as 'Wessex Heights' (47) suggests, the space of Hardy's poetry. Wessex had of course been created and mapped by the novels, but it was the guides to the 'Hardy country' produced in the period after 1900 which fully delineated its boundaries – with Hardy attempting to 'police' the process (see Millgate 1982: 421–3). In the 'General Preface' of 1911 he justified the use of Wessex as the 'stage' for his actions – that is, in terms of art rather than the social reality of a region. Indeed, as 'Wessex Heights' suggests, 'Wessex' would be the achievement of a writer supposedly liberated from the contingent nature of his background by his already long career as a novelist, a fully imagined area over which Hardy might brood as its presiding genius.

This idealization of Hardy's region has been attacked strongly. George Wotton argues that the Wessex of the *Life* (and implicitly the poems) is the space of consciousness, while the Wessex of the novels is, more productively, the space of contested social values (Wotton 1985: 38–40). Peter Widdowson has criticized a tradition of criticism which sees Hardy's work as the essence of a nostalgic rural 'Englishness', abstracted from its historical context (Widdowson 1989). In fact Hardy's poems register a more complex reality; there is a resistance within his work to the idealization of Wessex. The 'General Preface' acknowledges the need for a fidelity to his region, and recognizes that there is a conflict between reality and the needs of the writer: 'I have instituted inquiries to correct tricks of memory, and striven against temptation to exaggerate, in order to preserve for my own satisfaction a fairly true record of a vanishing life'. Hardy was placed in a difficult position. As a member of a metropolitan élite, dining with cabinet ministers and nobility, he represented the values of disinterested 'intelligence', with all that implied in terms of assumptions about provincial and rural life. But as the memorialist of a region, born the son of a rural tradesman, he had allegiances to a fast-vanishing way of life, threatened by the very forces that issued from the urban world (mechanized agriculture, newspapers, increased material expectations). The tensions between these two viewpoints is often apparent in his novels. He has been accused of tailoring his descriptions of rural Dorset to the tastes of the educated Victorian reading public (Snell 1985); yet he was also concerned to represent the views of that other, unspoken rural constituency. In his essay 'The Dorsetshire Labourer' he laments the way in which the people whom he calls the 'workfolk' are being converted into paid labourers, moving about at random, with an accompanying loss of village traditions and continuity. Here and in poems like 'Drummer Hodge' (12) he attacks the rural stereotype of the 'yokel'. The aim of his memorialization of village life is thus partly to represent (even as it commodifies) those local values at the point of their vanishing – hence Hardy's recording of family traditions, folk-tales, popular songs and dances, and the vanishing vocabulary of the Wessex dialect; and his registering the impact of railways and other changes of rural life. The meticulous dating of traditions from the nineteenth century and earlier, the footnotes concerning forgotten usages and places, all attest to the tension between fidelity and the needs of an audience, and suggest Hardy's location in a history which he constantly registers.

The 'time' of Wessex is, it is often noticed, the time of one of

Hardy's favourite modes, the ballad. As Thom Gunn points out, ballads seek a generality of feeling which resists precise periodization, and which link them to the oral tradition. They suggest the ever-present 'story' of romance, of the 'maid and her wight' in 'In Time of "The Breaking of Nations"' (109), in contrast to 'war's annals' which provide that poem's immediate context in 1916. For Gunn, the ballad's omission of details, its tendency to present isolated scenes, its iterative rhetoric, all link it to the past; ballads are 'the perfect repositories for his laments about passing time' (Gunn 1972: 35). Yet Hardy's ballads (or ballad-like poems) also register the specifics of time: 'The Convergence of the Twain' (45) attaches itself to an occasion; 'The Trampwoman's Tragedy' (31) is meticulous in its documenting of vanished inns; 'The Mock Wife' (144) indicates its source in a historical event; 'To an Unborn Pauper Child' (17) has in manuscript a note which suggests its origins in a sitting of the local courts. Even those poems which borrow the ballad's stripped-down interest in narrative repetition, like 'The Five Students' (100), in which characters drop out one by one, has a source in Hardy's own experience, and relates to much more precisely located poems. Hardy was always conscious of the way his poems embody a philosophy of history which balances past against present.

Hardy's style

Among the first things which readers of Hardy's poems noticed was their idiosyncracy of style – a strangeness in terms of diction, syntax, and movement which caused his work to be compared to Browning's. One need go no further than the (much-revised) opening stanzas of the first poem of *Wessex Poems* to encounter it:

> 'Cherish him can I while the true one forthcome –
> Come the rich fulfiller of my prevision;
> Life is roomy yet, and the odds unbounded.'
>   So self-communed I.

Most readers have had the experience of picking their way back through a poem by Hardy in search of the grammatical thread. This strangeness, or 'harshness', as Isobel Grundy calls it (Grundy 1980), when combined with the highly wrought nature of the poems, their elaborate rhyme-schemes, sound patterning, and other symmetrical effects, is part of an unmistakable style, parodied by Beerbohm, Betjeman and others. Given that he was a highly conscious craftsman who remained committed to the problems of craft and pattern, we need to ask why Hardy's poems read the way they do. Why are they so strange?

The Gothic art-principle

One answer is that they are strange in the way in which other Victorian poetry is: Browning, Clough, Christina Rossetti, Swinburne, and Dowson all write poems in which stylistic pressures suggest a rethinking of the genres that were inherited from the past, as well as implying a restless 'modernism' which reflects Victorian uncertainties about religion, history, gender and the self. But Hardy's own defence of his style rested on a more specific point: the relationship between his work and the Gothic revival movement in architecture, which he elaborates in his autobiography:

> He knew that in architecture cunning irregularity is of enormous worth, and it is obvious that he carried on into his verse, perhaps in part unconsciously, the Gothic art-principle in which he had been trained – the principle of spontaneity, found in mouldings, tracery, and such like – resulting in the 'unforeseen' (as it has been called) character of his metres and stanzas, that of stress rather than syllable, poetic texture rather than poetic veneer; the latter kind of thing, under the name of 'constructed ornament', being what he, in common with every Gothic student, had been taught to avoid as the plague. (*LY* 78–9)

The principles contained here are drawn from A.N. Pugin's famous architectural polemic *Contrasts*, and from Ruskin's essay on 'The Nature of Gothic' in *The Stones of Venice* (1853), particularly Ruskin's description of Gothic 'variety' and restlessness in sections 26–40 of the essay. Indeed, many of Ruskin's six defining features of the Gothic (Savageness, Changefulness, Naturalism, Grotesqueness, Rigidity, Redundancy) might be applied to Hardy's poetry, to its combination of a rigidity of structure with subtle variations and 'grotesque' detail. To take just one of these characteristics which has seldom been remarked on, 'Redundancy' for Ruskin signified a richness which is, paradoxically, part of the 'humility' of the work, in contrast to the 'haughty' simplicity of the classical style. Hardy's approach is similar: his copiousness of output, his ability to 'turn' a poem for any occasion, his desire to produce a multi-faceted oeuvre, all suggest parallels with the Gothic craftsman.

The Gothic aesthetic thus implies that the poet is a craftsman, exploiting materials with skill, economy, and an eclectic energy – as D. Drew Cox points out, Hardy's word for this in both writing and architecture is 'technicist' (1972: 57–8). The Gothic, moreover, provides a vocabulary perfectly adjusted to Hardy's preoccupation with shapes and structures. Words like 'tracery', 'moulding', 'mark', 'measure', 'chiselled', 'upfingered' link perfectly with Hardy's concern with shapes which outline themselves in memory and in the landscape (many of these are 'out' compounds: outshape, outleant, outskeleton; see Elliott 1984: 198). Dennis Taylor interestingly extends the architectural comparison, relating the curves of Gothic tracery to the family trees of Darwin's evolutionary diagrams, so that the 'Gothic' becomes an aesthetic which expresses twisting and branching patterns of experience, carried across time (Taylor 1981: 39–81).

Not all critics have accepted this parallel. James Richardson is suspicious of the 'Gothic' aesthetic, which he sees as exhausted by the time Hardy used it (1977: 76–7), while Donald Davie sees in it a licence for the poetic equivalent of some of the monstrosities of Victorian gothic, 'decoration' on factories and so on. But we should at least register its importance for Hardy's self-understanding, and mark its call for an attention to the details of his poetry, and to its deliberate distortions. If Hardy's work is 'rough' and difficult, the passage above suggests that is a deliberate effect rather than ignorance of propriety. Just as he wrote in an early note that 'Art is a disproportioning – i.e. distorting, throwing out of proportion – of realities, to show more clearly the features that matter in those realities' (*EL* 299), Hardy's harshness aims at revealing the edges of experience, in all its freshness. In another passage in the *Life* he quotes Herrick's 'A sweet disorder in the dress' to justify irregularity before shifting to the metaphor of a coin: a smooth style is 'like a worn half-pence – all the fresh images wound off by rubbing, and no crispness or movement at all' (*EL* 138). Hardy's coinages are similarly rough, their new-minted state representing a determination to reappraise and revalue words and expressions. In 1926 Hardy was still defending his work in these terms, writing to an American professor 'you may discover as you get older that the harshness you say you note in some of his poems is deliberate, as a reaction from the smooth alterations of the Victorian poets' (*CL* VII, 18).

Words

One aspect of Ruskin's definition of the Gothic which is reflected closely in Hardy's poetry is the restless eclecticism of his diction and syntax. The oddness of his word-choice and syntax and its violation of the rules of decorum were remarked upon by most of the early reviewers of his work. F.R. Leavis's comments are typical in their mixture of irritation and admiration:

> If one says that he seems to have no sensitiveness for words, one recognizes at the same time that he has made a style out of stylelessness.

There is something extremely personal about the gauche, unshrinking mismarriages – group-mismarriages – of his diction, in which, with naïf aplomb, he takes as they come the romantic-poetical, the prosaic banal, the stilted literary, the colloquial, the archaistic, the erudite, the technical, the dialect word, the brand-new Hardy coinage.
(Leavis 1940: 88)

All these features are, indeed, present in Hardy's verse; but their cause is not insensitivity or ignorance. In part, they are justified by the 'Gothic art principle', with its emphasis on the grotesque juxtaposition. But they also reflect the word-choice of a poet whose origins are ex-centric in relation to the central position from which Eliot, Leavis, Brooks, and other critics of Hardy's diction speak: a poet largely self-educated, entering the world of letters obliquely by writing architectural essays, gradually gaining recognition as a regional writer, and only then becoming a major 'tragic' novelist. Hardy's word-choice preserves intact the fractures in his relation to his origins and his career: the dialect words coexist with obscure latinate terms, just as the ballads coexist with the sapphics and fashionable rondeaux. The Dorset dialect, he insisted when writing of Barnes, is 'a tongue, and not a corruption'; yet he was also keen to stress Barnes's classicism (Barnes 1908: viii). What is absent – and this is despite Hardy's sensitivity about his origins, and his insistence that he had never actually *spoken* the dialect – is any central standard of decorum, of the 'right words in the right order' defined in terms of the poetic norms of an élite, educated oligarchy, rather than in terms of the poem's intention. Instead, there are competing voices and allegiances, like those registered in his novels.

In this sense, at least, Hardy is a modernist, breaking the standards of diction – not in the way in which Eliot includes dialect in *The Waste Land*, where 'aberrant' voices are still coordinated with respect to an ironic central consciousness, but by abandoning the standards of neutrality, and subordinating language to the aims of the poem. But Hardy's attitude to language must also be considered within the context of his historical awareness. If he regarded the whole range of English usage as available to him, it is in a Darwinian context within which all words struggle for survival, and within which linguistic 'fossils' preserve valuable facts about origins, processes, and types, and perhaps even, as Patricia Ingham says, suggest the way in which the human subject is trapped in time (Ingram 1980). The fading of Dorset usage under the pressures of education and standardization is described in the introduction to his selection from Barnes's poems: 'the process is always the same: the word is ridiculed by the newly taught; it gets into disgrace; it is heard in holes and corners only; it dies; and, worst of all, it leaves no synonym' (Barnes 1908: iii). The legacy of Barnes's *Philological Grammar* was Hardy's own contribution to dialect dictionaries, and his sense of himself as the last continuator of the Dorset tradition, 'translating' it to the larger world.

Thus, rather than being insensitive to the historical associations of words as Leavis implies, Hardy was acutely aware of etymologies, and where he uses an archaic or ambiguous word or even a pun it is often to suggest that a buried meaning lies hidden in its history. When he says 'as whilom' in 'Old Furniture' (99), meaning 'as formerly', the archaism itself conveys the vanishing of things (as well as perhaps recalling Dryden's 'MacFlecknoe'). 'The Convergence of the Twain' (45) is in part an exploration of the hidden meanings of words: of 'smart', which is brisk and fashionable, but also signifies a hurt ('smart-money' is paid to seamen's widows); of things being 'co-incident', both accidental and parts of a hidden unity; of objects being 'bent', which can mean either 'directed by an external force' or 'determined, self-willed'. Such ambiguities are consciously placed – in this case to raise the question of whether the *Titanic* disaster was attributable to a malignant external fate or to a wilful human blindness.

Hardy's coinages and compound-words similarly involve ideas of competing and emergent meanings. The 'years-heired' face in 'Heredity' (81) suggests both time and succession, as does the 'siresown tree' of 'The Pedigree' (91). In 'Tess's Lament' (27) the cry 'I'd have my life unbe' suggests both undoing life, ending it, and never having lived at all. 'Unvision', a negative compound in 'The Shadow on the Stone' (106), means not seeing the person there when one turns to look, but also 'unvisioning' in the sense of consciously ceasing to 'vision' something which one has been imagining into existence. The double negative in 'Nay, I'll not unvision' carries a tremendous freight of idealism, against an equal weight of doubt. Coinages (whether of actual words or usage) like 'deeplier' ('The Obliterate Tomb' (72)) and 'deedily' ('The New Dawn's Business' (154)) testify to Hardy's willingness to squeeze new meanings from both familiar and obsolete words. And as Richardson (1977: 97) remarks, he 'calls attention to language as a material on which shape is being imposed' in the process.

Hardy's use of syntactic oddity and periphrasis is also often, like Browning's, the product of a desire to register the nuances of situation. The central character of 'The Respectable Burgher' (22) has a stilted speech which reflects his prudishness (the numbingly repetitive rhyme-scheme reinforces that effect). The syntactic awkwardness of 'Neutral Tones' (3), ll. 7–8, which at first seems merely clumsy, suggests a debate on meaning and time. Moreover, Hardy's distinctive words – whether those he uses repeatedly or rare words – provide important clues to what Walter de la Mare called 'the bias of the recorder' in his work (see p. 244). One can characterize Hardy's poetry in terms of what Margaret Faurot calls a 'lexicon', a set of linked terms or groups of terms which are repeated constantly and which carry a particular conceptual freight (Faurot 1990). Such groupings in Hardy's work include those relating to writing and reading (trace, script, scan, mark, hieroglyphic), those relating to shapes (shape, form, frame, lineament), words suggesting a sense of belatedness and repetition (continue, continuator, abide, fade, masquings, repetitions; even the deleted rarity 'concatenations' in 'Family Portraits' (175)), words describing the 'pilgrimage' of existence (stalk, pace, perambulate, orbit, track, earth-track). Some of these words are Hardy's own, others carry a freight of poetic association – for example, 'blank', which echoes from Milton (the 'universal blank' of *Paradise Lost* III, 48) to Tennyson ('on the bald street breaks the blank day', *In Memoriam* 7), and for Hardy usually signifies a state of negativity; an 'unvision' or a bereftness which reflects his sense of thin-skinned exposure to the world.

Prosody

It may seem a large claim to argue that Hardy's poetry comes as the climax of the accentual-syllabic tradition in English poetry – that tradition which begins with the introduction of classical and renaissance models in the sixteenth century, and effectively ends with Ezra Pound's modernist declaration that 'To overthrow the pentameter . . . is the first heave'. But it is a view that was put by Pound himself, in *A Guide to Kulchur* (1938), and subsequent critics have (with varying degrees of approval) pointed out Hardy's ceaseless metrical experimentation, to the extent that his versification is more varied than that of any other English poet. Throughout his career he explored a wide variety of metres and stanza-forms, from the classical to the traditional, and varying from the relative simplicity of ballad stanza and common metre (the verse-form of many hymns) to the sonnet and complex forms like the villanelle and rondeau, as well as numerous irregular stanzas of several different line lengths.

These verse-forms were inspired by the study of a range of sources, in two different periods. In the 1860s he read widely in English poetry, copying passages into a notebook labelled 'Studies, Specimens &c' from the Old Testament, Spenser, Shakespeare, Burns, Byron, Wordsworth, Shelley, Tennnyson, Inglow, Barnes, and Swinburne (Millgate 1982: 87–8). He studied Milton in detail, Lodge, Vaughan, Thomson, Gray, James Montgomery, and numerous others in Palgrave's anthology *The Golden Treasury* which his friend Horace Moule gave him in 1862. He was also exposed, from an early age, to Keble's *The Christian Year*, with its variety of verse-forms, and to a huge ballad tradition which ranges from orally transmitted local ballads to the Scottish balladeers (Burns, Mickle) and the Romantic ballads of Wordsworth, Coleridge and others (see Gunn 1972; Taylor 1986). In the late 1890s, when he returned to poetry after a quarter-century devoted mainly to writing novels, he again studied verse-forms, spending time at the British Museum reading Latin hymns, and producing a diagram illustrating the kinds of verse and the way in which 'Poetic Diction' is related to the 'Language of Common Speech' (*LY* 85–6). This interest in the theory of prosody is reflected in continued note-taking from articles on metre, on ballads, and on individual poets like Swinburne. He read classical poetry and attempted translations from Sophocles, Catullus, Sappho, Heine, and others. Throughout his life Hardy continued to experiment: with French forms in the 1890s, with a number of long and complex stanza patterns from about 1910. In late life he even responded to the 'free-verse' revolution, writing lines from the young T.S. Eliot into his notebooks, and justifying his own more traditional practice to correspondents.

As Dennis Taylor has pointed out in his recent book on *Hardy's Metres and Victorian Prosody* (1988), Hardy's experimentation with metre and stanza shape came as the climax of an increasingly refined and philosophically sophisticated Victorian debate on metrics. In particular, there was a new flexibility in the way in which the relationship between metre and the poetic line was understood. English prosody, the study of poetic metres, is derived from the study of the classical rules of metre, which were based in turn on the relatively orderly patternings of syllables in Greek and Latin poetry. But English verse, with its much less orderly rhythms, had never fitted well with classical prosody. In the work of Victorian theorists like Coventry Patmore and George Saintsbury there emerged for the first time an awareness of the dialectical interplay between the rhythms of speech and what Hardy (following Saintsbury and Robert Bridges) called the 'verse skeleton', the pattern of stressed syllables theoretically demanded by a particular metre. The result was that Hardy, as Taylor puts it, was 'perhaps the first major poet in the tradition of Sidney to know a theory of accentual-syllabic metre adequate to the richness of the verse' (1988: 59). Patmore and others enabled metre to be seen not as a 'grid' which the poem would fit, but as a more abstracted presence: a pattern which is recognized even where the poem deviates markedly from it. So long as we 'hear' the tune, it is present in the subtle interplay of speech patterns and the 'expected' stress patterns.

Indeed, Hardy's subtle employment of a variety of metrical and sound effects is rooted in a close observation of speech rhythms and verbal resources, as well as an understanding of metrics. In his diary for July 1884 we find him visiting the court in Dorchester and noticing that 'Witnesses always begin their evidence in sentences containing ornamental words, evidently prepared beforehand, but when they get into the thick of it this breaks down to a struggling grammar and lamentably jumbled narrative' (*EL* 218). This is presented as an observation on rural ways, but a parallel effect is used in Hardy's own poetry – for example, when under the pressure of grief the careful triple rhythm of 'The Voice' (59) breaks down into the 'faltering' metre of the final stanza.

Hardy's technical proficiency has produced a tradition of hostile reaction. A number of critics have complained that Hardy's 'verse skeletons' are simply imposed arbitrarily on poems, like 'boxes' into which the meaning is dropped. James Southworth complained in 1947 that 'the greatest obstacle to the poet's successful communication ... lies in his frequent attempts at enclosing the thought in a predetermined pattern, ill-fitted for the purpose' (Southworth 1947: 166), and a number of subsequent critics have made similar claims (see Hynes 1961: 75; Hollander 1975: 137). Donald Davie, one of Hardy's best critics, presents a more sophisticated version of the argument when he argues that Hardy's metrical skill represents a poetic version of the Victorian preoccupation with technology, so that he becomes 'the laureate of engineering' (Davie 1973: 17), marring his work through an over-emphasis on symmetry and metrical variation. In 'The Convergence of the Twain' (45), for example, Davie suggests that 'the poem itself is an engine, a sleek and powerful machine; its rhythms slide home like pistons inside cylinders, ground exactly to fractions of a millimetre'.

Davie's comment on the latter poems suggests, however, that Hardy's metres *can* usually be related closely to his poems. The occasional rigidity of his forms is part of the story which his poems tell. Form is Fate in Hardy's work, the 'arbitrary' yet also 'necessary' accident of a rhyme or a stanza-form encapsulating a larger irony (see Mahar 1978). Even a colon or a dash can reproduce the accidents of existence, as in the 'elsewhere' of 'Beeny Cliff' (65):

> What if still in chasmal beauty looms that wild weird western shore,
> The woman now is – elsewhere – whom the ambling pony bore,
> And nor knows nor cares for Beeny, and will laugh there nevermore.

The 'elsewhere' here is itself a signal of time's depredations, and the final line's modulation of a few basic sounds into an inevitable conclusion is almost diagrammatic. The idea of 'verse skeletons' of ideal form has repercussions for the poet as 'memorialist', who shapes the material of the past. Often metres are 'ghostly' presences for Hardy: remembered tunes, ironic reminders of Fate's action, or a mark of human intentionality in general, so that when metre breaks down or shifts under the pressure of feeling, it signals the fragility of all human constructs. Moreover, the abstract and highly experimental nature of metrical form, the fact that metre is itself ghostly, means that it is difficult to separate a reading of the metres of many of Hardy's poems from an interpretation of the poem: we necessarily read one through the other, as the dialogue of expectation and (belated) recognition. Jean Brooks's comment is useful here: 'the reader's uncertainties on the placing of stress may be art rather than incompetence – a required contribution to the sense of the difficulties of emergent human consciousness struggling with the intractable denseness of matter' (1971: 46). Encountering Hardy's poems involves us in a struggle like that of his protagonists, fraught with conjecture and an often retroactive understanding that a pattern has emerged.

Consider 'Exeunt Omnes' (74), the penultimate poem of the main sequence of *Satires of Circumstance* (followed only by the 'Satires' which were originally earlier in the volume). Encountering the first line, the poem seems to be in a falling metre, initially three-beat. But the second line immediately makes that interpretation difficult: a rising (iambic) metre ends with a possible double-beat (easily realized in reading the poem), making the line seem four-beat rising with an implied off-beat:

> And Í still léft where the fáir wás? . . .

The third line begins with a Tennysonian cadence, and again seems iambic tetrameter, with a feminine ending:

> Much háve I séen of néighbour loúngers

By the end of the stanza, however, the poem seems to have reverted to a falling rhythm:

> Máking a lústy shówing,
> Eách now pást all knówing.

The metrical possibilities here are expanded and reinterpreted by the second stanza, where the second line is anapaestic, pushed in that direction by the interpolated (and grammatically unnecessary) 'the':

In the stréet and the líttered spáces.

This line makes us re-read the second line of the previous stanza, where the comparison between the feminine ending above ('spácĕs') and 'fair was' tends to suggest that the latter is not in fact a double stress, but a feminine ending with the stress on 'was' demoted: 'fáir wăs' – a reading put into place when we encounter the return to 'fair was' in the second line of stanza three: now clearly a falling cadence, perhaps a falling-away.

The poem as a whole thus offers two possibilities: a falling metre which is reinforced by the feminine endings throughout, which in turn involve the suppression of the 'was' of line 2 of the first and last stanza – a suppression which suggests the vacating of the past. This is counterpointed by the flickering of the Tennysonian iambics, a rising metre which in its context (the 'Much have I seen and known' of 'Ulysses') signals hopeful aspiration. But the iambics are constantly diluted and distorted by the 'wisening' forces of the poem's form, its tendency to 'dribble' into the falling metre which dominates each stanza's opening and ending. The metrical uncertainties reflect the dialogue between the present location ('As I wait alone') and its sliding away into the past ('wás/wăs') as the fair collapses into the 'spaces' opened up by reverie. The rhymes reinforce the point: 'going' becomes 'past knowing', 'hither' becomes 'thither'. The poet and his poem inhabit a space between the passing of things and his own extinction, and this is something which we can read into, as well as from, the poem's metre.

Numerous other poems have such a metrical 'plot'. 'A Singer Asleep' (48) experiments with various stanzas before resolving into Swinburne's own *ottava rima* in the final stanza. Poems like 'The Walk' (53) are 'shaped' so as to suggest an excursion and a 'return'; the stanza of 'The Convergence of the Twain' (45) even seems to imitate the shape of a ship. Dennis Taylor notices how a number of poems 'enact the emergence of a more regular hymnal form out of a rougher ballad or original form' while others do the opposite, disrupting a regular form and the comfortable pattern of expectation which it has generated (1988: 215). Such 'plots' also operate in detail: 'Snow in the Suburbs' (140) begins with a declarative and end-stopped falling rhythm which is 'released' into iambics (and enjambment) only when the action moves on after four lines. In 'The Whitewashed Wall' (128) the speed of the metre and internal rhyme of the first half of the last stanza mimics the 'rush' of the brush which covers the wall, like time itself, before the stanza breaks down into a turbulent irregular metre which reflects the 'labouring' sleep of the mother. Here, the caesurae, enjambment, and repetitions of 'him' combine to suggest what is almost a 'draught' (draft) second set of line-endings, buried in the line as the picture of the woman's son is buried under the whitewash:

> 'Yes', he said: 'My brush goes on with a rush,
>   And the draught is buried under;
> When you have to whiten old cots and brighten,
>   What else can you do, I wonder?'
> But she knows he's there. And when she yeans
>   For him, deep in the labouring night,
> She sees him as close at hand, and turns
>   To him under his sheet of white.

Such 'ghostly' effects suggest the way in which the forms of human experience shape our world, asserting their presence in a language which is both a 'snare' (the web of words) and a means of resistance.

Hardy and literary tradition

I have already suggested the extent of Hardy's debt to other writers in terms of metrical variety and inherited images. Like all poets, he was involved in a dialogue with his predecessors – visible in some of the allusions documented in the annotations (the poem numbers given as illustration below are by no means definitive, and the allusions suggested are necessarily often tentative or just illustrative of a common topos). His closeness to Browning has often been noted – most thoroughly by James Richardson (1977) – in terms of interest in history, in the grotesque, in dramatic monologue, and in his writing of overtly philosophical poetry (to this I would add his borrowings from Browning's love-poetry: see for example poems 6, 40, 50, 80, 94, 112, 163). His relations with Tennyson have been less well documented, but there is in his elegiac poetry in particular a sustained debate with Tennyson (e.g. poems 5, 16, 21, 51, 63, 68, 106, 134, 174); while in poems like 'A Sign-Seeker' (5) Tennyson is blended with Shelley as a seeker after the secrets of the universe. Tennyson's melancholy meditations on time and fame also seem to have been important to Hardy (74, 75, 102, 153, 179). Beyond that, there are any number of influences in and allusions to classical, seventeenth-century, eighteenth-century and Romantic literature: Virgil (13, 65), Horace (59, 102), Dante, Shakespeare (extensive allusions to the plays), Jonson (17), Vaughan (82, 102, 146, 161), Milton (21, 87, 106), Dryden (99, 114, 165), Gray (57, 112), Goldsmith (128), Cowper (21), Byron (25), Wordsworth (21, 23, 54, 68, 112), Shelley (5, 16, 24, 71, 77, 91, 102, 151, 178), Keats (21, 117) – though Hardy was also capable of borrowing from

Victorian poets and near-contemporaries like Elizabeth Barrett Browning (3, 102, 161), Keble, Arnold (45, 84, 133, 161), Swinburne (1, 3, 17, 48, 107), Fitzgerald (69), Meredith (41, 63), Patmore (particularly his elegies: see 51), Barnes (95, 97, 98, 159), even perhaps from Yeats (69) and Dickinson (121). His work is remarkably dense in its echoes and allusions – many of them in that mode which Harold Bloom and John Hollander call 'transumptive', with Hardy seeming to echo with voices which he has made peculiarly his own. Who can read Shelley's 'Ode to Autumn' without remembering Hardy's chorus in 'During Wind and Rain' (102)?

In his own lifetime, Hardy saw a gradual acceptance from critics of his poetic achievements. While there continued to be a good deal of negative criticism of his grimness and awkwardness, a large number of writers acknowledged the power of his verse, and its skill – recognized, often, that its apparent defects were part of its fascination. But Hardy never lacked followers. He received, in particular, praise from a number of fellow writers: Swinburne, Ezra Pound, T.E. Lawrence, Sigfried Sassoon, Walter de la Mare, Robert Graves, to be followed by accolades from later poets like D.H. Lawrence, Dylan Thomas, W.H. Auden. Many of them visited him and seemed to draw strength from his presence, perhaps because in old age he represented (as he recognized) a link with the past: 'It bridges over the years to think that Gray might have seen Wordsworth in his cradle, and Wordsworth might have seen me in mine' (*EL* 187).

For all the praise, in poems like 'So Various' (165), 'A Poet's Thought (162), and 'Not Known' Hardy meditates on his relationship with his readers, and suggests that the 'real' Hardy remains hidden – not least because of his own attempts at editing the image he bequeathed to posterity in the *Life*. The subsequent story of that bequest, from the battle over his body between Wessex and the Abbey, to Somerset Maugham's satirical portrayal of Hardy and his wife in *Cakes and Ale*, to Robert Gittings's aggressively iconoclastic biography in the 1970s, to the appearance of a 'restored' version of the *Life* in the 1980s, is a story replete with ironies worthy of the poet (see Millgate 1992).

Of course, the legacy of all writers, their place in that fractured entity we call 'literary tradition', is always contested. Hardy's afterlife as a poet is a reflection of twentieth-century literary history. Despite the fact that Pound claimed him briefly for Imagism, in the middle part of this century his work seemed closer to the Victorians than to the poetry of Modernism, and received relatively little attention from critics (with the exception of lukewarm praise from F.R. Leavis, John Crowe Ransome, and R.P. Blackmur). It was with the arrival of the 'Movement' in England in the 1950s that Hardy became a focus in the construction of a distinctly English tradition. Philip Larkin was the most influential of the poets who claimed Hardy as ancestor. For Larkin, Hardy is the poet of his maturity, the one towards whom he turned after abandoning his early enthusiasm for Yeats, a touchstone of candour and honesty. Other poets and critics connected to the Movement have developed the idea of a Hardyean tradition in English poetry, separate from the European and American modernist mainstream, and perhaps even from the dominant Victorian modes. David Wright argues that 'the true and indigenous line of English poetry, through most of the nineteenth century, went underground', and he suggests that before Hardy it surfaces mainly in the works of Clare, Barnes, and Tennyson (Wright 1972: 68).

Tom Paulin identifies a similar native and anti-Parnassian tradition in Hopkins and other poets whom he sees as rooted in the vernacular (Paulin 1987). Thom Gunn praises Hardy's adherence to the ballad-tradition, 'the chief native source of our literature' (Gunn 1972). The most influential (and ambivalent) such argument has been that of Donald Davie in *Thomas Hardy and British Poetry* (1973). Davie places Hardy at the head of a line of English poets from Edward Thomas to Larkin and beyond, all of whom tend to emphasize honesty, diminished claims about the power of poetry, and a refusal of the grand gesture. Davie is both attracted to this honesty, and repelled by what he sees as its selling short of the Romantic and modernist tradition of the poet as the seer and reformer.

Such claims are 'political', in the sense that all battles over the ancestry which artists and thinkers claim are political. Depending on one's perspective, it is possible to see Hardy, as Harold Bloom does, as a diminished late Romantic; or, like David Peck, to perceive a 'modernity' in 'the studied asymmetry of phrase and metre, the sudden shifts in diction and tone, or the quietly lunar phrase' (1972: 124). In the case of a poet whose work confronts the worlds of Darwin and Einstein, Tennyson and T.S. Eliot, both are possible, for Hardy is, surely, a genuinely transitional figure, a poet who stands self-consciously between one world and another, declaring his allegiances to the past but fascinated by the speed of its replacement. Part of the power of his work, moreover, is an awareness of the painful historicity of the human subject which is one of the continuities between Victorian and Modern literature. On that, his poems speak for themselves.

Selecting Hardy

The scope, size, and variety of Hardy's corpus means that selection is inevitably difficult, indeed in some ways impossible. As Terri Witek suggests, 'Hardy's most anthologized poems are often his least typical', since the 'typical' Hardy poem is often quirkier and less polished than anthology-pieces like 'The Oxen' (Witek 1990). For that reason, it is important to read a range of Hardy's verse, including what could be called 'bad' poems: those full of macabre humour or bitterness; those seemingly inappropriate in style like 'Last Words to a Dumb Friend' (124), which deploys an elegiac solemnity for a pet. All these must be placed alongside the seemingly central poems like the great wind-and-time series climaxing in 'During Wind and Rain' (102), or the visionary intensities of 'The Pedigree' (91), or the 'Poems of 1912–13'. Between F.R. Leavis's detection of genius in a very few poems and Philip Larkin's declaration that he would not lose one of them is the world of Hardy's everyday achievement: observation, memory, reflection, and the effort of creation.

Necessarily, any anthology from almost a thousand poems will differ from its predecessors. As Trevor Johnson suggests in his analysis of ten anthologies, there has been remarkably little unanimity among compilers of selections, outside a narrow core of reguarly anthologized pieces: there are only 37 poems which are included in more than half the anthologies (Johnson 1979). The choice here is biased towards the later poetry, and necessarily towards the shorter lyrics. It is designed to reflect the consensus on 'core' poems, including Hardy's own preferences. But it also aims to represent the different areas of his achievement: elegiac and narrative verse; ballads, classical experiments, dialogues, epitaphs, translations.

I have also attempted to retain some sense of the structure of Hardy's volumes, with their subtitled groupings. The poems are printed in the order in which they appear in the *Collected Poems* of 1928. Many selections rearrange Hardy's poems in thematic groups. That seems a mistake, partly because in some cases there are links between adjacent poems, but also because thematic groupings implicitly confirm the view that Hardy has 'no chronology', no development. The case is put by Samuel Hynes: Hardy 'did not develop through new styles as he grew older (as Yeats did) ... he simply learned to use better what he already had' (1961: 139). The reference to Yeats seems unfair (few other poets would stand the comparison), and while Hardy's poetics did not change radically, there are changes in his style, for example in his metrics and use of irregular stanzas. More importantly, time is crucial for Hardy, in terms of the patterns traced across a life.

A note on the annotations

The annotations to the poems include headnotes giving details of composition, sources, and publication, where available, relevant biographical material, and in some cases references to critical commentary and related poems in Hardy's corpus (those in this selection are identified by poem number). General annotations are introduced by a line number followed by full point, or a phrase and colon, thus:

15. breath while: short time (see Elliott 1984: 175).

Annotations cover points relating to individual lines, including glosses, allusions, interpretive comments, and interrelations with other poems. Textual annotations are introduced by a line number and half-bracket, followed by details of variants and relevant editions, thus:

24. showance] showings WE 1912, *CP* 1919.

Variants and (more sparingly) manuscript readings are given wherever they seem relevant: in general I have given fuller lists of variants for the lyric poems than the narrative poems, particularly where Hardy's revisions have a bearing on interpretation. Accidentals of punctuation, spelling, capitalization, etc., have largely been ignored.

Each poem has in addition a metrical note giving the stanza form and, in superscript, the number of beats in each line. This is followed by an indication of the rhythm using the following conventions: d = duple metre (two beats to the metrical foot), t = triple metre (three beats to the foot), r = rising metre, and f = falling metre. The convention $aabb^4$ tr thus indicates couplets in anapaestic tetrameter, $a^6b^5a^6b^5$ df a rhymed quatrain in a combination of trochaic pentameter and hexameter, aa^4 dtr tetrameter couplets in a combination of iambic and anapaestic metres. Capital letters refer to a repeated line or refrain. I have occasionally offered or reproduced other comments on form. Readers would be wise to remember that metres are always debatable, and that (as I occasionally suggest) various metrical possibilities are present in most poems.

A note on the text

There are two main 'lines of descent' (as Samuel Hynes calls them) of Hardy's texts, which were not properly collated in his lifetime. One is based on revisions which he began to make in 1909, when a complete collection of his poetry was suggested by his publisher. That project was delayed by the war, and only completed by the appearance of the *Collected Poems* in 1919. More revisions were incorporated into successive editions of the *Collected Poems* from 1919 through to 1928. The other line of descent is based on a separate set of revisions which Hardy made in 1911 for the Wessex Edition of 1912, and continued to make in Wessex Edition texts, as well as in related editions like the Mellstock Edition of 1920 (see Hynes, *CPW* I, xi–xxiii; Schweik 1984). The first series of revisions began with the *Wessex Poems* and *Poems of the Past and the Present*, which were set in 1909 and then left, Hynes suggests, almost a decade. It is in the two early volumes that the differences between the two lines of transmission are most apparent, and where there is sometimes an uncertainty about the exact point at which revisions were made in the *Collected Poems* line. In the later volumes, the differences are smaller, partly because Hardy made sporadic attempts at collation, though in general his texts remained in relative disarray, with separate corrections made in reprints of individual volumes as well as those in the collected editions.

Of the two modern editors of Hardy's poems, James Gibson used the *Collected Poems* of 1928 and 1930 as copy-text for his *Variorum Edition*; while Samuel Hynes, in preparing the three-volume *Complete Poetical Works*, used the first editions as copy-text, and then followed the more rigorous procedure of referring to the latest revision in either line of transmission. He also made use of corrections Hardy made to reprints of individual volumes, to master copies he kept of both editions (now in the Dorset County Museum), to his *Selected Poems* and its expanded version the *Chosen*

Poems, and to the Mellstock Edition. Hynes procedures are in some cases speculative, however, since it is at times impossible to date revisions, or to tell whether a discrepancy between readings is a result of Hardy's second thoughts or his failure to collate revisions.

This selection takes the *Collected Poems* of 1930 as copy-text. It has been corrected to take account of major revisions in other editions which are of later provenance than those in the *Collected Poems* (including the revised prefaces of the Wessex Edition). Obvious errors in the text have been corrected, titles regularized, and stanzas in manuscript omitted from a number of poems are given in footnotes. The manuscript used as printer's copy is located in the headnotes to each volume; other manuscripts or corrections made in Hardy's copies of his works are occasionally referred to in notes (for a full listing of such manuscripts, see Rosenbaum 1990).

The Poems

Wessex Poems and Other Verses (1898)

Hardy had been considering the publication of his first volume of verse for several years, before *Wessex Poems* was published by Harper & Bros in December 1898. A third of the poems dated from his first period of poetic production, the 1860s, a few were from the intervening two decades of novel-writing, and the rest were from the last decade, during which he had returned to writing poetry. There is evidence of anxiety surrounding their production: the fair copy he prepared for the printer (a manuscript now in the Birmingham City Museum and Art Gallery) was much revised, and more changes were made to the proofs. The volume included Hardy's own illustrations to 31 of the poems.

The reviewers of *Wessex Poems* were generally respectful, but often puzzled by Hardy's switch in genre, and critical of his pessimism, drawing comparisons with the late novels in this respect. A few were hostile: an anonymous reviewer in the *Saturday Review*, 7 January 1899, called the ballads 'some of the most amazing balderdash that ever found its way into a book of verse' (Cox 1970: 320). Perhaps the most positive reviewer was E.K. Chambers in the *Athenaeum*, who found the poems narrow in range but anticipated later reviewers (and Ezra Pound) in finding Hardy's work 'of a kind with which modern poetry can ill afford to dispense. There is no finish or artifice about it: the note struck is strenuous, austere, forcible' (Cox 1970: 327). Hardy paid more attention to the reviews of his first volume of poetry than to any subsequent one: he thanked Lionel Johnson and William Archer for kindly comments, but was stung by criticism. He later argued that 'Almost all the fault-finding was, in fact, based on the one great antecedent conclusion that an author who has published prose first, and that largely, must necessarily express himself badly in verse' (*LY* 76), adding that 'In the reception of this and later volumes of Hardy's poems there was, he said, as regards form, the inevitable ascription to ignorance of what was really choice after full knowledge' (*LY* 78).

A corrected second edition of *Wessex Poems* was issued by Macmillan in 1903, after they had taken over from Harper as Hardy's publishers, as volume XVIII of the new Uniform Edition of his works. The volume was substantially revised for the Wessex Edition in 1912, and (in the same period) for the *Collected Poems* which finally appeared in 1919; other editions contain minor revisions (for commentary on revisions, see Zeitlow 1974: 29–35).

Preface

The first of a series of defensive prefaces which Hardy wrote for his volumes. Paul Zeitlow, in his reading of the Preface, sees in it a deliberate amateurishness expressive of the 'tension between the desire to commit himself and the desire to remain invulnerable' (1974: 35–7).

> Of the miscellaneous collection of verse that follows, only four pieces have been published, though many were written long ago, and others partly written. In some few cases the verses were turned into prose and printed as such in a novel, it not having been anticipated at that time that they might see the light in their original shape.
>
> Here and there, when an ancient and legitimate word still current in the district, for which there was no close equivalent in received English, suggested itself, it has been made use of, on what seemed good grounds.
>
> The pieces are in a large degree dramatic or personative in conception; and the dates attached to some of the poems do not apply to the rough sketches given in illustration, which have been recently made, and, as may be surmised, are inserted for personal and local reasons rather than for their intrinsic qualities.
>
> T.H.

September 1898.

1 The Temporary the All
(Sapphics)

The opening poem of *Wessex Poems*, subsequently included in *Selected Poems* (1916). It was accompanied by Hardy's illustration of a sundial and shadow on a tower of Hardy's house, Max Gate, suggesting the theme of time and contingency (the sundial was designed by Hardy, but only installed after his

---

4. turned into prose: a number of Hardy's poems relate to episodes in his novels, or expand on them (see annotations).
7. ancient and legitimate word: despite this defence of dialect, Hardy cut a number of dialect-words when revising for the *Collected Poems*.
11. dramatic or personative: cf. the Preface to Hardy's next volume, and Browning's disclaimer in *Dramatic Lyrics*, that his poems were 'so many utterances of so many imaginary persons, not mine'.
12. conception; and the dates] conception; and this even where they are not obviously so. The dates *WP* 1989, 1903, *CP*.
Subtitle: Sapphics] added *SP* 1916.

death). The manuscript is heavily revised, and Hardy made a number of changes to later editions (as in all subsequent poems, variants are given selectively here).

Most critics have agreed with James Richardson's description of this poem as 'militantly odd' in style, as if signalling Hardy's poetic intentions from the outset. Richardson comments that 'the terrible restraint and the difficulty of the whole performance are clues that the poem deals with what is for Hardy the most painful of issues' (Richardson 1977: 15–17; cf. Zeitlow 1974: 26–35; Grundy 1980: 1–3).

Metre: as the subtitle states, the poem is in sapphics, named for the Greek poet Sappho (*c.* 600 BC), whose work Hardy imitates in 'Sapphic Fragment'. In Sapphics, strictly defined, three lines of eleven syllables are followed by a shorter line of five syllables. Swinburne had used the form in his *Poems and Ballads*. Hardy combines it with a use of alliteration and compound words perhaps borrowed from the Dorset poet William Barnes, and with archaizing inversions ('Can I', 'Bettered not'). This is the only unrhymed poem in *Wessex Poems*.

> Change and chancefulness in my flowering youthtime,
> Set me sun by sun near to one unchosen;
> Wrought us fellowlike, and despite divergence,
>   Fused us in friendship.
>
> 'Cherish him can I while the true one forthcome –   5
> Come the rich fulfiller of my prevision;
> Life is roomy yet, and the odds unbounded.'
>   So self-communed I.
>
> 'Thwart my wistful way did a damsel saunter,
> Fair, albeit unformed to be all-eclipsing;   10
> 'Maiden meet,' held I, 'till arise my forefelt
>   Wonder of women.'

1. cf. Browning's 'Any Wife to Any Husband', 9: 'Chance cannot change that love, nor time impair . . .'
1. flowering] bloothing MS (the latter a dialect term).
2. one unchosen: perhaps Henry Robert Bastow, whom Hardy worked with as an architectural assistant (Bailey 1970: 48).
3–4] Wrought us fellowy, and despite divergence, / Friends interblent us. *WP* 1898, 1903; Friends interknit us. MS.
5. forthcome: comes forth.
6. prevision: foresight. Tess is described as 'previsioned by suffering' (*Tess of the D'Urbervilles*, ch. 36, p. 269).
9. 'Thwart: athwart, across.
10] Fair not fairest, good not best of her feather; MS, *WP* 1898.
11. forefelt: anticipated.

Long a visioned hermitage deep desiring,
Tenements uncouth I was fain to house in:
'Let such lodging be for a breath-while,' thought I,   15
  'Soon a more seemly.

'Then high handiwork will I make my life-deed,
Truth and Light outshow; but the ripe time pending,
Intermissive aim at the thing sufficeth.'
  Thus I.... But lo, me!   20

Mistress, friend, place, aims to be bettered straightway,
Bettered not has Fate or my hand's achievement;
Sole the showance those of my onward earth-track –
  Never transcended!

2 Hap

'Hap' is the earliest poem in this selection. It is one of the few poems not included in *Selected Poems* (1916) but subsequently selected for *Chosen Poems* (1929), suggesting a reappraisal on Hardy's part.

'Hap' or chance is a resonant word for Hardy, suggesting both randomness and that which simply 'happens'. His use of it straddles his career, from this early poem to the 'neutral-tinted haps and such' of 'He Never Expected Much' (168), written some sixty years later. He had noted the phrase 'heavy hap' in his copy of *The Faerie Queen* III, 20 (Taylor 1990: 54).

Metre: abab[5] dr. John Lucas writes of 'the appalling, flat rhythms' which 'enact a frightening blanking-out of the spirit' (Lucas 1986: 35).

> If but some vengeful god would call to me
> From up the sky, and laugh: 'Thou suffering thing,
> Know that thy sorrow is my ecstasy,
> That thy love's loss is my hate's profiting!'

14. *Tenements uncouth*: a rented flat or part of a house rather than the American 'tenement block' (probably Westbourne Park Villas, where Hardy lived in the 1860s).
14. *fain*: reluctant.
15. *breath-while*: a short time (on such compounds, see Elliott 1984: 175).
17. *high handiwork*] achievement large MS.
20. *lo, me!*] woe me, MS.
23–4] They as tokens sole of my sorry earth-way / Stand in their scantness! MS.
23. *showance*] showings WE 1912, *SP* 1916, *CP* 1919.
Title] Chance MS.

Then would I bear it, clench myself, and die, 5
Steeled by the sense of ire unmerited;
Half-eased in that a Powerfuller than I
Had willed and meted me the tears I shed.

But not so. How arrives it joy lies slain,
And why unblooms the best hope ever sown? 10
– Crass Casualty obstructs the sun and rain,
And dicing Time for gladness casts a moan. . . .
These purblind Doomsters had as readily strown
Blisses about my pilgrimage as pain.
  1866.

3 Neutral Tones

As in the case of 'Hap', the poem's date suggests that its context is Hardy's disappointed love affair in the 1860s. The governing metaphor suggested by the title is that of a picture or etching in 'neutral tones', inscribed on the memory like the recollections described in 'In a Former Resort after Many Years' (133) (on etching, cf. 'Lying Awake' (160), written near the end of Hardy's career). Subsequently included in *Selected Poems* (1916).

  Metre: $a^4b^4b^4a^3$ dtr, perhaps best seen as a variant on the *In Memoriam* metre, though Dennis Taylor's suggestion of Elizabeth Barrett Browning's 'The Deserted Garden' as model is persuasive, given the thematic parallels between the poems (1988: 230).

8. *meted*: alloted.
10. the failure of flowers to bloom and crops to ripen is a common elegiac trope (used by Hardy in his own elegies): cf. Milton's 'Lycidas', ll. 42–9; and Shelley's 'Adonais' 6:
      The bloom, whose petals nipped before they they blew
      Died on the promise of the fruit, is waste . . .
10. *unblooms*: fails to bloom. Hardy often uses negative componds like 'unbe', 'unblind', 'unsee', 'unknow', 'unvision' (Elliott 1984: 191–6). Richardson suggests that they are inherently dialectical and involve 'a deliberate exclusion [of the root concept], a negative vector rather than zero' (1977: 103–4).
11. *Crass Casualty*: Hardy glossed this as 'insensible' chance (Bailey 1970: 52). 'Casualty' also suggests 'causality,' i.e. the Fate which determines events and lives.
12. *dicing*: throwing dice. Cf. 'Sine Prole' (138) l. 18.
13. *purblind Doomsters*: dim-sighted or stupid Fates.
Date] WE 1912 adds location: W.P.V. (16 Westbourne Park Villas).

We stood by a pond that winter day,
And the sun was white, as though chidden of God,
few leaves lay on the starving sod;
    – They had fallen from an ash, and were gray.

Your eyes on me were as eyes that rove   5
Over tedious riddles of years ago;
And some words played between us to and fro
    On which lost the more by our love.

The smile on your mouth was the deadest thing
Alive enough to have strength to die;   10
And a grin of bitterness swept thereby
    Like an ominous bird a-wing. . . .

Since then, keen lessons that love deceives,
And wrings with wrong, have shaped to me
Your face, and the God-curst sun, and a tree,   15
    And a pond edged with grayish leaves.

1867.

---

2. chidden of God: cf. Milton, Sonnet XIV: 'To serve therewith my Maker, and present / My true account, lest he returning chide, / 'Doth God exact day-labour, light denied?'; or the gods of Swinburne's 'Ilicet' (1866), a poem which has a number of echoes in Hardy: 'Before their eyes all life stands chidden' (l. 137).

6. of] solved   Editions before *CP* 1923.

7–8. there is a grammatical ambiguity in these lines. Morgan (1974) suggests that they are interrogative: ie. there was an exchange between the lovers 'On which [of us] lost the more' in love. Docherty and Taylor (1974) perhaps over-ingeniously suggest other alternatives, arguing that 'played . . . to and fro on' should be seen as a unit, so that the lines mean:
        And some words [were] played on between us to and fro
        Which [words] lost the more by our love.

7. some words] a query MS del.; words WE, *SP* 1916.

7. fro] fro –   All editions before *CP* 1919.

8] MS has: Which was most wrecked by our love? (del.).
        On which the more lost by our love.

9–10. the oxymoron is Swinburnian: cf. 'Hermaphroditus', ll. 3–4, for example: Of all things tired thy lips look weariest,
        Save the long smile that they are wearied of.

Date] *SP* 1916 adds location: Westbourne Park Villas.

4 The Peasant's Confession

One of a group of narrative poems in *Wessex Poems* set in the Napoleonic Wars, many of them related to Hardy's novel *The Trumpet-Major* (1880), to *The Dynasts*, and to material remembered from childhood stories reaching back to the Napoleonic era. A note in the *Life* describes how in 1898 'Hardy did some reading at the British Museum with a view to *The Dynasts*, and incidentally stumbled upon some details that suggested to him the Waterloo episode embodied in a poem called "The Peasant's Confession"' (*LY* 74). The larger events which frame those in this poem are dealt with in *The Dynasts*, Part III, vi–vii. After publication Hardy described it as 'a mere romance, purporting to account for Grouchy's absence from Waterloo: not (what some careless reviewers say) anything about Wellington' (*CL* II, 211). *Wessex Poems* includes as illustration Hardy's sketch of what appears to be the rainy scene of the poem's opening.

Metre: $a^5b^3a^5b^3$ dr, used for a number of poems and perhaps modelled on Vaughan's 'Confession' (Taylor 1988: 228).

> 'Si le maréchal Grouchy avait été rejoint par l'officier que Napoléon lui avait expédié la veille à dix heures du soir, toute question eût disparu. Mais cet officier n'était point parvenu à sa destination, ainsi que le maréchal n'a cessé de l'affirmer toute sa vie, et il faut l'en croire, car autrement il n'aurait eu aucune raison pour hésiter. Cet officier avait-il été pris? avait-il passé à l'ennemi? C'est ce qu'on a toujours ignoré.' – Thiers, *Histoire de l'Empire*. 'Waterloo.'

Title: *Confession*: the monologue is in the form of a confession to a priest, with a prayer of contrition at the end.
Epigraph. from Adolphe Thiers's monumental *Histoire du Consulat et de l'Empire* (Paris, 1862), XX, 258. Hardy also owned a translation of the work by D. Forbes Campbell (London, 1862), marked at this passage:

> There would have been an end put to all discussion had the officer whom Napoleon had sent to the Marshal at ten o'clock on the previous evening arrived. But he did not, as Marshal Grouchy frequently repeated during his life, and we must give credit to what he said, for he could not otherwise have had any motive for hesitation. The fate of this officer has never been ascertained, and whether he was captured or whether he deserted to the enemy, is alike unknown. (XX, 143–4)

Bailey suggests that another source is Victor Hugo's *Les Miserables* I, viii, ix: 'it may almost be said that from this shake of a peasant's head came the catastrophe of Napoleon' (Bailey 1970: 71–2). However, none of the sources includes Hardy's story of the officer and the peasant.

Good Father! ... It was eve in middle June,
    And war was waged anew
By great Napoleon, who for years had strewn
    Men's bones all Europe through.

Three nights ere this, with columned corps he'd cross'd   5
    The Sambre at Charleroi,
To move on Brussels, where the English host
    Dallied in Parc and Bois.

The yestertide we'd heard the gloomy gun
    Growl through the long-sunned day   10
From Quatre-Bras and Ligny; till the dun
    Twilight suppressed the fray;

Albeit therein – as lated tongues bespoke –
    Brunswick's high heart was drained,
And Prussia's Line and Landwehr, though unbroke,   15
    Stood cornered and constrained.

And at next noon-time Grouchy slowly passed
    With thirty thousand men:
We hoped thenceforth no army, small or vast,
    Would trouble us again.   20

My hut lay deeply in a vale recessed,
    And never a soul seemed nigh
When, reassured at length, we went to rest –
    My children, wife, and I.

But what was this that broke our humble ease?   25
    What noise, above the rain,

---

1. *eve in middle June*: 17 June 1815, the day before the battle of Waterloo.
5–8. French troop movements leading up to the battle are contrasted with British inaction (cf. Byron's *Childe Harold*, and the famous Ball in Brussels, described in Thackeray's *Vanity Fair*).
5. *three nights*: on 15 June, in fact.
8. *Parc and Bois*: park and wood.
11. *Quatre-Bras and Ligny*: preliminary battles. On 16 June Napoleon defeated a Prussian force at Ligny, and left the Marquis de Grouchy, in command of his right wing, to pursue them while he turned his attention to the British under Wellington. Grouchy's failure to return forms the subject of the poem.
13–16] stanza not in MS.
13. *as lated tongues bespoke*: as later witnesses testified.
14. *Brunswick's*: (troops from) the Duchy of Brunswick.
15. *Landwehr*: army.

Above the dripping of the poplar trees
    That smote along the pane?
— A call of mastery, bidding me arise,
    Compelled me to the door,   30
At which a horseman stood in martial guise —
    Splashed — sweating from every pore.

Had I seen Grouchy! Yes? What track took he?
    Could I lead thither on? —
Fulfilment would ensure much gold for me,   35
    Perhaps more gifts anon.

'I bear the Emperor's mandate,' then he said,
    'Charging the Marshal straight
To strike between the double host ahead
    Ere they co-operate,   40

'Engaging Blücher till the Emperor put
    Lord Wellington to flight,
And next the Prussians. This to set afoot
    Is my emprise to-night.'

I joined him in the mist; but, pausing, sought   45
    To estimate his say.
Grouchy had made for Wavre; and yet, on thought,
    I did not lead that way.

I mused: 'If Grouchy thus and thus be told,
    The clash comes sheer hereon;   50
My farm is stript. While, as for gifts of gold,
    Money the French have none.

'Grouchy unwarned, moreo'er, the English win,
    And mine is left to me —
They buy, not borrow.' — Hence did I begin   55
    To lead him treacherously.

And as we edged Joidoigne with cautious view
    Dawn pierced the humid air;
And still I easted with him, though I knew
    Never marched Grouchy there.   60

---

35. much gold for me,] gold pieces three, Editions before *CP* 1919 (paralleling Judas's bargain and the 'mite' of l. 135).
38–44. the plan to split the British and the Prussians failed; the return of the Prussian forces under Blücher marked the decisive moment in the battle.
44. emprise: (military) undertaking.
57. Joidoigne: the peasant leads him eastwards, away from Waterloo.

Near Ottignies we passed, across the Dyle
    (Lim'lette left far aside),
And thence direct toward Pervez and Noville
    Through green grain, till he cried:

'I doubt thy conduct, man! no track is here –   65
    I doubt thy gagèd word!'
Thereat he scowled on me, and prancing near,
    He pricked me with his sword.

'Nay, Captain, hold! We skirt, not trace the course
    Of Grouchy,' said I then: 70
'As we go, yonder went he, with his force
    Of thirty thousand men.'

– At length noon nighed; when west, from Saint-John's-Mound,
    A hoarse artillery boomed,
And from Saint-Lambert's upland, chapel-crowned,   75
    The Prussian squadrons loomed.

Then leaping to the wet wild path we had kept,
    'My mission fails!' he cried;
'Too late for Grouchy now to intercept,
    For, peasant, you have lied!'   80

He turned to pistol me. I sprang, and drew
    The sabre from his flank,
And 'twixt his nape and shoulder, ere he knew,
    I struck, and dead he sank.

I hid him deep in nodding rye and oat –   85
    His shroud green stalks and loam;
His requiem the corn-blade's husky note –
    And then I hastened home. . . .

– Two armies writhe in coils of red and blue,
    And brass and iron clang   90

61–4. they move haphazardly past villages to the southeast.
66. *gagèd*: pledged.
73. they have circled back to a hill a few miles south of Waterloo.
85–8: the hasty epitaph (ironically) borrows the pastoral elegance of classical elegy, before the bathetic l. 88. Hardy was criticized by William Archer for making his peasant too sophisticated, and responded: 'Concluding that the tale must be regarded as a translation of the original utterance of the peasant I thought an impersonal wording admissable' (*CL* II, 207).
89–90: cf. the description of 'writhing' nations in the 'Fore Scene' of *The Dynasts* (p. 27).

From Goumont, past the front of Waterloo,
   To Pap'lotte and Smohain.

The Guard Imperial wavered on the height;
   The Emperor's face grew glum;
'I sent,' he said, 'to Grouchy yesternight,   95
   And yet he does not come!'

'Twas then, Good Father, that the French espied,
   Streaking the summer land,
The men of Blücher. But the Emperor cried,
   'Grouchy is now at hand!'   100

And meanwhile Vand'leur, Vivian, Maitland, Kempt,
   Met d'Erlon, Friant, Ney;
But Grouchy – mis-sent, blamed, yet blame-exempt –
   Grouchy was far away.

By even, slain or struck, Michel the strong,   105
   Bold Travers, Dnop, Delord,
Smart Guyot, Reil-le, l'Heriter, Friant,
   Scattered that champaign o'er.

Fallen likewise wronged Duhesme, and skilled Lobau
   Did that red sunset see;   110
Colbert, Legros, Blancard! ... And of the foe
   Picton and Ponsonby;

With Gordon, Canning, Blackman, Ompteda,
   L'Estrange, Delancey, Packe,
Grose, D'Oyly, Stables, Morice, Howard, Hay,   115
   Von Schwerin, Watzdorf, Boek,

Smith, Phelips, Fuller, Lind, and Battersby,
   And hosts of ranksmen round. . . .
Memorials linger yet to speak to thee
   Of those that bit the ground!   120

The Guards' last column yielded; dykes of dead
   Lay between vale and ridge,

---

91. Goumont: contraction of 'Hougoumont'.
101–20. the names are of French, British, Prussians involved in the battle, many killed or wounded (for details see Bailey 1970: 75). The list of combatants is a standard device of classical epic.
105. even: evening.
105. struck: wounded.
108. champaign: countryside or field of battle: see 'The Eve of Waterloo' (180), l. 5n.
109. wronged Duhesme: he was killed as a prisoner.

>   As, thinned yet closing, faint yet fierce, they sped
>   In packs to Genappe Bridge.
>   Safe was my stock; my capple cow unslain;   125
>   Intact each cock and hen;
>   But Grouchy far at Wavre all day had lain,
>   And thirty thousand men.
>
>   O Saints, had I but lost my earing corn
>   And saved the cause once prized!   130
>   O Saints, why such false witness had I borne
>   When late I'd sympathized! ...
>
>   So now, being old, my children eye askance
>   My slowly dwindling store,
>   And crave my mite; till, worn with tarriance,   135
>   I care for life no more.
>
>   To Almighty God henceforth I stand confessed,
>   And Virgin-Saint Marie;
>   O Michael, John, and Holy Ones in rest,
>   Entreat the Lord for me!

5 A Sign-Seeker

'A Sign-Seeker' has often been read as a pessimistic reply to Tennyson's attempt to find meaning in the face of death (see McCarthy 1980; Zeitlow 1974: 16; Buckler 1983a: 151). But it invokes a tradition of poetic aspirations to knowledge which extends back to Vergil's 'Happy the man who, studying Nature's laws, / Through known effects can trace the secret cause' (see note below). Hardy's illustration in *Wessex Poems* depicts a shooting star or comet over the Dorchester skyline.

Metre: $a^5b^4b^4a^6$ dr, perhaps alluding to the $abba^4$ stanza of *In Memoriam*.

>   I mark the months in liveries dank and dry,
>   The noontides many-shaped and hued;

---

125. capple: white-muzzled.
135. mite: insignificant amount (lit. a small coin).
135. tarriance: delay.
137–40. formal conclusion to the 'confession'.
1. liveries: uniforms (cf. *A Midsummer Night's Dream* II, i, 112–13: 'The chiding autumn, angry winter, change / Their wonted liveries').
2. noontides] day-tides MS, *WP* 1898. 'Noontide' is mid-day; cf. the final poem of *Wessex Poems*.

I see the nightfall shades subtrude,
And hear the monotonous hours clang negligently by.

I view the evening bonfires of the sun   5
   On hills where morning rains have hissed;
   The eyeless countenance of the mist
Pallidly rising when the summer droughts are done.

I have seen the lightning-blade, the leaping star,
   The cauldrons of the sea in storm,   10
   Have felt the earthquake's lifting arm,
And trodden where abysmal fires and snow-cones are.

I learn to prophesy the hid eclipse,
   The coming of eccentric orbs;
   To mete the dust the sky absorbs,   15
To weigh the sun, and fix the hour each planet dips.

I witness fellow earth-men surge and strive;
   Assemblies meet, and throb, and part;
   Death's sudden finger, sorrow's smart;
– All the vast various moils that mean a world alive.   20

But that I fain would wot of shuns my sense –
   Those sights of which old prophets tell,
   Those signs the general word so well,
As vouchsafed their unheed, denied my long suspense.

---

3. subtrude: thrust themselves in stealthily (Hardy's is the only usage listed in OED).
9–12. the imagery is partly apocalyptic (see Revelation 8).
13–16. cf. the invocation of the muses in Vergil's second Georgic, translated by Dryden:
   Give me the ways of wandering stars to know,
   The depths of heaven and earth below;
   Teach me the various labours of the moon,
   And whence proceed the eclipses of the sun. . . .
14. eccentric orbs: comets.
15. mete: measure.
16. weigh the sun: a phrase from Tennyson's 'Locksley Hall', l. 186.
19. sudden] soothing MS, *WP* 1898, 1903.
20. moils: labours, toils.
21. i.e. 'But that which I would like to understand escapes me'. The diction in this stanza is deliberately difficult.
23–4. i.e. 'Those signs [which] most people speak of glibly as given to them freely, in their unheedlessness, are denied to me, despite all my waiting.'
24. long suspense] watchings tense MS, *WP* 1898.

In graveyard green, where his pale dust lies pent   25
  To glimpse a phantom parent, friend,
  Wearing his smile, and 'Not the end!'
Outbreathing softly: that were blest enlightenment;

Of, if a dead Love's lips, whom dreams reveal
  When midnight imps of King Decay   30
  Delve sly to solve me back to clay,
Should leave some print to prove her spirit-kisses real;

  Or, when Earth's Frail lie bleeding of her Strong,
  If some Recorder, as in Writ,
  Near to the weary scene should flit   35
And drop one plume as pledge that Heaven inscrolls the wrong

– There are who, rapt to heights of trancelike trust,
  These tokens claim to feel and see,
  Read radiant hints of times to be –
Of heart to heart returning after dust to dust.   40

Such scope is granted not to lives like mine . . .
  I have lain in dead men's beds, have walked

25] In graveyard green, behind his monument MS, *WP* 1898, 1903.
31. *solve*: dissolve.
34. *Recorder, as in Writ*: recording angel, as in the book of Revelation.
37–40. cf. Tennyson's 'trance', *In Memoriam* 95:
> So word by word, and line by line,
>   The dead man touched me from the past,
>   And all at once it seemed at last
> The living soul was flashed on mine,
>
> And mine in this was wound, and whirled
>   About empyreal heights of thought,
>   And came on that which is, and caught
> The deep pulsations of the world. . . .

37] There are who, blest with store of stoic trust MS.
40. *dust to dust*: from the Burial Service: 'we therefore commit his body to the ground; earth to earth, ashes to ashes, dust to dust; in sure and certain hope of the Resurrection to eternal life.'
41. *not to lives like mine*] not my powers indign *WP* 1898.
42–5. alludes to Shelley's *Alastor*, ll. 23–9:
> I have made my bed
> In charnels and on coffins, where black death
> Keeps record of the trophies won from thee,
> Hoping to still these obstinate questionings
> Of thee and thine, by forcing some lone ghost
> Thy messenger, to render up the tale
> Of what we are.

The tombs of those with whom I had talked,
Called many a gone and goodly one to shape a sign,
And panted for response. But none replies; 45
   No warnings loom, nor whisperings
   To open out my limitings,
And Nescience mutely muses: When a man falls he lies.

6 Friends Beyond

'Friends Beyond' accompanies the frontispiece of *Wessex Poems*, which depicts the entrance gate of Stinsford churchyard at dusk. The poem features characters from Hardy's novels as well as real people in the company of the dead, and makes use of dialect in registering their speech (though some of those usages were removed in revision). It was subsequently included in *Selected Poems* (1916). Hardy returns to this subject in a similar style in 'Voices from Things Growing in a Churchyard' (121).

Metre: the unusual $a^8b^4a^8$ df stanza-form seems to borrow its catalectic long lines from Tennyson's 'Locksley Hall', though Paulin (1982: 92–3) suggests the poem alludes and 'replies' to Browning's 'A Toccata of Galuppi's', also in trochaic octameter. There is an allusion to *terza rima* in the rhyming of the first and third lines of each stanza with the middle line of each previous stanza. Taylor sees in the poem a 'sound symbolism' which creates a 'ghostly whispering' of subterranean voices (1988: 153). John Betjeman lovingly parodies its effects in his poem 'Dorset'.

William Dewey, Tranter Reuben, Farmer Ledlow late at plough,
   Robert's kin, and John's, and Ned's,
And the Squire, and Lady Susan, lie in Mellstock churchyard now!
'Gone,' I call them, gone for good, that group of local hearts and heads;
   Yet at mothy curfew-tide, 5

48. *Nescience*: lack of knowledge (used *EL* 191).
1–3. William Dewey and his son Reuben (a Tranter or carter), Farmer Ledlow, and Robert Penny appear in *Under the Greenwood Tree* and other novels (the latter based on a boot-maker, Robert Reason, mentioned *LY* 198, 242–3). John and Ned are obscure, the Squire has a number of possible models, and 'Lady Susan' was Susan O'Brien of Stinsford House, daughter of the Earl of Ilchester, portrayed in Hardy's short story 'The Noble Lady's Tale' (*EL* 11, 213–14; *LY* 12–13).
5. *mothy curfew-tide*: traditionally the curfew-bell was sounded at 8 o'clock. According to Hardy in a letter to E.B. Poulton (*CL* VI, 251–2), a folk-belief held that moths were connected with the souls of the dead: cf. 'Afterwards' (112).

And at midnight when the noon-heat breathes it back from walls
    and leads,
They've a way of whispering to me – fellow-wight who yet abide –
    In the muted, measured note
Of a ripple under archways, or a lone cave's stillicide:
'We have triumphed: this achievement turns the bane to
    antidote,   10
    Unsuccesses to success,
Many thought-worn eves and morrows to a morrow free of
    thought.
'No more need we corn and clothing, feel of old terrestial stress;
    Chill detraction stirs no sigh;
Fear of death has even bygone us: death gave all that we
    possess.'   15
W.D. – 'Ye mid burn the old bass-viol that I set such value
    by.'
Squire. – 'You may hold the manse in fee,
    You may wed my spouse, may let my children's memory of
        me die.'
Lady S. – 'You may have my rich brocades, my laces; take each
    household key;
    Ransack coffer, desk, bureau;   20
    Quiz the few poor treasures hid there, con the letters kept by
        me.'

---

6. *leads*: lead roofing. Hardy often uses the night time radiation of heat from stones as a metaphor for the persistence of memory (see Paulin 1975: 173–4).
7. *fellow-wight*: fellow-being.
9. *stillicide*: the falling of drops (from L. *stillicidium*: previous usage cited by the OED is seventeenth century). The word takes on ominous overtones from its parallels with 'homicide', 'suicide'.
10. *turns the bane to antidote*: i.e. makes that which had been destructive harmless.
16. *mid*: may.
16. *old*] wold MS, *WP* 1898, 1903.
16. *value*] vallie MS, *WP* 1898, 1903.
17. *hold the manse in fee*: own the manor by hereditary right.
21. *Quiz*: mock.
19–21. cf. Mother Cuxsom in *The Mayor of Casterbridge*, ch. 18 (p. 142): 'All her shining keys will be took from her, and her cupboards opened; and little things a'didn't wish seen, anybody will see; and her wishes and ways will be as nothing.'
21. *con*: examine.

Far. – 'Ye mid zell my favourite heifer, ye mid let the charlock
           grow,
       Foul the grinterns, give up thrift.'
Far. Wife. – 'If ye break my best blue china, children, I shan't
           care or ho.'
All. – 'We've no wish to hear the tidings, how the people's
           fortunes shift;   25
       What your daily doings are;
   Who are wedded, born, divided; if your lives beat slow or
           swift.
'Curious not the least are we if our intents you make or mar,
       If you quire to our old tune,
If the City stage still passes, if the weirs still roar afar.'   30
– Thus, with very gods' composure, freed those crosses late
           and soon
       Which, in life, the Trine allow
(Why, none witteth), and ignoring all that haps beneath the
           moon,
William Dewy, Tranter Reuben, Farmer Ledlow late at plough,
       Robert's kin, and John's, and Ned's,   35
And the Squire, and Lady Susan, murmur mildly to me now.

7 Thoughts of Phena
At News of Her Death

The occasion of the poem is described in a diary entry for 5 March 1890, recorded in the *Life*: 'In the train on the way to London. Wrote the first four or six lines of "Not a line of her writing have I". It was a curious instance of sympathetic telepathy. The woman whom I was thinking of – a

22. *Ye mid zell*: You may sell.
22. *charlock*: a weed, field mustard.
23. *grinterns*: granary bins.
24. *ho*: be anxious.
31. *god's composure*: ie. the Stoic philosophy of indifference as expounded by Lucretius, Epicurius and other Greek philosophers.
32. *Trine*: Trinity.
33. *none witteth*: no one knows.
33. *haps*: chances.
Title] early versions of the title suggest a desire to avoid too explicit reference to Tryphena: T——a MS; Thoughts of Ph——a *WP* 1898; At News of a Woman's Death *SP* 1916.

cousin – was dying at the time, and I was quite in ignorance of it. She died six days later. The remainder of the piece was not written till after her death' (*EL* 293). The cousin was Tryphena Sparks, who died on 17 March 1890. It has been suggested Hardy was in love with her in the late 1860s; but he had not seen her since her marriage in 1877. The illustration shows the body of a woman covered by a shroud, laid out on a monumental-looking divan. Subsequently included in *Selected Poems* (1916).
  Metre: $a^3b^2a^5b^2c^3d^2c^5d^2$ tr.

>   Not a line of her writing have I,
>   Not a thread of her hair,
> No mark of her late time as dame in her dwelling, whereby
>   I may picture her there;
>   And in vain do I urge my unsight   5
>   To conceive my lost prize
> At her close, whom I knew when her dreams were upbrimming with light,
>   And with laughter her eyes.
>
>   What scenes spread around her last days,
>   Sad, shining, or dim?   10
> Did her gifts and compassions enray and enarch her sweet ways
>   With an aureate nimb?
>   Or did life-light decline from her years,
>   And mischances control
> Her full day-star; unease, or regret, or forebodings, or fears   15
>   Disennoble her soul?
>
>   Thus I do but the phantom retain
>   Of the maiden of yore
> As my relic; yet haply the best of her – fined in my brain
>   It may be the more   20
>   That no line of her writing have I,
>   Nor a thread of her hair,

5. *unsight*: a word also used in 'To Meet, or Otherwise'. On such negatives, see note on 'unblooms' in 'Hap' (2).
10–12] MS has:
    Sad, sharp, or serene?
  Did the Fates and Affections combine to embow her sweet ways
    With an irisèd sheen?
12, aureate nimb: glowing light (as the MS makes clear, a rainbow is suggested).
19. fined: refined.

No mark of her late time as dame in her dwelling, whereby
    I may picture her there.
March 1890.

8 Nature's Questioning

'Nature's Questioning' reflects Hardy's engagement with a range of nineteenth-century thought on progress, religion, and the nature of creation in the absence of a personal deity. It is particularly linked to his attempt in *The Dynasts* to formulate a view of history which would allow for some notion of non-random direction to human affairs, in the face of a seemingly meaningless universe (see Wright 1967). Paul Zeitlow comments on the poem's series of bizzarly shifting metaphors (1974: 17–19).
    The poem's illustration depicts a broken key. Roger Ebbatson comments: 'That emblem sums up his position, which insists upon the unknowability of the universe and man's bafflement at his role – part victim, part agent – within the process' (1982: 39). In *Far from the Madding Crowd*, ch. 33 (p. 234), Maryann says that 'Breaking a key is a dreadful bodement'.
    Metre: $a^4b^3b^3a^6$ dr (cf. 'A Sign-Seeker' (5)).

> When I look forth at dawning, pool,
>   Field, flock, and lonely tree,
>   All seem to gaze at me
> Like chastened children sitting silent in a school;
>
>   Their faces dulled, constrained, and worn,   5
>   As though the master's way
>   Through the long teaching day
> Had cowed them till their early zest was overborne.
>
>   Upon them stirs in lippings mere
>   (As if once clear in call,   10
>   But now scarce breathed at all) –
> 'We wonder, ever wonder, why we find us here!

23–4] No mark of her late time, her bower, her lattice, whereby / I may image her there. MS.
1–4. the classroom images suggest Wordsworth's 'Intimations' Ode, though Hardy's use of that poem is implicitly negative (I. Grundy 1980: 14).

'Has some Vast Imbecility,
    Mighty to build and blend,
    But impotent to tend, 15
Framed us in jest, and left us now to hazardry?
'Or come we of an Automaton
    Unconscious of our pains? ...
    Or are we live remains
Of Godhead dying downwards, brain and eye now gone? 20
'Or is it that some high Plan betides,
    As yet not understood,
    Of Evil stormed by Good,
We the Forlorn Hope over which Achievement strides?'

13–16. this and the following 'explanations' of existence caricature different philosophical attempts to solve the problems of Freewill and Necessity. Here the suggestion is of a 'blind Clockmaker' – i.e. that the maker of the universe might be impotent to actually direct Creation once it was set in motion (a view which derives ultimately from Hume's essay 'On Miracles'). Hardy's notebooks contain a comment on 'This strange absentee government of the universe [by the God of the Deists]' (Björk entry 1604, Hardy's parentheses).

19–20. the suggestion that life represents a 'falling away' from an original unity is a Platonic commonplace: cf. Wordsworth's 'Intimations' Ode, stanza 5. The lines can also be read as describing the 'death of God' as a result of increased scepticism (cf. 'God's Funeral'). Lawrence Jones relates the eye/brain image to Leslie Stephen's essay 'Are We Christians?', first published in the *Fortnightly Review*, March 1873, in which he describes unbelief in the 'thinking class' as like nerve impulses which only slowly make their way from the active brain to duller subsidiary organs (Jones 1980: 191).

21–4. the idea of evolutionary improvement towards some as yet unrealized goal was expounded by J.S. Mill and occasionally espoused by Hardy before 1914. Mill writes:

> The only admissable moral theory of creation is that the Principle of Good *cannot* at once and altogether subdue the powers of evil, either physical or moral; could not place mankind in a world free from the necessity of an incessant struggle with maleficient powers ... (quoted Wright 1967: 32, from Mill's 1874 essay 'Nature', in *Three Essays on Religion*).

Hardy's copied passages from Leslie Stephen's article 'An Attempted Philosophy of History' (1880) into his notebooks, including this one:

> [By Darwinism] we are no longer forced to choose between a fixed order imposed by supernatural sanction, & accidental combination capable of instantaneous & arbitrary reconstruction, [but] recognise in society, as in individuals, the development of an *organic structure* by slow secular processes. (Björk entry 1194)

  Thus things around. No answerer I . . .   25
   Meanwhile the winds, and rains,
   And Earth's old glooms and pains
 Are still the same, and Life and Death are neighbours nigh.

9 In a Eweleaze near Weatherbury

The date and the setting, a field near Puddleton used for village festivities, suggest that memories of Hardy's cousin Tryphena Sparks are involved in the poem: she had lived at Puddleton, and her death on 17 March 1890 must have triggered memories of her (see 'Thoughts of Phena' (7)). Pinion suggests that some details are related to *The Return of the Native* IV, 3 (1976: 25). The illustration, one of Hardy's oddest, depicts a pair of spectacles superimposed on the poem's scene.

'In a Eweleaze near Weatherbury' establishes a pattern repeated in many subsequent pieces: memories of dancing or singing, the 'defacing' action of Time, and a realization of loss. Included in *Selected Poems* (1916).

Metre: ababcdcd^3 dr, alternating feminine and masculine endings; a favourite hymn stanza, as in 'Redeem'd, Restored, Forgiven' (Taylor 1988: 248).

   The years have gathered grayly
    Since I danced upon this leaze
   With one who kindled gaily
    Love's fitful ecstasies!
   But despite the term as teacher,   5
    I remain what I was then
   In each essential feature
    Of the fantasies of men.

   Yet I note the little chisel
    Of never-napping Time   10

26. see note to title of 'During Wind and Rain' (102).
28] the resonant second clause evolved slowly:
  and gladdest Life dawns but to die. MS.
  and gladdest Life Death neighbours nigh. *WP* 1898, 1903.
  and Death and glad Life neighbour nigh. *CP* 1919.
Title. Eweleaze: sheep-pasture.
Title: *Weatherbury*: 'Wessex' name for Puddleton.
7. each essential] many a mental MS del.
8] And in fervours hid from men. MS del.
9–10. Time is depicted as a sculptor in a number of subsequent poems: cf. 'Time's transforming chisel' in 'The Revisitation' (30), l. 109.

>   Defacing wan and grizzel
>   The blazon of my prime.
>   When at night he thinks me sleeping
>   I feel him boring sly
>   Within my bones, and heaping   15
>   Quaintest pains for by-and-by.
>
>   Still, I'd go the world with Beauty,
>   I would laugh with her and sing,
>   I would shun divinest duty
>   To resume her worshipping.   20
>   But she'd scorn my brave endeavour,
>   She would not balm the breeze
>   By murmuring 'Thine for ever!'
>   As she did upon this leaze.
>
>   1890.

10 'I look into my glass'

The last of a final group of five poems in *Wessex Poems*, published under the heading 'Additions' in the first edition; subsequently included in *Selected Poems* (1916). The poem's use of the mirror is often related to Hardy's diary entry for 18 October 1892: 'I look in the glass. Am conscious of the humiliating sorriness of my earthly tabernacle. ... Why should a man's mind have been thrown into such close, sad, sensational, inexplicable relations with such a precarious object as his own body!' (*EL* 13–14). Cf. also the scene in which the ageing Pierston catches sight of himself in the mirror in *The Well-Beloved* III, 4 (pp. 121–2).

Metre: $a^3b^3a^4b^3$ dr, 'short' hymn stanza, the metre of the doxology in Hardy's Hymn-book.

>   I look into my glass,
>   And view my wasting skin,
>   And say, 'Would God it came to pass
>   My heart had shrunk as thin!'
>
>   For then, I, undistrest   5
>   By hearts grown cold to me,

11. wan] ghast *WP* 1898, 1903, WE 1912.
11. wan and grizzel: pale and grey.
12. blazon: boastfulness, self-display (lit. a coat of arms).
22. balm: soothe.
23. Thine for ever!: Pinion suggests that the hymn 'Thine for ever, God of love' is alluded to (1976: 25).

Could lonely wait my endless rest
With equanimity.

But Time, to make me grieve,
Part steals, lets part abide;
And shakes this fragile frame at eve
With throbbings of noontide.

11. frame: body.
12. noontide: suggesting midlife here (cf. also Shelley's 'The Sensitive Plant', I, 90: 'The quivering vapours of dim noontide').

Poems of the Past and the Present (1901)

Poems of the Past and the Present was published November 1901, but post-dated 1902 on the title-page. The original title Hardy agreed with Harper & Bros was 'Poems of Feeling, Dream, and Deed' (Purdy 1954: 118). In contrast to Hardy's first volume, it consisted mostly of poems written since he had abandoned the novel, though some earlier poems were included.

Hardy's increasing momentum as a poet is suggested by the fact that fourteen poems had been previously published in periodicals (including a group of Boer War poems). He was pessimistic about the book, writing in September 1901: 'Alas for that volume! I feel gloomy in the extreme when I think of it, & hope they will let it down easily. Can there be anything more paralyzing that features, subjects, forms, & methods, adopted advisedly, will be set down to blundering, lack of information, pedantry, & the rest' (*CL* II, 300). However, by early 1902 he was preoccupied with transferring his contracts to Macmillan, and seems to have paid less attention to its reception than to that of other volumes.

The reviews were mixed. T.H. Warren, Master of Magdalene College, Cambridge, commented in *The Spectator* that Hardy was 'a master of fiction, but not a master of music' (Cox 1970: xxxviii). The *Saturday Review* compared Hardy to Browning and praised his sincerity while criticizing his style, concluding 'But so far as it is possible to be a poet without a singing voice, Mr. Hardy is a poet, and a profoundly interesting one' (Cox 1970: 331).

In 1903 *Poems of the Past and the Present* was republished (from the corrected Harper plates) by Macmillan, as volume XIX of their Uniform Edition. In 1912 it was revised for the first verse volume of the Wessex Edition, and the *Collected Poems* of 1919 also involved substantial revision, some of it done around the same time as the Wessex Edition revisions. The manuscript, a fair copy used by the printers, is in the Bodleian library.

Preface

Herewith I tender my thanks to the editors and proprietors of the *Times*, the *Morning Post*, the *Daily Chronicle*, the *Westminster Gazette, Literature*, the *Graphic, Cornhill, Sphere*, and other papers, for permission to reprint from their pages such of the following pieces of verse as have already been published.

As was said of *Wessex Poems*, of the subject-matter of this volume much is dramatic or impersonative even where not explicitly so. And that portion which may be regarded as individual comprises a series of feelings and fancies written down in widely differing moods and circumstances, and at various dates; it will probably be found, therefore, to possess little cohesion of thought or harmony of colouring. I do not greatly regret this. Unadjusted impressions have their value, and the road to a true philosophy of life seems to lie in humbly recording diverse readings of its phenomena as they are forced upon us by chance and change.

T.H.

August 1901.

11 V.R. 1819–1901
A Reverie

The introductory poem of *Poems of the Past and the Present* stands alone, followed immediately by the 'War Poems'. The Victorian era ended with the death of the Queen on 22 January 1901. 'V.R. 1819–1901' was published in *The Times* on 29 January, two days after it was written, and reprinted in a commemorative volume, *The Passing of Victoria*, edited by J.A. Hammerton later that year. Hardy wrote to Mrs Henniker a few weeks later that the lines 'have all the crudeness of an unrevised performance' (*CL* II, 280). He was to describe Queen Victoria to Lytton Strachey in 1921 as 'a most uninteresting woman' but 'a good queen, well suited to her time & circumstances, in which perhaps a smarter woman would have been disastrous' (*CL* VI, 84).

Metre: $a^5b^3a^5a^3b^6b^6a^3$ dr, unique example.

8. *dramatic or impersonative*: the same disclaimer as in the preface to the previous volume (MS has 'personative').
13. *little cohesion of thought*: a claim Hardy continued to make throughout his career – cf. Preface to *Winter Words*, and *LY* 217.
17–18. *chance and change*: see opening of 'The Temporary the All' (1).

> The mightiest moments pass uncalendared,
>   And when the Absolute
> In backward Time pronounced the deedful word
>   Whereby all life is stirred:
> 'Let one be born and throned whose mould shall constitute   5
> The norm of every royal-reckoned attribute,'
>   Nor mortal knew or heard.
>
> But in due days the purposed Life outshone –
>   Serene, sagacious, free;
> Her waxing seasons bloomed with deeds well done,   10
>   And the world's heart was won ...
> Yet may the deed of hers most bright in eyes to be
> Lie hid from ours – as in the All-One's thought lay she –
>   Till ripening years have run.

Sunday Night,
  27th January 1901.

12 Drummer Hodge

First printed in *Literature*, 25 November 1899, in *Poems of the Past and the Present*, the seventh of the section called 'War Poems' on the Boer War (1899–1902). Most were first published in newspapers, Hardy now taking on the role of a public poet (see King and Morgan 1979). On 11 October 1899 he wrote to Florence Henniker: 'I constantly deplore the fact that "civilized" nations have not learnt some more excellent & apostolic ways of settling disputes than the old & barbarous one, after all these centuries; but when I feel that it must be, few persons are more martial than I, or like better to write of war in prose & rhyme' (*CL* II, 232). However, he was distressed by Swinburne's jingoistic poem 'The Transvaal', and three years later he was more negative, defending his war poems in a letter to Arthur

2. *the Absolute*: a term borrowed from Herbert Spencer, and one of Hardy's many names for the abstract and unknowable principle behind the Universe (cf. the final poem of *Poems of the Past and the Present*).
3. *backward Time*: earlier; but also with the suggestion of Time's being 'unenlightened', just as the 'Absolute' is blind, unconscious, or only slowly coming to consciousness. Cf. also Shakespeare's 'dark backward and abysm of time', *Tempest* I, ii, 50.
13. *All-One's*: i.e. the Absolute's.
Title] The Dead Drummer MS, *Literature*, *PP* 1901–3. In *Literature* it had a headnote: 'One of the Drummers killed was a native of a village near Casterbridge [Dorchester]'.
Title. Hodge: a nick-name for an agricultural labourer. In *Tess of the D'Urbervilles*, ch. 18 and in his 1883 essay 'The Dorsetshire Labourer' (*PW* 168–89), Hardy attacks those who employ such disparaging terms.

Quiller-Couch: 'The romance of *contemporary* wars has withered for ever, it seems to me: we see too far into them – too many details. Down to Waterloo war was romantic, was believed in ...' (*CL* III, 51). On Hardy and War, see also Orel 1976: 129; Taylor 1981: 118–35.

A month before 'Drummer Hodge' was published Hardy made a notebook cutting of a poem entitled 'War' by Herbert Cadett, published in the *Daily Chronicle*, 28 October 1899. It begins:

> Private Smith of the Royals; the veldt and a slate-black sky.
> Hillocks of mud, brick-red with blood, and a prayer – half curse
>   – to die.
> A lung and a Mauser bullet; pink froth and a half-choked cry.
>   (Björk entry 2017).

Metre: $a^4b^3a^4b^3a^4b^3$ dr, extended common metre: cf. Byron's 'The Days are Done' (Taylor 1988: 241). The spare technique has features in common with A.E. Houseman's in *A Shropshire Lad*, published three years earlier; there are also echoes of Wordsworth's 'A Slumber Did My Spirit Steal'.

I

They throw in Drummer Hodge, to rest
    Uncoffined – just as found:
His landmark is a kopje-crest
    That breaks the veldt around;
And foreign constellations west   5
    Each night above his mound.

II

Young Hodge the Drummer never knew –
    Fresh from his Wessex home –
The meaning of the broad Karoo,
    The Bush, the dusty loam,   10
And why uprose to nightly view
    Strange stars amid the gloam.

III

Yet portion of that unknown plain
    Will Hodge for ever be;
His homely Northern breast and brain   15
    Grow to some Southern tree,
And strange-eyed constellations reign
    His stars eternally.

3. *kopje-crest*: hill-crest (Afrikaans).
4. *veldt*: grasslands.
5. *west*: move west.
7. *young Hodge*: Drummers were often boys.
9. *Karoo*: a barren plateau in South Africa.
12. *gloam*: twilight.
15–16. cf. the body-and-tree image of Hardy's 'Transformations'.

13 The Souls of the Slain

Ninth of the 'War Poems', comparable to Hardy's later poem on the First World War, '"And There was a Great Calm"' (116), in its synoptic view and emphasis on pity. Hardy's vision of a crowd of spirits has a number of possible models, including Dante's *Inferno*, Coleridge's 'The Rhyme of the Ancient Mariner', and Shelley's 'The Triumph of Life'.

For the poem's first publication in *The Cornhill Magazine*, April 1900, Hardy supplied a headnote:

> The spot indicated in the following poem is the Bill of Portland, which stands, roughly, on a line drawn from South Africa to the middle of the United Kingdom; in other words, the flight of a bird along a 'great circle' of the earth, cutting through South Africa and the British Isles, might land him at Portland Bill. The 'Race' is the turbulent sea-area off the Bill, where contrary tides meet. 'Spawls' are the chips of freestone left by the quarriers.

It was subsequently included in *Selected Poems* (1916).

Metre: $a^3b^2c^2c^3a^4b^2$ tr. Taylor sees it as one of a 'wind and water' series beginning with 'Friends Beyond' (6), and notes that the rhythm, 'with its pointed use of iambic and anapaestic interplay and greater relishing of assonance ... captures nicely the interweaving motions of mind and ocean' (1988: 154). Gittings suggests that the alliterative effects and stanza-shape are Swinburnian (1978: 142).

I

The thick lids of Night closed upon me
    Alone at the Bill
    Of the Isle by the Race –
Many-caverned, bald, wrinkled of face –
And with darkness and silence the spirit was on me   5
    To brood and be still.

II

No wind fanned the flats of the ocean,
    Or promontory sides,
    Or the ooze by the strand,
    Or the bent-bearded slope of the land,   10
Whose base took its rest amid everlong motion
    Of criss-crossing tides.

Title. perhaps echoing Revelation 6: 9–10, 'I saw under the altar the souls of them that were slain for the word of God. . . . And they cried with a loud voice, saying How long, O Lord. . . .'
9. ooze] spawls *Cornhill* (see headnote).
10. bent-bearded: grass-covered.

III

Soon from out of the Southward seemed nearing
  A whirr, as of wings
    Waved by mighty-vanned flies,   15
  Or by night-moths of measureless size,
And in softness and smoothness well-nigh beyond hearing
  Of corporal things.

IV

And they bore to the bluff, and alighted –
  A dim-discerned train   20
    Of sprites without mould,
  Frameless souls none might touch or might hold –
On the ledge by the turreted lantern, far-sighted
  By men of the main.

V

And I heard them say 'Home!' and I knew them   25
  For souls of the felled
    On the earth's nether bord
  Under Capricorn, whither they'd warred,
And I neared in my awe, and gave heedfulness to them
  With breathings inheld.   30

VI

Then, it seemed, there approached from the northward
  A senior soul-flame
    Of the like filmy hue:

13–30. Paulin (1975: 50) compares Diomede's lament, *Aeneid* XI:
  The Gods have envy'd me the sweets of Life,
  My much lov'd Country, and my more lov'd wife:
  Banish'd from both, I mourn; while in the Sky
  Transform'd to Birds, my lost Companions fly:
  Hov'ring about the Coasts they make their Moan;
  And cuff the Cliffs with Pinions not their own.
  What squalid Spectres, in the dead of Night
  Break my short Sleep, and skim before my sight.
              (Dryden's translation, ll. 417–24)
15. mighty-vanned: with mighty wings.
16. night-moths: associated with death: cf. 'Afterwards' (112).
18. corporal: earthly.
21. sprites without mould: spirits without flesh.
23. turreted lantern: the lighthouse on the Bill.
24. main: sea.
27. earth's nether bord: its bottom end (i.e. South Africa).
28. Capricorn: a constellation of the Southern skies.

And he met them and spake: 'Is it you,
O my men?'   Said they, 'Aye!   We bear homeward and hearthward 35
To feast on our fame!'

VII

'I've flown there before you,' he said then:
'Your households are well;
But – your kin linger less
On your glory and war-mightiness 40
Than on dearer things.' – 'Dearer?' cried these from the dead then,
'Of what do they tell?'

VIII

'Some mothers muse sadly, and murmur
Your doings as boys –
Recall the quaint ways 45
Of your babyhood's innocent days.
Some pray that, ere dying, your faith had grown firmer,
And higher your joys.

IX

'A father broods: "Would I had set him
To some humble trade, 50
And so slacked his high fire,
And his passionate martial desire;
And told him no stories to woo him and whet him
To this dire crusade!"'

X

'And, General, how hold out our sweethearts, 55
Sworn loyal as doves?'
– 'Many mourn; many think
It is not unattractive to prink
Them in sables for heroes. Some fickle and fleet hearts
Have found them new loves.' 60

XI

'And our wives?' quoth another resignedly,
'Dwell they on our deeds?'
– 'Deeds of home; that live yet
Fresh as new – deeds of fondness or fret;

---

53. *whet him*: sharpen his desire.
58. *prink*: decorate.
59. *sables*: furs used for mourning.

Ancient words that were kindly expressed or unkindly, 65
    These, these have their heeds.'

XII
– 'Alas! then it seems that our glory
    Weighs less in their thought
    Than our old homely acts,
And the long-ago commonplace facts 70
Of our lives – held by us as scarce part of our story,
    And rated as nought!'

XIII
Then bitterly some: 'Was it wise now
    To raise the tomb-door
    For such knowledge? Away!' 75
But the rest: 'Fame we prized till to-day;
Yet that hearts keep us green for old kindness we prize now
    A thousand times more!'

XIV
Thus speaking, the trooped apparitions
    Began to disband 80
    And resolve them in two:
Those whose record was lovely and true
Bore to northward for home: those of bitter traditions
    Again left the land,

XV
And, towering to seaward in legions, 85
    They paused at a spot
    Overbending the Race –
That engulphing, ghast, sinister place –
Whither headlong they plunged, to the fathomless regions
    Of myriads forgot. 90

XVI
And the spirits of those who were homing
    Passed on, rushingly,

---

82. cf. Phil. 4: 8: 'Finally, bretheren, whatsoever things are true, whatsoever things are honest, whatsoever things are just, whatsoever things are pure, whatsover things are lovely, whatsoever things are of good report; if there be any virtue, and if there be any praise, think on these things' (also alluded to in 'Surview' (130)).

88. ghast: ghastly, frightening.

Like the Pentecost Wind;
And the whirr of their wayfaring thinned
And surceased on the sky, and but left in the gloaming   95
Sea-mutterings and me.

December 1899.

14 Rome
Building a New Street in the Ancient Quarter
(*April* 1887)

The fifth of the 'Poems of Pilgrimage', a group which originated in Hardy's tours to Italy and Switzerland in the summers of 1887 and 1897. One of Hardy's series of architectural poems, and one of a number in which the values of the ancient and the modern worlds clash: see 'Christmas in the Elgin Room' (176) for an example at the end of Hardy's career. Hardy's visit to Rome and the meditation which occasioned the poem are described *EL* 247-8:

> There was a great spurt of building going on at this time, on which he remarks, 'I wonder how anybody can have any zest to erect a new building in Rome, in the overpowering presence of decay on the mangy and rotting walls of old erections, originally of fifty times the strength of the new.'

Metre: one of a number of variations on the Petrarchan sonnet, here abba abba cddccd^5 dr (see Taylor 1988: 255-6).

These umbered cliffs and gnarls of masonry
Outskeleton Time's central city, Rome;

93. *Pentecost Wind*: the 'rushing mighty wind' described in Acts 2: 1-2 inspires the Apostles to speak in tongues and be heard by all. Given the silence here, the image is ironic.
95. *surceased*: came to an end.
95. *gloaming*: twilight.
96. *me*: the word also ends l. 1, ie. the poem returns to the isolated observer.
1. umbered: dark brown, stained (from L. *umbra*, shade).
2. outskeleton: not in OED. Hardy's 'out'-compounds, 'outleant', 'outshape', 'outstand', etc., form a significant grouping, often in words expressive of shape and lineament (see Elliott 1984: 198ff; Faurot 1990: 154).
2. Time's Central City, Rome: see Hardy's Paterian meditation on Rome's 'measureless layers of history', *EL* 247.

Whereof each arch, entablature, and dome
Lies bare in all its gaunt anatomy.
And cracking frieze and rotten metope   5
Express, as though they were an open tome
Top-lined with caustic monitory gnome;
'Dunces, Learn here to spell Humanity!'

And yet within these ruins' very shade
The singing workmen shape and set and join   10
Their frail new mansion's stuccoed cove and quoin
With no apparent sense that years abrade,
Though each rent wall their feeble works invade
Once shamed all such in power of pier and groin.

15 Rome
At the Pyramid of Cestius near the Graves of Shelley and Keats
(1887)

The seventh of the 'Poems of Pilgrimage' (the second of the series, 'Shelley's Skylark', is another tribute to Shelley). The MS gives a more precise date, 'April, 1887'. Subsequently included in *Selected Poems* (1916).

Keats and Shelley (the latter's heart only) are buried in the Protestant Cemetery in Rome, near the massive (116 ft) obelisk of Cestius. Hardy visited the graves on 31 March, 1887, and copied the inscription on Keats's grave: 'Here lies one whose name was writ in water.' On Hardy and Keats, see Pinion 1976: 210–11, Bailey 1970: 132–3, 441–2, 454–5; Björk entry 416n; and cf. 'At Lulworth Cove a Century Back' (118). On his more ambivalent feelings about Shelley, see Björk entry 1175n; Pinion 1968: 213–14; Pinion 1977: 148–57.

Metre: $a^3b^3a^6b^3$ dr.

3. *entablature*: the decoration above a classical column.
5. *frieze*: a horizontal decorative band near the top of the entablature or below the ceiling.
5. *metope*: part of a frieze.
7. *monitory gnome*: warning aphorism.
11. *cove and quoin*: curved surfaces and corners.
14. *pier*: pillar.
14. *groin*: edge where vaults join.
Title. Caius Cestius was an obscure Roman Tribune, d. *c.* 30BC.

> Who, then, was Cestius,
>> And what is he to me? –
> Amid thick thoughts and memories multitudinous
>> One thought alone brings he.
>
>> I call recall no word   5
>>> Of anything he did;
> For me he is a man who died and was interred
>> To leave a pyramid
>
>> Whose purpose was exprest
>>> Not with its first design,   10
> Nor till, far down in Time, beside it found their rest
>> Two countrymen of mine.
>
>> Cestius in life, maybe,
>>> Slew, breathed out threatening;
> I know not. This I know: in death all silently   15
>> He does a finer thing,
>
>> In beckoning pilgrim feet
>>> With marble finger high
> To where, by shadowy wall and history-haunted street,
>> Those matchless singers lie. . . .   20
>
>> – Say, then, he lived and died
>>> That stones which bear his name
> Should mark, through Time, where two immortal Shades abide;
>> It is an ample fame.

16 A Commonplace Day

This and the following poems through to 'Tess's Lament' (27) belong to the largest grouping in *Poems of the Past and the Present*, the 'Miscellaneous Poems'. It was heavily revised in manuscript (see *CPW* I, 148–9). Included in *Selected Poems* (1916).

Metre: a³b⁷a³b⁷b³ dr. Taylor suggests that the trimeter–heptameter line matches the flickering light-effects of the poem (Taylor 1988: 162).

14. cf. Acts 9: 1, 'And Saul, yet breathing out threatenings and slaughter against the disciples of the Lord, went unto the high priest.'
16. finer] sweeter MS; kindlier PP 1901–3; rarer WE 1912.
17–19. see Shelley's own description of Keats's burial place in *Adonais*, preface and 49–50.

       The day is turning ghost,
And scuttles from the kalendar in fits and furtively,
       To join the anonymous host
Of those that throng oblivion; ceding his place, maybe,
       To one of like degree.   5

       I part the fire-gnawed logs,
Rake forth the embers, spoil the busy flames, and lay the ends
       Upon the shining dogs;
Further and further from the nooks the twilight's stride extends,
       And beamless black impends.   10

       Nothing of tiniest worth
Have I wrought, pondered, planned; no one thing asking
  blame or praise,
       Since the pale corpse-like birth
Of this diurnal unit, bearing blanks in all its rays –
       Dullest of dull-hued Days!   15

       Wanly upon the panes
The rain slides, as have slid since morn my colourless
  thoughts; and yet
       Here, while Day's presence wanes,
And over him the sepulchre-lid is slowly lowered and set,
       He wakens my regret.   20

       Regret – though nothing dear
That I wot of, was toward in the wide world at his prime,
       Or bloomed elsewhere than here,
To die with his decease, and leave a memory sweet, sublime,
       Or mark him out in Time. . . .   25

---

2. *kalendar*: a spelling since 1800 used mainly in the context of the Church calendar.
8. *dogs*: metal bars on which logs are placed in a fire.
13–15. Bailey compares the description of dawn in *The Woodlanders*, ch. 4 (p. 55): 'the bleared white visage of a sunless winter day emerged like a dead-born child' (Bailey 1970: 142). Cf. also Shelley's *Hellas* l. 228: 'And Day peers forth with her blank eyes'; and Tennyson's *In Memoriam* 7: 'On the bald street breaks the blank day.'
14. *diurnal*: daily (as in Wordsworth's 'A slumber did my spirit steal').
22. *wot*: know.
22. *toward*: impending, promising.
24. *sublime*: Hardy often uses the word 'sublimation' in the context of memory (see Introduction).

– Yet, maybe, in some soul,
In some spot undiscerned on sea or land, some impulse rose,
    Or some intent upstole
Of that enkindling ardency from whose maturer glows
    The world's amendment flows;   30
    But which, benumbed at birth
By momentary chance or wile, has missed its hope to be
    Embodied on the earth;
And undervoicings of this loss to man's futurity
    May wake regret in me.   35

17 To an Unborn Pauper Child

Quoted as one of 'Mr. Thomas Hardy's New Poems', *Academy*, 23 November 1901 (stanzas 3–5 only, with 5 and 4 transposed); subsequently included in *Selected Poems* (1916). An epigraph in the manuscript suggests that the poem is based on a court hearing relating to the plight of a woman: '"She must go to the Union-house [i.e. Work-house] to have her baby." *Petty Sessions*.'

In the 1890s Hardy wrote a number of poems on it being better not to be born (see 'Thoughts from Sophocles' (179) and the 'In Tenebris' poems (24–6)). The undesirability of life is a topic these poems inherit from *Tess of the D'Urbervilles* and *Jude the Obscure*, while poverty contributes to the desire for self-annihilation in figures like Little Father Time and Tess (see Giordano 1984). The poem also draws on a tradition of elegies for children, including Swinburne's 'A Baby's Epitaph' (with similar sound-effects), and Ben Jonson's pessimistic meditation in 'To ... Sir Lucius Cary and Sir H. Morison' (*Under-wood* LXX):

> Wise child, did'st hastily returne,
> And mad'st thy Mother's wombe thine urne.

Metre: $a^4a^4b^2b^2c^4c^5$ dr, unique (though Hardy uses the same rhyme scheme for other elegiac poems in tetrameter: cf. 'A Necessitarian's Epitaph' and 'Last Words to a Dumb Friend' (124)).

29–30. Hardy's doctrine of gradual improvement or 'evolutionary meliorism'. Pinion compares the optimistic ending of Shelley's *The Revolt of Islam* IX, 28 (1976: 40).
32. *wile*: trick or ruse.
Title] To an Unborn Child MS del.

I

Breathe not, hid Heart: cease silently,
And though thy birth-hour beckons thee,
   Sleep the long sleep:
   The Doomsters heap
Travails and teens around us here, 5
And Time-wraiths turn our songsingings to fear.

II

Hark, how the peoples surge and sigh,
And laughters fail, and greetings die:
   Hopes dwindle; yea,
   Faiths waste away, 10
Affections and enthusiasms numb;
Thou canst not mend these things if thou dost come.

III

Had I the ear of wombèd souls
Ere their terrestrial chart unrolls,
   And thou wert free 15
   To cease, or be,
Then would I tell thee all I know,
And put it to thee: Wilt thou take Life so?

IV

Vain vow! No hint of mine may hence
To theeward fly: to thy locked sense 20
   Explain none can
   Life's pending plan:
Thou wilt thy ignorant entry make
Though skies spout fire and blood and nations quake.

V

   Fain would I, dear, find some shut plot 25
Of earth's wide wold for thee, where not

---

4. *Doomsters*: used in 'Hap' (2), l. 13.
5. *teens*: pains, annoyances.
13–24. cf. Jonson (cited above), ll. 17–20:
    Sword, fire, and famine, with fell fury met;
    And all on utmost ruine set;
    As, could they but lifes miseries fore-see,
    No doubt all Infants would returne like thee?
13. ear of wombèd] circuit of all MS del, *Academy*.
14. terrestial chart: the image suggests a pedigree.
22. pending] dismal MS, *Academy*.

>   One tear, one qualm,
>   Should break the calm.
>   But I am weak as thou and bare;
>   No man can change the common lot to rare.   30
>
>   VI
>   Must come and bide. And such are we –
>   Unreasoning, sanguine, visionary –
>   That I can hope
>   Health, love, friends, scope
>   In full for thee; can dream thou wilt find   35
>   Joys seldom yet attained by humankind!

18 Her Reproach

'Her Reproach' dwells on the possibility that a life of writing may involve the sacrifice of lived experience – a ancient *topos*, dealt with in contemporary novels (e.g. George Eliot's *Middlemarch*) and often in Hardy's fiction. The epigraph to *Jude the Obscure*, 'The letter killeth' (from 2 Corinthians 3: 6 'for the letter killeth, but the spirit giveth life') underlines the conflict between books and love in that novel (esp. I, vii). The distinction between the bitterness of books and the sweetness of life is explored in 'In Tenebris III' (26).

Metre: Spenserian sonnet, abab bcbc cdcd ee[5] dr.

>   Con the dead page as 'twere live love: press on!
>   Cold wisdom's words will ease thy track for thee;
>   Aye, go; cast off sweet ways, and leave me wan
>   To biting blasts that are intent on me.
>
>   But if thy object Fame's far summits be,   5
>   Whose inclines many a skeleton overlies
>   That missed both dream and substance, stop and see
>   How absence wears these cheeks and dims these eyes!
>
>   It surely is far sweeter and more wise
>   To water love, than toil to leave anon   10
>   A name whose glory-gleam will but advise

30] No man can move the stony gods to spare! MS del., *Academy*.
30. *common lot to rare*: cf. 'He Abjures Love' (33), ll. 34.
1. Con: read.
3. wan: pale, sickly.
7. dream and substance: united here, but the traditional distinction between shadow and substance (or dream and reality) is often used by Hardy.

Invidious minds to eclipse it with their own,
And over which the kindliest will but stay
A moment; musing, 'He, too, had his day!'
   Westbourne Park Villas, 1867.

19 His Immortality

Also published in a group of 'Mr. Thomas Hardy's New Poems', *Academy*, 23 November 1901. A companion-piece to a poem from *Wessex Poems*, 'Her Immortality', which similarly dwells on the increasingly attenuated persistence of memories of the dead in those who live on.
Metre: $a^4a^4b^5b^3$ (modified hymn stanza).

I

I saw a dead man's finer part
Shining within each faithful heart
Of those bereft. Then said I: 'This must be
   His immortality.'

II

I looked there as the seasons wore,   5
And still his soul continuously bore
A life in theirs. But less its shine excelled
   Than when I first beheld.

III

His fellow-yearsmen passed, and then
In later years I looked for him again;   10
And found him – shrunk, alas! into a thin
   And spectral mannikin.

IV

Lastly I ask – now old and chill –
If aught of him remain unperished still;
And find, in me alone, a feeble spark,   15
   Dying amid the dark.

February 1899.

12. eclipse] quench MS, *PP* 1901–3; dull *CP* 1919.
13–14. cf. the similar claims about love and fame in 'A Poet' (75).
5] I looked there on a later day, MS del., *Academy*.
6] And still his soul outshaped, as when in clay MS del., *Academy*.
9. fellow yearsmen: contemporaries. A 'yearsman' is also, in local usage, a labourer hired by the year. Cf. 'daysman' in 'He Abjures Love' (33), l. 3.
12. mannikin: small man (pejorative).

20 Winter in Durnover Field

One of a group of five bird-poems (with one other poem interspersed), the climax of which is 'The Darkling Thrush' (21). Hardy's compassion for birds is well documented: see Introduction; Bailey 1970: 163–5.
  Metre: the third of three triolets: $A^4B^4a^4A^4a^4b^4A^4B^4$ dr. Hardy redistributes the lines among three voices. This, the villanelle which precedes the grouping, and a later rondeau, reflect Hardy's interest in complex French verse-forms (see note to ' "When I set out for Lyonnesse" ' (46)).

> Scene. – *A wide stretch of fallow ground recently sown with wheat, and frozen to iron hardness. Three large birds walking about thereon, and wistfully eyeing the surface. Wind keen from north-east: sky a dull grey.*

(Triolet)

> *Rook.* – Throughout the field I find no grain;
>   The cruel frost encrusts the cornland!
> *Starling.* – Aye: patient pecking now is vain
>   Throughout the field, I find ...
> *Rook.* –   No grain!
> *Pigeon.* – Nor will be, comrade, till it rain,   5
>   Or genial thawings loose the lorn land
>   Throughout the field.
> *Rook.* –   I find no grain:
>   The cruel frost encrusts the cornland!

21 The Darkling Thrush

Despite the date given in the subscript, the poem was first printed as an occasional piece entitled 'By the Century's Deathbed' in *The Graphic*, 29 December 1900. The MS has a deletion in the original subscript: 'The Century's End, 1899 (del.) 1900'. Bernard Jones argues that this suggests

6. *lorn*: desolate, forlorn.
Title] By the Century's Deathbed *Graphic*.
Title. *Darkling*: in darkness. The word is used of Pierston's gloomy meditation in *The Well-Beloved* III, 7, and in 'God's Funeral', l. 38. It has strong poetic associations, suggesting Milton's *Paradise Lost* III, 37–9, 'the wakeful Bird / Sings darkling, and in shadiest Covert hid / Tunes her nocturnal Note ...'; Keats's 'Ode to a Nightingale': 'Darkling, I listen. ...'; Keble's 'The Twenty-first Sunday after Trinity' in *The Christian Year*, 'Contented in his darkling round'; and the 'darkling plain' in Matthew Arnold's 'Dover Beach' (see Hollander 1981: 90ff).

either composition in 1899, or a momentary uncertainly in Hardy's mind over the dating of the end of the century when he prepared the fair copy for the printers in 1901. Either supposition fits the fact that there had been a controversy over dating the official beginning of the new century, before 1 January 1901 rather than 1 January 1900 was settled on (Jones 1981). Always calendar-conscious, Hardy wrote a number of such end-of-year poems (see Pinion 1990: 307–33). This was subsequently included in *Selected Poems* (1916).

Perhaps Hardy's most allusive poem, 'The Darkling Thrush' also forms one of a series of poems on birds which spans his career as a poet (see Introduction). Among the huge tradition of bird-poems those of Cowper, Keble, and particularly Keats seem to lie behind Hardy's; Wordsworth's 'To a Sky-Lark' and 'To the Cuckoo', and Meredith's 'The Thrush in February' also invite comparison.

Metre: $a^4b^3a^4b^3c^4d^3c^4d^3$ dr, combined hymn stanzas, modelled perhaps on William Barnes's 'The Wife a-Lost' (Taylor 1988: 249), or on Cowper's 'To the Nightingale', which is in hymn stanza (Jones 1981: 227).

> I leant upon a coppice gate
>   When Frost was spectre-gray,
> And Winter's dregs made desolate
>   The weakening eye of day.
> The tangled bine-stems scored the sky   5
>   Like strings of broken lyres,
> And all mankind that haunted nigh
>   Had sought their household fires.
>
> The land's sharp features seemed to be
>   The Century's corpse outleant,   10
> His crypt the cloudy canopy,
>   The wind his death-lament.

1. coppice: wood of small trees.
2–4. cf. the winter landscape of 'Neutral Tones' (3), and the scene-setting of the previous poem.
2. Frost was] shades were *Graphic*.
5. bine-stems: dried-out stems of bindweed. The metaphor which follows suggests the Romantic Aeolian lyre or wind-harp: see Björk entry 1172; Abrams 1960; and cf. the opening of Coleridge's 'Ode to the Departing Year': 'Spirit who sweepest the wild Harp of time'. Hardy uses a similar image in 'To My Father's Violin', in *Moments of Vision*: 'your strings a tangled wreck'.
10. outleant: strictly 'leaning out'; but here it seems to mean 'stretched out'. Hardy uses many such compounds: 'outflickers', 'outshapes', 'outbursts' (Elliott 1984: 198–9).
11–12. cf. Shelley's 'Ode to the West Wind', ll. 23–15: 'Thou dirge / Of the dying year, to which this closing night / Will be the dome of a vast sepulchre'.

The ancient pulse of germ and birth
    Was shrunken hard and dry,
And every spirit upon earth   15
    Seemed fervourless as I.

At once a voice arose among
    The bleak twigs overhead
In a full-hearted evensong
    Of joy illimited;   20
An aged thrush, frail, gaunt, and small,
    In blast-beruffled plume,
Had chosen thus to fling his soul
    Upon the growing gloom.

So little cause for carolings   25
    Of such ecstatic sound
Was written on terrestrial things
    Afar or nigh around,

13–16. perhaps an echo of Tennyson's *In Memoriam* 85:
         And every pulse of wind and wave
            Recalls, in change of light or gloom
            My old affection of the tomb
         And my prime passion in the grave.
17. arose] outburst MS, *Graphic, PP* 1901–3; burst forth *CP* 1919. The more muted present form dates from WE 1912.
19. full-hearted evensong: cf. Keats's 'full-throated ease' in 'Ode to a Nightingale', l. 10; and Milton's nightingale in 'Il Penseroso': 'Thee chantress oft the woods among, / I woo to hear thy evensong' (ll. 63–4).
21–4. it has been suggested by Bailey and others that this description of a missel-thrush, which sings in winter, is derived from W.H. Hudson's *Nature in Downland* (London, 1900), pp. 251–2; but see Jones 1981: 227 for an argument against Hudson's influence.
25–32. cf. Cowper's 'To the Nightingale':
        Or sing'st thou rather under force
           Of some divine command,
        Commission'd to presage a course
           Of happier days at hand?

        Thrice welcome then! for many a long
           And joyless year have I,
        As thou to-day, put forth my song
           Beneath a wintry sky.
26. ecstatic sound: cf. the 'ecstasy' of Keats's 'Ode', l. 58.

That I could think there trembled through
    His happy good-night air   30
Some blessed Hope, whereof he knew
    And I was unaware.

31 *December* 1900.

22 The Respectable Burgher
on 'The Higher Criticism'

One of a number of early poems which Hardy wrote on Victorian doubts about religion and the eventual sense of the 'Death' of God, or his replacement by a humanistic entity: cf. 'A Sign-Seeker' (5), 'Nature's Questioning' (8), 'The Impercipient', 'God-Forgotten', 'By the Earth's Corpse', 'New Year's Eve', 'God's Education', 'God's Funeral'. The progress of scepticism is chronicled in a similar way, at the end of Hardy's career, in 'Drinking Song' (171).

Metre: iambic tetrameter, each line rhymed or near-rhymed on the opening 'declare' for a deliberately excessive effect.

    Since Reverend Doctors now declare
    That clerks and people must prepare
    To doubt if Adam ever were;

31. some blessed hope: perhaps echoing Wordsworth's 'O blessèd bird!' in 'To the Cuckoo'. Tennyson less tentatively suggests hope in the song of a bird 'in the darkening leaf' in *In Memoriam* 88: 'in the midmost heart of grief / Thy passion clasps a secret joy.'
Date. 31 December 1900] The Century's End, 1899 (del.) 1900 MS; December 1900 All editions to 1930 (revised in Hardy's copy of *CP* 1923, in DCM). A date assigned as the poem's 'moment' rather than a date of composition (see headnote).
Title. 'Burgher' (G. citizen) has overtones of middle-class respectability.
Subtitle. the 'Higher Criticism' was the critical appraisal of the Bible's texts and their contexts associated with David Strauss and other German writers in the late eighteenth and nineteenth centuries: the result of their efforts was to cast doubt on the literal truth of the Bible.
1. Reverend Doctors: the Higher Critics and, implicitly, the more recent authors of *Essays and Reviews* (1860), the volume of essays by Mark Pattison, Benjamin Jowett, Rowland Williams, Charles Godwin (the one layman), and three other liberal clergymen, in which the sceptical impact of the Higher Criticism was most strongly felt in England. Their aim, Jowett said in the collection's most notorious phrase, was to 'interpret the Bible like any other book'.
3. Rowland William's essay on 'Bunsen's Biblical Researches' suggested that many of the biblical (esp. Old Testament) stories could best be treated as myths.

> To hold the flood a local scare;
> To argue, though the stolid stare, 5
> That everything had happened ere
> The prophets to its happening sware;
> That David was no giant-slayer,
> Nor one to call a God-obeyer
> In certain details we could spare, 10
> But rather was a debonair
> Shrewd bandit, skilled as banjo-player:
> That Solomon sang the fleshly Fair,
> And gave the Church no thought whate'er,
> That Esther with her royal wear, 15
> And Mordecai, the son of Jair,
> And Joshua's triumphs, Job's despair,
> And Balaam's ass's bitter blare;
> Nebuchadnezzar's furnace-flare,
> And Daniel and the den affair, 20
> And other stories rich and rare,
> Were writ to make old doctrine wear
> Something of a romantic air:
> That the Nain widow's only heir,

4. as Charles Goodwin suggested in *Essays and Reviews*, nineteenth-century geological research implied that the biblical 'deluge' (Genesis 7–9) had not happened, while scholars pointed to similar flood legends in such Middle-Eastern texts as the *Epic of Gilgamesh*.

5–7. Williams argued that the prophetic books were a type of moralized history rather than being truly predictive.

8–12. the lines throw doubt on the story of David and Goliath (1 Samuel 17), mock his skill as a musician (1 Samuel 16: 14–23), and hint at the impropriety of his relations with Bathsheba (2 Samuel 11).

13–14. the Song of Solomon had traditionally been read as an allegory of Christ's love for the Church, rather than as describing physical love.

15–20. the Old Testament stories and miracles doubted here include that of Esther and her guardian Mordecai, who succeeded in reconciling King Ahasuerus to the Jews; of Joshua and his feat of making the sun and moon stand still; of Job's persecution by God; of the angel and Balaam's talking ass; of King Nebuchadnezzar's 'burning fiery furnace' from which Shadrach, Meshach, and Abednego emerge unscathed; and of Daniel in the Lion's den (Books of Esther, Joshua, Job; Numbers 22: 21–34; Daniel 3: 19–26; Daniel 6: 16–23).

24–30. New and Old Testament stories: Jesus's raising of the dead (Luke 7: 11–15, John 11: 1–45); Jael's murder of Sisera by nailing him through the head, so that 'the children of Israel prospered' (Judges 4: 18–24); Pontius Pilate's condemnation of Christ (which the new critics tended to historicize as administrative routine); and Peter's cutting off the ear of the High Priest's servant (John 18: 10).

And Lazarus with cadaverous glare 25
(As done in oils by Piombo's care)
Did not return from Sheol's lair:
That Jael set a fiendish snare,
That Pontius Pilate acted square,
That never a sword cut Malchus' ear: 30
And (but for shame I must forbear)
That —— —— did not reappear! ...
—Since thus they hint, nor turn a hair,
All churchgoing will I forswear,
And sit on Sundays in my chair, 35
And read that moderate man Voltaire.

23 The Self-Unseeing

Hardy wrote a number of poems on memories of music-making in childhood (cf. 'In the Small Hours' (123)). A similar episode is described in the *Life*:

> He was of ecstatic temperament, extraordinarily sensitive to music, and among the endless jigs, hornpipes, reels, waltzs, and country-dances that his father played of an evening in his early married years, and to which the boy danced a *pas seul* in the middle of the room, there were three or four that always moved the child to tears, though he strenuously tried to hide them. ... This peculiarity in himself troubled the mind of 'Tommy' as he was called, and set him wondering at a phenomenon to which he ventured not to confess. (*EL* 18–19, cf. 29–30)

The title also suggests connections with other poems on watching but not being conscious of the meaning of a scene: see 'Self-Unconscious' (49) and

26. Piombo: the Italian painter Sebastiano Luciani (1485–1547) whose 'Raising of Lazarus' Hardy studied in the National Gallery in London.
32. —— ——: Jesus Christ (the pious reluctance to spell out his name is the Burgher's rather than Hardy's). The conflicting accounts of the Gospels cast doubts on their description of the Resurrection.
36. Voltaire: François Marie Arouet (1694–1778), the French philosopher who often served as the 'type' of a rational, urbane scepticism directed at church and state. In *Jude* III, iv Jude complains of Sue's 'Voltairean' reading of the Song of Solomon. The notebooks show considerable interest in 'the great scoffer-mocker Voltaire' (see Björk entry 52), especially the account in John Morley's *Voltaire* (London, 1886). In one excerpt from Morley, Voltaire's 'relentless fire' from a hostile position is contrasted with modern critics who undermine belief from within, as *Essays and Reviews* seemed to do (Björk entry 1589).
Title] Unregarding MS del.

'Overlooking the River Stour' (97). It was subsequently included in *Selected Poems* (1916).

Metre: abbb³, in a generally falling rhythm.

> Here is the ancient floor,
> Footworn and hollowed and thin,
> Here was the former door
> Where the dead feet walked in.
>
> She sat here in her chair,   5
> Smiling into the fire;
> He who played stood there,
> Bowing it higher and higher.
>
> Childlike, I danced in a dream;
> Blessings emblazoned that day;   10
> Everything glowed with a gleam;
> Yet we were looking away!

24 In Tenebris I

The first of three poems of the same title, written in the period of crisis and depression around 1895–6, during which Hardy abandoned novel-writing. In early editions they were published under the title 'De Profundis' ('From the depths'), alluding to the opening of Psalm 130, 'Out of the deep I have called unto thee, O Lord'. Pinion (1978: 99) links the winter imagery used throughout the opening poem to Shelley's in 'The Sensitive Plant'.

Metre: a²b³b³a² dr. Green notes the 'syntactic thrust into the third line', and the 'consonantal pressure' of many lines (1990: 129).

> 'Percussus sum sicut foenum, et aruit cor meum.' – PS. CI.

1–4. cf. Hardy's comments on the memoried and worn floor of St Mark's, Venice, *EL* 253; and the 'indentations' of worn objects in 'Old Furniture' (99).

9–11. *dream ... gleam*: the same rhyme occurs in Wordsworth's 'Intimations' Ode, ll. 57–8 (for a comparison see Simpson 1979):
> Whither is fled the visionary gleam?
> Where is it now, the glory and the dream?

10–12. *day ... away*: perhaps another rhyme from the 'Intimations' Ode, ll. 77–8:   At length the Man perceives it die away,
                And fade into the light of common day.

Title] De Profundis *PP* 1901–3. MS has both titles, del.

Title. *In Tenebris*: L. In Darkness.

Epigraph. Psalm 101: 5 from the Vulgate (Latin) Bible, translated by Coverdale as 'My heart is smitten down, and withered like grass' (Psalm

Wintertime nighs;
But my bereavement-pain
It cannot bring again:
    Twice no one dies.

Flower-petals flee;
But, since it once hath been,
No more that severing scene
    Can harrow me.

Birds faint in dread:
I shall not lose old strength
In the lone frost's black length:
    Strength long since fled!

Leaves freeze to dun;
But friends can not turn cold
This season as of old
    For him with none.

Tempests may scath;
But love can not make smart
Again this year his heart
    Who no heart hath.

Black is night's cope;
But death will not appal
One who, past doubtings all,
    Waits in unhope.

102: 4: the English versions of the Psalms have a slightly different numbering to those in the Vulgate).
4. cf. Jude 12–13 on the ungodly: 'twice dead, plucked up by the roots; raging waves of the sea, foaming out of their own shame; wandering stars, to whom is reserved the blackness of darkness for ever.'
18. smart: as in 'The Convergence of the Twain' (45), Hardy seems to invoke both meanings of smart: hurt (the primary sense here), and bright, in good order.
24. an ironic reference to the Psalm which supplied the original title: 'I wait for the Lord, my soul doth wait, and in his word do I hope' (Psalm 130: 5, Authorized Version).
24. unhope: on such negatives, see 'Hap' (2), l. 10n.

25 In Tenebris II

As the metrical parallels between the two poems suggest, 'In Tenebris II' is close to 'Wessex Heights' (47), written in the same period, in its emphasis on the poet as 'shaped awry' and needing to remove himself from society. The only poem of the three which Hardy included in *Selected Poems* (1916). It was heavily revised in manuscript (detailed *CPW* I, 207–8).

Metre: aabb[7] dtr, an ancient form, the metre of 'Wessex Heights', another poem of troubled thoughts (cf. also 'The Mock Wife' (144) and 'Our Old Friend Dualism' (170)). Taylor suggests a number of possible models including Byron's 'There's Not a Joy', in Palgrave (Taylor 1988: 222).

> 'Considerabam ad dexteram, et videbam; et non erat qui cognosceret me. . . . Non est qui requirat animam meam.' – PS. CXLI.

When the clouds' swoln bosoms echo back the shouts of
    the many and strong
That things are all as they best may be, save a few to be
    right ere long,
And my eyes have not the vision in them to discern what
    to these is so clear,
The blot seems straightway in me alone; one better he
    were not here.

Title] De Profundis *PP* 1901–3. MS has both titles, del.
Title. In Tenebris: L. In Darkness.
Epigraph. Psalm 141: 5 in the Vulgate, 'I looked also upon my right hand: and saw that there was no man that would know me. . . . no man cared for my soul' (Psalm 142: 4–5). A cancelled Latin epigraph in the MS is from Psalm 2: 1: 'Why do the heathen so furiously rage together: and why do the people imagine a vain thing?'
1. cf. 1 Thessalonians 4: 16–17, 'For the Lord himself shall descend from heaven with a shout, with the voice of the archangel, and with the trump of God: and the dead in Christ shall rise first: then we which are alive and remain shall be caught up together with them in the clouds'.
1. swoln: swollen.
2–4. Bailey (1970: 182) cites a later defence of pessimism: 'The motto or practice of the optimists is: Blind the eyes to the real malady, and use empirical panaceas to suppress the symptoms' (*LY* 183).

The stout upstanders say, All's well with us: ruers have
    nought to rue! 5
And what the potent say so oft, can it fail to be somewhat
    true?
Breezily go they, breezily come; their dust smokes around
    their career,
Till I think I am one born out of due time, who has no
    calling here.

Their dawns bring lusty joys, it seems; their evenings all
    that is sweet;
Our times are blessed times, they cry: Life shapes it as
    is most meet, 10
And nothing is much the matter; there are many smiles
    to a tear;
Then what is the matter is I, I say. Why should such an
    one be here? ...

Let him in whose ears the low-voiced Best is killed by the
    clash of the First,

5–6. in a note made on 17 October 1896 Hardy wrote: 'Poetry. Perhaps I can express more fully in verse ideas and emotions which run counter to the inert crystallized opinion – hard as rock – which the vast body of men have vested interests in supporting' (*LY* 57).
5. say] chime WE 1916.
7. career: the older meaning of 'rapid motion' is recalled.
8. cf. 1 Corinthians 15: 8, where St Paul says of Christ: 'And last of all he was seen of me also, as of one born out of due time.' The dedicatory stanzas to William Morris's *The Earthly Paradise* allude to the same text:

> Dreamer of dreams, born out of my due time,
> Why should I strive to set the crooked straight?

9. evenings all that is sweet] eves exultance sweet MS, *PP* 1901–3, *CP* 1919.
11. nothing is much the matter: ironically inverted some 26 years later in '"Nothing matters much"' (149).
13. Let him in whose ears] Maybe (Haply) all to whose ears MS del.
13. in] to MS, *PP* 1901–3, *CP* 1919.
13. is killed] seems stilled MS, *PP* 1901–3, *CP* 1919; a more passive phrase.

Who holds that if way to the Better there be, it exacts a
    full look at the Worst,
Who feels that delight is a delicate growth cramped by
    crookedness, custom, and fear,   15
Get him up and be gone as one shaped awry; he disturbs
    the order here.
1895–96.

26 In Tenebris III

'In Tenebris III' can be related to the unpublished but contemporary 'Thoughts from Sophocles' (179) and 'Tess's Lament' (27) in its wish for an 'ending', and to 'To an Unborn Pauper Child' (17) in its emphasis on avoiding life's pain.

Metre: abba⁶, in a rather turbulent metre, mainly tf with the b-lines having feminine endings. Taylor suggests that it 'might be considered a loose accentual-syllabic imitation of the dactylic hexameter or "heroic" line [of classical metrics]' (1988: 262–3).

'Heu mihi, quia incolatus meus prolongatus est! Habitavi cum habitantibus Cedar; multum incola fuit anima mea.' – PS. CXIX.

There have been times when I well might have passed and the
    ending have come –
Points in my path when the dark might have stolen on me,
    artless, unrueing –

14. Hardy cites this line defending his pessimism in the 'Apology' to *LL* (p.246 below). Cf. the journal entry for 1 January 1902: 'Pessimism (or rather what is called such) is, in brief, playing the sure game. You cannot lose at it; you may gain. It is the only view of life in which you can never be disappointed' (*LY* 91).
16] Should up and be gone as men shaped awry; or as weird ghosts wandering here MS del. (another example of Hardy's self-perceived 'ghostliness').
Title] De Profundis *PP* 1901–3. MS has both titles, del.
Title. In Tenebris: L. In Darkness.
Epigraph. Psalm 119 in the Vulgate, 'Woe is me, that I am constrained to dwell with Mesech: and to have my habitation among the tents of Kedar. My soul hath long dwelt among them: that are enemies unto peace' (Psalm 120: 4–5).
2. artless] passive MS del.
2. unrueing: unrepentant (cf. l. 5 of previous poem).

Ere I had learnt that the world was a welter of futile doing:
Such had been times when I well might have passed, and the ending have come!

Say, on the noon when the half-sunny hours told that April was nigh,
And I upgathered and cast forth the snow from the crocus-border,
Fashioned and furbished the soil into a summer-seeming order,
Glowing in gladsome faith that I quickened the year thereby.

Or on that loneliest of eves when afar and benighted we stood,
She who upheld me and I, in the midmost of Egdon together,
Confident I in her watching and ward through the blackening heather,
Deeming her matchless in might and with measureless scope endued.

Or on that winter-wild night when, reclined by the chimney-nook quoin,
Slowly a drowse overgat me, the smallest and feeblest of folk there,
Weak from my baptism of pain; when at times and anon I awoke there –
Heard of a world wheeling on, with no listing or longing to join.

Even then! while unweeting that vision could vex or that knowledge could numb,

---

3. *welter*: restless motion (cf. '"Why Do I?"' (153), l. 3).
10. *She who upheld me*: Bailey suggests this is Hardy's mother (1970: 182).
10. *Egdon*: 'Egdon Heath', described in the opening of *Return of the Native*, the Wessex name for the heathland east of Stinsford.
13. *quoin*: corner.
14. *overgat*: overtook.
16. *listing*: desire, wish.
17. *unweeting*: ignorant.

>   That sweets to the mouth in the belly are bitter, and tart, and
>   untoward,
>   Then, on some dim-coloured scene should my briefly raised
>   curtain have lowered,
>   Then might the Voice that is law have said 'Cease!' and the
>   ending have come.   20
>   1896.

27 Tess's Lament

The lyric is spoken by the heroine of Hardy's *Tess of the D'Urbervilles*. Hardy may have been inspired to write it by the 1897 stage adaptation in America, but this is only one of a number of poems containing characters from his novels – ranging from Tess and Little Father Time to minor rustic characters. In his revisions for the *Collected Poems*, Hardy regularized its use of dialect to some extent (see Gifford 1972). However in the novel, Tess abandons her dialect as she moves away from Marlott and gains in experience, so that this poem could be seen as returning to her an earlier (or private) self. In its negation of life, it can clearly be related to the 'In Tenebris' poems, as well as to the effacement and silence of Tess in the novel (see Giordano 1984; Higonnet 1990).

Metre: $A^4A^2a^4b^3c^4c^4b^3$ dr.

I

> I would that folk forgot me quite,
>   Forgot me quite!
> I would that I could shrink from sight,
>   And no more see the sun.
> Would it were time to say farewell,   5
> To claim my nook, to need my knell,
> Time for them all to stand and tell
>   Of my day's work as done.

18. cf. Revelation 10: 10, 'And I took the little book out of the angel's hand, and ate it up; and it was in my mouth sweet as honey: and as soon as I had eaten it, my belly was bitter.' On the bitterness of books, cf. 'Her Reproach' (18).
20. perhaps alluding to Revelation 16: 17, 'there came a great voice out of the temple of heaven, from the throne, saying, It is done.'
Title] A Lament MS del.
1–8. cf. the episode in the novel in which Tess wishes for death, ch. 41.

II

Ah! dairy where I lived so long,
        I lived so long;
Where I would rise up staunch and strong,
        And lie down hopefully.
'Twas there within the chimney-seat
He watched me to the clock's slow beat –
Loved me, and learnt to call me Sweet,
        And whispered words to me.

III

And now he's gone; and now he's gone; . . .
        And now he's gone!
The flowers we potted perhaps are thrown
        To rot upon the farm.
And where we had our supper-fire
May now grow nettle, dock, and briar,
And all the place be mould and mire
        So cozy once and warm.

IV

And it was I who did it all,
        Who did it all;
'Twas I who made the blow to fall
        On him who thought no guile.
Well, it is finished – past, and he
Has left me to my misery,
And I must take my Cross on me
        For wronging him awhile.

V

How gay we looked that day we wed,
        That day we wed!
'May joy be with ye!' they all said
        A-standing by the durn.
I wonder what they say o'us now,

---

9. the dairy is Talbothays, where the bucholic third part of *Tess* is set.
13. the chimney-seat in which Angel Clare sat at breakfast admiring Tess is described in ch. 18.
19–21. events not in the novel.
19. perhaps] p'rhaps   All editions except *CP*.
33. Tess's wedding is in ch. 33.
35. they all] all o'm   All editions except *CP*.
36. durn: doorpost.
37. o'us] o's   All editions except *CP*.

And if they know my lot; and how
She feels who milks my favourite cow,
    And takes my place at churn!   40

VI

It wears me out to think of it,
    To think of it;
I cannot bear my fate as writ,
   I'd have my life unbe;
Would turn my memory to a blot,   45
Make every relic of me rot,
My doings be as they were not,
    And leave no trace of me!

28 Sapphic Fragment

The first of six poems under the heading 'Imitations, etc.' This is a translation of a well-known poem by Sappho, which Hardy knew in Henry Thornton Wharton's 1895 edition (Björk entry 522n). He had marked Swinburne's rendition of these lines in *Poems and Ballads*, and in 1897 wrote to Swinburne 'Those few words present, I think, the finest *drama* of Death and Oblivion, so to speak, in our tongue' (*LY* 61). On Hardy, Swinburne, and Sappho, cf. 'The Temporary the All' (1) and 'A Singer Asleep' (48).

    Metre: $a^3a^3b^5c^3c^3b^5$ dr. Taylor suggests Keble's 'Third Sunday after Easter' as a model (1988: 239).

43. as writ: as written (but also as a text, as in 'holy writ').
44. unbe: on such negatives, see 'Hap' (2), l. 10n.
48] this is the WE reading. Variants include:
    And what they've brought to me! MS, *PP* 1901–3.
    And gone all trace of me! *CP*.

Epigraphs. from Edward Fitzgerald's *The Rubáiyát of Omar Khayyám* (1859): 'Thou shall be – Nothing – Thou shall not be less' (stanza 47 in the first edition); Shakespeare, *Henry V* I, ii, 229. The MS has a cancelled epigraph, from Ecclesiastes 9: 5, 'Neither have they [the dead] any more a reward; for the memory of them is forgotten' – as Hynes points out, Hardy also considered this as an epigraph for 'The To-Be-Forgotten' (*CPW* I, 376).

'Thou shalt be – Nothing.' – Omar Khayyám.
'Tombless, with no remembrance.' – W. Shakespeare.

>Dead shalt thou lie; and nought
>Be told of thee or thought,
>For thou hast plucked not of the Muses' tree:
>And even in Hades' halls
>Amidst thy fellow-thralls 5
>No friendly shade shall keep thee company!

29 'ΑΓΝΩΣΤΩι ΘΕΩι

The last of the final three poems of *Poems of the Past and the Present*, collectively labelled 'Retrospect'. In 1906 Hardy suggested that *'ΑΓΝΩΣΤΩι ΘΕΩι* should be included with 'Hap' and three other poems in *The Ways of God* (1907), a religious anthology edited by A.C. Gowans (*CL* III, 232). Heavily revised in manuscript (see *CPW* I, 228).
  Metre: $a^5b^3b^3a^5b^3$ dr (cf. 'Plena Timoris', iambic tetrameter abbab).

>Long have I framed weak phantasies of Thee,
>   O Willer masked and dumb!
>   Who makest Life become, –
>As though by labouring all-unknowingly,
>   Like one whom reveries numb. 5
>
>How much of consciousness informs Thy will,
>   Thy biddings, as if blind,
>   Of death-inducing kind,
>Nought shows to us ephemeral ones who fill
>   But moments in Thy mind. 10

6. *shall keep thee*] thy shade shall *PP* 1901–3, *CP* (revised WE 1912).
Title. 'To the Unknown God'. From Acts 17: 23, where St Paul finds an altar with that inscription and declares: 'Whom, therefore, ye ignorantly worship, him declare I unto you.'
4] By labouring all unknowingly, maybe, MS, *PP* 1901–2.
6–15. Hardy often thought of the Will or power behind Creation as only gradually coming to consciousness: see *LY* 124–5 and 'God's Education'.

Perhaps Thy ancient rote-restricted ways
    Thy ripening rule transcends;
    That listless effort tends
To grow percipient with advance of days,
    And with percipience mends. 15

For, in unwonted purlieus, far and nigh,
    At whiles or short or long,
    May be discerned a wrong
Dying as of self-slaughter; whereat I
    Would raise my voice in song. 20

11–12. a reference to the law-giving God of the Old Testament, already superseded by the New Testament.
11. Perhaps] Haply MS, *PP* 1901–2.
11. rote-restricted] tentative, slow MS del; automatic MS del, *PP* 1901.
16. unwonted purlieus: unusual places.
17. i.e. at short or long intervals.
19. self-slaughter] self-vision MS del. (an antithetical term).
20. Would] Do *PP* 1901–2 (Hardy hestitated: MS has both del. and 'Would' restored).

Time's Laughingstocks and Other Verses (1909)

Hardy wrote to Edward Clodd on 30 August 1909 that he was preparing his new volume 'for a public which does not desire a line of it' (*CL* IV, 42). *Time's Laughingstocks* was published by Macmillan (Hardy's publishers since 1902) on 3 December 1909. With the exception of the group from the 1860s entitled 'More Love Lyrics', a large proportion of the poems were recently written, and the fact that 29 (of 94) had been previously published suggests that Hardy was under more pressure from editors to supply poems. Robert Gittings comments that 'the general tone ... contrasts with his previous collection' in being more intimate and family-centred than the generally 'philosophic, skeptical, and quasi-religious' *Poems of the Past and the Present* (Gittings 1978: 133); in fact the volume is a combination of differing groups, including a large number of the ballad-like narratives which Hardy believed were popular.

The title is from Tennyson's *The Princess* IV, 496: 'The drunkard's football, laughing-stocks of Time'. In 1920 Hardy defended it against the accusation that it implied a malignant Fate, writing to Alfred Noyes: 'The words "Time's Laughingstocks" are legitimate imagery all of a piece with such expressions as "Life, Time's fool", and thousands in poetry and I am amazed that you should see any *belief* in them' (*LY* 217).

The reception of the volume was enthusiastic to a degree which seemed to surprise Hardy. Many reviewers commented on his skill, the critic for *The Athenaeum* writing that 'his execution has everywhere a vibrating precision' (8 January 1910, pp. 34–5). The reviewer in *The Times Literary Supplement* (9 December 1909, pp. 473–4) judged the volume the best of the year, contrasting the 'sense of big issues' in Hardy's work with the cleverness of younger poets: 'again and again throughout the volume is the old sense of the vastness of Time and the littleness of human doings and suffering that gives them a tone of something humbly akin to sublimity.' Hardy showed some of his usual sensitivity to adverse reviews, but was gratified that the collection sold out and had to be reprinted early in 1910.

As Samuel Hynes comments, the manuscript and draft table of contents in the Fitzwilliam Museum, Cambridge, show that 'Hardy had considerable trouble in selecting and ordering the poems to his satisfaction' (*CPW* I, 379). He changed the titles and ordering of groups of poems, and removed and added pieces. The volume was reordered slightly for the Wessex Edition, Verse Vol. III (1913), though the *Collected Poems* retained the original ordering (the sequence of the selection here is the same in both texts). Further revisions were made for the *Collected Poems* (1919).

Preface

In collecting the following poems I have to thank the editors and proprietors of the periodicals in which certain of them have appeared for permission to reclaim them.

Now that the miscellany is brought together, some lack of concord in pieces written at widely severed dates, and in   5
contrasting moods and circumstances, will be obvious enough. This I cannot help, but the sense of disconnection, particularly in respect of those lyrics penned in the first person, will be immaterial when it is borne in mind that they are to be regarded, in the main, as dramatic   10
monologues by different characters.

As a whole they will, I hope, take the reader forward, even if not far, rather than backward. I should add that some lines in the early-dated poems have been rewritten, though they have been left substantially unchanged.   15

T.H.

September 1909.

30 The Revisitation

The title of the first section of the volume, 'Time's Laughingstocks', is taken from this poem, entitled 'Time's Laughingstocks / A Summer Romance' when first published in the *Fortnightly Review*, 1 August 1904. Both echoing *The Well-Beloved* and anticipating some of Hardy's later poems on the passing of love, 'The Revisitation' has been seen as marking a stage in Hardy's development: Patricia Clements compares it to 'My Cicely' in *Wessex Poems*, with its 'measuring repetition' in which 'experience overpowers expectation' (1980: 142–3); Dennis Taylor refers it to later 'love-journey poems' in which 'the present reverie . . . seems to recapitulate the lover's entire dream-led life' (1981: 20–1). Hardy revised the poem lightly for volume publication (see *CPW* I, 237–43).

4–7. lack of concord . . . disconnection: Hardy's standard disclaimer; cf. Preface to previous volume.
Title] Time's Laughingstocks / A Summer Romance *Fortnightly*.

Metre: Taylor suggests that it is dipodic, $a^4b^8a^8b^4$ df or $a^3b^7a^7b^3$ dr, the two rhythms 'ghosting' each other (1988: 96–7). The latter possibility seems much easier to realize.

  As I lay awake at night-time
In an ancient country barrack known to ancient cannoneers,
And recalled the hopes that heralded each seeming brave and
    bright time
  Of my primal purple years,

  Much it haunted me that, nigh there,   5
I had borne my bitterest loss – when One who went, came
    not again;
In a joyless hour of discord, in a joyless-hued July there –
  A July just such as then.

  And as thus I brooded longer,
With my faint eyes on the feeble square of wan-lit window
    frame,   10
A quick conviction sprung within me, grew, and grew yet
    stronger,
  That the month-night was the same,

  Too, as that which saw her leave me
On the rugged ridge of Waterstone, the peewits plaining
    round;
And a lapsing twenty years had ruled that – as it were to
    grieve me –   15
  I should near the once-loved ground.

  Though but now a war-worn stranger
Chance had quartered here, I rose up and descended to the
    yard.
All was soundless, save the troopers' horses tossing at the
    manger,
  And the sentry keeping guard.   20

  Through the gateway I betook me
Down the High Street and beyond the lamps, across the
    battered bridge,

2. *country barrack*: in Dorchester.
4. *primal purple years*: on 'purples', see 'Beeny Cliff' (65), l. 9n.
10. *wan-lit*: barely lit (cf. ll. 99–100).
14. *Waterstone*: northeast of Dorchester.
14. *peewits plaining*: the mornful cry of the bird is suggested by its name. Cf. the scene in 'Overlooking the River Stour' (97).

Till the country darkness clasped me and the friendly shine
    forsook me,
  And I bore towards the Ridge,
    With a dim unowned emotion   25
Saying softly: 'Small my reason, now at midnight, to be
    here . . .
Yet a sleepless swain of fifty with a brief romantic notion
  May retrace a track so dear.'

    Thus I walked with thoughts half-uttered
Up the lane I knew so well, the grey, gaunt, lonely Lane of
    Slyre;   30
And at whiles behind me, far at sea, a sullen thunder muttered
    As I mounted high and higher.

    Till, the upper roadway quitting,
I adventured on the open drouthy downland thinly grassed,
While the spry white scuts of conies flashed before me,
    earthward flitting,   35
  And an arid wind went past.

    Round about me bulged the barrows
As before, in antique silence – immemorial funeral piles –
Where the sleek herds trampled daily the remains of flint-tipt
    arrows
  Mid the thyme and chamomiles;   40

    And the Sarsen stone there, dateless,
On whose breast we had sat and told the zephyrs many a
    tender vow,
Held the heat of yester sun, as sank thereon one fated
    mateless
  From those far fond hours till now.

    Maybe flustered by my presence   45
Rose the peewits, just as all those years back, wailing soft
    and loud,

---

30. *Lane of Slyre*: Slyre's Lane is the road from Dorchester to Waterstone.
33. the poem's walker turns off the road down a track called Ridge Way.
34. *drouthy*: arid.
35. *conies*: rabbits.
37. *barrows*: burial mounds.
41. *Sarsen stone*: marker-stone. 'Sarsen' is a corruption of 'Saracen' or Infidel (upright stones were often associated with pre-Christian worship).
42. *zephyrs*: breezes.
43. *yester sun*: the sun of the previous day. Cf. the radiation of leads, 'Friends Beyond' (6).

And revealing their pale pinions like a fitful phosphorescence
    Up against the cope of cloud,
  Where their dolesome exclamations
Seemed the voicings of the self-same throats I had heard
    when life was green, 50
Though since that day uncounted frail forgotten generations
  Of their kind had flecked the scene. –

  And so, living long and longer
In a past that lived no more, my eyes discerned there,
    suddenly,
That a figure broke the skyline – first in vague contour, then
    stronger, 55
  And was crossing near to me.

  Some long-missed familiar gesture,
Something wonted, struck me in the figure's pause to list and
    heed,
Till I fancied from its handling of its loosely wrapping vesture
  That it might be She indeed. 60

  'Twas not reasonless: below there
In the vale, had been her home; the nook might hold her
    even yet,
And the downlands were her father's fief; she still might
    come and go there; –
  So I rose, and said, 'Agnette!'

  With a little leap, half-frightened, 65
She withdrew some steps; then letting intuition smother fear
In a place so long-accustomed, and as one whom thought
    enlightened,
  She replied: 'What – *that* voice? – here!'

  'Yes, Agnette! – And did the occasion
Of our marching hither make you think I *might* walk where
    we two –' 70
'O, I often come,' she murmured with a moment's coy evasion,
  '('Tis not far), – and – think of you.'

  Then I took her hand, and led her
To the ancient people's stone whereon I had sat. There now
    sat we;

---

50. *self-same throats*: recalls Keats's 'selfsame song', 'Ode to a Nightingale',
l. 65 (see 'The Selfsame Song' (117)).
58. *list*: listen.
63. *fief*: property.

And together talked, until the first reluctant shyness fled her,   75
   And she spoke confidingly.
'It is *just* as ere we parted!'
Said she, brimming high with joy. – 'And when, then, came
      you here, and why?'
'– Dear, I could not sleep for thinking of our trystings when
      twin-hearted.'
   She responded, 'Nor could I.   80

'There are few things I would rather
Than be wandering at this spirit-hour – lone-lived, my
      kindred dead –
On this wold of well-known feature I inherit from my father:
   Night or day, I have no dread. . . .

   'O I wonder, wonder whether   85
Any heartstring bore a signal-thrill between us twain or no? –
Some such influence can, at times, they say, draw severed
      souls together.'
   I said; 'Dear, we'll dream it so.'

   Each one's hand the other's grasping,
And a mutual forgiveness won, we sank to silent thought,   90
A large content in us that seemed our rended lives reclasping,
   And contracting years to nought.

   Till I, maybe overweary
From the lateness, and a wayfaring so full of strain and stress
For one no longer buoyant, to a peak so steep and eery,   95
   Sank to slow unconsciousness. . . .

   How long I slept I knew not,
But the brief warm summer night had slid when, to my swift
      surprise,
A red upedging sun, of glory chambered mortals view not,
   Was blazing on my eyes,   100

   From the Milton Woods to Dole-Hill
All the spacious landscape lighting, and around about my feet
Flinging tall thin tapering shadows from the meanest mound
      and mole-hill,
   And on trails the ewes had beat.

---

79. trystings: meetings.
83. wold: pasture.
99. chambered mortals: people in bed.
101. Milton Woods to Dole-Hill: Milton Woods are northeast of Waterstone Ridge, Dole's Hill Plantation is to the northeast, above Puddletown.

> She was sitting still beside me, 105
> Dozing likewise; and I turned to her, to take her hanging
>   hand;
> When, the more regarding, that which like a spectre shook
>   and tried me
>   In her image then I scanned;
>   That which Time's transforming chisel
> Had been tooling night and day for twenty years, and tooled
>   too well, 110
> In its rendering of crease where curve was, where was raven,
>   grizzle –
>   Pits, where peonies once did dwell.
>   She had wakened, and perceiving
> (I surmise) my sigh and shock, my quite involuntary dismay,
> Up she started, and – her wasted figure all throughout it
>   heaving – 115
>   Said, 'Ah, yes: I am *thus* by day!
>   'Can you really wince and wonder
> That the sunlight should reveal you such a thing of skin and
>   bone,
> As if unaware a Death's-head must of need lie not far under
>   Flesh whose years out-count your own? 120
>   'Yes: that movement was a warning
> Of the worth of man's devotion! – Yes, Sir, I am *old*,' said she,
> 'And the thing which should increase love turns it quickly into
>   scorning –
>   And your new-won heart from me!'
>   Then she went, ere I could call her, 125
> With the too proud temper ruling that had parted us before,
> And I saw her form descend the slopes, and smaller grow and
>   smaller,
>   Till I caught its course no more. ...

107–20. cf. the moment when Pierston awakens to realize his own age, *The Well-Beloved* III, 4 (pp. 121–2).
109. Time's transforming chisel: cf. 'In a Eweleaze near Weatherbury' (9) and other poems in which Time is portrayed as a sculptor.
111. where was raven, grizzle: her formerly black hair was now grey.
114. surmise: guess.
120. Flesh] One *TL* 1909–10.
127. and smaller grow and smaller: cf. the 'shrinking, shrinking' vision in 'At Castle Boterel' (66), l. 31.

True; I might have dogged her downward;
– But it *may* be (though I know not) that this trick on us of
     Time   130
Disconcerted and confused me. – Soon I bent my footsteps
     townward,
Like to one who had watched a crime.

Well I knew my native weakness,
Well I know it still. I cherished her reproach like physic-wine,
For I saw in that emaciate shape of bitterness and bleakness   135
     A nobler soul than mine.

Did I not return, then, ever? –
Did we meet again? – mend all? – Alas, what greyhead
     perseveres! –
Soon I got the Route elsewhither. – Since that hour I have
     seen her never:
Love is lame at fifty years.   140

31 A Trampwoman's Tragedy
(182–)

Written in 1902, 'A Trampwoman's Tragedy' was printed in the *North American Review*, November 1903. The poem had been originally offered to *The Cornhill Magazine*, who turned it down as unsuitable for a 'family periodical' (*LY* 100–1). Hardy later cited the fate of this poem and 'A Sunday Morning Tragedy' (which deals with abortion) as evidence of censorship, but in fact he had commented on its 'lurid picturesqueness' when submitting it to the *Cornhill*, and wrote a number of such racy narratives in this period (*CL* III, 58). It was privately printed by Florence Hardy in 1917, and while Hardy did not reprint it in *Selected Poems* (1916), he included it in his *Chosen Poems* (1929). There were a number of minor revisions after first publication (see *CPW* I, 243–7).

The *Life* states that this was 'a ballad based on some local story of an event more or less resembling the incidents embodied, which took place between 1820 and 1830. Hardy considered this, upon the whole, his most successful poem' (*LY*, 92–3). In the *North American Review* it had a headnote stating 'The incidents on which this tale is based occurred in 1827' (Purdy 1954: 138), and in a letter to Gosse he identified the woman in the poem as Mary Ann Taylor (*CL* III, 83). 'On Martock Moor' has a comparable scenario.

134. physic-wine: medicine.
139. Route: marching-orders.
Title] The original title was 'The Tramp's Tragedy', but Hardy considered that title too likely to have been used before (*CL* III, 75).

Metre: $a^4a^2a^4b^3c^4c^4c^4b^3$ dr (extended tail-rhyme with refrain in line 2: cf. Wordsworth's 'The Green Linnet' and Hardy's poems 'I Need Not Go', 'The Mongrel', 'Genitrix Laesa' for rhyme scheme). Donald Hogan comments on the pattern of 'holding' in the refrain and 'release' in the triplet (quoted Bailey 1970: 198).

I

From Wynyard's Gap the livelong day,
    The livelong day,
We beat afoot the northward way
    We had travelled times before.
The sun-blaze burning on our backs,   5
Our shoulders sticking to our packs,
By fosseway, fields, and turnpike tracks
    We skirted sad Sedge-Moor.

II

Full twenty miles we jaunted on,
    We jaunted on, –   10
My fancy-man, and jeering John,
    And Mother Lee, and I.
And, as the sun drew down to west,
We climbed the toilsome Poldon crest,
And saw, of landskip sights the best,   15
    The inn that beamed thereby.

III

For months we had padded side by side,
    Ay, side by side
Through the Great Forest, Blackmoor wide,
    And where the Parret ran.   20
We'd faced the gusts on Mendip ridge,

---

1. Wynard's Gap: the opening stanzas describe a journey from Winyard's Gap, north of Beaminster, to Marshal's Elm Inn, some 25 miles north in the Poldon hills near Glastonbury (Hardy's 'Glaston').
7. fosseway: sunken road.
7. turnpike tracks: toll-roads.
8. Sedge-Moor: King's Sedge Moor, southwest of Marshal's Elm; 'sad' perhaps because of the defeat of the Duke of Monmouth there in 1685 (Bailey 1970: 197).
15. landskip: landscape.
19. Great Forest, Blackmoor wide: the New Forest, in Hampshire; and Blackmoor Vale, through which the river Parret runs (described as 'the Vale of Little Dairies' in *Tess*, ch. 2).
21. Mendip: the Mendip Hills, north of Glastonbury.

Had crossed the Yeo unhelped by bridge,
Been stung by every Marshwood midge,
    I and my fancy-man.

IV

Lone inns we loved, my man and I,
    My man and I;
'King's Stag,' 'Windwhistle' high and dry,
    'The Horse' on Hintock Green,
The cosy house at Wynyard's Gap,
'The Hut' renowned on Bredy Knap,
And many another wayside tap
    Where folk might sit unseen.

V

Now as we trudged – O deadly day,
    O deadly day! –
I teased my fancy-man in play
    And wanton idleness.
I walked alongside jeering John,
I laid his hand my waist upon;
I would not bend my glances on
    My lover's dark distress.

VI

Thus Poldon top at last we won,
    At last we won,
And gained the inn at sink of sun
    Far-famed as 'Marshal's Elm.'
Beneath us figured tor and lea,

---

22. *Yeo*: a tributary of the Parret.
23. *Marshwood*: the Vale of Marshwood, in South Dorset.
25. *lone inns*: a number of Wessex inns are described in the lines which follow, some no longer in existence when Hardy wrote the poem.
27. '"Windwhistle" (Stanza IV). The highness and dryness of Windwhistle Inn was impressed upon the writer two or three years ago, when, after climbing on a hot afternoon to the beautiful spot near where it stands and entering the inn for tea, he was informed by the landlady that none could be had, unless he would fetch water from a valley half a mile off, the house containing not a drop, owing to its situation. However a tantalizing row of full barrels behind her back testified to a wetness of a certain sort, which was not at that time desired' (Hardy's note).
31. *tap*: tavern.
44. '"Marshal's Elm" (Stanza VI), so picturesquely situated, is no longer an inn, though the house, or part of it, still remains. It used to exhibit a fine old swinging sign' (Hardy's note).
45. *tor and lea*: hills and pastures.

From Mendip to the western sea —
I doubt if finer sight there be
    Within this royal realm.

VII

Inside the settle all a-row —
    All four a-row
We sat, I next to John, to show
    That he had wooed and won.
And then he took me on his knee,
And swore it was his turn to be
My favoured mate, and Mother Lee
    Passed to my former one.

VIII

Then in a voice I had never heard,
    I had never heard,
My only Love to me: 'One word,
    My lady, if you please!
Whose is the child you are like to bear? —
His? After all my months o' care?'
God knows 'twas not! But, O despair!
    I nodded — still to tease.

IX

Then up he sprung, and with his knife —
    And with his knife
He let out jeering Johnny's life,
    Yes; there, at set of sun.
The slant ray through the window night
Gilded John's blood and glazing eye,
Ere scarcely Mother Lee and I
    Knew that the deed was done.

X

The taverns tell the gloomy tale,
    The gloomy tale,
How that at Ivel-chester jail
    My Love, my sweetheart swung;
Though stained till now by no misdeed
Save one horse ta'en in time o' need;

---

49. *settle*: high-backed wooden bench.
60. *lady*] doxy *TL* 1909.

(Blue Jimmy stole right many a steed
    Ere his last fling he flung.)   80

XI

Thereaft I walked the world alone,
    Alone, alone!
On his death-day I gave my groan
    And dropt his dead-born child.
'Twas nigh the jail, beneath a tree,   85
None tending me; for Mother Lee
Had died at Glaston, leaving me
    Unfriended on the wild.

XII

And in the night as I lay weak,
    As I lay weak,   90
The leaves a-falling on my cheek,
    The red moon low declined –
The ghost of him I'd die to kiss
Rose up and said: 'Ah, tell me this!
Was the child mine, or was it his?   95
    Speak, that I rest may find!'

XIII

O doubt not but I told him then,
    I told him then,
That I had kept me from all men
    Since we joined lips and swore.   100
Whereat he smiled, and thinned away
As the wind stirred to call up day ...
– 'Tis past! And here alone I stray
    Haunting the Western Moor.

April 1902.

---

79. '"Blue Jimmy" (Stanza X) was a notorious horse-stealer of Wessex in those days, who appropriated more than a hundred horses before he was caught, among others one belonging to a neighbour of the writer's grandfather. He was hanged [on 25 April 1827] at the now demolished Ivelchester or Ilchester jail above mentioned – that building formerly of so many sinister associations in the minds of the local peasantry, and the continual haunt of fever, which at last led to its condemnation.

'Its site is now an innocent-looking green meadow' (Hardy's note).

101. thinned: Pinion (1976: 65) points out the ghostly associations of this word in Hardy's work.

104. the Western Moor: Exmoor, the large expanse of wild country west of Exeter.

32 In the Mind's Eye

Part of the second section of 26 poems in *Time's Laughingstocks*, 'More Love Lyrics'. In Hardy's own copy he underlined the title and wrote 'Ghost-face' in the margin (DCM). Included in *Selected Poems* (1916). 'In the Mind's Eye' both continues the general emphasis on memory of poems like 'His Immortality' (19), and anticipates the personal tone, vocabulary, and movement of the later 'Poems of 1912-13', with its shift from third-person description to direct address.

Metre: abcb^3 (rhyme scheme as for ballad measure), df but the short (rhymed) lines drop a syllable to produce a masculine rhyme.

>   That was once her casement,
>   And the taper nigh,
>   Shining from within there,
>   Beckoned, 'Here am I!'
>
>   Now, as then, I see her   5
>   Moving at the pane;
>   Ah; 'tis but her phantom
>   Borne within my brain! –
>
>   Foremost in my vision
>   Everywhere goes she;   10
>   Change dissolves the landscapes,
>   She abides with me.
>
>   Shape so sweet and shy, Dear,
>   Who can say thee nay?
>   Never once do I, Dear,   15
>   Wish thy ghost away.

33 He Abjures Love

Final poem of 'More Love Lyrics', and in some ways a traditional farewell to love, like those which end many sonnet-sequences. Included in *Selected Poems* (1916). The poem is one of only five dated in the 1880s.

Metre: a^{3}b^{2}c^{3}d^{2}a^{3}b^{2}c^{3}d^2 dr (stanzas 1, 3, 4, 5) and a^{3}b^{2}b^{3}c^{2}a^{3}d^{2}d^{3}c^2 dr (stanzas 2, 6).

Title] The Face in the Mind's Eye *SP* 1916; The Phantom *TL* 1909–10, WE 1913, *CP* 1919–28. Hardy changed the title to avoid confusion with 'The Phantom Horsewoman', which echoes this poem.
1. casement: window.
7–12. cf. 'The Phantom Horsewoman' (68), ll. 18–27.

At last I put off love,
  For twice ten years
The daysman of my thought,
  And hope, and doing;
Being ashamed thereof,
  And faint of fears
And desolations, wrought
  In his pursuing,

Since first in youthtime those
  Disquietings
That heart-enslavement brings
  To hale and hoary,
Became my housefellows.
  And, fool and blind,
I turned from kith and kind
  To give him glory.

I was as children be
  Who have no care;
I did not shrink or sigh,
  I did not sicken;
But lo, Love beckoned me,
  And I was bare,
And poor, and starved, and dry,
  And fever-stricken.

Too many times ablaze
  With fatuous fires,
Enkindled by his wiles
  To new embraces,
Did I, by wilful ways
  And baseless ires,
Return the anxious smiles
  Of friendly faces.

No more will now rate I
  The common rare,

---

3. daysman: the usual meaning is 'arbitrator', but the alternative meaning of 'day-labourer' would also work here, in the sense of 'daily accompaniment' (cf. 'yearsman' in 'His Immortality' (19)).
15. kith and kind: plays on the proverbial 'kith and kin', aquaintances and family. 'Kind' is more general, meaning humanity and its ways.
19. shrink] think   Editions before *CP* 1919.
33–4. i.e. 'No more will I see that which is common as rare, or the drizzle as dew' (Hardy omits the conjunction 'as' and collapses the paired

> The midnight drizzle dew, 35
>   The gray hour golden,
> The wind a yearning cry,
>   The faulty fair,
> Things dreamt, of comelier hue
>   Than things beholden! ... 40
>
> – I speak as one who plumbs
>   Life's dim profound,
> One who at length can sound
>   Clear views and certain.
> But – after love what comes? 45
>   A scene that lours,
> A few sad vacant hours,
>   And then, the Curtain.
> 1883.

34 Let Me Enjoy
(Minor Key)

The introductory poem to the 18 poems which comprise the third section of *Time's Laughingstocks*, 'A Set of Country Songs', described by Paul Zeitlow as 'Hardy's fullest lyric presentation of the countryside' (1974: 85). 'Let Me Enjoy' was first published in *The Cornhill Magazine* in April 1909, and the same text in *Putnam's Magazine* (New York), April; subsequently revised for volume publication. It was singled out for praise by a number of reviewers of *Time's Laughingstocks*, and Hardy included it in *Selected Poems* (1916).

   Metre: abab⁴ dr, the 'long metre' of many hymns and over a dozen other poems by Hardy.

I

> Let me enjoy the earth no less
> Because the all-enacting Might
> That fashioned forth its loveliness
> Had other aims than my delight.

antitheses). 'Common' and 'rare' are also opposed in 'To an Unborn Pauper Child' (17), l. 30.
37. cf. the meditation on the sound of the wind in 'The Voice' (59).
37] The wind a jealous cry, MS; The creak a jealous cry, *TL* 1909–10.
38] The day a care, MS; The speech a snare, *TL* 1909.
46. *lours*: darkens.
2. *Might*: Will, Absolute, etc. (see Introduction, p. 17).

II

About my path there flits a Fair, 5
Who throws me not a word or sign;
I'll charm me with her ignoring air,
And laud the lips not meant for mine.

III

From manuscripts of moving song
Inspired by scenes and dreams unknown 10
I'll pour out raptures that belong
To others, as they were my own.

IV

And some day hence, towards Paradise
And all its blest – if such should be –
I will lift glad, afar-off eyes, 15
Though it contain no place for me.

35 Julie-Jane

Number thirteen in 'A Set of Country Songs', a dialect-poem with links to Hardy's *Tess of the D'Urbervilles*, and thus comparable to 'We Field-women' (167), at the end of his career.

Metre: Taylor suggests $a^3b^3a^4b^2$ dr but with an 'increasingly trisyllabic' measure (1988: 224). Giordano (1979: 93) notes 'the frequent pauses, the abundant punctuation, the halting and inverted phrasing' and links this to 'the narrator's reluctance ... to get on with her sorrowful story'.

Sing; how 'a would sing!
How 'a would raise the tune
When we rode in the waggon from harvesting
By the light o' the moon!

Dance; how 'a would dance! 5
If a fiddlestring did but sound

---

5. *Fair*: ie. fair person.
7] I will find charm in her loth air, *Cornhill*.
  I will find charm in her uncare, *TL* 1909–10.
9. *moving song*] rapturous strain MS; tender song *Cornhill*.
10. *dreams*] souls MS, *Cornhill*, *TL* 1909–10, *CP* 1919–23.
13. *And some day hence*] Perhaps some day MS, *TL* 1909–10 (*Cornhill* has present reading, restored WE 1913).
15. *I will lift*] I will cast *Cornhill*; I shall lift MS, *TL* 1909–10.
1. *how 'a would sing*: how she would sing.

She would hold out her coats, give a slanting glance,
    And go round and round.
  Laugh; how 'a would laugh!
    Her peony lips would part   10
As if none such a place for a lover to quaff
    At the deeps of a heart.

  Julie, O girl of joy,
    Soon, soon that lover he came.
Ah, yes; and gave thee a baby-boy,   15
    But never his name. . . .

  –Tolling for her, as you guess;
    And the baby too. . . . 'Tis well.
You knew her in maidhood likewise? – Yes,
    That's her burial bell.   20

  'I suppose,' with a laugh, she said,
    'I should blush that I'm not a wife;
But how can it matter, so soon to be dead,
    What one does in life!'

  When we sat making the mourning   25
    By her death-bed side, said she,
'Dears, how can you keep from your lovers, adorning
    In honour of me!'

  Bubbling and brightsome eyed!
    But now – O never again.   30
She chose her bearers before she died
    From her fancy-men.

36 The Dead Quire

First published in *The Graphic*, Christmas 1901, and thus one of Hardy's series of Christmas Poems, as well as one of a number of narrative poems written in this period, partly in response to their popularity. It is comparable to other ballad-like reminiscences of the Mellstock Quire, including 'The

7. *coats*: 'old name for petticoats' (Hardy's note).
10. *peony lips*: cf. Tess's 'mobile peony mouth', *Tess of the D'Urbervilles*, ch. 2 (p. 39).
25–6. 'It is, or was, a common custom in Wessex, and probably other country places, to prepare the mourning beside the death-bed, the dying person sometimes assisting, who also selects his or her bearers on such occasions' (Hardy's note).
Title. *Quire*: choir.

Rash Bride', the poem which precedes it (subtitled 'An Experience of the Mellstock Quire'), and 'The Paphian Bell' in *Human Shows* (subtitled 'Another Christmas Experience of the Mellstock Quire'). It appeared in a revised form in 'Pieces Occasional and Various' the fourth section of *Time's Laughingstocks*; subsequently included in *Selected Poems* (1916).

Hardy describes the Mellstock Quire in *Under the Greenwood Tree*, where William Dewey suggests the subject of the poem (the failure to adhere to pious tradition) when he tells his grandson Dick that dancing cannot take place until Christmas day is over (I, 7). The ghostly Quire of the poem follows the route of the Quire in the novel, heading towards the churchyard for refreshments (I, 4–5).

Metre: $a^4b^4a^4b^2$ dr, the metre of one of Hardy's favourite hymns and of Jean Ingelow's 'Song of the Going Away' (Taylor 1988: 226).

I

Beside the Mead of Memories,
Where Church-way mounts to Moaning Hill,
The sad man sighed his phantasies:
    He seems to sigh them still.

II

"Twas the Birth-tide Eve, and the hamleteers   5
Made merry with ancient Mellstock zest,
But the Mellstock quire of former years
    Had entered into rest.

III

'Old Dewy lay by the gaunt yew tree,
And Reuben and Michael a pace behind,   10
And Bowman with his family
    By the wall that the ivies bind.

1–2. Bailey suggests that the 'mead' or meadow is by the Frome, down the hill from Stinsford ('Mellstock') Church; 'Moaning Hill' the rising ground to the northwest. The rest of the poem's geography closely follows that of the area between Bockhampton and Stinsford (see Bailey 1970: 236–7).

3. sad] meek *TL* 1909–10.

3. sighed] spoke *Graphic*.

4. sigh] speak *Graphic*.

5. Birth-tide Eve: Christmas Eve.

9–10. characters from *Under the Greenwood Tree*. William Dewey appears in a number of Hardy's poems; in *Tess of the D'Urbervilles*, ch. 17, William Crick says: 'I can tell you to a foot where he's a-lying in Mellstock Churchyard at this very moment – just between the second yew-tree and the north aisle' (p. 139).

9. gaunt] great *Graphic*.

IV

'The singers had followed one by one,
Treble, and tenor, and thorough-bass;
And the worm that wasteth had begun 15
    To mine their mouldering place.

V

'For two-score years, ere Christ-day light,
Mellstock had throbbed to strains from these;
But now there echoed on the night
    No Christmas harmonies. 20

VI

'Three meadows off, at a dormered inn,
The youth had gathered in high carouse,
And, ranged on settles, some therein
    Had drunk them to a drowse.

VII

'Loud, lively, reckless, some had grown, 25
Each dandling on his jigging knee
Eliza, Dolly, Nance, or Joan –
    Livers in levity.

VIII

'The taper flames and hearthfire shine
Grew smoke-hazed to a lurid light, 30
And songs on subjects not divine
    Were warbled forth that night.

IX

'Yet many were sons and grandsons here
Of those who, on such eves gone by,
At that still hour had throated clear 35
    Their anthems to the sky.

X

'The clock belled midnight; and ere long
One shouted, "Now 'tis Christmas morn;

---

14. thorough-bass: person who sings a bass *continuo* part.
21. dormered: with a dormer (gable) window.
27] Eliza, Betsy, Nancy, Joan, *Graphic*.
28. livers: people who are alive, active.
29–30] *Graphic* has: The taper-flame and chimney-shine
                      Grew hazed with smoke and lurid light;
31. not] scarce *Graphic*.
33, many] some *Graphic*.
35. throated] voiced out *Graphic*.
37] 'Midnight resounded; and ere long *Graphic*.

Here's to our women old and young,
    And to John Barleycorn!"   40

XI
'They drink the toast and shout again:
The pewter-ware rings back the boom,
And for a breath-while follows then
    A silence in the room.

XII
'When nigh without, as in old days,   45
The ancient quire of voice and string
Seemed singing words of prayer and praise
    As they had used to sing:

XIII
'*While shepherds watch'd their flocks by night*, –
Thus swells the long familiar sound   50
In many a quaint symphonic flight –
    To, *Glory shone around*.

XIV
'The sons defined their fathers' tones,
The widow his whom she had wed,
And others in the minor moans   55
    The viols of the dead.

XV
'Something supernal has the sound
As verse by verse the strain proceeds,
And stilly staring on the ground
    Each roysterer holds and heeds.   60

XVI
'Towards its chorded closing bar
Plaintively, thinly, waned the hymn,
Yet lingered, like the notes afar
    Of banded seraphim.

---

40. John Barleycorn: the rustic 'god' of drink.
41] 'They drink it; and they shout again; *Graphic*.
42. pewter-ware] dresser-ware *Graphic*.
43. breath-while: short time.
50. long] once *Graphic*.
53. defined] discerned *Graphic*.
57. supernal: supernatural.
58. strain] Quire *Graphic*.
59. stilly: quietly.
60. roysterer: reveler (derived from L. *rusticus*, rustic). *holds*] lists *Graphic*.

XVII

'With brows abashed, and reverent tread,   65
The hearkeners sought the tavern door:
But nothing, save wan moonlight, spread
    The empty highway o'er.

XVIII

'While on their hearing fixed and tense
The aerial music seemed to sink,   70
As it were gently moving thence
    Along the river brink.

XIX

'Then did the Quick pursue the Dead
By crystal Froom that crinkles there;
And still the viewless quire ahead   75
    Voiced the old holy air.

XX

'By Bank-walk wicket, brightly bleached,
It passed, and 'twixt the hedges twain,
Dogged by the living; till it reached
    The bottom of Church Lane.   80

XXI

'There, at the turning, it was heard
Drawing to where the churchyard lay:
But when they followed thitherward
    It smalled, and died away.

XXII

'Each headstone of the quire, each mound,   85
Confronted them beneath the moon;
But no more floated therearound
    That ancient Birth-night tune.

---

66. *hearkeners*] listeners *Graphic*.
70. *aerial*] aetherial *Graphic*. 'Aerial Music' is a stage-direction often used in *The Dynasts*.
74] By flowery Froom that meanders there; *Graphic*.
76. *Voiced*] Tuned *Graphic*.
77–80] not in MS, *Graphic*.
77. *wicket*: gate.
81–84. *Graphic* has: 'Till, where the cascade's cry is heard,
              The music took the churchyard side;
              But when they followed thitherward
                  It paused, and there it died.
85. *headstone*] gravestone *TL* 1909–10.
88. *Birth-night*] Bethlehem *Graphic*.

XXIII

'There Dewy lay by the gaunt yew tree,
There Reuben and Michael, a pace behind,   90
And Bowman with his family
    By the wall that the ivies bind. . . .

XXIV

'As from a dream each sobered son
Awoke, and musing reached his door:
'Twas said that of them all, not one   95
    Sat in a tavern more.'

XXV

– The sad man ceased; and ceased to heed
His listener, and crossed the leaze
From Moaning Hill towards the mead –
    The Mead of Memories.   100

1897

37 Night in the Old Home

Hardy raises domestic ghosts in a number of poems: compare, for example, 'The Self-Unseeing' (23) and 'Old Furniture' (99), and see Knoepflmacher 1990 on houses and memories. Included in *Selected Poems* (1916).
    Metre: $a^5b^6a^5b^6$ dr (complement of 'Afterwards' (112) $a^6b^5a^6b^5$).

When the wasting embers redden the chimney-breast,
And Life's bare pathway looms like a desert track to me,
And from hall and parlour the living have gone to their rest,
My perished people who housed them here come back to me.

They come and seat them around in their mouldy places,   5
Now and then bending towards me a glance of wistfulness,
A strange upbraiding smile upon all their faces,
And in the bearing of each a passive tristfulness.

89–92] not in *Graphic*.
97–100. a framing conclusion which returns to the poem's opening, reminiscent of romantic ballads and narratives: cf. Coleridge's 'The Rhyme of the Ancient Mariner' and the conclusion of Wordsworth's *The Excursion*, Book I.
4. My perished] The bygone MS; The Perished TL 1909–10 (the phrase becoming more intimate with revision).
6. wistfulness: cf. the coinage 'wistlessness' and its rhyme with 'listlessness' in 'The Voice' (59), another poem about a ghostly presence.

'Do you uphold me, lingering and languishing here,
A pale late plant of your once strong stock?' I say to them; 10
'A thinker of crooked thoughts upon Life in the sere,
And on That which consigns men to night after showing the
    day to them?'
'— O let be the Wherefore! We fevered our years not thus:
Take of Life what it grants, without question!' they answer
    me seemingly.
'Enjoy, suffer, wait: spread the table here freely like us, 15
And, satisfied, placid, unfretting, watch Time away beamingly!'

38 After the Last Breath
(J.H. 1813–1904)

The 'occasion' for this rather formal elegy is the death of Hardy's mother, Jemima Hardy, on Easter Sunday, 3 April 1904 (see *LY* 106). Included in *Selected Poems* (1916).
  Metre: $a^5b^5a^5b^2$ dr. Taylor suggests that Hardy's model may have been Grant Allen's poem 'Forget-Me-Not', from *The Lower Slopes* (London, 1894); a similar metre is used for another of Hardy's commemorative poems, 'The Inscription' (1988: 228–9).

> There's no more to be done, or feared, or hoped;
> None now need watch, speak low, and list, and tire;
> No irksome crease outsmoothed, no pillow sloped
>   Does she require.
>
> Blankly we gaze. We are free to go or stay; 5
> Our morrow's anxious plans have missed their aim;
> Whether we leave to-night or wait till day
>   Counts as the same.
>
> The lettered vessels of medicaments
> Seem asking wherefore we have set them here; 10

10. pale late plant: cf. the idea of Hardy as the end of his line in 'Sine Prole' (138).
11. A thinker of crooked thoughts: Hardy often suggested that consciousness was a burden, and that over-sensitive humanity's perceptions had outgrown its biological development: see *Jude the Obsure* VI, 2 (pp. 346–8).
11. Life in the sere: the autumn of life ('sere' is withered or dried up: Hardy often quoted *Macbeth* V, iii, 22–3: 'I have lived long enough: my way of life / Is fall'n into the sere, the yellow leaf').
2. list: listen.

Each palliative its silly face presents
   As useless gear.

And yet we feel that something savours well;
We note a numb relief withheld before;
Our well-beloved is prisoner in the cell   15
   Of Time no more.

We see by littles now the deft achievement
Whereby she has escaped the Wrongers all,
In view of which our momentary bereavement
   Outshapes but small.   20

1904.

39 One We Knew
(M.H. 1772–1857)

First published in *The Tatler*, 2 December 1903, and in *Harper's Weekly* in America, 12 December 1903. The poem is dedicated to the memory of Hardy's paternal grandmother, Mary (Head) Hardy, who died aged 84 in January 1857. For the first sixteen years of Hardy's life she lived with the Hardy family in Bockhampton (*LY* 231). Mrs Martin, the aged repository of 'the parish history for the last sixty years' in *Two on a Tower* 2 is often seen as a portrait of her. One of only eight poems in *Selected Poems* (1916) which Hardy dropped from *Chosen Poems* (1929).
Metre: $a^5b^3a^5b^3$ dtr (triplets often dominate the long lines: cf. 'Lying Awake' (160)).

She told how they used to form for the country dances –
   'The Triumph,' 'The New-rigged Ship' –
To the light of the guttering wax in the panelled manses,
   And in cots to the blink of a dip.

15–16. the cell / Of time: see Ingham 1980 for a commentary on this phrase as typifying Hardy's sense of the self's entrapment in Time.
18. Wrongers: gossips in general, perhaps; but Hardy was stung after his mother's death by comments in the press on her humble origins, and attempted to counter the suggestion that he neglected her (*CL* III, 119; Millgate 1982: 435).
20. Outshapes: appears; the usage is unusual, OED cites only Hardy. Cf. 'outleant', 'The Darkling Thrush' (21).
Title] Remembrance *Harper's* (no subtitle).
2. The Triumph: the name of the dance which opens the Christmas party in *Under the Greenwood Tree* I, 7 (p. 66). Hardy's family owned a number of manuscript books with this and other songs or dances in it (now in DCM).
3. manses: mansions.
4. cots: cottages.
4. dip: tallow candle.

She spoke of the wild 'poussetting' and 'allemanding'   5
  On carpet, on oak, and on sod;
And the two long rows of ladies and gentlemen standing,
  And the figures the couples trod.

She showed us the spot where the maypole was yearly planted,
  And where the bandsmen stood   10
While breeched and kerchiefed partners whirled, and panted
  To choose each other for good.

She told of that far-back day when they learnt astounded
  Of the death of the King of France:
Of the Terror; and then of Bonaparte's unbounded   15
  Ambition and arrogance.

Of how his threats woke warlike preparations
  Along the southern strand,
And how each night brought tremors and trepidations
  Lest morning should see him land.   20

She said she had often heard the gibbet creaking
  As it swayed in the lightning flash,
Had caught from the neighbouring town a small child's
    shrieking
  At the cart-tail under the lash. . . .

With cap-framed face and long gaze into the embers –   25
  We seated around her knees –
She would dwell on such dead themes, not as one who
    remembers,
  But rather as one who sees.

5. *poussetting*: dancing in a circle.
5. *allemanding*: dancing a 'German' dance.
6. *sod*] green *Harper's*.
8] And the couples that tripped between *Harper's*.
9. *maypole*: described in *The Return of the Native* VI, 1 (p. 385) as a dying popular custom.
11. *kerchiefed*: with scarfs around their necks.
13–20. a month after this poem was written Hardy began the first draft of *The Dynasts*. He had always been interested in folk-memories of the Naploeonic era, and one focus of the 'epic' was the way in which these European events affected the working people of Dorset: in 1916 he wrote approvingly of a production of *Wessex Scenes from The Dynasts*, 'embracing scenes of a local character only, from which could be gathered in echoes of drum and trumpet and alarming rumours, the events going on elsewhere' (*LY* 172). Cf. 'The Alarm'.
13. *far-back*] distant *Tatler, Harper's*.
19. *tremors*] terrors *Tatler, Harper's*.
21. *gibbet*: gallows.

> She seemed one left behind of a band gone distant
>   So far that no tongue could hail: 30
> Past things retold were to her as things existent,
>   Things present but as a tale.

May 20, 1902.

40 George Meredith
(1828–1909)

George Meredith was the novelist who had helped Hardy early in his career when, as a reader for Chapman and Hall, he turned down Hardy's 'The Poor Man and the Lady' but encouraged him to write a second novel. In his autobiography, Hardy describes seeing a newspaper poster announcing Meredith's death, and going to his club where he wrote the poem (*LY* 137). It was published in *The Times* on the day of Meredith's funeral, 22 May 1909, and subsequently included in *Selected Poems* (1916).

Metre: *terza rima* on the tetrameter model of Browning's 'The Statue and the Bust', aba⁴ bcb⁴ cdc⁴ etc. dr.

> Forty years back, when much had place
> That since has perished out of mind,
> I heard that voice and saw that face.
>
> He spoke as one afoot will wind
> A morning horn ere men awake; 5
> His note was trenchant, turning kind.
>
> He was of those whose wit can shake
> And riddle to the very core
> The counterfeits that Time will break. . . .
>
> Of late, when we two met once more, 10
> The luminous countenance and rare
> Shone just as forty years before.

31–2. cf. Florence Hardy's 1919 description of Hardy: 'He forgets things that have happened only a day or two before, and people he has seen or heard from, though of course his memory of his early life is miraculous' (Meynell 1940: 302).
4. wind: blow.
6. turning] smart, but *Times*.
7. wit] words *Times*.
9. counterfeits] falsities *Times*.

> So that, when now all tongues declare
> His shape unseen by his green hill,
> I scarce believe he sits not there.   15
>
> No matter. Further and further still
> Through the world's vaporous vitiate air
> His words, wing on – as live words will.
> *May* 1909.

41 Yell'ham-Wood's Story

The poem Hardy seems to have originally seen as closing the volume (see headnote to next poem). Included in *Selected Poems* (1916). Cornelia Cook links it to Meredith's 'Woodland Peace', which may explain its placement immediately after the elegy (1980: 95). Lines 19–23 of Meredith's poem are closest to Hardy:

> And this the woodland saith:
> I know not hope or fear;
> I take whate'er may come;
> I raise my head to aspects fair,
> From foul I turn away.

Metre: a⁴b³a⁴b²b²C²a³ dr (the last line heavily spondaic).

> Coomb-Firtrees say that Life is a moan,
>   And Clyffe-hill Clump says 'Yea!'
> But Yell'ham says a thing of its own:
>   It's not 'Gray, gray
>   Is Life alway!'   5
>   That Yell'ham says,
> Nor that Life is for ends unknown.

14. His shape] He is *Times*.
14. his green hill: Meredith lived at Box Hill in Surrey.
17. vaporous vitiate: polluted, enfeebling.
18. His words wing on: 'winged words' is a classical epithet which Hardy echoes in his auto-elegies; see '"Why do I?"' (153).
18. live] strong *Times*.
Title. Yellowham Wood is a beech wood north of Puddletown, where Hardy grew up.
1. Coomb-Firtrees: a wood to the east.
2. Clyffe-hill Clump: another patch of firs to the east.

> It says that Life would signify
>   A thwarted purposing:
> That we come to live, and are called to die. 10
>   Yes, that's the thing
>   In fall, in spring,
>   That Yell'ham says: —
> 'Life offers — to deny!'
> 1902.

42 A Young Man's Epigram on Existence

Final poem of the volume, but placed before 'George Meredith' in the manuscript. The 'Epigram' would have been drafted when Hardy was 26 and working as an architect's assistant in London. When in 1920 Alfred Noyes used this poem as an example of Hardy's 'pessimism', Hardy replied: 'The lines you allude to, "A Young Man's Epigram", dated 1866, I remember finding in a drawer, and printed them merely as an amusing instance of early cynicism' (*LY* 217).

Metre: aabb^4 dr, best seen here as two epigrammatic couplets.

> A senseless school, where we must give
> Our lives that we may learn to live!
> A dolt is he who memorizes
> Lessons that leave no time for prizes.
>   16 Westbourne Park Villas, 1866

12. *In fall, in spring*: beeches are deciduous (unlike the fir).
Title] Epigram on Existence MS.

Satires of Circumstance, Lyrics and Reveries (1914)

Satires of Circumstance, Lyrics and Reveries was published on 17 November 1914. In contrast to Hardy's three previous volumes, most of the poems were recently written. Thirty-five had been published previously (Purdy 1954: 172). The manuscript fair copy used by the printers is in the Dorset County Museum.

Hardy hesitated over the arrangements and contents of this volume, since it spanned the period of his wife's death and the group of poems which gave the volume its title, the 'Satires of Circumstance' (1910), seemed at odds with the elegiac tone of much of the rest of the book. He wrote of 'the harsh contrasts which the accidents of my life during the past few years had forced into the poems & which I could not remove, so many of them having been printed in periodicals – those in fact that I liked least' (*CL* V, 70). In the first edition and second impression (1915) the 'Satires' were placed near the beginning of the volume, before the 'Poems of 1912–13', but in subsequent editions (beginning with the Wessex Edition, Verse Vol. IV, 1919) they were moved to the end. Other changes were made to the ordering of the elegies (see headnote to the 'Poems of 1912–13'); and 'Men Who March Away', published as a postscript on the war in the first edition, was later moved to *Moments of Vision*.

The volume's reception was indicative of an evolving consensus that Hardy's poetry had a harsh genius, though most reviewers found the volume melancholy in tone. Lytton Strachey, writing in the *New Statesman*, 19 December 1914, described it as 'a very interesting, and in some ways a baffling book' and commented that 'what gives Mr. Hardy's poems their unique flavour is their utter lack of romanticism, their common, undecorated presentments of things. They are, in fact, modern as no other poems are' (Cox 1970: 435–7). Laurence Binyon in the *Bookman* praised the 'Poems of 1912–13', but registered doubts about Hardy's bluntness and negativity: 'if we could understand these poems of a great artist's old age, we should perhaps refrain from asking why he seems so insistently, as with a morbid absorption in the theme, to harp on that familiar note of the implanted crookedness of things and the inbred malignity of chance' (Cox 1970: 441).

43 In Front of the Landscape

The first poem of the opening section of *Satires of Circumstance*, entitled 'Lyrics and Reveries'. In the manuscript table of contents it occupied the present place of 'Wessex Heights', before they were transposed, and it is clearly related to 'Wessex Heights' in its use of a visionary landscape and ghost-ridden speaker (see Miller 1990). The poem's mist-shrouded scene may be Came Down, south of Dorchester, which matches the details in stanza 2 (Bailey 1970: 261–2). Included in *Selected Poems* (1916).

Metre: complex: $a^5b^2c^5d^2e^5b^2$ (except last stanza, which ends ded) tf with the short lines heavily catalectic. There are link-rhymes between stanzas (d/b). The long and short lines suggest the speaker's agitation: 'the rhyme / Sung by the sea-swell' (ll. 52–3). The style has attracted much comment: Zeitlow suggests that 'the frequent breaking of lines into smaller units consisting of heavily accented alliterative phrases echoes the elegiac pace of Anglo-Saxon alliterative poetry', linking this to the ancient landscape (1974: 181). Miller writes that 'the dactylic metre fits the thematic mood and the organizing figure, affirming that memories are like the inundating waters of great sea-swells' (Miller 1990: 197–8).

> Plunging and labouring on in a tide of visions,
>   Dolorous and dear,
> Forward I pushed my way as amid waste waters
>   Stretching around,
> Through whose eddies there glimmered the customed landscape   5
>   Yonder and near
>
> Blotted to feeble mist. And the coomb and the upland
>   Coppice-crowned,
> Ancient chalk-pit, milestone, rills in the grass-flat
>   Stroked by the light,   10
> Seemed but a ghost-like gauze, and no substantial
>   Meadow or mound.
>
> What were the infinite spectacles featuring foremost
>   Under my sight,
> Hindering me to discern my paced advancement   15
>   Lengthening to miles;

2] Bitterly dear, MS; Corpse-like, yet dear, MS del.
5. *customed landscape*: Paulin (1975: 124) notices that 'customed', 'visions', and 'landscape' all appear in a passage in *The Hand of Ethelberta*, ch. 2 (p. 52).
7. *coomb*: small valley.
8. *coppice*: wood of young trees.
9. *rills*: small streams.
11. Paulin (1975: 123–4) compares the light-effects here and elsewhere in the poem to those in Turner's late works, which Hardy admired.

What were the re-creations killing the daytime
    As by the night?
O they were speechful faces, gazing insistent,
    Some as with smiles,   20
Some as with slow-born tears that brinily trundled
    Over the wrecked
Cheeks that were fair in their flush-time, ash now with
        anguish,
    Harrowed by wiles.

Yes, I could see them, feel them, hear them, address them –   25
    Halo-bedecked –
And, alas, onwards, shaken by fierce unreason,
    Rigid in hate,
Smitten by years-long wryness born of misprision,
    Dreaded, suspect.   30

Then there would breast me shining sights, sweet seasons
    Further in date;
Instruments of strings with the tenderest passion
    Vibrant, beside
Lamps long extinguished, robes, cheeks, eyes with the earth's
        crust   35
    Now corporate.

Also there rose a headland of hoary aspect
    Gnawed by the tide,
Frilled by the nimb of the morning as two friends stood there
    Guilelessly glad –   40
Wherefore they knew not – touched by the fringe of an ecstasy
    Scantly descried.

Later images too did the day unfurl me,
    Shadowed and sad,

17–18. cf. Amos 5.8: '[The Lord] maketh the day dark with night.'
24. harrowed by wiles: marked by deceits.
29. misprision: neglect or misunderstanding (perhaps also relevant is 'misprision of felony', the crime of concealing an offence). Misunderstanding the dead is a common topic: cf. the 'hurt, misrepresented names' of 'Spectres that Grieve'.
31–6. Paulin links these lines, via *A Pair of Blue Eyes*, ch. 3, to a memory of Hardy's courtship, and a prophecy of lost love carried by the song Elfride sings in the novel, part of Shelley's 'When the Lamp is Shattered' (Paulin 1975: 28–9).
31. breast me: draw up to me (but the word can mean 'oppose').
39. nimb: nimbus, glowing cloud.
42. descried: seen.

Clay cadavers of those who had shared in the dramas, 45
  Laid now at ease,
Passions all spent, chiefest the one of the broad brow
  Sepulture-clad.
So did beset me scenes, miscalled of the bygone,
  Over the leaze, 50
Past the clump, and down to where lay the beheld ones;
  – Yea, as the rhyme
Sung by the sea-swell, so in their pleading dumbness
  Captured me these.

For, their lost revisiting manifestations 55
  In their live time
Much had I slighted, caring not for their purport,
  Seeing behind
Things more coveted, reckoned the better worth calling
  Sweet, sad, sublime. 60

Thus do they now show hourly before the intenser
  Stare of the mind
As they were ghosts avenging their slights by my bypast
  Body-borne eyes,
Show, too, with fuller translation than rested upon them 65
  As living kind.

Hence wag the tongues of the passing people, saying
  In their surmise,
'Ah – whose is this dull form that perambulates, seeing nought
  Round him that looms 70
Whithersoever his footsteps turn in his farings,
  Save a few tombs?'

47. Passions all spent: cf. the final line of Milton's 'Samson Agonistes,' 'And calm of mind all passion spent'.
47. the one of the broad brow: probably Emma Hardy; cf. 'A Dream or No' (62), l. 8.
49. miscalled of the bygone: wrongly said to be past.
50. leaze: pasture.
52–3: cf. metaphor of the sea in the poem's opening.
60. sublime: on 'sublimation', see Introduction, p. 23.
63. bypast: past, earlier.
65. translation: the word also refers to the artistic process of rendering images from one medium to another (Paulin 1975: 123). See Miller 1990: 207–12 for an discussion of writing as a 'translation' of the dead.
69. perambulates: walks (cf. 'Childhood Among the Ferns' (161), l. 15n).

44 Channel Firing

Published four months before the beginning of the First World War in the *Fortnightly Review*, 1 May 1914. Hardy could thus later call the poem 'prophetic' in its sense of an approaching catastrophe (*LY* 161). In the manuscript table of contents it was originally placed later, after 'Tolerance'.
Metre: abab[4] dr, 'long' hymn stanza.

> That night your great guns, unawares,
> Shook all our coffins as we lay,
> And broke the chancel window-squares,
> We thought it was the Judgment-day
>
> And sat upright. While drearisome   5
> Arose the howl of wakened hounds:
> The mouse let fall the altar-crumb,
> The worms drew back into the mounds,
>
> The glebe cow drooled. Till God called, 'No;
> It's gunnery practice out at sea   10
> Just as before you went below;
> The world is as it used to be:
>
> 'All nations striving strong to make
> Red war yet redder. Mad as hatters
> They do no more for Christés sake   15
> Than you who are helpless in such matters.
>
> 'That this is not the judgment-hour
> For some of them's a blessed thing,
> For if it were they'd have to scour
> Hell's floor for so much threatening. . . .   20
>
> 'Ha, ha. It will be warmer when
> I blow the trumpet (if indeed
> I ever do; for you are men,
> And rest eternal sorely need).'
>
> So down we lay again. 'I wonder,   25
> Will the world ever saner be,'

1–4. alludes to the sounding of the last trump and the end of creation as described in 1 Corinthians 15: 52, and in the book of Revelation.
9. glebe cow: one pastured on church land.
10. suggests the practice of firing cannon over water to loosen and raise drowned bodies (Taylor 1981: 123). The actual gunnery practice which Mrs Hardy reported in this period was at Portland.
14. red war: more apocalyptic imagery: the second of the four beasts of the apocalypse is a red horse, symbolizing War (Revelation 6: 4).
15. Christés: Christ's.

Said one, 'than when He sent us under
In our indifferent century!'

And many a skeleton shook his head.
'Instead of preaching forty year,'
My neighbour Parson Thirdly said,
'I wish I had stuck to pipes and beer.'

Again the guns disturbed the hour,
Roaring their readiness to avenge,
As far inland as Stourton Tower,
And Camelot, and starlit Stonehenge.

April 1914.

45 The Convergence of the Twain
(Lines on the loss of the 'Titanic')

The White Star liner *Titanic* struck an iceberg on her maiden voyage on 15 April 1912, with loss of 1513 lives including many famous people, some of whom Hardy knew. After the disaster, there was widespread criticism of the ship's excessive luxury, of differential survival rates between first-class and steerage passengers, of the arrogance of the (alleged) claim that it was 'unsinkable', and even of the ship's name, which was seen as inviting disaster – the Titans were the violent gods defeated by the more 'civilized' Olympians. Titanism is often linked with crisis in Romantic literature: cf. Hardy's description of the Heath in *The Return of the Native*: 'Every night its Titanic form appeared to await something; but it had waited thus, unmoved, during so many centuries, through the crisis of so many things, that it could only be imagined to await one last crisis – the final overthrow' (p. 34). The poem can be read as an ambiguous meditation on catastrophe and the forces behind history (see Armstrong 1992).

The manuscript dates the poem 24 April 1912. It was published in the souvenir programme of the 'Dramatic and Operatic Matinée in Aid of the "Titanic" Disaster Fund', given at Covent Garden on 14 May. It was subsequently reprinted with alterations and stanza V added, in the *Fortnightly Review*, June 1912, in a limited edition for the American collector George McCutcheon in August, and in *Selected Poems* (1916). A

31. Parson Thirdly: the sermonizing parson in *Far from the Madding Crowd*.
35–6. Bailey points out that three past civilizations are recalled by the place-names: Stourton Tower is a monument (erected 1766) commemorating Alfred's victory over the Danes in 879, Camelot the legendary court of King Arthur, and Stonehenge the neolithic site north of Salisbury (1970: 263).
Headnote] Improvised on the loss of 'The Titanic' *Souvenir Programme*.

possible model is 'The Iceberg' by the American Celia Thaxter, written more than thirty years earlier and published in *The Spectator* on 20 April 1912, p. 620, as an interesting anticipation of the wreck.

Metre: a³a³a⁶ dr. The stanzas are often seen as 'shaped' to suggest a ship low in the water.

I

In a solitude of the sea
Deep from human vanity,
And the Pride of Life that planned her, stilly couches she.

II

Steel chambers, late the pyres
Of her salamandrine fires,
Cold currents thrid, and turn to rhythmic tidal lyres.

5

III

Over the mirrors meant
To glass the opulent
The sea-worm crawls – grotesque, slimed, dumb, indifferent.

1–6. cf. the opening of R.S Hawker's 'The Fatal Ship', which Hardy knew:
   Down the deep sea, full fourscore fathoms down,
   —An iron vault hath clutched five hundred men!
1] In the solitudes of the sea, *Souvenir Programme*.
2. vanity: the word takes on its biblical overtones of worldliness and futility (cf. Ecclesiastes 1–2). In a letter written on 17 December 1911 Hardy wrote 'Yes: the vanity of life – the *cui bono*? is overwhelmingly borne in upon us with the years. . . . I was reading Ecclesiastes only this morning' (*CL* VII, 154).
3. Pride of Life: I John 2: 15–17: 'Love not the world, neither the things that are in the world. . . . For all that is in the world, the lust of the flesh, and the lust of the eyes, and the pride of life, is not of the Father, but is of the world. And the world passeth away. . . .' Given that the *Titanic* was widely seen as representing a peak in mechanical progress, the final stanza of Matthew Arnold's 'Progress' is an interesting juxtaposition:
   'Children of men! not that your age excel
   In pride of life the ages of your sires,
   But that ye think clear, fear deep, bear fruit well,
   The friend of man desires.'
3. stilly: quietly (as in Coleridge's 'The Aeolian Harp', l. 11: 'The stilly murmur of the distant sea').
4] In retorts that were the pyres *Souvenir Programme*.
5. salamandrine: according to legend, salamanders were able to live in fire.
6] The cold, calm currents strike their rythmic tidal lyres. *Souvenir Programme*.
6. thrid: thread. On 'tidal lyres' see 'The Darkling Thrush' (21), l. 6n.
8–9] To flash forms opulent / The sea-worm creeps – grotesque, unweeting, mean, content. *Souvenir Programme*.

IV

Jewels in joy designed   10
To ravish the sensuous mind
Lie lightless, all their sparkles bleared and black and blind.

V

Dim moon-eyed fishes near
Gaze at the gilded gear
And query: 'What does this vaingloriousness down here?' ... 15

VI

Well: while was fashioning
This creature of cleaving wing,
The Immanent Will that stirs and urges everything

VII

Prepared a sinister mate
For her – so gaily great –   20
A Shape of Ice, for the time far and dissociate.

VIII

And as the smart ship grew
In stature, grace, and hue,
In shadowy silent distance grew the Iceberg too.

IX

Alien they seemed to be: 25
No mortal eye could see
The intimate welding of their later history.

13–15] not in *Souvenir Programme*.
14–15] The daintily gilded gear / Gaze querying: 'What does this sumptuousness down here?' *Fortnightly*.
15–30. Thaxter's poem similarly describes the 'dread appointment' of iceberg and ship, and how 'with matchless grace, / The stately ship, unconscious of her foe, / Drew near the trysting-place'. Other poems by Hardy describe two entities that are 'secret sharers': cf. 'The Felled Elm and She'.
16. Well: Clements (1980: 153) points out that the poem hinges on this word, like 'The Contretemps'. *Souvenir Programme* has 'For'.
17] This ship of swiftest wing, *Souvenir Programme*, *Fortnightly*, Limited Edn.
19. mate: see l. 30n.
22. smart: i.e. elegant, fashionable; but the word here retains overtones of its older meaning: hurt, and especially 'suffering of the nature of punishment or retribution' (OED). 'Smart-money' is paid to the widows of seamen.
27] How closely welded was their later history, *Souvenir Programme*.

X
      Or sign that they were bent
      By paths coincident
On being anon twin halves of one august event.   30

XI
      Till the Spinner of the Years
      Said 'Now!' And each one hears,
And consummation comes, and jars two hemispheres.

46 'When I set out for Lyonnesse'
(1870)

The poem's background is Hardy's first visit to St Juniot, Cornwall, on 7 March 1870, where he met Emma Gifford, his future wife (*EL* 85–7, 98–9). In a letter to Florence Henniker on 23 December 1914, he wrote 'It is exactly what happened 44 years ago'; later he called it 'my favourite lyric' (*CL* V, 70, 204). The setting is Upper Bockhampton. Included in *Selected Poems* (1916).

28–30] And so coincident / In course as to be meant / To form anon ... *Souvenir Programme* (the revision produces a greater ambiguity: see l. 28n).
28. bent: like other words in the poem, 'bent' encompasses antithetical meanings: 'bent' in the sense of shaped by an outside force, or 'bent' in the sense of being motivated.
30. anon: soon; but the older meanings of the word are also present: 'in one body, company, or mass ... in unity' and 'in one course or direction' (OED).
30. twin halves: perhaps alludes to the idea, in Plato's *Symposium*, of an original self split into male and female halves; thus the 'consummation' of l. 33 is also the sexual (re)union of the two 'mates' which Plato sees as the root of heterosexual desire.
30. august: grand (the root sense of the word also implies something prepared by augury and brought to fruition).
31. Spinner] Mover *Souvenir Programme*. Hardy revises in the direction of a emphasis on aesthetic pattern: cf. the 'World-weaver' of 'Doom and She' and the 'spinner's wheel' of 'According to the Mighty Working', both suggesting the Fates who spin and cut the web of life.
32. And each one] The which each *Souvenir Programme, Fortnightly*.
33. consummation comes: recalls Christ's final words on the Cross, in the Vulgate *consummatum est* ('it is finished', John 19: 30). The word also has sexual overtones (see l. 30n above).
33. jars] clouds *Souvenir Programme*.
Title. '"Lyonnesse" is a vague term denoting the north & north west coast of Cornwall generally' (*CL* V, 289). Hardy borrowed it from the Arthurian romances of Tennyson and Swinburne. He considered calling *A Pair of*

Metre: $A^4B^3b^3a^4A^4B^3$ dr. As Hardy wrote in 1924, 'The Poem ... is one of the many varieties of Roundelay, Roundel, or Rondel' (Bailey 1970: 270). Taylor points out that French forms were fashionable in the 1870s and 1880s, and that Hardy studied Gleeson White's *Ballades and Rondeaus* (1887). His use of the form is non-traditional, though it remains a 'rondeau' in that the first two lines 'come round' again (Taylor 1988: 253).

> When I set out for Lyonnesse,
>   A hundred miles away,
>   The rime was on the spray,
> And starlight lit my lonesomeness
> When I set out for Lyonnesse   5
>   A hundred miles away.
>
> What would bechance at Lyonnesse
>   While I should sojourn there
>   No prophet durst declare,
> Nor did the wisest wizard guess   10
> What would bechance at Lyonnesse
>   While I should sojourn there.
>
> When I came back from Lyonnesse
>   With magic in my eyes,
>   All marked with mute surmise   15
> My radiance rare and fathomless,
> When I came back from Lyonnesse
>   With magic in my eyes!

Blue Eyes 'Elfride of Lyonnesse', and the novel which Elfride writes as 'Ernest Field' in the book is subtitled 'A Romance of Lyonnesse'.
3. *rime*: hoar-frost, frozen mist (perhaps punning on the alternative spelling of 'rhyme').
7. *bechance*: happen by chance.
9. *durst*: dares to.
15–16] None managed to surmise / What meant my godlike gloriousness, MS, SC 1914–15.
15. *mute surmise*: silent conjecture (cf. the 'wild surmise' of Cortez's men discovering a new ocean in Keats's 'On First Looking into Chapman's Homer').

47 Wessex Heights
(1896)

The poem with which Hardy originally wished to open *Satires of Circumstance*, 'Wessex Heights' is dated 'December, 1896' in the manuscript, i.e. the same period as the 'In Tenebris' poems. It seems to mark Hardy's 'escape' from prose to verse (Giordano 1975). The four 'heights' in the poem form a rectangle taking in most of Wessex, so that Hardy is defining his poetic 'territory'; however the contrast between peopled lowlands and solitary highlands is also a common romantic gesture, as e.g. in Byron's *Childe Harold* III, 68–75 (see Miller 1990: 107–34 on the poem's use of place and time). Included in *Selected Poems* (1916).

The identity of the women in the poem is obscure. Bailey suggested they are Emma Hardy; Hardy's mother Jemima Hardy (the 'figure against the moon'); his cousin Tryphena Sparks (the 'ghost at Yell'ham Bottom'); and Florence Henniker ('one rare fair woman'), with whom he was in love in the mid–1890s (Bailey 1970: 275–8). However, only the identification of Mrs Henniker is well supported, and Bailey's inferences have been attacked. Michael Benson (1982) persuasively links the three other figures to heroines in Hardy's novels whom he might have associated with Florence Henniker: Bathsheba, Tess, and Sue.

Metre: aabb[7] dtr, an ancient form also used by Byron, Tennyson and others. Paulin comments that 'the enormous iambic couplets create a terrifying monotony.... The poem sounds what it is – a speech delivered by someone in a state of such acute depression that he has almost totally lost his own will' (1975: 128). The 'monotony' is, however, qualified by the caesura in most lines, which tend to resolve the metre into three- and four-beat sections (an effect reinforced by internal rhymes). Miller argues that the poem uses a sound-structure which attaches 'low vowels' ('o' and 'a') to lowland places and high vowels ('i') to 'Heights' (1990: 122).

> There are some heights in Wessex, shaped as if by a kindly hand
> For thinking, dreaming, dying on, and at crises when I stand,
> Say, on Ingpen Beacon eastward, or on Wylls-Neck westwardly,
> I seem where I was before my birth, and after death may be.
>
> In the lowlands I have no comrade, not even the lone man's friend –   5

---

3. *Ingpen Beacon*: Ingpen (or 'Inkpen') is a chalk 'height' or hill in northwest Wessex. 'Beacon' implies it was used for signal fires.
3. *Wylls-Neck*: hill northwest of Taunton, in Somerset.

Her who suffereth long and is kind; accepts what he is too
    weak to mend:
Down there they are dubious and askance; there nobody
    thinks as I,
But mind-chains do not clank where one's next neighbour is
    the sky.

In the towns I am tracked by phantoms having weird detective
    ways –
Shadows of beings who fellowed with myself of earlier days: 10
They hang about at places, and they say harsh heavy things –
Men with a wintry sneer, and women with tart disparagings.

Down there I seem to be false to myself, my simple self that
    was,
And is not now, and I see him watching, wondering what crass
    cause
Can have merged him into such a strange continuator as this,   15
Who yet has something in common with himself, my chrysalis.

I cannot go to the great grey Plain; there's a figure against
    the moon,
Nobody sees it but I, and it makes my breast beat out of tune;
I cannot got to the tall-spired town, being barred by the forms
    now passed
For everybody but me, in whose long vision they stand there
    fast.   20

There's a ghost at Yell'ham Bottom chiding loud at the fall of
    the night,
There's a ghost in Froom-side Vale, thin-lipped and vague, in
    a shroud of white,
There is one in the railway train whenever I do not want it
    near,
I see its profile against the pane, saying what I would not hear.

6. Her who suffereth long and is kind: 1 Corinthians 13: 4, 'Charity suffereth
long and is kind' (cf. 'The Blinded Bird' (87) and 'Surview' (130)).
15. continuator: word also used in the draft of 'The Pedigree' (91), l. 30n.
17. great grey Plain: perhaps Salisbury Plain, though Bailey suggests Egdon
Heath (1970: 276).
19. tall-spired town: variously seen as Salisbury or Christminster/Oxford.
22. cf. the mist-shrouded and spectral figures in 'In Front of the
Landscape' (43) and 'The Head Above the Fog'.
23. it near] her there MS del.

As for one rare fair woman, I am now but a thought of hers,   25
I enter her mind and another thought succeeds me that she
    prefers;
Yet my love for her in its fulness she herself even did not
    know;
Well, time cures hearts of tenderness, and now I can let her
    go.

So I am found on Ingpen Beacon, or on Wylls-Neck to the
    west,
Or else on homely Bulbarrow, or little Pilsdon Crest,   30
Where men have never cared to haunt, nor women have
    walked with me,
And ghosts then keep their distance; and I know some liberty.

48 A Singer Asleep
(Algernon Charles Swinburne, 1837–1909)

First published in the *English Review*, April 1910, and included in *Selected Poems* (1916). Swinburne died on 10 April 1909, and Hardy visited his grave at Bonchurch on the Isle of Wight the following March (*LY* 141). He read *Poems and Ballads* on their first appearance in 1866, and met Swinburne about 1887, remaining on friendly terms thereafter. He was particularly interested in Swinburne's metrical experiments, making notes from an article on his verse in 1909 (Björk entry 2461; on Hardy and Swinburne see also Murfin 1978).

Metre: in keeping with Swinburne's status as a master-metricist, the versification is deliberately virtuoso: a series of variations culminating in the final adapted *ottava rima* stanza, $a^5b^5a^5b^5a^5b^5c^5c^3$. Peter Sacks comments on the way in which the poem 'offers an intriguing continuation of the earlier poet's style and ideology' (1985: 228–34).

30. Bulbarrow: a hill in south Wessex, overlooking Blackmoor Vale ('barrow' suggests a burial-mound as well as a hill).
30. Pilsdon Crest: Pilsdon Pen in west Dorset, the highest hill in the county, site of an ancient hill-fort.
Title] A South-Coast Nocturne (del.) MS prepared for *English Review*.
1–3. cf. Swinburne's elegy for Baudelaire, 'Ave Atque Vale', e.g. ll. 14–16:
    Thine ears knew all the wandering watery sighs
      Where the sea sobs around Lesbian promontories,
        The barren kiss of piteous wave to wave ...
The opening lines of Swinburne's 'A Forsaken Garden' are similar:
    In a coign of the cliff between lowland and highland,
      At the sea-down's edge between windward and lee ...

I

In this fair niche above the unslumbering sea,
That sentrys up and down all night, all day,
From cove to promontory, from ness to bay,
The Fates have fitly bidden that he should be
    Pillowed eternally.

II

– It was as though a garland of red roses
Had fallen about the hood of some smug nun
When irresponsibly dropped as from the sun,
In fulth of numbers freaked with musical closes,
Upon Victoria's formal middle time
    His leaves of rhythm and rhyme.

III

O that far morning of a summer day
When, down a terraced street whose pavements lay
Glassing the sunshine into my bent eyes,
I walked and read with a quick glad surprise
    New words, in classic guise, –

IV

The passionate pages of his earlier years,
Fraught with hot sighs, sad laughters, kisses, tears;
Fresh-fluted notes, yet from a minstrel who
Blew them not naïvely, but as one who knew
    Full well why thus he blew.

---

3. ness: promontory.
5. pillowed: cf. Swinburne's 'A Swimmer's Dream': 'I lean my cheek to the cold grey pillow.'
6–11. the garland and leaves recall the opening stanza of 'Ave Atque Vale' and Swinburne's 'Sapphics' and other elegiac verse: cf. Milton's 'Lycidas', ll. 1–14.
9. fulth: fullness.
12–16. Hardy reported: 'I used to walk from my lodgings near Hyde Park to the draughting office every morning, and never without a copy of the first edition of the *Poems and Ballads* sticking out of my pocket' (Bailey 1970: 282–3).
17–21. the excessiveness of Swinburne's love poetry led to a reputation as a libertine: in 1905 Hardy related that 'We laughed and condoled with each other on having been the two most abused of living writers; he for *Poems and Ballads*, I for *Jude the Obscure*' (*LY* 112). Later, in 'A Refusal', Hardy mocked the church authorities who refused to bury Swinburne in Westminster Abbey.
19. naïvely: a word worth remarking in 1914: Lytton Strachey called it a 'horrid hybrid . . . a neologism exactly calculated to make the classic author of *Atalanta* [i.e. Swinburne] turn in his grave' (Cox 1970: 436).

V

I still can hear the brabble and the roar
At those thy tunes, O still one, now passed through
That fitful fire of tongues then entered new!
Their power is spent like spindrift on this shore; 25
    Thine swells yet more and more.

VI

– His singing-mistress verily was no other
Than she the Lesbian, she she the music-mother
Of all the tribe that feel in melodies;
Who leapt, love-anguished, from the Leucadian steep 30
Into the rambling world-encircling deep
    Which hides her where none sees.

VII

And one can hold in thought that nightly here
His phantom may draw down to the water's brim,
And hers come up to meet it, as a dim 35
Lone shine upon the heaving hydrosphere,
And mariners wonder as they traverse near,
    Unknowing of her and him.

VIII

One dreams him sighing to her spectral form:
'O teacher, where lies hid thy burning line; 40
Where are those songs, O poetess divine
Whose very orts are love incarnadine?'
And her smile back: 'Disciple true and warm,
    Sufficient now are thine.' ...

---

28. *she the Lesbian*: the Greek lyric poet Sappho, said to have thrown herself into the sea off the Island of Leucas when spurned in love. Hardy had imitated Swinburne's 'Sapphics' (see 'Sapphic Fragment' (28); Björk entry 522n).

36. *hydrosphere*: system of waters on the earth. Sacks (1985: 232) comments that the term's 'aggressive modernity' (first usage listed in OED 1887) is modified by its Greek root and invocation of Swinburne's world of water and mist.

42. *orts*: scraps, leavings. Sappho's work mainly survives in fragments, many of them quoted in other writers' works.

42. *incarnadine*: reddened, blood or flesh-coloured (also suggests 'incarnate'). In 'Ave Atque Vale' Swinburne asks the dead Baudelaire 'What of life is there, what ill or good? / Are the fruits grey like dust or bright like blood?'

IX

>   So here, beneath the waking constellations, 45
>   Where the waves peal their everlasting strains,
>   And their dull subterrene reverberations
>   Shake him when storms make mountains of their plains –
>   Him once their peer in sad improvisations,
>   And deft as wind to cleave their frothy manes – 50
>   I leave him, while the daylight gleam declines
>   Upon the capes and chines.
>   Bonchurch, 1910.

49 Self-Unconscious

The poem's title suggests a comparison with 'The Self-Unseeing' (23) and other poems on missed opportunities, blindness, and late realizations. Hardy's 1913 trip to Cornwall may have been the occasion.

Metre: $a^2 a^2 b^4 c^2 c^2 b^4 e$ dr (also used for 'Outside the Casement').

>   Along the way
>   He walked that day,
>   Watching shapes that reveries limn,
>   And seldom he
>   Had eyes to see 5
>   The moment that encompassed him.
>
>   Bright yellowhammers
>   Made mirthful clamours
>   And billed long straws with a bustling air,
>   And bearing their load 10
>   Flew up the road
>   That he followed, alone, without interest there.
>
>   From bank to ground
>   And over and round
>   They sidled along the adjoining hedge; 15
>   Sometimes to the gutter
>   Their yellow flutter
>   Would dip from the nearest slatestone ledge.

45–52. Swinburne's elegy also ends with images of sunset, dying wind, and stars.
52. chines: fissures in a cliff.
3. limn: illuminate, paint.
6] The life that lay in front of him. MS (ie. future rather than present).

>   The smooth sea-line
>   With a metal shine,
> And flashes of white, and a sail thereon,
>   He would also descry
>   With a half-wrapt eye
> Between the projects he mused upon.
>
>   Yes, round him were these
>   Earth's artistries,
> But specious plans that came to his call
>   Did most engage
>   His pilgrimage,
> While himself he did not see at all.
>
>   Dead now as sherds
>   Are the yellow birds,
> And all that mattered has passed away;
>   Yet God, the Elf,
>   Now shows him that self
> As he was, and should have been shown, that day.
>
>   O it would have been good
>   Could he then have stood
> At a clear-eyed distance, and conned the whole,
>   But now such vision
>   Is mere derision,
> Nor soothes his body nor saves his soul.
>
>   Not much, some may
>   Incline to say,
> To see therein, had it all been seen,
>   Nay! he is aware
>   A thing was there
> That loomed with an immortal mien.
>
>   Near Bossiney.

22. *descry*: see.
23. *half-wrapt*: half-covered or obscured (perhaps playing on 'rapt').
31. *sherds*: shards, fragments.
36. In respose to a query about this line, Hardy wrote: 'If he had realized then, when young, what he was, he would have acted differently. That is the tragedy of youth: when we know, it's too late to alter things' (Collins 1928: 24).
39. *clear-eyed*] focussed *SC* 1914–15; *conned the*] seen him MS del.
39. *conned*: studied, inspected.
45. *therein*] in him *SC* 1914.
48. *mien*: air, bearing.
Endnote. Near Bossiney: Bossiney Haven, a cove on the north coast of Cornwall, near where Emma Gifford lived when Hardy first met her.

50 Under the Waterfall

The last poem of the 'Lyrics and Reveries'. The poem describes an incident in the Vallency Valley, recalled in Emma Hardy's *Some Recollections*, p. 57 (Hardy's sketch of the scene is reproduced on a facing page). The hand-in-water motif recurs in a number of his novels, suggesting its importance to Hardy as one of the epiphanic moments in his romance (see Bailey 1970: 292–3).

Metre: irregular couplets, $a^4a^4b^4b^4c^2c^2d^2d^2e^4e^4$ etc. dr; ending in a sestet in tetrameter couplets. The first substantially irregular set of stanza-forms in this selection. Taylor suggests, rather implausibly, that the stanza-shapes suggest a waterfall, as in Vaughan's 'The Waterfall' (1988: 190).

'Whenever I plunge my arm, like this,
In a basin of water, I never miss
The sweet sharp sense of a fugitive day
Fetched back from its thickening shroud of gray.
    Hence the only prime   5
    And real love-rhyme
    That I know by heart,
    And that leaves no smart,
Is the purl of a little valley fall
About three spans wide and two spans tall   10
Over a table of solid rock,
And into a scoop of the self-same block;
The purl of a runlet that never ceases
In stir of kingdoms, in wars, in peaces;
With a hollow boiling voice it speaks   15
And has spoken since hills were turfless peaks.'

'And why gives this the only prime
Idea to you of a real love-rhyme?
And why does plunging your arm in a bowl
Full of spring water, bring throbs to your soul?'   20

'Well, under the fall, in a crease of the stone,
Though where precisely none ever has known,
Jammed darkly, nothing to show how prized,
And by now with its smoothness opalized,
    Is a drinking-glass: 25
    For, down that pass

Title. Hardy considered two alternative titles: 'The Lost Glass' and 'The Glass in the Stream' (*CPW* II, 45, 490n).
1–16. C. Day Lewis suggested a comparison of these lines with the reminiscent mode of Browning's 'By the Fireside' (Gibson 1979: 151).
24. opalized: made opaque by scouring.

My lover and I
Walked under a sky
Of blue with a leaf-wove awning of green,
In the burn of August, to paint the scene,   30
And we placed our basket of fruit and wine
By the runlet's rim, where we sat to dine;
And when we had drunk from the glass together,
Arched by the oak-copse from the weather,
I held the vessel to rinse in the fall,   35
Where it slipped, and sank, and was past recall,
Though we stooped and plumbed the little abyss
With long bared arms. There the glass still is.
And, as said, if I thrust my arm below
Cold water in basin or bowl, a throe   40
From the past awakens a sense of that time,
And the glass we used, and the cascade's rhyme.
The basin seems the pool, and its edge
The hard smooth face of the brook-side ledge,
And the leafy pattern of china-ware   45
The hanging plants that were bathing there.

'By night, by day, when it shines or lours,
There lies intact that chalice of ours,
And its presence adds to the rhyme of love
Persistently sung by the fall above.   50
No lip has touched it since his and mine
In turns therefrom sipped lovers' wine.'

Poems of 1912–13

Veteris vestigia flammae

Emma Hardy died suddenly at Max Gate on 17 November 1912. They had been more or less estranged from each other for a number of years, but Emma's death revived Hardy's passion for her, and created guilt at the way he had treated her. Both these feelings were accentuated by the writings which Emma left behind her: the vituperative notebook entitled 'What I

30. paint the scene: see headnote.
47. lours: looks dark.
48. chalice] glass MS del.
Epigraph. Veteris vestigia flammae. Virgil, *Aeneid* IV, 23, variously rendered as 'traces of the old flame', 'ashes from the old fire' (Peter Sacks points out

think of my Husband' (which he later destroyed) and the poignant memoir of her girlhood and courtship later published as *Some Recollections*. In March 1913 he revisited the scenes of their courtship in Cornwall. He hesitated over the publication of these elegiac poems, and seems to have seen them partly as an 'expiation' (Purdy 1954: 166).

In the first edition the sequence finished with 'The Phantom Horsewoman'. The final three poems were transferred into the sequence from the 'Lyrics and Reveries' section in the Wessex Edition and *Collected Poems* of 1919 (on other revisions, see Gifford 1972). Critics have interpreted the additions in very different ways. Davie sees the coda as a betrayal of the absolute truths of 'At Castle Boterel' and 'The Phantom Horsewoman', arguing that 'Hardy psychologizes his own metaphysical insights', denying his experience of the spiritual reality of the dead (1972: 155). Other writers have often contested that claim: Miller and Sacks see the additions as involving a necessary withdrawal from the intensities of the previous poems, and a recognition that Emma exists only as a memory (Miller 1970: 251; Sacks 1985: 257–8).

Criticism of the sequence has focused on a number of issues. Many critics have examined the overall shape of the sequence including Hardy's additions, often placing in the context of what Freud calls 'the work of mourning' (see Davie 1972; Morgan 1974; Buckler 1979; Murfin 1982; Sacks 1985; Sexton 1991). Others have raised the question of what extent the elegies represent a recovery of Emma's voice (Davie; Armstrong 1991); Sexton argues that voice in the sequence is always problematic and that Hardy ultimately seeks to create an image of the dead, a visual memory. David Gewanter discusses the interplay between the older and younger Emma in the sequence (1991). A number of critics have focused on the way in which Hardy revises the elegiac tradition which he inherits from Tennyson and earlier poets (Sacks; Morgan; Johnson 1977; Edmond 1981; Griffith 1989; Ramazani 1991; Campbell 1992).

that 'flammae' can signify the ruins of a fire as well as the fire itself (1985: 236)). The words are spoken by Dido when she feels the love which died with her husband Sychaeus rekindled as Aeneas tells his story, and as the events which lead to Aeneas's betrayal and her suicide are set in motion. Later in the *Aeneid* Aeneas travels to Hades where he meets Dido's accusing shade (as Hardy travels to Cornwall in search of Emma's ghost). The same phrase is quoted in the *Commedia* at the point where Dante meets the transfigured Beatrice: *conosco i segni dell' antica fiamma*, translated by Cary 'The old flame / Throws out clear tokens of reviving fire' (*Purgatorio* XXX). On Hardy, Virgil and Dante, see Björk entries 263–8n; Davie 1972; Miller 1970: 248–9; Armstrong 1991.

51 The Going

The first seven poems of the sequence express and attempt to deal with a sense of rupture and shock, a 'difference' (as 'The Walk' (53) puts it) between 'then' and 'now' which is succeeded by Emma's own voice in 'The Haunter' (58). They alternate between addressing her ('you' poems) and third-person recollections ('her' poems).

Hardy models the opening of his sequence on Coventry Patmore's 1877 volume of domestic elegies, *To the Unknown Eros* (Edmond 1981: 160). As Eric Griffith points out in his comparison of the two sequences (1989: 223–7), Patmore's 'Departure' opens more consolingly than Hardy's poem on lost opportunities:

> It was not like your great and gracious ways!
> Do you, that have nought other to lament,
> Never, my Love, repent
> Of how, that June afternoon,
> You went,
> With sudden, unintelligible phrase,
> And frighten'd eye,
> Upon your journey of so many days,
> Without a single kiss, or a good-bye?

Hardy included 'The Going' in *Selected Poems* (1916).

Metre: $a^4b^4a^4b^4c^2c^2b^4$ (stanzas 1, 3, 5), $a^3b^3a^4b^4c^2c^2b^4$ (stanzas 2, 4, 6) dr with a number of triplets and feminine endings on the dimeter lines. Partly modelled on Chatterton's 'Song from Aella', much marked in Hardy's edition (Taylor 1988: 245). Davie finds the symmetrical form over-rigid, 'the imperious verbal engineer still, even here, thwarting the true and truly suffering poet' (1973: 59).

> Why did you give no hint that night
> That quickly after the morrow's dawn,
> And calmly, as if indifferent quite,
> You would close your term here, up and be gone
>   Where I could not follow   5
>   With wing of swallow
> To gain one glimpse of you ever anon!
>
>   Never to bid good-bye,
>   Or lip me the softest call,

1. no hint: arguably Hardy exaggerates or even dissembles about his lack of knowledge of his wife's condition (see Gittings 1978: 206–7).

5–6. cf. Tennyson's flight after Hallam, *In Memoriam* 12. Griffith, however, notes that the rhyme echoes Tennyson's 'O Swallow, Swallow', the 'chirpy lyric' in *The Princess* 4, suggesting that 'Hardy gives the rhyme a bizzare double aspect, both tripping and dumpy ... to convey the bitterness which Hardy in actuality turns on poetical machineries which loft the poet like a bird' (1989: 226).

9. lip: give MS, *SC* 1914–15, *SP* 1916. Hardy's 'Spectres that Grieve' also

Or utter a wish for a word, while I 10
Saw morning harden upon the wall,
    Unmoved, unknowing
    That your great going
Had place that moment, and altered all.

Why do you make me leave the house 15
And think for a breath it is you I see
At the end of the alley of bending boughs
Where so often at dusk you used to be;
    Till in darkening dankness
    The yawning blankness 20
Of the perspective sickens me!

    You were she who abode
    By those red-veined rocks far West,
You were the swan-necked one who rode
Along the beetling Beeny Crest, 25
    And, reining nigh me,
    Would muse and eye me,
While Life unrolled us its very best.

Why, then, latterly did we not speak,
Did we not think of those days long dead, 30
And ere your vanishing strive to seek
That time's renewal? We might have said,
    'In this bright spring weather
    We'll visit together
Those places that once we visited.' 35

    Well, well! All's past amend,
    Unchangeable. It must go.
I seem but a dead man held on end

---

uses 'lipped' to suggest the mute voice of the dead, while in Barnes's 'Woak Hill' the narrator calls to his wife's ghost 'wi' lippens / All soundless to others' (Hardy 1908: 81).
23. *red-veined rocks*: the cliffs near St Juniot (with fleshly overtones: cf. the 'primaeval rocks' of 'At Castle Boterel' (66)).
25. *beetling*: projecting (coined by Shakespeare, *Hamlet* I, iv, 71, and used by Hardy in *A Pair of Blue Eyes*, ch. 7, p. 82).
27. *eye me*: as Hardy 'eyes' her at the end of the sequence, in 'The Phantom Horsewoman' (68).
36. *Well, well!*: again echoes Patmore's 'Departure', 'Well, it was well. . . .'
37. *It must go*: the word 'go' echoes through the sequence (see Gifford 1972: 131–2).

To sink down soon. . . . O you could not know
    That such swift fleeing   40
No soul foreseeing –
Not even I – would undo me so!
December 1912.

52 Your Last Drive

The second poem of the sequence sustains the direct address of the opening poem, and continues with the theme of the suddenness and unexpectedness of Emma's death, expressing the sense of hurt which necessarily precedes any elegiac recovery.
Metre: ababcc^4 dr, a common hymn sestet.

    Here by the moorway you returned,
    And saw the borough lights ahead
    That lit your face – all undiscerned
    To be in a week the face of the dead,
    And you told of the charm of that haloed view   5
    That never again would beam on you.

    And on your left you passed the spot
    Where eight days later you were to lie,
    And be spoken of as one who was not;
    Beholding it with a heedless eye   10
    As alien from you, though under its tree
    You soon would halt everlastingly.

    I drove not with you. . . . Yet had I sat
    At your side that eve I should not have seen
    That the countenance I was glancing at   15
    Had a last-time look in the flickering sheen,
    Nor have read the writing upon your face,
    'I go hence soon to my resting-place;

    'You may miss me then. But I shall not know
    How many times you visit me there,   20

Title. the drive to Puddletown is described in Hardy's autobiography (*LY* 154).
2. borough lights: i.e. Dorchester.
17. the writing upon your face: the idea that experience is 'inscribed' on the face occurs throughout Hardy's writings (see, e.g. the diary entry for 2 January 1886, *EL* 231; Björk entry 1061; and the description of Clym Yeobright's face at the beginning of *The Return of the Native* III, 1).

Or what your thoughts are, or if you go
There never at all. And I shall not care.
Should you censure me I shall take no heed,
And even your praises no more shall need.'

True: never you'll know. And you will not mind.   25
But shall I then slight you because of such?
Dear ghost, in the past did you ever find
The thought 'What profit,' move me much?
Yet abides the fact, indeed, the same, –
You are past love, praise, indifference, blame.   30

December 1912.

53 The Walk

Emma's last drive is succeeded by Hardy's habitual walk, which spans the point of her death. This is the final poem in the opening group of three poems addressed to Emma ('you'), replaced by the 'her' of the two poems which follow.

Metre: $a^3a^3b^2b^2c^2c^2d^4d^4$ dr, a shaped stanza with the last line of the poem suggesting a 'return' with a 'difference', anapaestics after the mainly iambic long lines.

You did not walk with me
Of late to the hill-top tree
   By the gated ways,
   As in earlier days;
   You were weak and lame,   5
   So you never came,
And I went alone, and I did not mind,
Not thinking of you as left behind.

I walked up there to-day
Just in the former way;   10
   Surveyed around
   The familiar ground

28] Me one whom consequence influenced much. MS del. (Hardy hesitated: the line printed is also del. in MS).
30. if 'indifference' is the median, the implicit final term of the spectrum, 'hate', is elided.
2. Bailey suggests Culliford Tree, 3 miles southwest of Max Gate (1970: 295).

>   By myself again:
>   What difference, then?
> Only that underlying sense 15
> Of the look of a room on returning thence.

54 Rain on a Grave

'Rain on a Grave' uses the association of mourning with tears, and secondarily with rain and the vegetative cycle of flowering and re-growth, common in elegiac verse (see Sacks 1985: 18–34). It thus might be seen as expressing Hardy's first stirrings of recovery, moving towards a greater objectification of the dead woman who is now addressed as 'her'.

Metre: irregular 9-line stanzas, ab^2 etc. dtr, with many feminine endings, but perhaps better read as two-beat dipodic, given the great flexibility over numbers of syllables per line and the ordering of main stresses. Pinion notes the apparent incongruity of the 'dance rhythm' (1990: 305).

>   Clouds spout upon her
>   Their waters amain
>   In ruthless disdain, –
>   Her who but lately
>   Had shivered with pain 5
>   As at touch of dishonour
>   If there had lit on her
>   So coldly, so straightly
>   Such arrows of rain:
>
>   One who to shelter 10
>   Her delicate head
>   Would quicken and quicken
>   Each tentative tread
>   If drops chanced to pelt her
>   That summertime spills 15
>   In dust-paven rills
>   When thunder-clouds thicken
>   And birds close their bills.
>
>   Would that I lay there
>   And she were housed here! 20
>   Or better, together
>   Were folded away there

Title] Rain on Her Grave MS del.
22. *Were folded*] We both slept MS del.

> Exposed to one weather
> We both, – who would stray there
> When sunny the day there.   25
>   Or evening was clear
>   At the prime of the year.
>
> Soon will be growing
>   Green blades from her mound,
> And daisies be showing   30
>   Like stars on the ground,
> Till she form part of them –
> Ay – the sweet heart of them,
> Loved beyond measure
> With a child's pleasure   35
>   All her life's round.
>
> 31 *January* 1913

55 'I found her out there'

The poem describes Hardy's first meeting with Emma in Cornwall, and thus presages the voyage to the scenes of their courtship described later in the sequence. Here the scene is mediated through written memories, Hardy's in *A Pair of Blue Eyes* and Emma's in *Some Recollections*, pp. 50–1 (see also *EL* 90–3). A date of composition is added in *Selected Poems* (1916), December 1912.

Metre: abbacdcd² dtr, close to Byron's in 'When We Two Parted', and with a similar anapaestic release to 'The Walk' (Taylor 1988: 156).

24] Who often would stay there MS del.
28–31. flowers growing on a grave are a common elegiac topos: cf. *In Memoriam* 21, and *Hamlet* V, i, 232–4:
> Lay her i'the earth,
> And from her fair and unpolluted flesh
> May violets spring. . . .

30–6. the reference to stars and to Emma as a 'child' suggests Wordsworth's 'Lucy' in 'She Dwelt Among the Untrodden Ways':
> A violet by a mossy stone
>   Half hidden from the eye!
> – Fair as a star, when only one
>   Is shining in the sky.

35. cf. the final two lines of the following poem.
36. life's round: again cf. Wordsworth: 'Rolled round in earth's diurnal course' ('A Slumber Did My Spirit Seal').

I found her out there
On a slope few see,
That falls westwardly
To the salt-edged air,
Where the ocean breaks   5
On the purple strand,
And the hurricane shakes
The solid land.

I brought her here,
And have laid her to rest   10
In a noiseless nest
No sea beats near.
She will never be stirred
In her loamy cell
By the waves long heard   15
And loved so well.

So she does not sleep
By those haunted heights
The Atlantic smites
And the blind gales sweep,   20
Whence she often would gaze
At Dundagel's famed head,
While the dipping blaze
Dyed her face fire-red;

And would sigh at the tale   25
Of sunk Lyonnesse,
As a wind-tugged tress
Flapped her cheek like a flail;

---

1. there: 'there' in this poem is Cornwall, to the west, and the 'here' of l. 9 is Dorset, far from the sea; the dialogue between the two places continues throughout the sequence.
4. salt-edged] sharp-edged MS del., *SC* 1914.
6. purple strand: see 'Beeny Cliff' (65), l. 9n.
14. loamy cell: grave (cf. the 'tiny cell' of 'Lament' (57), l. 11).
22. Dundagel: Tintagel head, near Boscastle, legendary birthplace of King Arthur.
24. see 'After a Journey' (63), l. 8n.
26. Lyonnesse: northwest Cornwall.
27–8. references to Emma's hair appear in 'Beeny Cliff' and later poems including 'The Wind's Prophecy' (101) and 'This Summer and Last' (148). Peter Coxon indicates parallel passages in the novels (e.g. Elfride in *A Pair of Blue Eyes*), and discusses the erotic connotations of hair in Victorian literature (Coxon 1982).

>   Or listen at whiles
>   With a thought-bound brow 30
>   To the murmuring miles
>   She is far from now.
>
>   Yet her shade, maybe,
>   Will creep underground
>   Till it catch the sound 35
>   Of that western sea
>   As it swells and sobs
>   Where she once domiciled,
>   And joy in its throbs
>   With the heart of a child. 40

56 Without Ceremony

'Without Ceremony' returns to direct address ('you') in a more muted fashion than the opening poems. It was one of the eight poems from his *Selected Poems* (1916) which Hardy dropped for the *Chosen Poems* (1929). The prosaic tone contrasts with the more conventionally elegiac images of the previous two poems (see Sacks 1985: 246). Griffith points out a number of echoes of Patmore's 'Departure' (1989: 224–5).

Metre: abccb^3 dr, with link-rhymes between the a-lines.

>   It was your way, my dear,
>   To vanish without a word
>   When callers, friends, or kin
>   Had left, and I hastened in
>   To rejoin you, as I inferred. 5
>
>   And when you'd a mind to career
>   Off anywhere – say to town –
>   You were all on a sudden gone
>   Before I had thought thereon,
>   Or noticed your trunks were down. 10

34. creep] glide *SC* 1914 (corrected to MS reading *SC* 1915). The relative physicality of 'creep' is often noticed.
38. domiciled: lived.
39–40. images of rebirth are often associated with elegy: cf. ending of the previous poem.
2. vanish] have retired MS del.; be gone MS, *SC* 1914–15.
5. as I inferred: contemporary reviewers objected to this phrase as unpoetic. Richardson defends it: 'he uses the slowness, the difficulty, to express the tentativeness, and ultimately the error, of the speaker's inference' (1977: 84).

> So, now that you disappear
> For ever in that swift style,
> Your meaning seems to me
> Just as it used to be:
> 'Good-bye is not worth while!' 15

57 Lament

A return to elegiacs, and the end of the opening sequence of laments. Sacks comments that 'the poem is made up of a series of conjurings and banishings' in which Emma's presence is negated in a series of scenes (1985: 246).
Metre: ababccddeee^2 dtr. '"I thought, my heart"' (105) has the same rhyme-scheme in more varied metres. The repetitive 'she is shut' reinforces the effect of closure suggested by the stanza's narrowing shape.

> How she would have loved
> A party to-day! –
> Bright-hatted and gloved,
> With table and tray
> And chairs on the lawn 5
> Her smiles would have shone
> With welcomings. ... But
> She is shut, she is shut
>   From friendship's spell
>   In the jailing shell 10
>   Of her tiny cell.
>
> Or she would have reigned
> At a dinner to-night
> With ardours unfeigned,
> And a generous delight; 15
> All in her abode
> She'd have freely bestowed
> On her guests. ... But alas,
> She is shut under grass
>   Where no cups flow, 20
>   Powerless to know
>   That it might be so.

5. *chairs on the lawn*: phrase repeated in 'During Wind and Rain' (102).
11. *tiny cell*: cf. Gray's 'Elegy', l. 15: 'Each in his narrow cell for ever laid'. Hardy often stresses the closeness of the grave: cf. '"Not only I"' (145).
19] She is shut, she is shut MS del. (Hardy varying the refrain here and l. 30).

And she would have sought
With a child's eager glance
The shy snowdrops brought   25
By the new year's advance,
And peered in the rime
Of Candlemas-time
For crocuses . . . chanced
It that she were not tranced   30
    From sights she loved best;
    Wholly possessed
    By an infinite rest!

And we are here staying
Amid these stale things,   35
Who care not for gaying,
And those junketings
That used so to joy her,
And never to cloy her
As us they cloy! . . . But   40
She is shut, she is shut
    From the cheer of them, dead
    To all done and said
    In her yew-arched bed.

24. child's eager glance: cf. the child references of 'Rain on a Grave' (54) and 'I found her out there' (55).
27. rime: frost.
28. Candlemas-time: the Feast of the Purification of the Virgin, 2 February.
29–30] But / She is shut, she is shut MS del.
30. tranced: entranced; but the older, obsolete, meaning of the word is 'to pass away or die' (F. *transir*). Patmore calls death 'tranced breath' in 'The Toys'.
37. junketings: feasts, picnics.
39. cloy: Sacks (1985: 247) rather implausibly relates the word to the ME *acloien*, to lame, and the MF *enclouer*, to drive in a nail, suggesting crucifixion.
44. yew-arched: yew trees are grown in churchyards (cf. Gray's 'Elegy', l. 13).

58 The Haunter

The first poem in the sequence in which Hardy takes on the voice of Emma's ghost, here addressing the reader as an intermediary between wife and a husband who is addressed in the third person. Sexton suggests that this ghost (the ghost of 'here', the older Emma) is more passive and associated with voice, while the young Emma (the ghost of 'there', Cornwall) is wilder and associated with vision (Sexton 1991: 218).

Metre: $a^4b^3c^4b^3d^4e^3f^4e^3$ dr (combined ballad quatrains, first two stanzas), then $a^4b^3a^4b^3c^4d^3c^4d^3$ (combined hymn stanzas), with repeated and double rhymes linking stanzas. Taylor suggests that the metrical 'plot' of the poem is the emerging of the more regular hymn form from the 'rougher' ballad stanzas (1988: 215, 249).

> He does not think that I haunt here nightly:
>   How shall I let him know
> That whither his fancy sets him wandering
>   I, too, alertly go? –
> Hover and hover a few feet from him   5
>   Just as I used to do,
> But cannot answer the words he lifts me –
>   Only listen thereto!
>
> When I could answer he did not say them:
>   When I could let him know   10
> How I would like to join in his journeys
>   Seldom he wished to go.
> Now that he goes and wants me with him
>   More than he used to do,
> Never he sees my faithful phantom   15
>   Though he speaks thereto.
>
> Yes, I companion him to places
>   Only dreamers know,
> Where the shy hares print long paces,
>   Where the night rooks go;   20
> Into old aisles where the past is all to him,
>   Close as his shade can do,

Title] Hardy pencilled and erased 'His' above 'The' in the MS.
7. *the words he lifts*] his words addressed MS, *SC* 1914–15.
8. *thereto*: this word (ending each stanza) can be linked to the 'Hereto' which opens 'After a Journey' (Sexton 1991: 218).
12. *Seldom he wished*] He did not wish MS del.
17. *companion*] accompany MS, *SC* 1914–15.
19. *print long paces*] show their faces MS, *SC* 1914; limp long paces *SC* 1915.

>   Always lacking the power to call to him,
>   Near as I reach thereto!
>   What a good haunter I am, O tell him!   25
>   Quickly make him know
>   If he but sigh since my loss befell him
>   Straight to his side I go.
>   Tell him a faithful one is doing
>   All that love can do   30
>   Still that his path may be worth pursuing,
>   And to bring peace thereto.

59 The Voice

'The Voice' takes up the argument of the previous poem in questioning whether Hardy can hear his dead wife's voice, even as that voice is described. Gewanter argues that the voice is also equivocal in period, the opening stanza sliding in complex fashion between 'young-Emma' and 'old-Emma', with Hardy attempting to expunge the latter (1991: 201). Included in *Selected Poems* (1916).

Metre: abab^4 tf, alternating full and truncated lines, with triple rhymes on the full lines ('call to me/all to me') which suggest the receding and echoing voice of the woman. Jean Brooks suggests that the triple measure is based, ironically, on 'Haste to the Wedding', one of Hardy's favourite songs (1971: 83). The metre breaks down into an irregular a^{3}b^{3}a^{4}b^2 df in the final stanza, emphasizing its removal from the more visionary and flowing earlier stanzas (for a full analysis see Neuman 1980: 49; and esp. Attridge 1982: 329–33).

>   Woman much missed, how you call to me, call to me,
>   Saying that now you are not as you were
>   When you had changed from the one who was all to me,
>   But as at first, when our day was fair.

29–32] *SC* 1914:   And if it be that at night I am stronger,
                          Go, too, by day I do: (Little harm day can do; MS)
                       Please, then, keep him in gloom no longer,
                          Even ghosts tend thereto! –

1. some critics have followed I.A. Richards in comparing the cadences of the opening line to Horace, *Odes* II, 14 (in Alcaic stanza), 'Eheu fugaces, Postume, Postume' (Richards 1979: 5; Coxon 1983).
1. Woman much missed] O woman weird MS.
3. all to me: Griffith (1989: 233–5) provides an extensive comparison with Robert Browning's 'I would that you were all to me' in 'Two in the Campagna', arguing that the poem is indebted to Browning throughout.

Can it be you that I hear? Let me view you, then, 5
Standing as when I drew near to the town
Where you would wait for me: yes, as I knew you then,
Even to the original air-blue gown!

Or is it only the breeze, in its listlessness
Travelling across the wet mead to me here, 10
You being ever dissolved to wan wistlessness,
Heard no more again far or near?

    Thus I; faltering forward,
    Leaves around me falling,
Wind oozing thin through the thorn from norward, 15
    And the woman calling.

December 1912.

---

6. *the town*: presumably Boscastle, near where Hardy first met Emma Gifford.

9–16. I.A. Richards points to the context of the debate between Jesus and the doubting Nicodemus in John 3: 5–8. Jesus says: 'The wind bloweth where it listeth, and thou hearest the sound thereof, but canst not tell whence it cometh, and wither it goeth: so is every one that is born of the Spirit.' Nicodemus's reply is 'How can these things be?' Richards comments: 'The poem is, I take it, dissenting, as definitely as Nicodemus, from the attribution to the wind of "desire or choice", the full sense of "listeth". It is quietly but firmly denying that the wind has any such vocational independence' (Richards 1979: 6; but see Weatherby 1983 for a more equivocal use of the same passage).

11] to F.R. Leavis's disapproval (1940: 93), the line was revised in 1923 from: You being ever consigned to existlessness, MS, *SC* 1914–15
    You being ever dissolved to existlessness, *CP* 1919, WE
Henry Gifford suggests that the change 'restores Emma very faintly to the borders of life' (1972: 135).

11. wan wistlessness: pale inattentiveness ('wistlessness' is Hardy's coinage; the older sense of 'wan' is ghostly, deficient). Cf. the 'wistfulness/tristfulness' rhyme of 'Night in the Old Home' (37), another poem on ghostly presences and echoing voices, and the 'wistful/tristful' of 'The Statue of Liberty' (88), ll. 4–5.

15. cf. the wind-sounds opening *Under the Greenwood Tree*.

60 His Visitor

This is the second poem in the sequence in which Emma is given voice, now addressing Hardy as 'you' rather than 'he', and meditating on the 'change' at Max Gate. Hardy could thus be said to have externalized the then/now division of the opening poems.

Metre: abcbb dr. Taylor suggests the poem is dipodic with four major stresses to the line in the long lines (1988: 95). The final two-beat lines of each stanza, which refer the reader back to the past, seem both metrically isolated and connected via the rhyme.

> I come across from Mellstock while the moon wastes weaker
> To behold where I lived with you for twenty years and more:
> I shall go in the gray, at the passing of the mail-train,
> And need no setting open of the long familiar door
>   As before.   5
>
> The change I notice in my once own quarters!
> A formal-fashioned border where the daisies used to be,
> The rooms new painted, and the pictures altered,
> And other cups and saucers, and no cosy nook for tea
>   As with me.   10
>
> I discern the dim faces of the sleep-wrapt servants;
> They are not those who tended me through feeble hours and strong,
> But strangers quite, who never knew my rule here,
> Who never saw me painting, never heard my softling song
>   Float along.   15
>
> So I don't want to linger in this re-decked dwelling,
> I feel too uneasy at the contrasts I behold,
> And I make again for Mellstock to return here never,
> And rejoin the roomy silence, and the mute and manifold
>   Souls of old.   20
>
>   1913.

1. *Mellstock*: fictional name for Stinsford, where Emma Hardy was buried.
6. *the change*: by late 1912 Florence Dugdale was helping with the domestic arrangements at Max Gate. Later she was to report Hardy's own resistance to any household changes.
7. *formal-fashioned*] brilliant budded Editions before *CP* 1923 (i.e. the line itself was 'changed' with time).
14. *softling*: soft in nature.
16–20. Emma 'leaves' Max Gate at this point in the sequence, forcing Hardy to undertake a journey in search of her.
17. *contrasts*: a resonant word in the context of Hardy's 'Gothic' aesthetic, the title of A.W. Pugin's 1841 diatribe on the tragic differences between mediaeval and modern towns.
19. *manifold*: having many forms.

61 A Circular

One of a number of poems by Hardy on messages gone astray or made redundant, or on remnants of a dead person (cf. 'The Flower's Tragedy' and 'On a Discovered Curl of Hair'). As Sacks notes, Hardy's elegies constitute a similarly undeliverable message to a dead recipient (1985: 251).
  Metre: a⁴b⁴a⁴b³ dr. Here, as elsewhere, Hardy seems to borrow the metre of a hymn he associated with Emma: no. 119 in his *Hymns* (1889), 'His are the Thousand Sparkling Rills', is marked E.L.H. (Taylor 1988: 226).

> As 'legal representative'
> I read a missive not my own,
> On new designs the senders give
>   For clothes, in tints as shown.
>
> Here figure blouses, gowns for tea,   5
> And presentation-trains of state,
> Charming ball-dresses, millinery,
>   Warranted up to date.
>
> And this gay-pictured, spring-time shout
> Of Fashion, hails what lady proud?   10
> Her who before last year ebbed out
>   Was costumed in a shroud.

62 A Dream or No

'A Dream or No' initiates the sequence's movement to Cornwall, as Hardy meditates on the possibility of a trip there. Like 'Without Ceremony' (56), this poem was in *Selected Poems* (1916) but dropped in *Chosen Poems* (1929).
  Metre: a⁴b²b²a⁴ tr (the rhyme-scheme is that of 'In Memoriam').

> Why go to Saint-Juliot? What's Juliot to me?
>   Some strange necromancy
>   But charmed me to fancy
> That much of my life claims the spot as its key.

4. tints as shown: the diction mimics the stilted language of the advertisement.
Title] A Dream Indeed? MS. Hardy also pencilled and erased another possible title, 'The Fancy'.
1. Saint-Juliot: village a few miles east of Boscastle, overlooking the Valency Valley. Emma Gifford was living there when Hardy first met her.
2–3] I've been (I was *SC* 1915) but made fancy / By some necromancy *SC* 1914–15.
2. necromancy: magic involving communication with the dead.

Yes. I have had dreams of that place in the West, 5
    And a maiden abiding
      Thereat as in hiding;
Fair-eyed and white-shouldered, broad-browed and brown-tressed,

And of how, coastward bound on a night long ago,
    There lonely I found her 10
      The sea-birds around her,
And other than nigh things uncaring to know.

So sweet her life there (in my thought has it seemed)
    That quickly she drew me
      To take her unto me, 15
And lodge her long years with me. Such have I dreamed.

But nought of that maid from Saint-Juliot I see;
    Can she ever have been here,
      And shed her life's sheen here,
The woman I thought a long housemate with me? 20

Does there even a place like Saint-Juliot exist?
    Or a Vallency Valley
      With stream and leafed alley,
Or Beeny, or Bos with its flounce flinging mist?

   February 1913.

---

13. thought] dreams MS del.
16] And tarry long years with her. MS.
17. maid from Saint-Juliot] woman of Juliot MS del. ('maid' suggests the context of romance).
19. life's sheen: see Introduction, p. 27.
22. Vallency: the river Valency enters the sea at Boscastle Harbour. In response to a printer's query about the different spelling of the word in 'A Death-Day Recalled', Hardy replied 'No: the two spellings are because of two pronunciations, which the metres require. The river is called either way indifferently' (*CPW* II, 491).
24. Beeny, or Bos: Beeny Cliff, northwest of St Juniot; and either Boscastle or Bossiney Haven, both on the north coast of Cornwall.

63 After a Journey

The turning point in the sequence, moving it from Dorset to Cornwall and the landscape of memory and romance. Hardy visited Cornwall in 1913: 'On March 6 – almost to a day, forty-three years after his first journey to Cornwall – he started for St Juniot, putting up at Boscastle, and visiting Pentargan Bay and Beeny Cliff, on which he had not once set foot in the long interval' (*LY* 156). The poem was included in *Selected Poems* (1916).

Metre: difficult. Taylor suggests $a^4b^4a^4b^4c^4d^4d^2c^4$ (dipodic, often with the possibility of a pentameter reading but tending towards tetrameter), commenting that this is 'perhaps [Hardy's] most metrically interesting poem'. He provides an extensive discussion of its metrics, comparing it to Meredith's 'Love in the Valley' and Tennyson's 'In the Valley of Cauterez' (1988: 82–100, 167–9). Davie describes it as 'English hendacasyllables', i.e. eleven-syllable verse based on the classical metre (1973: 57). The rhyme-scheme is used skilfully, with e.g. the suggestion of echo in the 'hollow/follow' of stanza 3.

> Hereto I come to view a voiceless ghost;
>   Whither, O whither will its whim now draw me?
> Up the cliff, down, till I'm lonely, lost,
>   And the unseen waters' ejaculations awe me.
> Where you will next be there's no knowing, 5
>   Facing round about me everywhere,
>   With your nut-coloured hair,
> And gray eyes, and rose-flush coming and going.
>
> Yes: I have re-entered your olden haunts at last;
>   Through the years, through the dead scenes I have tracked
>   you; 10
> What have you now found to say of our past –

1. view a voiceless ghost] interview a ghost MS, *SC* 1914–15, *SP* 1916 (the revision removes the possibility of dialogue). The opening line, Sexton argues (1991: 218–19), picks up the 'Thereto' of 'The Haunter' and shifts the sequence's stress from voice to vision.

4. ejaculations] soliloquies MS, *SC* 1914; Hardy drawing on a phrase from *A Pair of Blue Eyes*, 'the eternal soliloquy of the waters' (Gifford 1972: 136). Cf. also the 'huzza' of the waves in 'The Voice of Things'.

8. rose-flush: Hardy often refers to Emma's colouring as a 'rose' flush, just as he portrayed the fictional Elfride in *A Pair of Blue Eyes* as flushed with passion. He wrote to the rector of St Juniot on 22 August 1913 that the parishioners 'may perhaps recall her golden curls and rosy colour as she rode about, for she was very attractive at that time' (*CL* IV, 297). Cf. the colours in 'Places', l. 17, 'The Phantom Horsewoman', l. 25, and '"Not only I"', l. 14; and see Paulin's comments on the association between vision and irradiated flesh throughout Hardy's works (1975: 201).

    Scanned across the dark space wherein I have lacked you?
Summer gave us sweets, but autumn wrought division?
    Things were not lastly as firstly well
        With us twain, you tell?   15
But all's closed now, despite Time's derision.

I see what you are doing: you are leading me on
    To the spots we knew when we haunted here together,
The waterfall, above which the mist-bow shone
    At the then fair hour in the then fair weather,   20
And the cave just under, with a voice still so hollow
    That it seems to call out to me from forty years ago,
        When you were all aglow,
And not the thin ghost that I now frailly follow!

Ignorant of what there is flitting here to see,   25
    The waked birds preen and the seals flop lazily,
Soon you will have, Dear, to vanish from me,
    For the stars close their shutters and the dawn whitens
        hazily.
Trust me, I mind not, though Life lours,
    The bringing me here; nay, bring me here again!   30
        I am just the same as when
Our days were a joy, and our paths through flowers.

    Pentargan Bay

---

12. Scanned] Viewed MS, *SC* 1914–15, *SP* 1916. The word suggests 'scansion' and the metrical 'space' between 'tracked you' and 'lacked you'.
14. lastly as firstly: the biblical overtones are of 'first and last', Edenic innocence versus the corrupted 'last' days.
15. you tell?: Paulin compares the conversational 'do you say?' of Browning's 'A Toccata of Galuppi's' (1975: 72).
25. Matthew Campbell points out that this chimes with and perhaps answers Tennyson's 'Oh! that 'twere possible' (later *Maud* II, iv), which in its original context described Tennyson's desire to see Hallam's ghost: 'A shadow flits before me – / Not thou, but like to thee' (Campbell 1992).
27–8. traditionally ghosts disappear at dawn. Buckler sees an allusion to the myth of Tithonius and Aurora (1979: 105).
29. lours: looks gloomy.
Pentargan Bay: northwest of St Juniot.

64 A Death-Day Recalled

The manuscript table of contents places this poem earlier, after 'Rain on a Grave' (54), but it falls more naturally within the Cornwall group, where Hardy placed it in *Satires of Circumstance*. Here the failure of Emma to register or Hardy to 'read' her approaching death is reflected in the landscape's indifference.

Metre: ababcdcd³ df, alternating masculine and feminine endings and with much alliteration in the opening stanza. The metre is that of a number of hymns, including Hardy's favourite 'Redeemed, Restored, Forgiven' (Taylor 1988: 248).

>   Beeny did not quiver,
>   Juliot grew not gray,
>   Thin Valency's river
>   Held its wonted way.
>   Bos seemed not to utter   5
>   Dimmest note of dirge,
>   Targan mouth a mutter
>   To its creamy surge.
>
>   Yet though these, unheeding,
>   Listless, passed the hour   10
>   Of her spirit's speeding,
>   She had, in her flower,
>   Sought and loved the places –
>   Much and often pined
>   For their lonely faces   15
>   When in towns confined.
>
>   Why did not Valency
>   In his purl deplore
>   One whose haunts were whence he
>   Drew his limpid store?   20
>   Why did Bos not thunder,
>   Targan apprehend
>   Body and Breath were sunder
>   Of their former friend?

Title] A Death-day (del.) MS table of contents (cf. title of 'St. Launce's Revisited' (70)).
1. Beeny: Beeny Cliff, overlooking Pentargan Bay.
2. Juniot: St Juniot.
3. Valency: on the spelling of the river's name, see 'A Dream or No' (62), l. 22n.
18. purl: twisting.
22. Targan: Pentargan Bay (setting of previous poem).

65 Beeny Cliff
March 1870–March 1913

As the subtitle suggests, 'Beeny Cliff' spans the period between Hardy's first visit to Cornwall and his later pilgrimage. The former is described by Emma, *SR* 50, and by Hardy, *EL* 99: '*March* 10 [1870]. Went with E.L.G. to Beeny Cliff. She on horseback. . . . On the cliff. . . . "The tender grace of a day", etc. The run down to the edge. The coming home' (Hardy's ellipsis: the reference is to Tennyson's 'Break, Break, Break'). On the March 1913 visit, see 'After a Journey' (63). Included in *Selected Poems* (1916).

Metre: seems aaa[7] dr with variations, including an occasionally falling rhythm (see Paulin 1975: 73–5 for analysis). But as Taylor points out (1988: 95), the line can be scanned as dipodic, with a tetrameter rhythm of strong beats alternating with weaker: 'The wŏman whóm I lŏved so, aňd who lŏyallý loved mĕ'.

I

O the opal and the sapphire of that wandering western sea,
And the woman riding high above with bright hair flapping
    free –
The woman whom I loved so, and who loyally loved me.

II

The pale mews plained below us, and the waves seemed far
    away
In a nether sky, engrossed in saying their ceaseless babbling
    say,   5
As we laughed light-heartedly aloft on that clear-sunned
    March day.

III

A little cloud then cloaked us, and there flew an irised rain,
And the Atlantic dyed its levels with a dull misfeatured stain,

---

2. on Emma's hair, see '"I found her out there"' (55), ll. 27–8n.
4. pale mews] puffins MS. Mews are gulls.
5. nether sky: lower sky (i.e. the border between sky and sea is unclear). But 'nether skies' is used by both Dryden and Shelley to describe the underworld.
7. irised rain: Paulin compares Browning's 'own soul's iris-bow' in the prologue to *Asolando* (1971: 73).

And then the sun burst out again, and purples prinked the
   main.

IV
— Still in all its chasmal beauty bulks old Beeny to the sky,   10
And shall she and I not go there once again now March is
   nigh,
And the sweet things said in that March say anew there by
   and by?

V
What if still in chasmal beauty looms that wild weird western
   shore,
The woman now is — elsewhere — whom the ambling pony
   bore,
And nor knows nor cares for Beeny, and will laugh there
   nevermore.   15

66 At Castle Boterel

The poem which is at the core of Hardy's 're-visioning' of the landscape of romance, and which seems to assert most strongly the possibility of recovering lost time (see Davie 1972: 154–5). Included in *Selected Poems* (1916).

Metre: $a^4b^4a^4b^4b^2$ dr (with some trisyllables and alternated masculine and feminine endings). Common metre with a supplementary disyllable, perhaps modelled on Swinburne's 'Félise' (Taylor 1988: 180, 236). There is a tension between the clogging caesurae and internal rhyme, and the release of the final line of the stanza (see Paulin 1982: 89–90).

   As I drive to the junction of lane and highway,
      And the drizzle bedrenches the waggonette,

9. *purples*: Bailey links this colour with the light-effects at Beeny (1970: 302); but Donald Davie argues convincingly that they have Virgilian overtones, recalling the 'purple light' or *purpureus* of Hades in *Aeneid* VI, 641, lines alluded to by Hardy in *A Pair of Blue Eyes*, ch. 4 and *The Woodlanders*, ch. 24, and associated with sexual passion (Davie 1972; Armstrong 1991). Cf. 'The Change' (89), l. 4.
9. *prinked the main*: adorned the sea.
13. *What if*] Nay. Though MS del., *SC* 1914; What if MS (restored second edition).
15. *laugh there*] see it MS, *SC* 1914–15, *SP* 1916. Cf. the matching indifference of Beeny in the opening of the previous poem.
Title. *Castle Boterel*: Hardy's name for the town of Boscastle.
2. *waggonette*: an open carriage.

I look behind at the fading byway,
    And see on its slope, now glistening wet,
        Distinctly yet   5

Myself and a girlish form benighted
    In dry March weather. We climb the road
Beside a chaise. We had just alighted
    To ease the sturdy pony's load
        When he sighed and slowed.   10

What we did as we climbed, and what we talked of
    Matters not much, nor to what it led, –
Something that life will not be balked of
    Without rude reason till hope is dead,
        And feeling fled.   15

It filled but a minute. But was there ever
    A time of such quality, since or before,
In that hill's story? To one mind never,
    Though it has been climbed, foot-swift, foot-sore,
        By thousands more.   20

Primaeval rocks form the road's steep border,
    And much have they faced there, first and last,
Of the transitory in Earth's long order;
    But what they record in colour and cast
        Is – that we two passed.   25

And to me, though Time's unflinching rigour,
    In mindless rote, has ruled from sight

---

3. *I look behind*: perhaps suggesting Orpheus's backward look at Eurydice (see headnote to 'The Shadow on the Stone' (106)); but also 'hindsight', which Sexton argues represents a recovery which is painfully achieved rather than an easy recollection (1991: 223).
8. *chaise*: a light cart.
14. *rude reason*] good reason (del.) sore pressure MS. A puzzling phrase: perhaps 'rude' in the sense of 'robust, healthy'.
17. *time of such quality*: cf. *A Pair of Blue Eyes*, ch. 20: 'It was to him [Knight] a gentle innocent time – a time which, though there may not be much of it, seldom repeats itself in a man's life, and has a peculiar dearness when glanced at retrospectively' (p. 207). Davie asserts that in this poem 'love triumphs over time', though only briefly (Davie 1972: 149).
21–5. Hardy often suggests that stones absorb human feelings, and 'hold' them as memorials: cf. 'The Shadow on the Stone' (106) and 'In the British Museum'. The context is partly that of the fossil record in Darwinian geology (see *A Pair of Blue Eyes*, ch. 22).
25. *we two*: in contrast to 'one mind', l. 18.
27. *rote*: mechanical operation.

>   The substance now, one phantom figure
>   Remains on the slope, as when that night
>   Saw us alight. 30
>   I look and see it there, shrinking, shrinking,
>   I look back at it amid the rain
>   For the very last time; for my sand is sinking,
>   And I shall traverse old love's domain
>   Never again. 35
>   *March* 1913.

67 Places

One of a number of poems in which Hardy gathers material from his wife's memoir, *Some Recollections*, the manuscript of which he read and annotated after her death (though here the material relates to her childhood and youth rather than to a period of shared memories: cf. 'During Wind and Rain' (102)). Davie sees this poem as 'the fulcrum on which the whole series turns', since Hardy turns away from Cornwall to Plymouth and, Davie suggests, continues to assert the primacy of the romance-landscape (1972: 150). The setting is, in fact, both Plymouth and Cornwall.

Metre: $a^4b^4b^4a^4c^4b^2c^2$ dr (with some triplets).

>   Nobody says: Ah, that is the place
>   Where chanced, in the hollow of years ago,
>   What none of the Three Towns cared to know –
>   The birth of a little girl of grace –
>   The sweetest the house saw, first or last; 5
>   Yet it was so
>   On that day long past.
>
>   Nobody thinks: There, there she lay
>   In a room by the Hoe, like the bud of a flower,
>   And listened, just after the bedtime hour, 10
>   To the stammering chimes that used to play
>   The quaint Old Hundred-and-Thirteenth tune

33. *my sand is sinking*: in the hour-glass (i.e. his life seems over). See 'The Obliterate Tomb', l. 12, and 'Quid Hic Agis?', l. 27, and the hour-glass illustration to 'Amabel' in *Wessex Poems*.
3. *Three Towns*: the adjacent towns of Plymouth, Stonehouse, and Devonport. Emma lived in Plymouth until she was 19.
9. *the Hoe*: Plymouth Hoe, the open area fronting the sea at Plymouth.
11–12. follows *Some Recollections*:
  The Churches of Plymouth were not numerous as now – I believe five only St. Andrew's being the finest which had a curfew bell regularly

> In Saint Andrew's tower
> Night, morn, and noon.
>
> Nobody calls to mind that here   15
> Upon Boterel Hill, where the waggoners skid,
> With cheeks whose airy flush outbid
> Fresh fruit in bloom, and free of fear,
> She cantered down, as if she must fall
> > (Though she never did),   20
> > To the charm of all.
>
> Nay: one there is to whom these things,
> That nobody else's mind calls back,
> Have a savour that scenes in being lack,
> And a presence more than the actual brings;   25
> To whom to-day is beneaped and stale,
> > And its urgent clack
> > But a vapid tale.
>
> Plymouth, *March* 1913.

tolled and chimes which played every four hours that fine old tune [the 'Old 113th'].
  I have good reason to remember it – as we lived for five years not far away, and that tune with its haltings and runs plays up in my head often even now. (*SR* 11–12)
13. *Saint Andrew's*: Emma Gifford (later Hardy) was baptized there.
15–21. cf. Emma's description of riding near Boscastle:
  scampering up and down the hills on my beloved mare alone, wanting no protection, the rain going down my back. . . . The Villagers stopped to gaze when I rushed down the hills. A butterman laid down his basket once to exclaim loudly for no one dared except myself to ride in such wild fearless fashion. (*SR* 50–1)
17. *airy flush*: see 'After a Journey', l. 8n.
26. *beneaped*: (of a ship) left aground after a high (neap) tide.
Plymouth, March 1913: Hardy visited Plymouth on his return from the pilgrimage to Cornwall described in the previous poems. However, as Davie points out, the 'here' of the poem is *not* Plymouth, but Cornwall. The poem thus asserts 'the superior reality of the domain of love and loyalty'.

68 The Phantom Horsewoman

'The Phantom Horsewoman', with its more distanced third-person description of Hardy and its final 'turn' away from Emma's ghost in Cornwall, marks the end of the original sequence of 'Poems of 1912–13'. It was included in *Selected Poems* (1916).

Metre: a⁴b²c²b²c²b²c²a²a⁴ dtr. Another 'oceanic' rhythm imitating the 'swing' of the tide. Davie notes 'the internal rhyme and sudden ripple of elated anapaests which make the last line so buoyant' (1972: 151).

I
Queer are the ways of a man I know:
    He comes and stands
    In a careworn craze,
    And looks at the sands
    And the seaward haze,   5
    With moveless hands
    And face and gaze,
    Then turns to go ...
And what does he see when he gazes so?

II
They say he sees as an instant thing   10
    More clear than to-day,
    A sweet soft scene
    That was once in play
    By that briny green;
    Yes, notes alway   15
    Warm, real, and keen,
    What his back years bring –
A phantom of his own figuring.

III
Of this vision of his they might say more:
    Not only there   20
    Does he see this sight,
    But everywhere

---

3. *craze*: fit of madness.
13. *was once*] once was Editions before *CP* 1930 (the corrected reading is more affirmative, perhaps).
15. *alway*: always.
10–18. the fixing of an image of the beloved is described as 'sublimation' in *The Hand of Ethelberta*, ch. 40 (quoted in Introduction, p. 23 above).
19–27. Taylor suggests a comparison of these lines with Wordsworth's 'The Solitary Reaper', ll. 25–32 (1986: 442).

                    In his brain – day, night,
                    As if on the air
                    It were drawn rose-bright –   25
                    Yea, far from that shore
              Does he carry this vision of heretofore:
                                IV
              A ghost-girl-rider. And though, toil-tried,
                    He withers daily,
                    Time touches her not,   30
                    But she still rides gaily
                    In his rapt thought
                    On that shagged and shaly
                    Atlantic spot,
                    And as when first eyed   35
              Draws rein and sings to the swing of the tide.
              1913.

69 The Spell of the Rose

This more allegorical treatment of missed opportunities and mourning was printed after 'Under the Waterfall' (50) in *Satires of Circumstance* (1914), and only added to the sequence as it stands (with the two poems below) in the Wessex Edition of 1919. For comments on the additions, see the headnote to the sequence.

Emma Hardy planted a rose shortly before her death. As well as the traditional associations of the rose and love, the title plays on Hardy's 'rose-bright' vision of Emma in the previous poem. The manuscript has a deleted date, 1913.

Metre: $a^4b^3b^3c^4a^4a^4b^3$ dr, a highly symmetrical form with a number of inter-stanza links, especially between c-lines.

23. In his brain: Paulin argues that this phrase involves depicting the mind as 'an electro-chemical organism, rather than a transcendental unity' (1975: 203).
25. rose bright: Emma's colouring; but the word also provides a link to the next poem.
28–30. cf. Tennyson's 'Tithonius', ll. 5–6: 'Me only cruel immortality / Consumes; I wither slowly in thine arms'.
35. eyed: in a reciprocal manner, Emma 'eyes' Hardy in the first poem of the sequence.

'I mean to build a hall anon,
    And shape two turrets there,
    And a broad newelled stair,
And a cool well for crystal water;
    Yes; I will build a hall anon,
    Plant roses love shall feed upon,
    And apple-trees and pear.'

He set to build the manor-hall,
    And shaped the turrets there,
    And the broad newelled stair,
And the cool well for crystal water;
    He built for me that manor-hall,
    And planted many trees withal,
    But no rose anywhere.

And as he planted never a rose
    That bears the flower of love,
    Though other flowers throve
Some heart-bane moved our souls to sever
    Since he had planted never a rose;
    And misconceits raised horrid shows,
    And agonies came thereof.

'I'll mend these miseries,' then said I,
    And so, at dead of night,
    I went and, screened from sight,
That nought should keep our souls in severance,
    I set a rose-bush. 'This,' said I,
    'May end divisions dire and wry,
    And long-drawn days of blight.'

But I was called from earth – yea, called
    Before my rose-bush grew;
    And would that now I knew

1–7. the romantic scene perhaps suggests Edward FitzGerald's 'The Rubáiyát of Omar Khayyám', which also contains a good deal of rose-imagery (Hardy visited Fitzgerald's grave in 1901, and saw there a rose-bush raised from hips taken from Omar's grave in Persia, *PN* 254).
3. newelled: with a central pillar (newel).
5. anon: soon.
18. Some heart-bane] A frost-wind MS, *SC* 1914–15.
22–28. the idea of the rose as a healing image is reminiscent of Yeats's 'The Lover Tells of the Rose in His Heart', in *The Wind Among the Reeds*, one of Hardy's two choices as a 'Favourite Book' for 1899 (Bies 1980: 193).
29. called from earth: cf. ll. 26–7 of the following poem.

What feels he of the tree I planted,
   And whether, after I was called
To be a ghost, he, as of old,
   Gave me his heart anew!   35

Perhaps now blooms that queen of trees
   I set but saw not grow,
And he, beside its glow –
Eyes couched of the mis-vision that blurred me –
   Ay, there beside that queen of trees   40
He sees me as I was, though sees
   Too late to tell me so!

70 St Launce's Revisited

Printed after 'Under the Waterfall' (50) and 'The Spell of the Rose' (69) in *Satires of Circumstance* (1914), and only included in the 'Poems of 1912–13' in 1919, providing a more sceptical version of the return to Cornwall. 'St Launce's' is Hardy's name for Launceston, the closest point by rail to St Juniot in the 1870s. On his first visit he 'hired a conveyance for the additional sixteen or seventeen miles' distance by the Boscastle road towards the north coast' (*EL* 86). The manuscript has a deleted date, 1913.
 Metre: $a^2b^3b^3b^3$ df, with variations.

Slip back, Time!
Yet again I am nearing
Castle and keep, uprearing
   Gray, as in my prime.

At the inn   5
Smiling nigh, why is it
Not as on my visit
   When hope and I were twin?

39. *couched of the mis-vision*: cleared (to 'couch' is to remove a cataract).
Title] At St Launce's MS del. (cf. the change towards an emphasis on recovering the ground in the title of 'A Death-Day Recalled' (64)).
3. *Castle*: Robert of Mortain's castle overlooks the town.
4. since 'Gray' is associated with late life, the line presents an irony.
5. *inn*: the White Harte Hotel.
6. *nigh*] close MS, *SC* 1914–15.

>   Groom and jade
>   Whom I found here, moulder;   10
>   Strange the tavern-holder,
>   Strange the tap-maid.
>
>   Here I hired
>   Horse and man for bearing
>   Me on my wayfaring   15
>   To the door desired.
>
>   Evening gloomed
>   As I journeyed forward
>   To the faces shoreward,
>   Till their dwelling loomed.   20
>
>   If again
>   Towards the Atlantic sea there
>   I should speed, they'd be there
>   Surely now as then? ...
>
>   Why waste thought,   25
>   When I know them vanished
>   Under earth; yea, banished
>   Ever into nought!

71 Where the Picnic Was

Originally printed after 'The Place on the Map' in 1914, added to the 'Poems of 1912–13' in 1919. Included in *Selected Poems* (1916). In the last poem of the sequence in its extended final version, Hardy returns to a winter scene in Dorset, probably the Ridgeway overlooking Portland, now 'quite readily' reading his own experience into the scene and, finally, closing the eyes of the dead.

Metre: nine-line stanzas becoming increasingly regular and culminating in the final aabbccdefdef[2] dtr.

>   Where we made the fire
>   In the summer time
>   Of branch and briar
>   On the hill to the sea,
>   I slowly climb   5

9. *groom and jade*: cart-horse and rider.
11. *tavern-holder*: publican.
12. *tap-maid*: barmaid.

Through winter mire,
And scan and trace
The forsaken place
Quite readily.

Now a cold wind blows, 10
And the grass is gray,
But the spot still shows
As a burnt circle – aye,
And stick-ends, charred,
Still strew the sward 15
Whereon I stand,
Last relic of the band
Who came that day!

Yes, I am here
Just as last year, 20
And the sea breathes brine
From its strange straight line
Up hither, the same
As when we four came.
– But two have wandered far 25
From this grassy rise
Into urban roar
Where no picnics are,
And one – has shut her eyes
For evermore. 30

[End of 'Poems of 1912–13']

7–15. the traces of the fire suggest the sequence's epigraph, and perhaps also the 'circle' of Hardy's experience. The trampling of ashes in Shelley's 'The Triumph of Life' is echoed:

'All that was, seemed as if it had been not;
And all the gazer's mind was strewn beneath
Her feet like embers; and she, thought by thought,
Trampled its sparks into the dust of death. . . .'

24. we four: perhaps refers to a picnic with W.B. Yeats and Henry Newbolt in June 1912 (see *EL* 152).
29. shut her eyes: closing the eyes of the dead is often a ritual act (Sacks 1985: 259).

72 The Obliterate Tomb

The poems in *Satires of Circumstance* which follow the 'Poems of 1912–13' are labelled 'Miscellaneous Pieces'. In this poem, Hardy seems to recall Emma Hardy's description of the tombs of her family, the Giffords, at Charles Church, Plymouth, mutilated during restoration: 'it is sad to see the stones removed which grand and great grandparents had put up in years gone by over their vaults, and wept and reflected upon' (*SR* 12). Hardy visited the graves in 1916 (*PN* 35–6). There are a number of other poems on funereal inscriptions: cf. 'The Levelled Churchyard', 'The Inscription' (127), 'The Memorial Brass: 186–'.

Metre: $a^3a^5b^5a^2$ dr with variations, perhaps best seen as a truncated form of the *Rubáiyát* stanza, $aaba^5$.

'More than half my life long
Did they weigh me falsely, to my bitter wrong,
But they all have shrunk away into the silence
    Like a lost song.

'And the day has dawned and come   5
For forgiveness, when the past may hold it dumb
On the once reverberate words of hatred uttered
    Half in delirium. . . .

'With folded lips and hands
They lie and wait what next the Will commands,   10
And doubtless think, if think they can: "Let discord
    Sink with Life's sands!"

'By these late years their names,
Their virtues, their hereditary claims,
May be as near defacement at their grave-place   15
    As are their fames.'

– Such thoughts bechanced to seize
A traveller's mind – a man of memories –
As he set foot within the western city
    Where had died these   20

Who in their lifetime deemed
Him their chief enemy – one whose brain had schemed
To get their dingy greatness deeplier dingied
    And disesteemed.

10. *Will*: on Hardy and the 'Creator', see Introduction, p. 17.
12. *Life's sand's*: another hour-glass image.
18. *man of memories*: cf. Hardy's description of himself in 'Memory and I'.
19. *western city*: Plymouth.

So, sojourning in their town,
He mused on them and on their once renown,
And said, 'I'll seek their resting-place to-morrow
    Ere I lie down,

    'And end, lest I forget,
Those ires of many years that I regret,
Renew their names, that men may see some liegeness
    Is left them yet.'

    Duly next night he went
And sought the church he had known them to frequent,
And wandered, lantern-bearing, in the precincts,
    Where they lay pent,

    Till by remembrance led
He stood at length beside their slighted bed,
Above which, truly, scarce a line or letter
    Could now be read.

    'Thus years obliterate
Their graven worth, their chronicle, their date!
At once I'll garnish and revive the record
    Of their past state,

    'That still the sage may say
In pensive progress here where they decay,
"This stone records a luminous line whose talents
    Told in their day."'

    While dreaming thus he turned,
For a form shadowed where they lay inurned,
And he beheld a stranger in foreign vesture,
    And tropic-burned.

    'Sir, I am right pleased to view
That ancestors of mine should interest you,
For I have fared of purpose here to find them....
    They are time-worn, true,

    'But that's a fault, at most,
Carvers can cure. On the Pacific coast

---

31. liegeness: faithfulness (Hardy's coinage).
33. night] day MS, *SC* 1914–15.
35] And wandered in the precincts, set on eying MS, *SC* 1914–15.
38. slighted bed: broken tomb.
49. dreaming] speaking MS, *SC* 1914–15.
55. fared] come MS, *SC* 1914–15.
55. find] trace MS, *SC* 1914–15.

I have vowed for long that relics of my forbears
    I'd trace ere lost,   60

   'And hitherward I come,
Before this same old Time shall strike me numb,
To carry it out.' – 'Strange, this is!' said the other;
    'What mind shall plumb

    'Coincident design!   65
Though these my father's enemies were and mine,
I nourished a like purpose – to restore them
    Each letter and line.'

    'Such magnanimity
Is now not needed, sir; for you will see   70
That since I am here, a thing like this is, plainly,
    Best done by me.'

    The other bowed, and left,
Crestfallen in sentiment, as one bereft
Of some fair object he had been moved to cherish,   75
    By hands more deft.

    And as he slept that night
The phantoms of the ensepulchred stood upright
Before him, trembling that he had set him seeking
    Their charnel-site   80

    And, as unknowing his ruth,
Asked us with terrors founded not on truth
Why he should want them. 'Ha,' they hollowly hackered,
    'You come, forsooth,

    'By stealth to obliterate   85
Our graven worth, our chronicle, our date,
That our descendant may not gild the record
    Of our past state,

    'And that no sage may say
In pensive progress near where we decay: 90
"This stone records a luminous line whose talents
    Told in their day."'

    Upon the morrow he went,
And to that town and churchyard never bent
His ageing footsteps till, some twelvemonths onward,   95
    An accident

---

83. hackered: stuttered.

Once more detained him there;
And, stirred by hauntings, he must needs repair
To where the tomb was. Lo, it stood still wasting
    In no man's care.

And so the tomb remained
Untouched, untended, crumbling, weather-stained,
And though the one-time foe was fain to right it
    He still refrained.

'I'll set about it when
I am sure he'll come no more. Best wait till then.'
But so it was that never the kinsman entered
    That city again.

Till doubts grew keen
If it had chanced not that the figure seen
Shaped but in dream on that dim doubtful midnight:
    Such things had been. . . .

So, the well-meaner died
While waiting tremulously unsatisfied
That no return of the family's foreign scion
    Would still betide.

And many years slid by,
And active church-restorers cast their eye
Upon the ancient garth and hoary building
    The tomb stood nigh.

And when they had scraped each wall,
Pulled out the stately pews, and smartened all,
'It will be well,' declared the spruce church-warden,
    'To overhaul

100] MS and *SC* 1914–15 have two extra stanzas here:
    'The travelled man you met
  The last time', said the sexton, 'has not yet
  Appeared again, though wealth he had in plenty.
    Can he forget?

    'The architect was hired
  And came here on smart summons as desired,
  But never the descendant came to tell him
    What he required.'
107. kinsman] stranger MS, *SC* 1914–15, WE.
109–12] not in MS, *SC* 1914–15.
119. garth: churchyard.

'And broaden this path where shown; 125
Nothing prevents it but an old tombstone
Pertaining to a family forgotten,
    Of deeds unknown.

'Their names can scarce be read,
Depend on't, all who care for them are dead.' 130
So went the tomb, whose shards were as path-paving
    Distributed.

Over it and about
Men's footsteps beat, and wind and waterspout,
Until the names, aforetime gnawed by weathers, 135
    Were quite worn out.

So that no sage can say
In pensive progress near where they decay,
'This stone records a luminous line whose talents
    Told in their day.' 140

73 The Workbox

A ballad-like tale of what Blackmur called 'crossed fidelities' (1940: 29, 40–2). Heavily revised in manuscript (see *CPW* II, 118).
  Metre: $a^4b^3a^4b^3$ dr, 'common metre' with variations. Hardy's most frequently used form.

'See, here's the workbox, little wife,
    That I made of polished oak.'
He was a joiner, of village life;
    She came of borough folk.

He holds the present up to her 5
    As with a smile she nears
And answers to the profferer,
    '"Twill last all my sewing years!'

'I warrant it will. And longer too.
    'Tis a scantling that I got 10
Off poor John Wayward's coffin, who
    Died of they knew not what.

131. Hardy deplores the use of grave-stones for this purpose (a common practice) in his 1906 essay 'Memories of Church Restoration' (*PW* 207–8).
10. scantling: piece of waste wood.

'The shingled pattern that seems to cease
    Against the box's rim
Continues right on in the piece   15
    That's underground with him.

'And while I worked it made me think
    Of timber's varied doom;
One inch where people eat and drink,
    The next inch in a tomb.   20

'But why do you look so white, my dear,
    And turn aside your face?
You knew not that good lad, I fear,
    Though he came from your native place?'

'How could I know that good young man,   25
    Though he came from my native town,
When he must have left far earlier than
    I was a woman grown?'

'Ah, no. I should have understood!
    It shocked you that I gave   30
To you one end of a piece of wood
    Whose other is in a grave?'

'Don't, dear, despise my intellect,
    Mere accidental things
Of that sort never have effect   35
    On my imaginings.'

Yet still her lips were limp and wan,
    Her face still held aside,
As if she had known not only John,
    But known of what he died.   40

74 Exeunt Omnes

The final two poems of *Satires of Circumstance* form its end-group, originally called 'Epilogue' (del.) in the manuscript. The 'Satires of Circumstance' which follow them were initially placed near the beginning of the volume.

Metre: $a^3b^3c^4a^3a^3$ with an irregular rhythm, mainly dtr but with feminine endings throughout and shading into df in the final two lines of each stanza (see Introduction, p. 38). Isobel Grundy contrasts the harshness of the middle stanza with the smoothness of the framing ones (1980: 12).

Title. L. 'all retire', the stage direction at the end of a scene or play.

I
Everybody else, then, going,
And I still left where the fair was? ...
Much have I seen of neigbour loungers
    Making a lusty showing,
    Each now past all knowing.   5

II
There is an air of blankness
In the street and the littered spaces;
Thoroughfare, steeple, bridge and highway
    Wizen themselves to lankness;
    Kennels dribble dankness.   10

III
Folk all fade. And whither,
As I wait alone where the fair was?
Into the clammy and numbing night-fog
    Whence they entered hither.
    Soon one more goes thither!   15

June 2, 1913.

1–5. the scene is similar to that in Thomas Moore's 'The Light of Other Days'.
2. the fair was in South Street, Dorchester (cf. 'After the Fair').
3–5. cf. Tennyson's 'Ulysses', ll. 13–14:
    Much have I seen and known – cities of men
    And manners, climates, councils, governments. ...
6–10. cf. Tennyson's *In Memoriam* 7:
        The noise of life begins again,
        And ghastly through the drizzling rain
        On the bald street breaks the blank day.
9. wizen: shrivel.
10. kennels: gutters.
15] Soon do I follow thither! Editions before *CP* 1923.
Date. Hardy's seventy-third birthday.

75 A Poet

The volume's end-piece alludes to the Horatian topos of the poet of 'double shape' who takes flight, leaving his earthly body behind. Like Shakespeare in Sonnet 71 ('The Triumph of Death' in Palgrave), Hardy emphasizes his humanity in imagining those mourning for him, rather than the monument he creates.

Metre: aabb[4] dr, a common hymn metre.

> Attentive eyes, fantastic heed,
> Assessing minds, he does not need,
> Nor urgent writs to sup or dine,
> Nor pledges in the rosy wine.
>
> For loud acclaim he does not care   5
> By the august or rich or fair,
> Nor for smart pilgrims from afar,
> Curious on where his hauntings are.
>
> But soon or later, when you hear
> That he has doffed this wrinkled gear,   10
> Some evening, at the first star-ray,
> Come to his graveside, pause and say:
>
> 'Whatever his message – glad or grim –
> Two bright-souled women clave to him';
> Stand and say that while day decays;   15
> It will be word enough of praise.

July 1914.

Title] The Poet MS del.
10. wrinkled gear. cf. the 'dusty cloak' and 'wondrous wings' of '"Why do I"?' (153), the end-poem of *Human Shows*.
13–16] MS, *SC* 1914–15 have versions which suggest a difficulty with the appropriate epithet to combine Emma and Florence:
> 'Whatever the message his to tell,
> Two thoughtful (spotless MS del.; bright-souled *SC* 1915)
>   women loved him well.'
> Stand and say that amid the dim:
> It will be praise enough for him.

Cf. the rejection of fame in 'Her Reproach' (18), and the conclusion of Tennyson's 'Epilogue':   The man remains, and whatsoe'er
>   He wrought of good or brave
>   Will mould him through the cycle-year
>   That dawns behind the grave.

76 VI. In the Cemetery

'In the Cemetery' was one of the eleven 'Satires of Circumstance' published in the *The Fortnightly Review*, 1 April 1911, a group expanded to fifteen in the volume to which it gives a title. They were placed early in the volume in 1914, but removed to the end in subsequent editions, as Hardy felt that their sardonic humour 'ill harmonized' (*LY* 164) and 'injured the others that I cared most about' (*CL* V 73).

The poem recalls Hardy's work as an architectural assistant in 1865, when he helped supervise the removal of 'bones in huge quantities' from Old St Pancras churchyard in London, so that a railway could be put through (*EL* 58–9). Similarly jumbled corpses are described in 'The Levelled Churchyard', 'mixed to human jam'. Solomon's judgement over the disputed child in 1 Kings 3: 16–28 may also be relevant.

Metre: modified sonnet form in tetrameter, ababccdd efefgg[4].

'You see those mothers squabbling there?'
Remarks the man of the cemetery.
'One says in tears, "*'Tis mine lies here!*"
Another, "*Nay, mine, you Pharisee!*"
Another, "*How dare you move my flowers*   5
And put your own on this grave of ours!"
But all their children were laid therein
At different times, like sprats in a tin.

'And then the main drain had to cross,
And we moved the lot some nights ago,   10
And packed them away in the general foss
With hundreds more. But their folks don't know,
And as well cry over a new-laid drain
As anything else, to ease your pain!'

4. *Pharisee*: hypocrite.
5–6] not in *Fortnightly*.
11. *foss*: ditch.

Moments of Vision and Miscellaneous Verses (1917)

Hardy's fifth volume of poems, his longest, most personal and most important collection, was published on 30 November 1917. Like the previous volume, it consisted mainly of recently written poems. A number had been previously published: most of the war poems and six others in periodicals, nine in the *Selected Poems* (1916), and six (including some of the above) appeared in the series of privately printed pamplets which Florence Hardy took over from Clement Shorter in 1916 (Purdy 1954: 207).

The volume's reception was mixed: even the generally favourable review in *The Times Literary Supplement* suggested that there was 'nothing so arresting as the greatest pieces in his earlier volumes' (*TLS*, 13 December 1917, pp. 603–4), while the reviewer in the *Athenaeum* claimed that 'his poems are written in a monotony of mournfulness, of dreary and dripping mournfulness' (12 January 1918, pp. 33–4). The writer in *Justice*, 10 January 1918, on the other hand, found the volume his best to date and called Hardy 'our greatest living English poet'. The review which Hardy read most carefully seems to have been Robert Lynd's in *The Nation*, 22 December 1917, pp. 412–13, entitled 'Mr. Hardy in Winter'. Lynd stressed Hardy's lack of musicality and 'dismal philosophy' but admired his genius: 'He builds his house lopsided, harsh, and with the windows in unusual places, but it is his own house, the house of a seer, of a personality' (see Hardy's comments on Lynd, *CL* V, 318–19, *LY* 79).

The manuscript used as printer's copy is in the Pepys Library, Magdalene College, Cambridge. It shows that Hardy reordered the poems slightly, removed one poem ('The Sound of Her'), and considered an alternative title for the volume, 'Moments from the Years'. He revised the volume for the Wessex Edition, Verse Vol. IV in 1919 (published with *Satires of Circumstance*), and for the *Collected Poems* published the same year.

77 Moments of Vision

The mirror of self-examination is an image which occurs elsewhere in Hardy's novels and poems: cf. 'The Pedigree' (91), 'The Burghers', and *The Well-Beloved* III, 4 (pp. 121–2). Bailey suggests it is derived from Von Hartmann's *Philosophy of the Unconscious*; another possible source is 'the world's vast mirror' in Shelley's *The Revolt of Islam* VIII, vi, in a passage which Hardy quotes on a number of occasions (Paulin 1975: 53–4, 183 discusses the passage from Shelley, but rejects it as a source for this poem). On mirrors, see also Joan Grundy 1979: ch. 4.
  Metre: $a^1b^4a^2b^5b^2$ dr.

>   That mirror
>   Which makes of men a transparency,
>   Who holds that mirror
> And bids us such a breast-bare spectacle see
>   Of you and me? 5
>
>   That mirror
>   Whose magic penetrates like a dart,
>   Who lifts that mirror
> And throws our mind back on us, and our heart,
>   Until we start? 10
>
>   That mirror
>   Works well in these night hours of ache;
>   Why in that mirror
> Are tincts we never see ourselves once take
>   When the world is awake? 15
>
>   That mirror
>   Can test each mortal when unaware;
>   Yea, that strange mirror
> May catch his last thoughts, whole life foul or fair,
>   Glassing it – where? 20

4. *breast-bare*] shudderful MS, breast-bared Editions before *CP* 1923.
14. *tincts*] tints MS. 'Tincts' are hues; though as a shortened form of 'tincture' the word also has alchemical overtones, 'the quintessence, spirit, or soul of a thing' (OED).
20. *Glassing*] Reflecting MS, *MV* 1917.

78 The Voice of Things

One of a number of poems in *Moments of Vision* which continue Hardy's meditation on the 'forty years' or more seperating his courtship and his return to Cornwall after the death of Emma Hardy. For a similar division of his life into three parts, cf. 'Quid Hic Agis?' (85) and '"I was the midmost"' (126).

Metre: a turbulent and difficult metre, $a^6b^5a^6b^4b^2$ dr with a number of variations and the possibility of a dipodic tetrameter reading. The rhyme-scheme is the same as the previous poem, but 'The Prospect' is closer in shape.

> Forty Augusts – aye, and several more – ago,
>   When I paced the headlands loosed from dull employ,
> The waves huzza'd like a multitude below,
>   In the sway of an all-including joy
>   Without cloy.   5
>
> Blankly I walked there a double decade after,
>   When thwarts had flung their toils in front of me,
> And I heard the waters wagging in a long ironic laughter
>   At the lot of men, and all the vapoury
>   Things that be.   10
>
> Wheeling change has set me again standing where
>   Once I heard the waves huzza at Lammas-tide;
> But they supplicate now – like a congregation there
>   Who murmur the Confession – I outside,
>   Prayer denied.   15

1. Augusts] years MS, *MV* 1917. Hardy's second visit to Cornwall was in August 1870. However, there is no recorded visit 'a double decade' after (stanza 2).
3. huzza'd: cried out. The same phrase is used in *The Hand of Ethelberta*, ch. 45, and 'The Wind's Prophecy' (101), l. 28.
6. blankly: see 'Exeunt Omnes' (74), l. 6n.
7. thwarts: obstructions.
12. Lammas-tide: 1 August, a harvest festival.
14–15. Hardy records a visit to Tintagel in September 1916 in which he and Florence were forced out of the church by the vicar's rudeness (*LY* 172–3); though 'prayer denied' is, of course, a more general comment on his situation.

79 Apostrophe to an Old Psalm Tune

Hardy's poems are often structured by the repeated hearing of a biblical passage or a tune within a situation in which meaning emerges with changing contexts (see Introduction, p. 11). The psalm heard here is that for the evening service on 13 August, Psalm 69. It has been set to various tunes: the poem contrasts an older tune with a newer. Cf. the reference to much-loved old hymn tunes in the opening chapter of *A Laodicean*, and 'On the Tune Called the Old-Hundred-and-Fourth' (120).
Metre: $a^5b^5b^5c^3c^2$ dr (unique example).

> I met you first – ah, when did I first meet you?
> When I was full of wonder, and innocent,
> Standing meek-eyed with those of choric bent,
>   While dimming day grew dimmer
>   In the pulpit-glimmer.   5
>
> Much riper in years I met you – in a temple
> Where summer sunset streamed upon our shapes,
> And you spread over me like a gauze that drapes,
>   And flapped from floor to rafters,
>   Sweet as angels' laughters.   10
>
> But you had been stripped of some of your old vesture
> By Monk, or another. Now you wore no frill,
> And at first you startled me. But I knew you still,
>   Though I missed the minim's waver,
>   And the dotted quaver.   15
>
> I grew accustomed to you thus. And you hailed me
> Through one who evoked you often. Then at last
> Your raiser was borne off, and I mourned you had passed
>   From my life with your late outsetter;
>   Till I said, ''Tis better!'   20
>
> But you waylaid me. I rose and went as a ghost goes,
> And said, eyes-full: 'I'll never hear it again!
> It is overmuch for scathed and memoried men
>   When sitting among strange people
>   Under their steeple.'   25

12. Monk: William Henry Monk (1823–89) edited *Hymns Ancient and Modern*, which became the standard hymn-book in 1861.
18. raiser: player (probably Emma Hardy).
19. outsetter: arranger.

Now, a new stirrer of tones calls you up before me
And wakes your speech, as she of Endor did
(When sought by Saul who, in disguises hid,
  Fell down on the earth to hear it)
    Samuel's spirit.   30

So, your quired oracles beat till they make me tremble
As I discern your mien in the old attire,
Here in these turmoiled years of belligerent fire
  Living still on – and onward, maybe,
    Till Doom's great day be!   35

Sunday, August 13, 1916.

80 At the Word 'Farewell'

First published in *Selected Poems* (1916). Hardy wrote that the recollection of his departure from St Juniot described in this poem was 'literally true' (*CL* V, 250; for other versions of the scene see *EL* 99; *A Pair of Blue Eyes*, ch. 6).
 Metre: $a^3b^2a^3b^2c^3d^2c^3d^2$ tr.

  She looked like a bird from a cloud
    On the clammy lawn,
  Moving alone, bare-browed
    In the dim of dawn.
  The candles alight in the room   5
    For my parting meal
  Made all things withoutdoors loom
    Strange, ghostly, unreal.

  The hour itself was a ghost,
    And it seemed to me then   10
  As of chances the chance furthermost
    I should see her again.

26. *new stirrer*: probably Hardy's second wife, Florence.
27. *she of Endor*: the Witch of Endor, who raises the spirit of the prophet Samuel in order to prophesy doom on Israel and inspire Saul (1 Samuel 28: 7–25). Hardy had always been interested in the story of the Witch of Endor (see *The Return of the Native* I, vi, *The Mayor of Casterbridge* xxvi, and the 'Apology' to *Late Lyrics and Earlier*), and in the period of the Great War it took on apocalyptic overtones for him (Taylor 1981: 135–8).
32. *mien*: bearing, characteristic air.
32. *old attire*: i.e. the original tune.

I beheld not where all was so fleet
  That a Plan of the past
Which had ruled us from birthtime to meet   15
  Was in working at last:
No prelude did I there perceive
  To a drama at all,
Or foreshadow what fortune might weave
  From beginnings so small;   20
But I rose as if quicked by a spur
  I was bound to obey,
And stepped through the casement to her
  Still alone in the gray.

'I am leaving you. . . . Farewell!' I said,   25
  As I followed her on
By an alley bare boughs overspread;
  'I soon must be gone!'
Even then the scale might have been turned
  Against love by a feather,   30
– But crimson one cheek of hers burned
  When we came in together.

81 Heredity

Hardy uses ideas about heredity derived from Darwin, Spencer, and others in a number of novels, and showed a consistent interest in the topic. In 1885 he copied part of an article in the *Contemporary Review* on 'the fatality of heredity' into his notebooks: 'tendencies . . . may be lying unsuspected at the very bottom of our nature, far below the level of consciousness' (Björk entry 1352). In February 1889 he wrote in his notebook the idea for ' "The story of a face which goes through three generations or more, would make a fine novel or poem on the passage of Time. The differences in personality to be ignored." [This idea was to some extent carried out in the novel *The Well-Beloved*, the poem entitled "Heredity", etc.]' (*EL* 284, Hardy's brackets). In 1890 he read August Weismann's *Essays on Heredity*, trans. Edward B. Poulton (Oxford, 1889), a work which J. Hillis Miller links to both 'Heredity' and 'The Pedigree' (91) (1982: 169). Cf. also 'Family Portraits' (175).

16. Was in working at last] Was accomplished at last MS, *MV* 1917.
17–24. Paulin (1975: 51) sees a parallel here with Browning's 'By the Fire-Side', 39–40, marked in the edition of Browning which Florence Henniker gave Hardy.
19. weave: see 'The Convergence of the Twain' (45), l. 31n.

Metre: ababab³ dr.

> I am the family face;
> Flesh perishes, I live on,
> Projecting trait and trace
> Through time to times anon,
> And leaping from place to place   5
> Over oblivion.
>
> The years-heired feature that can
> In curve and voice and eye
> Despise the human span
> Of durance – that is I;   10
> The eternal thing in man,
> That heeds no call to die.

82 Near Lanivet, 1872

Hardy included this poem in his list of those 'possibly among the best I have written', and selected it for *Chosen Poems* (1929). He reported that the events related took place between himself and Emma Gifford before their marriage (*CL* V, 250, 295; VI, 96). The manuscript has 'From an old note' (del.) at end.

The typological anticipation of a 'crucifixion' in the poem recalls Holman Hunt's famous painting 'The Shadow of Death', painted and much written-about 1869–73, in which Christ yawning in the carpenter's shop throws a shadow of the cross on the wall (see Introduction, p. 11).

Metre: a⁵b³a⁵b³ dr with variations (cf. 'The Peasant's Confession' (4), 'One We Knew' (39), 'Lying Awake' (160)). Taylor links this scheme to Vaughan's 'Corruption', another poem about loss (1988: 115–16n), while Thom Gunn comments on its closeness to ballad-metre (1972: 36).

> There was a stunted handpost just on the crest,
>   Only a few feet high:
> She was tired, and we stopped in the twilight-time for her
>   rest.
>   At the crossways close thereby.
>
> She leant back, being so weary, against its stem,   5
>   And laid her arms on its own,
> Each open palm stretched out to each end of them,
>   Her sad face sideways thrown.

4. *anon*: following.
7. *years-heired*] family MS, *MV* 1917.
10. *durance*: duration of life (with overtones of 'endurance' and imprisonment).

Her white-clothed form at this dim-lit cease of day
   Made her look as one crucified   10
In my gaze at her from the midst of the dusty way,
   And hurriedly 'Don't,' I cried.
I do not think she heard. Loosing thence she said,
   As she stepped forth ready to go,
'I am rested now. – Something strange came into my head;   15
   I wish I had not leant so!'

And wordless we moved onward down from the hill
   In the west cloud's murked obscure,
And looking back we could see the handpost still
   In the solitude of the moor.   20

'It struck her too,' I thought, for as if afraid
   She heavily breathed as we trailed;
Till she said, 'I did not think how 'twould look in the shade,
   When I leant there like one nailed.'

I lightly: 'There's nothing in it. For *you*, anyhow!'   25
   – 'O I know there is not,' said she ...
'Yet I wonder ... If no one is bodily crucified now,
   In spirit one may be!'

And we dragged on and on, while we seemed to see
   In the running of Time's far glass   30
Her crucified, as she had wondered if she might be
   Some day. – Alas, alas!

83 Copying Architecture in an Old Minster
(*Wimborne*)

This poem can be linked to a series of clock-poems, including 'A Broken Appointment', 'After the Fair', 'The Chimes', 'The Musical Box' (98), and 'On One Who Lived and Died Where He Was Born'. Taylor sees it as a paradigm for Hardy's meditative lyrics, in which the passing of time in the poem's reverie signals a larger forgetfulness (1981: 1–5).

30. *glass*: hour-glass (some commentators have suggested 'mirror', recalling the opening poem).
Headnote. *Wimborne*: Dorset town some 20 miles east of Dorchester. Hardy and his wife lived there 1881–3. The Minster (church) interested Hardy for its architectural variety and monuments.

Metre: a⁴b³a⁴c⁴b³ tr, with link-rhymes between stanzas on the c-lines 'like a recurrent clock chime' (Taylor 1988: 133).

> How smartly the quarters of the hour march by
>   That the jack-o'-clock never forgets;
> Ding-dong; and before I have traced a cusp's eye,
> Or got the true twist of the ogee over,
>   A double ding-dong ricochetts.   5
>
> Just so did he clang here before I came,
>   And so will he clang when I'm gone
> Through the Minster's cavernous hollows – the same
> Tale of hours never more to be will he deliver
>   To the speechless midnight and dawn!   10
>
> I grow to conceive it a call to ghosts,
>   Whose mould lies below and around.
> Yes; the next 'Come, come,' draws them out from their posts,
> And they gather, and one shade appears, and another,
>   As the eve-damps creep from the ground.   15
>
> See – a Courtenay stands by his quatre-foiled tomb,
>   And a Duke and his Duchess near;
> And one Sir Edmund in columned gloom,
> And a Saxon king by the presbytery chamber;
>   And shapes unknown in the rear.   20
>
> Maybe they have met for a parle on some plan
>   To better ail-stricken mankind;
> I catch their cheepings, though thinner than

2. *jack-o'-clock*: figure of a man who strikes a mechanical clock.
3. *cusp*: pointed ornament.
4. *ogee*: double or 'S' curve characteristic of Decorated Gothic architecture.
9. *tale*: tally, number.
16 *Courtenay*: despite the 'his', this is Gertrude, Marchioness of Exeter, d. 1558.
16. *quatre-foiled*: with openings in its tracery containing four leaves or petal-shapes.
17. *Duke and his Duchess*: John Beaufort, Duke of Somerset (d. 1444), and his wife Margaret.
18. *Sir Edmund*: Sir Edmund Uvedale (d. 1606).
19 *Saxon king*: Ethelred, succeeded by Alfred the Great in 871.
19. *presbytery chamber*: the space near the sanctuary, east of the choir.
21. *parle*: talk, conference.
22. *ail-stricken mankind*: could relate to the First World War rather than to 1881–3 (since the poem as a whole is concerned with one time 'ghosting' another).

>   The overhead creak of a passager's pinion
>   When leaving land behind.   25
>   Or perhaps they speak to the yet unborn,
>   And caution them not to come
>   To a world so ancient and trouble-torn,
>   Of foiled intents, vain lovingkindness,
>   And ardours chilled and numb.   30
>   They waste to fog as I stir and stand,
>   And move from the arched recess,
>   And pick up the drawing that slipped from my hand,
>   And feel for the pencil I dropped in the cranny
>   In a moment's forgetfulness.   35

84 To Shakespeare
After Three Hundred Years

Written on 14 February 1916 in response to a request from Professor Israel Gollancz of King's College London, who was preparing *A Book of Homage to Shakespeare*. It was published in the *Fortnightly Review* in June 1916 as well as appearing in Gollancz's book in April; in August Florence Hardy issued it as the first of the series of privately printed pamplets which she prepared with the aid of Sydney Cockrell (Purdy 1954: 177–8, 349–50; for variants in the different printings see *CPW* II, 173–4). 'To Shakespeare' reflects Hardy's view of writing as involving a clear distinction between the public nature of the works and the private individual who produces them.
  Metre: $a^5b^5b^5c^5a^2c^6$ dr (unique example).

>   Bright baffling Soul, least capturable of themes,
>   Thou, who display'dst a life of commonplace,
>   Leaving no intimate word or personal trace
>   Of high design outside the artistry
>   Of thy penned dreams,   5
>   Still shalt remain at heart unread eternally.

24. *passager's pinion*: migratory bird's wing.
24. *passager's*] puffin MS del.
26–30. Hardy often suggests that it is better not to have been born: cf. 'To an Unborn Pauper Child' (17).
1. *Bright baffling*] Daemonic MS del.
2–5. Arnold similarly stresses Shakespeare's anonymity in his sonnet 'Shakespeare'.
6. *unread eternally*: cf. Hardy on himself in 'Not Known'.

Through human orbits thy discourse to-day,
Despite thy formal pilgrimage, throbs on
In harmonies that cow Oblivion,
And, like the wind, with all-uncared effect   10
    Maintain a sway
Not fore-desired, in tracks unchosen and unchecked.

And yet, at thy last breath, with mindless note
The borough clocks but samely tongued the hour
The Avon just as always glassed the tower,   15
Thy age was published on thy passing-bell
    But in due rote
With other dwellers' deaths accorded a like knell.

And at the strokes some townsman (met, maybe,
And thereon queried by some squire's good dame   20
Driving in shopward) may have given thy name,
With, 'Yes, a worthy man and well-to-do;
    Though, as for me,
I knew him but by just a neighbour's nod, 'tis true.

'I'faith, few knew him much here, save by word,   25
He having elsewhere led his busier life;
Though to be sure he left with us his wife.'
– 'Ah, one of the tradesmen's sons, I now recall. . . .
    Witty, I've heard. . . .
We did not know him. . . . Well, good-day. Death comes to
    all.'   30

So, like a strange bright bird we sometimes find
To mingle with the barn-door brood awhile,
Then vanish from their homely domicile –

---

9. cow: intimidate.
10–12: cf. comments on the after-life of literature in 'A Poet's Thought' (162).
15. tower: of the church of Shakespeare's home town of Stratford-on-Avon, where he is buried. The river runs beside the church.
16. passing-bell: traditionally, one stroke was tolled for each year of the deceased's age. Hardy describes his own passing-bell in 'Afterwards' (112).
17. in due rote: according to custom.
26. left us with his wife: Shakespeare seems to have sent his wife to live in Stratford, *c.* 1596.
27. tradesmen's sons: Shakespeare's father was a tanner and merchant.
31. bright bird we sometimes find] bright-pinioned bird we find 1916 printings.

Into man's poesy, we wot not whence,
    Flew thy strange mind, 35
Lodged there a radiant guest, and sped for ever thence.
1916.

85 Quid Hic Agis?

Published in *The Spectator*, 19 August 1916 under the title of 'In Time of Slaughter'. Subsequently issued as a privately printed pamplet by Florence Hardy, with the title '"When I weekly knew"', revised and with 12 lines added (see *CPW* II, 175–7 for details). The poem draws on one of Hardy's favourite biblical passages, 1 Kings 19, and maps its text across his life to its wartime conclusion (see Introduction, p. 12).

Metre: aabb² etc. dr, an early English form used by Skelton, Drayton and others; more recently by Seamus Heaney.

I

When I weekly knew
An ancient pew,
And murmured there
The forms of prayer
And thanks and praise 5
In the ancient ways,
And heard read out
During August drought
That chapter from Kings
Harvest-time brings; 10
– How the prophet, broken
By griefs unspoken,
Went heavily away
To fast and to pray,

34. wot not whence: know not from where.
Date] Feb. 14 1916 MS, 1916 printings.
Title] In Time of Slaughter *Spectator*; 'When I weekly knew' MS, Private Printing.
Quid Hic Agis?: What does thou here? (from the Vulgate, 1 Kings 19: 9, 13). The words that God addresses to Elijah as he hides in the wilderness.
9. that chapter from Kings: 1 Kings 19, the reading for the eleventh Sunday after Trinity, one of the most heavily annotated in Hardy's Bible. Knight reads the passage in *A Pair of Blue Eyes*, ch. 19 (p. 193).
10. Harvest-time] The Trinity-time *Spectator*.
11–15. cf. 1 Kings 19:4: 'But he [Elijah]: himself went a day's journey into the wilderness, and came and sat down under a juniper tree: and he

And, while waiting to die, 15
The Lord passed by,
And a whirlwind and fire
Drew nigher and nigher,
And a small voice anon
Bade him up and be gone, – 20
I did not apprehend
As I sat to the end
And watched for her smile
Across the sunned aisle,
That this tale of a seer 25
Which came once a year
Might, when sands were heaping,
Be like a sweat creeping,
Or in any degree
Bear on her or on me! 30

II

When later, by chance
Of circumstance,
It befel me to read
On a hot afternoon
At the lectern there 35
The selfsame words
As the lesson decreed,
To the gathered few
From the hamlets near –
Folk of flocks and herds 40
Sitting half aswoon,
Who listened thereto
As women and men

requested for himself that he might die; and said, It is enough; now, O Lord, take away my life'.
16–19: cf. 1 Kings 19: 11–12: 'And behold, the Lord passed by, and a great and strong wind rent the mountains, and brake in pieces the rocks before the Lord; but the Lord was not in the wind: and after the wind an earthquake; but the Lord was not in the earthquake: And after the earthquake a fire; but the Lord was not in the fire: and after the fire a still small voice'.
20. 'And the Lord said unto him, Go, return on thy way to the wilderness of Damascus' (1 Kings 19: 15).
24. sunned] south *Spectator*, MS, pamphlet.
25. tale] theme *MV* 1919, *CP* 1919, *WE* 1919.
27. sands were heaping: another reference to the hour-glass, cf. 'At Castle Boterel' (66), l. 33n.
31–46] expanded from ten lines in *Spectator*.

Not overmuch
Concerned at such –   45
So, like them then,
I did not see
What drought might be
With me, with her,
As the Kalendar   50
Moved on, and Time
Devoured our prime.

III

But now, at last,
When our glory has passed,
And there is no smile   55
From her in the aisle,
But where it once shone
A marble, men say,
With her name thereon
Is discerned to-day;   60
And spiritless
In the wilderness
I shrink from sight
And desire the night,
(Though, as in old wise,   65
I might still arise,
Go forth, and stand
And prophesy in the land),
I feel the shake
Of wind and earthquake,   70
And consuming fire
Nigher and nigher,
And the voice catch clear,
'What doest thou here?'

The Spectator: 1916. During the War.

---

50. Kalendar: the spelling suggests the Church calendar.
55–60] not in *Spectator*.
71. consuming fire: alludes to Hebrews 12: 29, 'For our God is a consuming fire', the end of a passage typologically linked to 1 Kings 19.
During the War] added *CP* 1923.

86 On a Midsummer Eve

One of Hardy's most haunting lyrics, first published in *Selected Poems* (1916).

Metre: abab⁴ dr, 'long metre', with a move towards the anapaestic on the final line which John Lucas cites as an example of how 'again and again his poems start out of speech rhythms that drift near to song, or they begin with metrical regularity and then modulate into cadences that imply speech' (1986: 30–1).

> I idly cut a parsley stalk,
> And blew therein towards the moon;
> I had not thought what ghosts would walk
> With shivering footsteps to my tune.
>
> I went, and knelt, and scooped my hand   5
> As if to drink, into the brook,
> And a faint figure seemed to stand
> Above me, with the bygone look.
>
> I lipped rough rhymes of chance, not choice,
> I thought not what my words might be;   10
> There came into my ear a voice
> That turned a tenderer verse for me.

87 The Blinded Bird

One of Hardy's sequence of bird-poems (see Introduction, p. 15), using the fact that captive song-birds were blinded in the belief that it would make them sing better (in a parallel way, the idea of song as a compensation for blindness is traditionally applied to prophets and poets like Tiresias, Homer, Milton). Included in *Chosen Poems* (1929).

Metre: AbbaccA³ dr (unique, but other poems share the rhyme-scheme).

> So zestfully canst thou sing?
> And all this indignity,
> With God's consent, on thee!
> Blinded ere yet a-wing

Title. Midsummer Eve is traditionally a time of enchantment and phantasmagoria.
1–2. Firor reports the tradition that 'the cutting of parsley is a sign that the person so occupied will sooner or later be crossed in love' (1931: 51).
5–6. perhaps recalling the hand-in-water motif of the scene in 'Under the Waterfall' (50).
9. chance not choice: the same pairing opens 'The Temporary the All' (1).

> By the red-hot needle thou, 5
> I stand and wonder how
> So zestfully thou canst sing!
>
> Resenting not such wrong,
> Thy grievous pain forgot,
> Eternal dark thy lot, 10
> Groping thy whole life long,
> After that stab of fire;
> Enjailed in pitiless wire;
> Resenting not such wrong!
>
> Who hath charity? This bird. 15
> Who suffereth long and is kind,
> Is not provoked, though blind
> And alive ensepulchred?
> Who hopeth, endureth all things?
> Who thinketh no evil, but sings? 20
> Who is divine? This bird.

88 The Statue of Liberty

The 'investment' of the audience in a work of art, and the ability of superficial fairness to conceal ugliness fascinated Hardy, and he wrote a number of poems on the topic, e.g. 'The Collector Cleans His Picture' (119). The question of who controls the meanings of a commemorative work is similarly raised in 'The Obliterate Tomb' (72).

Metre: $a^4b^3c^4d^2d^2b^3$ dtr, a modified tail-rhyme (unique).

> This statue of Liberty, busy man,
>   Here erect in the city square,
> I have watched while your scrubbings, this early morning,
>   Strangely wistful,
>   And half tristful, 5

10. eternal dark: perhaps alluding to Milton's 'eternal Night' and 'ever-during dark' in *Paradise Lost* III, 18, 45.
15–20. cf. 1 Corinthians 13: 4–7: 'Charity suffereth long, and is kind. . . . Doth not behave itself unseemly, seeketh not her own, is not easily provoked, thinketh no evil. . . . Beareth all things, believeth all things, hopeth all things, endureth all things.' Hardy alludes to the same passage and uses bird imagery to describe Tess, *Tess of the D'Urbervilles*, ch. 36 (p. 267); see P. Griffith 1963.
4–5. the 'wistful / tristful' rhyme echoes that in 'Night in the Old Home' (37, see also 'The Voice' (59)).
5. tristful: sad.

Have turned her from foul to fair;
With your bucket of water, and mop, and brush,
   Bringing her out of the grime
That has smeared her during the smokes of winter
      With such glumness
      In her dumbness,
   And aged her before her time.

You have washed her down with motherly care –
   Head, shoulders, arm, and foot,
To the very hem of the robes that drape her –
      All expertly
      And alertly,
   Till a long stream, black with soot,

Flows over the pavement to the road,
   And her shape looms pure as snow:
I read you are hired by the City guardians –
      May be yearly,
      Or once merely –
   To treat the statues so?

'Oh, I'm not hired by the Councilmen
   To cleanse the statues here.
I do this one as a self-willed duty,
      Not as paid to,
      Or at all made to,
   But because the doing is dear.'

Ah, then I hail you brother and friend!
   Liberty's knight divine.
What you have done would have been my doing,
      Yea, most verily,
      Well, and thoroughly,
   Had but your courage been mine!

'Oh I care not for Liberty's mould,
   Liberty charms not me;
What's Freedom but an idler's vision,
      Vain, pernicious,
      Often vicious,
   Of things that cannot be!

'Memory it is that brings me to this –
   Of a daughter – my one sweet own.

---

6. foul to fair: recalls the witches's speech at the opening of *Macbeth*: 'Fair is foul and foul is fair'.

> She grew a famous carver's model, 45
>   One of the fairest
>   And of the rarest: –
> She sat for the figure as shown.
>
> 'But alas, she died in this distant place
>   Before I was warned to betake 50
> Myself to her side! ... And in love of my darling,
>   In love of the fame of her,
>   And the good name of her,
> I do this for her sake.'
>
> Answer I gave not. Of that form 55
>   The carver was I at his side;
> His child, my model, held so saintly,
>   Grand in feature,
>   Gross in nature,
> In the dens of vice had died. 60

89 The Change

One of Hardy's great series of memory-and-time poems in *Moments of Vision*, clearly linked through its refrain to 'During Wind and Rain' (102), and using the vocabulary of romance and loss developed in the 'Poems of 1912–13'.

Metre: $A^4b^4A^4c^3A^4a^3c^7$, dr, A-lines repeated through each stanza and b-lines repeated with variations throughout the poem. The scheme resembles that of the ballad 'Bonnie Susan Cleland' (Taylor 1988: 245).

> Out of the past there rises a week –
>   Who shall read the years O! –
> Out of the past there rises a week
>   Enringed with a purple zone.

48] MS has a deleted stanza:
>   'Alas for her calling. It suited her not;
>   She learnt ways sinister
>   And – died ... And tendance of this her image
>   With some gladness,
>   Though in sadness,
>   I give for love of her.'

2. *read*] know MS del. A revision followed up in the second line of each subsequent stanza, Hardy introducing more irregularity (see below).
3. *a week*: presumably Hardy's first visit to St Juniot, 7–11 March 1870.
4. *purple zone*: on 'purples', see 'Beeny Cliff' (65), l. 9n.

  Out of the past there rises a week
   When thoughts were strung too thick to speak,
And the magic of its lineaments remains with me alone.

  In that week there was heard a singing –
   Who shall spell the years, the years! –
  In that week there was heard a singing,
   And the white owl wondered why.
  In that week, yea, a voice was ringing,
   And forth from the casement were candles flinging
Radiance that fell on the deodar and lit up the path thereby.

  Could that song have a mocking note? –
   Who shall unroll the years O! –
  Could that song have a mocking note
   To the white owl's sense as it fell?
  Could that song have a mocking note
   As it trilled out warm from the singer's throat,
And who was the mocker and who the mocked when two felt all was well?

  In a tedious trampling crowd yet later –
   Who shall bare the years, the years! –
  In a tedious trampling crowd yet later,
   When silvery singings were dumb;
  In a crowd uncaring what time might fate her,
   Mid murks of night I stood to await her,
And the twanging of iron wheels gave out the signal that she
  was come.

  She said with a travel-tired smile –
   Who shall lift the years O! –
  She said with a travel-tired smile,
   Half scared by scene so strange;

9. *spell*] know MS del.
9. *the years, the years!*] the years O! MS, *MV* 1917.
12] In that week there was heard a singing, (MS, *MV* 1917).
14. *deodar*: cedar (there was one in the rectory garden at St Juniot).
15. *mocking note*: cf. the song in 'The Prophetess' (156).
16. *unroll*] know MS del.
18. *white owl*: cf. *SR* 35.
22, 24. *crowd yet*] crowd, far MS, *MV* 1917.
23. *bare*] know MS del.
23. *the years, the years!*] the years O! MS, *MV* 1917.
26] In a tedious trampling crowd, far later MS, *MV* 1917.
27. *Mid murks of*] In the filmy MS; In the murky *MV* 1917.
28. the scene is a London railway station, probably in 1873 or 1874.
30. *lift*] know MS del.

> She said, outworn by mile on mile,
> The blurred lamps wanning her face the while,
> 'O Love, I am here; I am with you!' ... Ah, that there should
>   have come a change! 35
>
> O the doom by someone spoken –
>   Who shall unseal the years, the years! –
> O the doom that gave no token,
>   When nothing of bale saw we:
> O the doom by someone spoken, 40
> O the heart by someone broken,
> The heart whose sweet reverberances are all time leaves to
>   me.

January–February 1913.

90 Lines
To a Movement in Mozart's E-Flat Symphony

Hardy wrote a number of poems on musical themes: cf. 'Apostrophe to an Old Psalm Tune' (79) and 'The Musical Box' (98) in the same volume. Mozart wrote four E-flat symphonies: a recent writer argues that the one alluded to in the subtitle is the second (andante) movement of Symphony No. 19 (Boone 1990).

Metre: $a^3 a^3 b^5 c^6 D^2$ dr, highly patterned with the a-lines close in form, link-rhymes between the b-lines, and D-lines identical. The final stanza involves even greater symmetry, rhyming aabaD. The poem's form suggests the movement of Mozart's rhythm, and the alliterative and heavily pointed fourth lines reinforce the musical effect. Davie, however, criticizes the poem as a monstrosity of 'heavy engineering' (1973: 17).

> Show me again the time
> When in the Junetide's prime
> We flew by meads and mountains northerly! –
> Yea, to such freshness, fairness, fulness, fineness, freeness,
>   Love lures life on. 5

34. *wanning*: making pale.
37. *unseal the years*: cf. Revelation 5: 2–3.
37. *unseal*] know MS del.
37. *the years, the years!*] the years O! MS.
38] O the doom by someone spoken MS, *MV* 1917.
39. *bale*: harm.
1. *time*: the time-references narrow throughout the poem: 'day', 'hour', 'moment'.

　　　　　Show me again the day
　　　　　When from the sandy bar
　　　　We looked together upon the pestered sea! –
　　Yea, to such surging, swaying, sighing, swelling, shrinking,
　　　　　　Love lures life on.   10

　　　　　Show me again the hour
　　　　　When by the pinnacled tower
　　　　We eyed each other and feared futurity! –
　　Yea, to such bodings, broodings, beatings, blanchings,
　　　　　　blessings,
　　　　　　Love lures life on.   15

　　　　　Show me again just this:
　　　　　The moment of that kiss
　　　　Away from the prancing folk, by the strawberry-tree! –
　　Yea, to such ratheness, rareness, ripeness, richness, rashness,
　　　　　　Love lures life on.   20
　　　Begun November 1898.

91 The Pedigree

'The Pedigree' is perhaps Hardy's most visionary and obscure poem, its dream-like series of transformations and crisis seeming to offer a key to his self-perception (for extended commentaries see Jacobus 1982, Miller 1990: 245–59; and the discussion of 'tree' patterns in Taylor 1981: ch. 2). The poem is perhaps influenced by Heine's 'Dream Pictures'.

Hardy wrote a series of poems on genealogy, family history: cf. 'Heredity' (81), 'Sine Prole' (138), 'Old Furniture' (99), and 'Family Portraits' (175). He was fascinated by pedigrees and drew up his own family tree, reaching back to the early seventeenth century (reproduced Millgate 1982: 464–5). See also Tess's tracing of her past in the D'Urberville window, *Tess of the D'Urbervilles*, ch. 52; and the discussion of pedigrees in the Preface to *A Group of Noble Dames* (*PW* 24).

Metre: highly irregular with each stanza having a different metrical scheme: $a^3b^5c^5a^7d^3c^7b^6$, $a^3b^5c^5a^3d^6c^6b^5$, etc., dr. The 'Gothic' complexity of the form mirrors the 'cynic twist' of Hardy's pedigree. The final stanza has an extra line.

14. bodings: forebodings, presages.
19] Yea, to such rashness, ratheness, rareness, ripeness, richness, All editions (correction in Hardy's copy of *CP* 1923, DCM).
19. ratheness: early ripeness (Elliott 1984: 209 suggests it is a Dorset survival of the OE hrædnes).

I

    I bent in the deep of night
      Over a pedigree the chronicler gave
As mine; and as I bent there, half-unrobed,
The uncurtained panes of my window-square let in the watery light
      Of the moon in its old age: 5
And green-rheumed clouds were hurrying past where mute and cold it globed
  Like a drifting dolphin's eye seen through a lapping wave.

II

      So, scanning my sire-grown tree,
  And the hieroglyphs of this spouse tied to that,
    With offspring mapped below in lineage,   10
      Till the tangles troubled me,
The branches seemed to twist into a seared and cynic face
  Which winked and tokened towards the window like a Mage
    Enchanting me to gaze again thereat.

III

      It was a mirror now,   15
  And in it a long perspective I could trace
Of my begetters, dwindling backward each past each
    All with the kindred look,

2. *pedigree*: genealogy.
4–5. cf. the moon-and-window imagery of 'Shut Out That Moon', 'The Moon Looks In', and '"I looked up from my writing"' (111). Stallworthy (1980) links these poems to the moon imagery of *The Well-Beloved*. Miller suggests the influence of Shelley's 'To the Moon' fragment, with its moon 'ever changing, like a joyless eye / That finds no object worth its constancy' (Miller 1990: 248). However, the 'eye of heaven' image is traditional (e.g. *Paradise Lost* V, 41–4).
6. *green-rheumed*] greenish MS. 'Rheum' is mucus or tears.
7. *drifting dolphin's*] this striking image evolved gradually: dying fish's MS; dying dolphin's *MV* 1917.
8–11. the branching lines of the family tree can be likened to both gothic tracery and the evolutionary trees drawn up by Darwin, patterns which mature through time (see Taylor 1981: 55–61, figs 3–5).
12. *cynic*: see l. 33n.
13. *tokened*: made a sign.
13. *Mage*: magician, seer (cf. 'Magians' in 'He Resolves to Say No More' (178)).
15. *mirror*: cf. 'that mirror' of 'Moments of Vision' (77), and the image of receding images in a mirror in 'Old Furniture' (99), ll. 12–15.
18. *kindred*] family MS, *MV* 1917.

> Whose names had since been inked down in their place
> On the recorder's book, 20
> Generation and generation of my mien, and build, and brow.
>
> IV
> And then did I divine
> That every heave and coil and move I made
> Within my brain, and in my mood and speech,
> Was in the glass portrayed 25
> As long forestalled by their so making it;
> The first of them, the primest fuglemen of my line,
> Being fogged in far antiqueness past surmise and reason's reach.
>
> V
> Said I then, sunk in tone,
> 'I am merest mimicker and counterfeit! – 30
> Though thinking, *I am I,
> And what I do I do myself alone.*'
> – The cynic twist of the page thereat unknit
> Back to its normal figure, having wrought its purport wry,

20. *recorder*: the 'chronicler' of l. 2; Hardy's *The Dynasts* includes 'Recording Angels' in its *dramatis personae*.
21. *mien*: bearing.
23. *heave and coil*: cf. the 'serpentine' coils of the giant brain in the 'Fore Scene' of *The Dynasts* (p. 28).
27. *fuglemen*: soldiers placed at the front of a file to lead the others in drill. Cf. the tree in *The Woodlanders*, ch. 13 with which old South identifies: 'As the tree waved South waved his head, making it his fugleman with abject obedience' (p. 119). Miller points out that 'to fugle' can also mean to mislead or trick (1990: 253).
30. *merest mimicker*] mere continuator MS, *MV* 1917 (the latter word also used in 'Wessex Heights').
30. *counterfeit*: the obsolete meaning 'made from a pattern' is relevant.
31–2. invokes a tradition of declarations of selfhood that have their origins on God's 'I am that I am' (Exodus 3: 14), e.g. Tennyson's 'Ulysses', l. 67, 'that which we are, we are' (cf. two later examples: Yeats's 'I am I, am I' in 'He and She', and Wallace Stevens's 'I have not but I am and as I am, I am' in 'Notes Towards a Supreme Fiction').
33. *cynic*: disillusioned, fault-finding; though 'cynic twist' here suggests the medical condition known as a 'cynic spasm', a facial twitch.
33. *thereat*: grammatically, the antecedent is not entirely clear: either the words which are spoken in ll. 29–30, or (more likely) the thoughts in ll. 31–2.
34. *wry*: perverse, ill-natured.

The Mage's mirror left the window-square, 35
And the stained moon and drift retook their places there.
1916.

92 His Heart
A Woman's Dream

'His Heart' is another poem on internal markings (cf. 133), and might be seen as relating to Hardy's reading of Emma's private journals after her death, with a reversal of positions which has her reading his 'heart'. The heart-rituals associated with the Dionysus legend may be relevant (see Sacks 1985: 31–2), but more plausibly the central image is a literalization of the colloquial phrase alluded to in Swinburne's 'Laus Veneris', l. 33: 'She holds my heart in her sweet open hands' – Hardy drawing on and adapting a long tradition of imagery relating to hearts and love, some of which pictures the cutting out of the heart. In this, it matches '"I thought, my Heart"' (105) in the same volume. Ironically, Hardy's heart was removed from his body after his death for burial in Dorset, while his ashes went to Westminster Abbey.

Metre: $a^5a^5b^6b^5$ dr (unique).

> At midnight, in the room where he lay dead
> Whom in his life I had never clearly read,
> I thought if I could peer into that citadel
> His heart, I should at last know full and well
>
> What hereto had been known to him alone, 5
> Despite our long sit-out of years foreflown,
> 'And if,' I said, 'I do this for his memory's sake,
> It would not wound him, even if he could wake.'
>
> So I bent over him. He seemed to smile
> With a calm confidence the whole long while 10
> That I, withdrawing his heart, held it and, bit by bit,
> Perused the unguessed things found written on it.
>
> It was inscribed like a terrestrial sphere
> With quaint vermiculations close and clear –
> His graving. Had I known, would I have risked the stroke 15
> Its reading brought, and my own heart nigh broke!

36. drift: clouds.
14. vermiculations: carved patterns resembling worm-tracks.
15. graving: engraving. Cf. 'In a Former Resort after Many Years' (133), l. 10n.

Yes, there at last, eyes opened, did I see
  His whole sincere symmetric history;
There were his truth, his simple singlemindedness,
  Strained, maybe, by time's storms, but there no less.   20

There were the daily deeds from sun to sun
  In blindness, but good faith, that he had done;
There were requests, at instances wherein he swerved
  (As he conceived) from cherishings I had deserved.

There were old hours all figured down as bliss –   25
  Those spent with me – (how little had I thought this!)
There those when, at my absence, whether he slept or waked,
  (Though I knew not 'twas so!) his spirit ached.

There that when we were severed, how day dulled
  Till time joined us anew, was chronicled: 30
And arguments and battlings in defence of me
  That heart recorded clearly and ruddily.

I put it back, and left him as he lay
  While pierced the morning pink and then the gray
Into each dreary room and corridor around,   35
  Where I shall wait, but his step will not sound.

93 The Oxen

One of Hardy's many Christmas-pieces, and one of his most anthologized poems, 'The Oxen' was first published in *The Times* on 24 December 1915, with copyright unreserved, and subsequently included in *Selected Poems* (1916). Hardy uses the same folk-tradition in *Tess of the D'Urbervilles*, ch. 17; he had learnt it from his mother as a child. Set at Higher Bockhampton.
  Metre: $a^4b^3a^4b^3$ dr with variations, 'common metre'. Lucas comments on the 'dance-like' anapaestics of the first two stanzas, suggesting folk-memory, compared to the stiffer iambics of the second two stanzas, set in the present (1986: 26–7).

> Christmas Eve, and twelve of the clock.
>   'Now they are all on their knees,'
> An elder said as we sat in a flock
>   By the embers in hearthside ease.
>
> We pictured the meek mild creatures where   5
>   They dwelt in their strawy pen,
> Nor did it occur to one of us there
>   To doubt they were kneeling then.

So fair a fancy few would weave
   In these years! Yet, I feel,   10
If someone said on Christmas Eve,
   'Come; see the oxen kneel

'In the lonely barton by yonder coomb
   Our childhood used to know,'
I should go with him in the gloom,   15
   Hoping it might be so.
1915.

94 The Photograph

The burning of materials from Hardy's past was a periodic ritual at Max Gate. Bailey (1970: 371) suggests that the photograph was of Hardy's cousin Tryphena Sparks, whom he had not seen since 1874 (see 'Thoughts of Phena' (7)).
   Metre: a⁵b⁵a³a⁵b⁵ dtr (cf. Herbert's 'The World' and Hardy's '"And There was a Great Calm"' (116) for similar schemes).

The flame crept up the portrait line by line
As it lay on the coals in the silence of night's profound,
   And over the arm's incline,
And along the marge of the silkwork superfine,
And gnawed at the delicate bosom's defenceless round.   5

Then I vented a cry of hurt, and averted my eyes;
The spectacle was one that I could not bear,
   To my deep and sad surprise;
But, compelled to heed, I again looked furtivewise
Till the flame had eaten her breasts, and mouth, and hair. 10

9. *would weave*] believe *Times*. The revision strengthens the sense of doubt.
13. *barton*: farmyard.
13. *coomb*: small valley.
1–10. perhaps playing on lines marked in 'Time's Revenges' in the *Selections from the Poetical Works of Robert Browning* (1893) which Florence Henniker gave Hardy in 1894:
   – So is my spirit, as flesh with sin,
   Filled full, eaten out and in
   With the face of her, the eyes of her,
   The lips, the little chin, the stir
   Of shadow round her mouth; and she
   – I'll tell you, – calmly would decree
   That I should roast at a slow fire,
   If that would compass her desire. . . .

4. marge] edge MS, *MV* 1917.

'Thank God, she is out of it now!' I said at last,
In a great relief of heart when the thing was done
    That had set my soul aghast,
And nothing was left of the picture unsheathed from the past
But the ashen ghost of the card it had figured on.   15

She was a woman long hid amid packs of years,
She might have been living or dead; she was lost to my sight,
    And the deed that had nigh drawn tears
Was done in a casual clearance of life's arrears;
But I felt as if I had put her to death that night! . . .   20

.   .   .   .

– Well; she knew nothing thereof did she survive,
And suffered nothing if numbered among the dead;
    Yet – yet – if on earth alive
Did she feel a smart, and with vague strange anguish strive?
If in heaven, did she smile at me sadly and shake her head?   25

95 The Last Signal
(*Oct.* 11, 1886)
A Memory of William Barnes

Hardy's friend and early mentor the Dorset dialect-poet William Barnes was buried on 11 October 1886. On Hardy's relations with Barnes, see *EL* 37, 42, 160–1, 210–11, 229–30, 240, and his obituary for Barnes, *PW* 100–6; as well as critical discussions in Zietlow 1969: 291–303; Hynes 1961: 23–32. *Moments of Vision* seems to show more of Barnes's influence than any of Hardy's other volumes, perhaps reflecting a response to Hardy's editing of the *Select Poems of William Barnes* (1908).

Metre: $a^5b^5c^5b^3$ dr, with variations. Hardy elaborates his tribute to Barnes by using Barnes's own theories about the metrics of ancient Celtic poetry (developed in his *Philological Grammar*), particularly 'union' (rhyming the end word of a line with the middle word of the next line) and *cynghanedd* (the use of regular consonant patterns within a line). Thus: 'road/abode', 'east/least'; 'the sudden shine sent from the livid east scene,' etc. (Hynes 1961: 29).

    Silently I footed by an uphill road
  That led from my abode to a spot yew-boughed;
    Yellowly the sun sloped low down to westward,
      And dark was the east with cloud.

1–2. Winterborne-Came Church, where Barnes was vicar and where he was buried, was a few hundred yards from Max Gate.

> Then, amid the shadow of that livid sad east, 5
> Where the light was least, and a gate stood wide,
> Something flashed the fire of the sun that was facing it,
> > Like a brief blaze on that side.
>
> Looking hard and harder I knew what it meant –
> The sudden shine sent from the livid east scene; 10
> It meant the west mirrored by the coffin of my friend there,
> > Turning to the road from his green,
>
> To take his last journey forth – he who in his prime
> Trudged so many a time from that gate athwart the land!
> Thus a farewell to me he signalled on his grave-way, 15
> > As with a wave of his hand.
>
> Winterborne-Came Path.

96 The Figure in the Scene

One of a group of poems on memories of his courtship in Cornwall, including '"Why did I sketch"' and '"It never looks like summer"' (see *EL* 104). Hardy drew two sketches of Beeny Cliff which he related to the poem (*CPW* II, 199). He included it in his list of 'the best I have written' (*CL* VI, 96).

Metre: $a^4b^3a^5b^3c^2d^5c^2d^5c^2$ dr (but with some trisyllables, l. 17 almost anapaestic). Taylor suggests that 'the jagged wavery form' of the verse mimes 'the interaction of writing and rain' (1988: 180).

> It pleased her to step in front and sit
> Where the cragged slope was green,
> While I stood back that I might pencil it
> > With her amid the scene;
> > > Till it gloomed and rained; 5

5. *amid*] below   Editions before *CP* 1923.
5. *livid sad east*: cf. '"Nothing Matters Much"' (149), l. 14.
7. *Something flashed the fire*] Flashed a reflection MS, *MV* 1917; Flashed back the fire *MV* 1919, *CP* 1919, WE.
11. *west*] sun *MV* 1917.
11. *mirrored*: Paulin points out that sheens and reflecting surfaces are common effects in Barnes's poetry (1975: 187–8). Cf. also the final mirror of 'Moments of Vision' (77).

>   But I kept on, despite the drifting wet
>   That fell and stained
> My draught, leaving for curious quizzings yet
>   The blots engrained.
>
>   And thus I drew here there alone,   10
>   Seated amid the gauze
> Of moisture, hooded, only her outline shown,
>   With rainfall marked across.
>   – Soon passed our stay;
> Yet her rainy form is the Genius still of the spot,   15
>   Immutable, yea,
> Though the place now knows her no more, and has known
>   her not
>   Ever since that day.
>
> *From an old note.*

97 Overlooking the River Stour

One of a group of three poems which Hardy wrote in 1916 after revisiting Riverside Villa at Sturminster Newton, where he and his first wife had spent their 'happiest days' in 1876–8 (*EL* 147, *LY* 172). Hardy also associated the area with William Barnes, whose love for 'the slow green river Stour' he records:

> Its multitudinous patches of water-lilies yellow and white, its pollard willows, its heavy-headed bullrushes, are for ever haunting him; and such is the loving fidelity with which the stream is depicted, that one might almost construct a bird's-eye view of its upper course by joining together the vignettes which are given of this and that point in its length. (*PW* 95–6)

Metre: $A^4B^3b^3a^4A^4B^3$ dr with variations, with the final repeated couplet in stanza four modulating via 'O' from statement to lament. Paulin comments that 'each stanza rhymes in what seems to be a modification of a triolet and in so doing describes a monotonous arc like the swallows'. He

6–9. as Paulin points out, rain-streaked drawings also feature in 'Beyond the Last Lamp' and 'The Abbey-Mason', suggesting the interaction of art, nature, and time (1975: 116).
8. *draught*: draft, drawing.
13. *rainfall*] rain-lines *MV* 1917 (emphasizing the graphic nature of what is described).
15. *Genius still of the spot*: the 'genius loci' or the tutelary spirit of a place.
15–18. cf. the conclusion of 'Beeny Cliff' (65).
Title] MS adds date: 1877.

links this effect to the poem's meditation on a hermetic gaze which reflects the scene before it perfectly, but excludes the emotional life behind the viewer's back (1975: 170).

> The swallows flew in the curves of an eight
>   Above the river-gleam
>   In the wet June's last beam:
> Like little crossbows animate
> The swallows flew in the curves of an eight   5
>   Above the river-gleam.
>
> Planing up shavings of crystal spray
>   A moor-hen darted out
>   From the bank therebout,
> And through the stream-shine ripped his way;   10
> Planing up shavings of crystal spray
>   A moor-hen darted out.
>
> Closed were the kingcups; and the mead
>   Dripped in monotonous green,
>   Though the day's morning sheen   15
> Had shown it golden and honeybee'd;
> Closed were the kingcups; and the mead
>   Dripped in monotonous green.
>
> And never I turned my head, alack,
>   While these things met my gaze   20
>   Through the pane's drop-drenched glaze,
> To see the more behind my back. . . .
> O never I turned, but let, alack,
>   These less things hold my gaze!

1–3. cf. Barnes's description of the Stour in 'Naighbour Playmeätes':
>   An' swifts did skim the water bright
>   Wi' whirlèn froth, in western light. . . .

7, 11. of crystal] made of MS, *MV* 1917.
7. the mechanical nature of this image (and that of l. 4), in contrast to the more organic imagery of stanza 3, has often been remarked upon (see Davie 1973: 23; Paulin 1975: 171).
22. more: part-rhymes with 'Stour' (i.e. the scene in *front* of the speaker).
19–24. cf. the conclusion of 'The Self-Unseeing' (23): 'Yet we were looking away!'. Other poems including 'The Esplanade' are also structured on an inability to look 'behind'; but later in *Moments of Vision*, in 'The Shadow on the Stone' (106), the refusal to turn and look becomes a positive act.

98 The Musical Box

The second of the poems relating to the Sturminster Newton idyll, and one of Hardy's many clock-and-time meditations: see 'Copying Architecture in an Old Minster' (83).

Metre: a²b⁴c⁴b⁴c⁴a² dtr, with the longer lines more trisyllabic. The metrical effects are designed to imitate the mechanical sounds of a musical box. Taylor suggests that 'the stanza form is like the obsolete form of the experience which time only later developed, like a delayed photographic "development" in the speaker's mind of what once was' (1988: 135).

        Lifelong to be
Seemed the fair colour of the time;
That there was standing shadowed near
A spirit who sang to the gentle chime
Of the self-struck notes, I did not hear,   5
        I did not see.

        Thus did it sing
To the mindless lyre that played indoors
As she came to listen to me without:
'O value what the nonce outpours –   10
This best of life – that shines about
        Your welcoming!'

        I had slowed along
After the torrid hours were done,
Though still the posts and walls and road   15
Flung back their sense of the hot-faced sun,
And had walked by Stourside Mill, where broad
        Stream-lilies throng.

        And I descried
The dusky house that stood apart,   20
And her, white-muslined, waiting there
In the porch with high-expectant heart,
While still the thin mechanic air
        Went on inside.

        At whiles would flit   25
Swart bats, whose wings, be-webbed and tanned,

10. *nonce*: occasion.
17–18. cf. the mill-side scene of Barnes's 'Naighbour Playmeätes', and his water-lily poem 'The Clote'.
26. *swart*: dark.

    Whirred like the wheels of ancient clocks:
    She laughed a hailing as she scanned
    Me in the gloom, the tuneful box
        Intoning it.   30

        Lifelong to be
    I thought it. That there watched hard by
    A spirit who sang to the indoor tune,
    'O make the most of what is nigh!'
    I did not hear in my dull soul-swoon –   35
        I did not see.

99 Old Furniture

Hardy wrote a number of poems on the 'radiation' of memory from old possessions, stones, etc. (see Paulin 1975: 121–45, 207). Here, as in 'Song to an Old Burden', it is also the music of the dead which is evoked.
    Metre: $a^4b^4a^4b^4b^2$ dr with variations, perhaps modelled on Swinburne's 'Félise' or a hymn stanza. Taylor argues that the stanza is a development of Sapphics (1988: 163, 260). 'At Castle Boterel' (66) is comparable in metre.

    I know not how it may be with others
        Who sit amid relics of householdry
    That date from the days of their mothers' mothers,
        But well I know how it is with me
             Continually.   5

    I see the hands of the generations
        That owned each shiny familiar thing
    In play on its knobs and indentations,
        And with its ancient fashioning
            Still dallying: 10

    Hands behind hands, growing paler and paler,
        As in a mirror a candle-flame
    Shows images of itself, each frailer
        As it recedes, though the eye may frame
            Its shape the same.   15

27. wheels] fly MS, *MV* 1917.
6–10. in *Far from the Madding Crowd*, p. 56, Hardy quotes Barnes's 'Woak Hill': 'my goods all a-sheenèn / Wi'long years o'handlèn'.
12–15. cf. the 'long perspective' and receding images in the mirror of 'The Pedigree' (91), l. 16.

On the clock's dull dial a foggy finger,
    Moving to set the minutes right
With tentative touches that lift and linger
      In the wont of a moth on a summer night,
        Creeps to my sight.   20

On this old viol, too, fingers are dancing –
    As whilom – just over the strings by the nut,
The tip of a bow receding, advancing
      In airy quivers, as if it would cut
        The plaintive gut.   25

And I see a face by that box for tinder,
    Glowing forth in fits from the dark,
And fading again, as the linten cinder
      Kindles to red at the flinty spark,
        Or goes out stark.   30

Well, well. It is best to be up and doing,
    The world has no use for one to-day
Who eyes things thus – no aim pursuing!
      He should not continue in his stay.
        But sink away.   35

---

20. *to*] on MS, *MV* 1917.
21. *viol*: violin.
22. *as whilom*] My father's MS (cf. 'To My Father's Violin').
22. *as whilom*: as formerly (cf. Dryden's 'MacFlecknoe', l. 35: 'My warbling lute, the lute I whilom strung').
22. *nut*: violin bridge.
26–30. MS has an different stanza at this point:
        From each curled eff-hole the ghosts of ditties
          Incanted there by his skill in his prime
        Quaver in whispers the pangs and pities
          They once could language, and in their time
            Would daily chime.
28. *linten*: made of soft linen (the 'tinder' which caught the spark to light a fire was often lint impregnated with saltpetre).
31. *well, well*: see 'He Never Expected Much' (168), l. 1n.
34–35. cf. the 'sinking' of 'The Going' (51), ll. 38–39.
34. *not continue*: cease continuing MS del. The word 'continue' carries much weight for Hardy: cf. 'continuator', 'Wessex Heights' (47), l. 15.

100 The Five Students

The first of three successive poems, all metrically complex, in which Hardy meditates on the course of his life ('The Change' (89), earlier in the volume, is comparable). Taylor comments, 'the three major journey poems of *Moments of Vision*, "The Five Students", "The Wind's Prophecy", and "During Wind and Rain", are placed together forming a triptych at the centre of the volume' (1981: 36). The passing of time is here subsumed within a seasonal cycle, ending in winter (cf. 'Afterwards' (112)).
Metre: $a^4b^3a^5b^3c^6c^2$ dr. Five separate line-types; the previous poem in *Moments of Vision*, 'The Ballet,' has the same rhyme-scheme and three line-types. The ballad-like incremental effect, with characters dropping out in turn, is like those in 'Looking Across' and 'Drinking Song' (171).

> The sparrow dips in his wheel-rut bath,
> The sun grows passionate-eyed,
> And boils the dew to smoke by the paddock-path;
> As strenuously we stride, –
> Five of us; dark He, fair He, dark She, fair She, I,   5
> All beating by.
>
> The air is shaken, the high-road hot,
> Shadowless swoons the day,
> The greens are sobered and cattle at rest; but not
> We on our urgent way, –   10
> Four of us; fair She, dark She, fair He, I, are there,
> But one – elsewhere.
>
> Autumn moulds the hard fruit mellow,
> And forward still we press
> Through moors, briar-meshed plantations, clay-pits yellow, 15
> As in the spring hours – yes,
> Three of us; fair He, fair She, I, as heretofore,
> But – fallen one more.
>
> The leaf drops: earthworms draw it in
> At night-time noiselessly,   20
> The fingers of birch and beech are skeleton-thin,
> And yet on the beat are we, –

3. cf. Barnes's 'Times o'Year' with its similar seasonal cycle: 'the zun, wi'eärly beams / Brighten'd streams, an' dried the dew'.
5. the identities of Hardy's friends are obscure: Pinion (1976: 143) suggests, in order, Horace Moule (d. 1873), Henry Moule (d. 1904), Helen Holder, Hardy's sister-in-law (d. 1900), Emma Hardy (d. 1912), though the former was the only person whom Hardy identified in the poem.
6. *beating*: tramping, as in Barnes's 'Waÿfeären': 'As I did beät the dowsty road'.
22. *beat*: habital round.

Two of us; fair She, I. But no more left to go
　　The track we know.
　　Icicles tag the chuch-aisle leads, 25
　　　The flag-rope gibbers hoarse,
The home-bound foot-folk wrap their snow-flaked heads,
　　Yet I still stalk the course –
One of us. . . . Dark and fair He, dark and fair She, gone:
　　　The rest – anon. 30

101 The Wind's Prophecy

The second poem in this short sequence is prospective: it looks forward to Hardy's marriage, where the other two look backwards from a point of loss. It describes Hardy's premonitions on his 1870 journey to Cornwall (in a later poem, 'A Man Was Drawing Near to Me', Hardy imagined the complementary situation: Emma's premonitions about his arrival). Hardy's cousin Typhena Sparks has been suggested (without real proof) as the city lover in the east contrasted with the as yet unseen one in the west. There are a number of manuscript revisions to the poem (see *CPW* II, 238).

Metre: abbaacdc^4 dr (unique), with a mockingly echoing internal rhyme within the d-lines. There is a general tendency to the adjective–noun combination, wedding landscape and subjective response, and each stanza is evenly divided between description and a dialogue between the narrator and the wind.

30] The rest – anon MS del.; Somewhither yon MS (the printed version leaves the emphasis on himself as survivor).
30. anon: to follow soon.
MS has two additional stanzas:
　　　　'And what do they say in that yon Pale Land
　　　　　Who trod the track with me,
　　　If there they dwell, and watch, and understand?
　　　　　They murmur, it may be,
　　　All of us – how we strode, as still does that lean thrall
　　　　　For nought at all!'

　　　　The Years may add: 'Peace; know ye not,
　　　　　Life's ashy track hence eyeing,
　　　That though gilt Vanity called your eyes somewhat,
　　　　　And ye were torn in trying,
　　　All of you, while you panted, saw aureola'd far
　　　　　Heaven's central star?'

I travel on by barren farms,
And gulls glint out like silver flecks
Against a cloud that speaks of wrecks,
And bellies down with black alarms.
I say: 'Thus from my lady's arms   5
I go; those arms I love the best!'
The wind replies from dip and rise,
'Nay; toward her arms thou journeyest.'

A distant verge morosely gray
Appears, while clots of flying foam   10
Break from its muddy monochrome,
And a light blinks up far away.
I sigh: 'My eyes now as all day
Behold her ebon loops of hair!'
Like bursting bonds the wind responds,   15
'Nay, wait for tresses flashing fair!'

From tides the lofty coastlands screen
Come smitings like the slam of doors,
Or hammerings on hollow floors,
As the swell cleaves through caves unseen.   20
Say I: 'Though broad this wild terrene,
Her city home is matched of none!'
From the hoarse skies the wind replies:
'Thou shouldst have said her sea-bord one.'

The all-prevailing clouds exclude   25
The one quick timorous transient star;
The waves outside where breakers are
Huzza like a mad multitude.
'Where the sun ups it, mist-imbued,'
I cry, 'there reigns the star for me!'   30
The wind outshrieks from points and peaks:
'Here, westward, where it downs, mean ye!'

Yonder the headland, vulturine,
Snores like old Skrymer in his sleep,

9–11. Hardy's familiar 'neutral tones' – Davie (1973: 19) suggests that the colours are those of the daguerrotype, an early form of photography.
17–20. nature is depicted here as a factory or industrial hammer. Davie argues that Hardy emphasizes the mechanical forces separating him and his lover, in order to assuage his guilt (see Davie 1973: 19; Paulin 1975: 75).
21. terrene: terrain.
28. Huzza: cry (also used of the waves in 'The Voice of Things' (78)).
34. old Skrymer: giant in Norse mythology. MS and *MV* 1917 have 'a giant'.

>And every chasm and every steep 35
>Blackens as wakes each pharos-shine.
>'I roam, but one is safely mine,'
>I say. 'God grant she stay my own!'
>Low laughs the wind as if it grinned:
>'Thy Love is one thou'st not yet known.' 40
>
>*Rewritten from an old copy.*

102 During Wind and Rain

Hardy described this poem as one of his best (*CL* VI, 96), a verdict which many have confirmed: Harold Bloom calls it 'as good a poem as our century has given us', Tom Paulin 'one of the best poems this century', Thom Gunn the poem in which 'the strengths and potentials of the ballad are more completely realized than in perhaps anything else he wrote', while Dennis Taylor sees it as the climax of a series of meditative lyrics (Bloom 1975: 20; Paulin 1975: 205–10; Gunn 1973: 28; Taylor 1981: 30–8). Details of the series of isolated scenes in the poem are derived from Emma Hardy's memories of family life in Plymouth, recorded in *Some Recollections*.

Metre: $a^3b^3c^3b^2c^3d^3a^4$ dr, with variations (but see Richardson 1977: 88 and Paulin 1982 for readings which emphasize spondaic final lines in each stanza). There is a ballad-like refrain on l. 6, and the 'framing' lines beginning and ending each stanza are reinforced by alliteration, assonance, and a tremendous metrical turbulence akin to the '*weather* and *ghost* music' which Hardy heard in Wagner (*EL* 137), and similar to that in 'The Change' (89).

36. *pharos*] lighthouse MS.
Title. cf. 'Nature's Questioning' ll. 26–8. The song which ends Shakespeare's *Twelfth Night* is usually cited as the source:
>With hey, ho, the wind and the rain,
>For the rain it raineth every day.

But perhaps a more apposite allusion would be to Vaughan's description of the grave in 'Burial' (marked in Hardy's copy in DCM):
>And scarce a room but wind, and rain
>   Beat through, and stain
>The seats, and cells within.

Another possible influence is Elizabeth Barrett Browning's 'Isobel's Child', with its variations on a refrain of 'The thunder tears through the wind and the rain, / As full on the lattice drives the rain.' Flickers of the same phrase are contained in a reference to Wordsworth in 1881 (*EL* 190) and a conversation with Grieg (*EL* 237).

> They sing their dearest songs –
> He, she, all of them – yea,
> Treble and tenor and bass,
>   And one to play;
> With the candles mooning each face.... 5
>   Ah, no; the years O!
> How the sick leaves reel down in throngs!
>
> They clear the creeping moss –
> Elders and juniors – aye,
> Making the pathways neat 10
>   And the garden gay;
> And they build a shady seat....
>   Ah, no; the years, the years;
> See, the white storm-birds wing across!
>
> They are blithely breakfasting all – 15
> Men and maidens – yea,
> Under the summer tree,
>   With a glimpse of the bay,
> While pet fowl come to the knee....
>   Ah, no; the years O! 20
> And the rotten rose is ript from the wall.

1–4. cf. *SR* 14: 'My father played the violin and my mother could play beautifully on the piano and sing like a professional.... They taught us to sing harmony and our four voices went well together'.
5. images of candles and faces or hands in mirrors are often used by Hardy: cf. 'Old Furniture' (99).
6. cf. the refrain of 'The Change' (89); and Horace, Odes 2:14, 'Eheu fugaces, Postume, Postume' ('Alas the swift years, Postumus, Postumûs').
7. wind-blown leaves are a traditional image for the passing of time and the souls of the dead, as in Shelley's 'Ode to the West Wind', ll. 2–5, where the leaves are 'pestilence-stricken multitudes' (Bloom 1982: 95–107 gives a history of the trope from its Homeric source).
7. sick leaves reel] sickened leaves drop MS del.
8–21. details of the garden from *SR* 5.
10. Making] shaping MS del.
13, 27, the years, the years] the years O! MS, *MV* 1917. As in 'The Change', Hardy introduced more 'cunning irregularity' into the poem by varying the refrain.
14. white] webbed white Editions before *CP* 1923.
19. fowl] birds MS, *MV* 1917.
21] And the wind-whipt creeper lets go the wall. MS.

> They change to a high new house,
> He, she, all of them – aye,
> Clocks and carpets and chairs
>   On the lawn all day, 25
> And brightest things that are theirs. ....
>   Ah, no; the years, the years;
> Down their carved names the rain-drop ploughs.

103 A Backward Spring

The implication of the seasonal cycle in mourning is present in a number of the poems in *Moments of Vision*: cf. 'Joys of Memory', '"It never looks like summer"', and even Hardy's auto-elegy 'Afterwards' (112). The trope is traditional: cf. Milton, *Paradise Lost*, III, 40–50; and Shelley, *Adonais*, 18: 'Ah, woe is me! Winter is come and gone, / But grief returns with the revolving year ...'

Metre: irregular, $a^4b^2a^4b^3c^4d^3$ $a^4b^4c^4d^3d^3c^4d^4e^4e^4$ dtr, with cd of the first stanzas rhyming with ab of the second.

> The trees are afraid to put forth buds,
> And there is timidity in the grass;
> The plots lie gray where gouged by spuds,
>   And whether next week will pass
> Free of sly sour winds is the fret of each bush 5
>   Of barberry waiting to bloom.

22. high new house: parallels Emma's description of the Gifford family's move to Bedford Terrace, *SR* 30–2.
24–5. chairs / On the lawn: a phrase also used in one of the 'Poems of 1912–13', 'Lament' (57).
28. carved] chiselled Editions before *CP* 1923. Hardy wrote 'On their chiselled names the lichen grows' (MS) before finding this striking image for the passing of time. Paulin (1975: 208–9) suggests that it is derived from Emma's description of the water-purifier at her family's house in Plymouth, with 'a huge stone basin, "a dripstone", and under which a bucket received the water drop by drop purified – a monster drop long a-coming, and long delaying its fall' (*SR* 67–8). Cf. also Tennyson's meditation on Horace's monumental images (and on Job 14:19) in 'Epilogue', ll. 57–60:   for Homer's fame,
>   Tho' carved in harder stone –
>   The falling drop will make his name
>   As mortal as my own.

1. cf. Meredith's 'Tardy Spring': 'The bitten buds dared not unfold'.
3. gouged] broken MS, *MV* 1917.
3. spuds: potatoes.
6. barberry: a thorny shrub.

Yet the snowdrop's face betrays no gloom,
And the primrose pants in its heedless push,
Though the myrtle asks if it's worth the fight
    This year with frost and rime   10
    To venture one more time
On delicate leaves and buttons of white
From the selfsame bough as at last year's prime,
And never to ruminate on or remember
What happened to it in mid-December.   15
    April 1917.

104 He Revisits His First School

One of a group of introspective poems in *Moments of Vision*: the volume as a whole tends to alternate such groups with less subjective poems. Hardy's account of this visit to the school at Lower Bockhampton which he attended in 1848 might be compared with W.B. Yeats's 'Among Schoolchildren'.
Metre: $a^3b^3b^3a^3c^2c^2c^2$ tr.

I should not have shown in the flesh,
I ought to have gone as a ghost;
It was awkward, unseemly almost,
Standing solidly there as when fresh,
    Pink, tiny, crisp-curled,   5
    My pinions yet furled
    From the winds of the world.

After waiting so many a year
To wait longer, and go as a sprite
From the tomb at the mid of some night   10
Was the right, radiant way to appear;
    Not as one wanzing weak
    From life's roar and reek,
    His rest still to seek:

12. *buttons*] buds MS, *MV* 1917.
13. *selfsame bough*: cf. the renewal of life in 'The Selfsame Song' (117).
6. *pinions*: wings.
12. *wanzing*: wasting (MS has the antithesis, 'growing').

>   Yea, beglimpsed through the quaint quarried glass   15
>   Of green moonlight, by me greener made,
>   When they'd cry, perhaps, 'There sits his shade
>   In his olden haunt – just as he was
>   When in Walkingame he
>   Conned the grand Rule-of-Three   20
>   With the bent of a bee.'
>
> But to show in the afternoon sun,
> With an aspect of hollow-eyed care,
> When none wished to see me come there,
> Was a garish thing, better undone.   25
>   Yes; wrong was the way;
>   But yet, let me say,
>   I may right it – some day.

105 'I thought, my Heart'

A poem of heart-scanning which matches 'His Heart' (92) in its literalization of romantic images associated with the heart.

Metre: $a^4 b^4 a^4 b^3 c^4 c^4 d^2 d^2 e^2 e^2 e^2$ dr (with variations).

>   I thought, my Heart, that you had healed
>   Of those sore smartings of the past,
>   And that the summers had overlooked
>   All mark of them at last.
>   But closely scanning in the night   5
>   I saw them standing crimson-bright
>   Just as she made them:
>   Nothing could fade them;
>   Yea, I can swear
>   That there they were –   10
>   They still were there!
>
>   Then the Vision of her who cut them came,
>   And looking over my shoulder said,
>   'I am sure you deal me all the blame
>   For those sharp smarts and red;   15
>   But meet me, dearest, to-morrow night,

---

15. *quarried glass*: diamond-shaped panes.
19. *Walkingame*: Francis Walkingame's *The Tutor's Assistant* was a standard arithmetic textbook.
20. *conned*: studied.
20. *Rule-of-Three*: 'a method for finding the fourth term of a proportion when three terms are given' (Bailey 1970: 403).

> In the churchyard at the moon's half-height,
>   And so strange a kiss
>   Shall be mine, I wis,
>   That you'll cease to know
>   If the wounds you show
>   Be there or no!'

106 The Shadow on the Stone

A poem on Emma's ghost, 'carried across' from a 1913 draft to a 1916 revision which itself ensures the 'dream' will not fade. It recalls the story of Orpheus, who enters the underworld in search of his dead lover Eurydice. His music charms the gods, and he is allowed to return with her to the world on condition that he does not turn and look at her. Just before reaching the air, he glances at her, and she is plucked back to the shades. Other poetical antecedents include Ovid, *Heroides* X, 9–14, Milton's Sonnet 19, and *In Memoriam* 13.

Metre: $a^3a^4b^4a^4c^4c^4d^4c^4$ dtr (octave comprised two aaba quatrains, the latter the rhyme-scheme of FitzGerald's *Rubáiyát*). Paulin comments that 'the poem's softly hesitant speech rhythms, its intimate, musing quality, suggest that he is conducting a conversation' (1975: 59).

> I went by the Druid stone
>   That broods in the garden white and lone,

19. *I wis*: to be sure.
23] a third verse was published in Ruth Head's *Pages from the Works of Thomas Hardy* (London, 1922), p. 171:
> That kiss so strange, so stark, I'll take
> When the world sleeps sound, and no noise will scare,
> And a moon-touch whitens each stone and stake:
>   Yes; I will meet her there –
> Just at the time she calls '*to-morrow*'
> But I call '*after the shut of sorrow*', –
>   And with her dwell –
>   Her parallel
>   In cease of pain,
>   And frost and rain,
>   And life's inane.

There are further small changes in a version of the Head text inserted in his copy of WE (*CPW* II, 260, 502).

1. *Druid stone*: a large stone which Hardy had erected at Max Gate in 1891 after it was found buried in the garden: 'Round the stone, which had been lying flat, they found a quantity of ashes and half charred bones' (*EL* 306). Hardy may have associated the stone with Emma because she was said to have burned his love-letters to her there.
2. *broods*] stands MS, *MV* 1917.

    And I stopped and looked at the shifting shadows
      That at some moments fall thereon
    From the tree hard by with a rhythmic swing,   5
      And they shaped in my imagining
    To the shade that a well-known head and shoulders
      Threw there when she was gardening.

      I thought her behind my back,
      Yea, her I long had learned to lack,   10
    And I said: 'I am sure you are standing behind me,
      Though how do you get into this old track?'
    And there was no sound but the fall of a leaf
      As a sad response; and to keep down grief
    I would not turn my head to discover   15
      That there was nothing in my belief.

      Yet I wanted to look and see
    That nobody stood at the back of me;
    But I thought once more: 'Nay, I'll not unvision
      A shape which, somehow, there may be.'   20
    So I went on softly from the glade,
      And left her behind me throwing her shade,
    As she were indeed an apparition –
      My head unturned lest my dream should fade.

    Begun 1913: *finished* 1916.

107 'For Life I had never cared greatly'

The final poem in the main sequence of *Moments of Vision*. It can be compared to other late poems of minimal expectation, and often of a reluctantly visionary nature, e.g. 'Childhood Among the Ferns' (161) and 'He Never Expected Much' (168).

    Metre: $a^3b^2c^2c^3a^5b^2$ tdr (cf. 'The Souls of the Slain' (13)).

4. fall thereon] there are thrown   Editions before *CP* 1923.
7–8. Cf. the impressions on stones in 'Beeny Cliff' (65) and 'The Whitewashed Wall' (128).
19. unvision: the verb 'vision' is used in 'Looking at a Picture on an Anniversary', five poems later in *MV* (the end of such 'visions' is described in 'Her Haunting-Ground'). On un-compounds, see Elliott 1984: 191–6.
24. cf. the quotation from Emerson which Hardy copied into his notebooks, *c.* 1882: 'I conceive a man as always spoken to from behind, & unable to turn his head & see the speaker' (Björk entry 1275).

For Life I had never cared greatly,
    As worth a man's while;
      Peradventures unsought,
   Peradventures that finished in nought,
Had kept me from youth and through manhood till lately   5
        Unwon by its style.

In earliest years – why I know not –
    I viewed it askance;
      Conditions of doubt,
   Conditions that leaked slowly out,   10
May haply have bent me to stand and to show not
        Much zest for its dance.

With symphonies soft and sweet colour
    It courted me then,
      Till evasions seemed wrong,   15
   Till evasions gave in to its song,
And I warmed, until living aloofly loomed duller
        Than life among men.

Anew I found nought to set eyes on,
    When, lifting its hand,   20
      It uncloaked a star,
   Uncloaked it from fog-damps afar,
And showed its beams burning from pole to horizon
        As bright as a brand.

And so, the rough highway forgetting,   25
    I pace hill and dale
      Regarding the sky,
   Regarding the vision on high,
And thus re-illumed have no humour for letting
        My pilgrimage fail.   30

---

3. Peradventures] Adventures MS ('Peradventures' are chance happenings).
11. haply: by chance.
21. uncloaked a star: cf. de Stancy's advice in *A Laodicean* I, 5: 'nobody is so unfortunate as not to have a lucky star in some direction or other . . . All I say is, discover your lucky star . . .' (the speech is borrowed from Balthasar Gracian's maxims: see Björk entry 904). Hardy may also have had in mind Swinburne's 'save his own soul he hath no star' (quoted *LY* 137), which echoes in turn Coleridge's 'Dejection: An Ode', ll. 53–4; but Hardy's revelation is passive, in contrast to the self-born energies of the Romantics.

108 The Pity of It

The sixth of the 'Poems of War and Patriotism', a group of poems on the First World War placed near the end of *Moments of Vision*. Hardy was horrified by the war: 'the contemplation of it led him to despair of the world's history thenceforward' (*LY* 162). He agreed to join a committee of men of letters 'for the organization of public statements of the strength of the British case and principles' (*LY* 163), and wrote some morale-boosting poems, but later refused to sign a manifesto entitled 'What We Are Fighting For?' drafted by Arnold Bennett.

'The Pity of It' was prompted by 'a contemporary article by Dr Caleb Williams Saleeby on "Eugenics"' (Purdy 1954: 189); Hardy sent Saleeby a manuscript. It was first published in *Fortnightly Review*, April 1915 (reprinted by Florence Hardy and in the *Dorset Year-book*, 1917), to a hostile response. Hardy intended to defend himself in the *Life*, and wrote a note (never inserted):

> Fussy Jingoes, who were hoping for knighthoods, attacked H for his assumption & asserted that we had no sort of blood relationship with Germany: But the Germans themselves, with far more commonsense, translated the poem, & approved of it, & remarked that when relations did fall out they fought more bitterly than any. (*PN* 291)

Metre: Petrarchan sonnet with Wordsworthian sestet, abba abba cdc ddc[5] dr (Wordsworth's political sonnets provide a model for this use of the form).

> I walked in loamy Wessex lanes, afar
> From rail-track and from highway, and I heard
> In field and farmstead many an ancient word
> Of local lineage like 'Thu bist,' 'Er war,'
>
> 'Ich woll,' 'Er sholl,' and by-talk similar,　　　　5
> Nigh as they speak who in this month's moon gird

Title. *Othello* IV, i, 192, 'But yet the pity of it, Iago!'
1–5. Hardy comments on similarities between archaic Dorset usages and German in *The Woodlanders*, ch. 17 and in a letter to Edmund Gosse on 26 October 1888: '"Ich". This & kindred words – e.g. – "Ich woll", "er woll", "er war", &c. are still used by old people in N.W. Dorset & Somerset. ... but it is dying rapidly' (*CL* I, 181).
2. rail-track: Hardy blamed the railways, above all other causes, for the death of local customs, and the assimilation of the rural to the cosmopolitan.
4. 'Thu bist', 'Er war': 'you are', 'he was'.
5. 'Ich woll', 'Er sholl': I will, you shall. On such dialect survivals of the Old English, see Elliott 1984: 92ff.
5. by-talk] small talk (del.) Saleeby MS.
6. Nigh] Even MS, *Fortnightly*, *MV* 1917, *CP* 1919.

At England's very loins, thereunto spurred
By gangs whose glory threats and slaughters are.

Then seemed a Heart crying: 'Whosoever they be
At root and bottom of this, who flung this flame   10
Between kin folk kin tongued even as are we,

'Sinister, ugly, lurid, be their fame;
May their familiars grow to shun their name,
And their brood perish everlastingly.'

April 1915.

109 In Time of 'The Breaking of Nations'

Published in the *Saturday Review*, 29 January 1916, with copyright not reserved (to encourage reprinting); subsequently reprinted in a 1917 pamphlet by Clement Shorter, and included in *Selected Poems* (1916). In his autobiography Hardy relates the poem to a memory of the Franco-Prussian war in 1870:

> On the day that the bloody battle of Gravelotte was fought they were reading Tennyson in the grounds of the rectory [at St Juniot]. It was at this time and spot that Hardy was struck by the incident of the old horse harrowing the arable field in the valley below, which, when in far later years it was recalled to him by a still bloodier war, he made into the little poem of three verses entitled 'In Time of "The Breaking of Nations"'. (*EL* 104)

Dennis Taylor suggests the context is larger, including the memories of Cornwall and his courtship which Hardy describes earlier in the same passage as 'smouldering in his mind for between forty and fifty years' before he wrote *The Famous Tragedy of the Queen of Cornwall* (*EL* 103; Taylor 1981: 89–93; cf. 'Prologue' (181)). The poem thus forms a paradigm for what Taylor calls 'Hardy's Apocalypse'.

9. *Whosoever they be*: In a letter to Florence Henniker accompanying the poem, Hardy suggested that the German people had been inflamed by 'oligarchs & munition-makers whose interest is war' (*CL* V, 86).
11. *kin folk*: the idea that England and Germany were both racially 'Anglo-Saxon' was a nineteenth-century commonplace (see MacDougall 1982: 89–124). Similar ideas are used in another poem in the group, 'England to Germany in 1914'.
14. *brood*] breed   All texts but *CP* (a more perpetual curse).
Title. Jeremiah 51: 20 (Hardy's note): 'Thou art my battle axe and weapons of war: for with thee will I break in pieces the nations, and with thee will I destroy kingdoms.'

Metre: $a^3b^2a^3b^2$ mainly tr, a folk-measure which Hardy could have derived from Burns and others. A number of subsequent poems are in variations of this metre: cf. 'The Bird-Catcher's Boy' (151). (For others, and other possible models, see Taylor 1988: 222.)

I

Only a man harrowing clods
   In a slow silent walk
With an old horse that stumbles and nods
   Half asleep as they stalk.

II

Only thin smoke without flame   5
   From the heaps of couch-grass;
Yet this will go onward the same
   Though Dynasties pass.

III

Yonder a maid and her wight
   Come whispering by: 10
War's annals will cloud into night
   Ere their story die.

      1915.

1. harrowing: there are overtones of God's harrowing of Babylon in Jeremiah 51, and the harvest of souls in Matthew 13: 30, Revelation 14: 25.
5–6. couch grass is a weed burnt off in autumn: see 'The Later Autumn' (136) and *Desperate Remedies* 10: 2 (p. 188), where Hardy notes that the 'volcano-like smoke' of couch grass can suddenly burst into flames, and describes such a fire. The parable of the separation of the wheat and the tares (weeds) in Matthew 13: 24–30 may also be relevant.
7–8. cf. the passage from Charles Reade which Hardy copied into his notebooks *c*. 1882: 'The chronic history of Waterloo field is to be ploughed & sowed & reaped & mowed: yet once in a way these acts of husbandry were diversified with a great battle, where hosts decided the fate of Empires. After that agriculture resumed its sullen sway' (Björk entry 1283).
9. wight: man (the usage is deliberately archaic).
11. annals: strictly, an annal documents a year (in contrast to the timelessness of 'story'). Cf. a passage from John Morley's *Voltaire* in Hardy's notebooks: 'We may say that three kinds of historian write history: the gazetteer or annalist, the statesman, and the philosopher' (Björk entry 1613).
11. cloud] fade MS, *Saturday Review*, SP 1916.

110 A New Year's Eve in War Time

Published in *The Sphere*, 6 January 1917, and privately printed by Florence Hardy in February 1917. One of a series of Christmas and New Year poems which Hardy wrote, including 'The Darkling Thrush' (21), 'End of the Year 1912', 'The Oxen' (93), 'Christmas: 1924', 'Christmastide', and the similarly sinister 'A Nightmare and the Next Thing' (see Pinion 1990: 307–33).

Metre: complex and highly symmetrical, $a^2b^2c^2d^2e^2$ tdr, with each stanza repeating the same rhymes, the first and last stanzas having an extra tetrameter e-line.

I

Phantasmal fears,
And the flap of the flame,
And the throb of the clock,
And a loosened slate,
And the blind night's drone,   5
Which tiredly the spectral pines intone!

II

And the blood in my ears
Strumming always the same,
And the gable-cock
With its fitful grate,   10
And myself, alone.

III

The twelfth hour nears
Hand-hid, as in shame;
I undo the lock,
And listen, and wait   15
For the Young Unknown.

IV

In the dark there careers –
As if Death astride came
To numb all with his knock –

9. *gable-cock*: weather-cock.
11. *myself*] ourselves *Sphere* (cf. l. 23).
13. *hand-hid*: i.e. at midnight the minute hand of the clock covers the hour hand.
14–16. Hardy describes the old custom of opening the door to 'let in' the new year (the 'Young Unknown').
17–21. cf. Revelation 6: 8: 'And I looked, and behold a pale horse: and his name that sat on him was death, and Hell followed with him. And power was given unto them over the fourth part of the earth, to kill with sword, and with hunger, and with death, and with the beasts of the earth.'

   A horse at mad rate   20
   Over rut and stone.

      V

   No figure appears,
   No call of my name,
   No sound but 'Tic-toc'
   Without check. Past the gate 25
   It clatters – is gone.

      VI

   What rider it bears
   There is none to proclaim;
   And the Old Year has struck,
   And, scarce animate,   30
   The New makes moan.

      VII

   Maybe that 'More Tears! –
   More Famine and Flame –
   More Severance and Shock!'
   Is the order from Fate   35
   That the Rider speeds on
To pale Europe; and tiredly the pines intone.

 1915–1916

20–1. After the poem appeared Hardy was sent a copy of Blake's print 'Pity' by S.C. Cockrell, and replied 'The incident of the horse galloping past precisely at the stroke of midnight between the old & the new year is, by the way, true; it happened here, & we never learnt what horse it was. It is strange that you should have lighted on the Blake picture which in some respects almost matches the verses' (*CL* V, 199). Cf. also the 'trotting does' of 'Signs and Tokens', l. 27, and the conclusion of 'A Nightmare, and the Next Thing' (164).
21] *Sphere* has an extra line: While tiredly the spectral pines intone.
23. my] our *Sphere* (cf. l. 11).
24. Tic-toc: cf. the clock-sounds of 'Copying Architecture in an Old Minster' (83), ll. 3, 5.
Date] 1916 MS; January 1917 *Sphere*.

111 'I looked up from my writing'

The last and most personal of the 'Poems of War and Patriotism', comparable to many other end-pieces or beginning-pieces in its stress on Hardy as a ghost-like survivor.
Metre: a³b³a³b³ dr (a common hymn-form).

    I looked up from my writing,
        And gave a start to see,
    As if rapt in my inditing,
        The moon's full gaze on me.

    Her meditative misty head   5
        Was spectral in its air,
    And I involuntarily said,
        'What are you doing there?'

    'Oh, I've been scanning pond and hole
        And waterway hereabout   10
    For the body of one with a sunken soul
        Who has put his life-light out.

    'Did you hear his frenzied tattle?
        It was sorrow for his son
    Who is slain in brutish battle,   15
        Though he has injured none.

    'And now I am curious to look
        Into the blinkered mind
    Of one who wants to write a book
        In a world of such a kind.'   20

    Her temper overwrought me,
        And I edged to shun her view,
    For I felt assured she thought me
        One who should drown him too.

1–4. cf. the 'inditing' gaze of the moon in 'Shut Out That Moon', and 'To the Moon'. Hardy's moon symbolism is discussed by Stallworthy (1980).
3. inditing: composing (but can also mean to dictate, enjoin).
9–16. cf. the 'killing' light in 'The New Dawn's Business' (154), ll. 8–14.
18. blinkered: cf. 'He Resolves to Say No More' (178), l. 17.

112 Afterwards

The final poem of the volume, 'Afterwards' was read at a memorial service for Hardy shortly after his death, and by W.H. Auden at the end of his inaugural address as Professor of Poetry at Oxford in 1956, in which he called it 'a rite of homage to sacred objects which are neither gods nor objects of desire' (Auden 1960: 436). As Timothy Hands points out (1989: 139), Hardy draws on the vocabulary of the funeral lesson in the *Book of Common Prayer* to create his own epitaph: 'Behold, I show you a Mystery, we shall not all sleep, but shall all be changed, in a moment, in the twinkling of an eye' (1 Corinthians 15). One could even see a sardonic response to that lesson's distinguishing between the 'flesh of beasts', 'birds', 'men', and 'celestial bodies' in Hardy's stress on animal creation.

Richardson (1977: 33–4) compares the poem's emphasis on curiosity with that of the poet in Browning's 'How It Strikes a Contemporary':

> He took such cognizance of men and things,
> If any beat a horse you felt he saw;
> If any cursed a woman, he took note. . . .

There are a number of parallels between the poem's imagination of Hardy's death and the conjectures about what 'some hoary-headed swain may say' in the last nine stanzas of Gray's 'Elegy Written in a Country Churchyard' (see Thatcher 1970). Taylor (1986: 442) suggests that it also draws on Wordsworth's 'A Poet's Epitaph', and notes that the poem involves a seasonal progression, beginning with a May day and moving through dusk to a winter night (1981: 147–8). It thus uses the vegetative cycle of the pastoral elegy.

Metre: $a^6b^5a^6b^5$ dtr, with the b-rhyme of the first stanza returning in the final stanza. The fourth line of each stanza tends to the iambic pentameter throb of the elegiac stanza.

> When the Present has latched its postern behind my
>   tremulous stay,
>   And the May month flaps its glad green leaves like wings,
> Delicate-filmed as new-spun silk, will the neighbours say,
>   'He was a man who used to notice such things'?

1] When night has closed its shutters on my dismantled day MS. C. Day-Lewis objected to the line as 'an intolerably over-written variant of "When I am dead"' (quoted Taylor 1981: 148).
1. When: the word occurs in each stanza, and locates its sense of Hardy's death in the same way that 'it came to an end' does in the previous poem.
1. postern: back-door.
1. tremulous: a favourite word, often used of Tess, particularly in the exchange between her and Angel Clare on the 'tremulous lives' of women, *Tess of the D'Urbervilles*, ch. 29.
2. Pinion compares *The Woodlanders*, ch. 47 (p. 367): 'the May month when beech trees have suddenly unfolded large limp leaves of the softness of butterflies' wings' (1976: 161).

If it be in the dusk when, like an eyelid's soundless blink,   5
    The dewfall-hawk comes crossing the shades to alight
Upon the wind-warped upland thorn, a gazer may think,
    'To him this must have been a familiar sight.'

If I pass during some nocturnal blackness, mothy and warm,
    When the hedgehog travels furtively over the lawn,   10
One may say, 'He strove that such innocent creatures should
        come to no harm,
    But he could do little for them; and now he is gone.'

If, when hearing that I have been stilled at last, they stand at
        the door,
    Watching the full-starred heavens that winter sees,
Will this thought rise on those who will meet my face no
        more,   15
    'He was one who had an eye for such mysteries'?

And will any say when my bell of quittance is heard in the
        gloom,
    And a crossing breeze cuts a pause in its outrollings,
Till they rise again, as they were a new bell's boom,
    'He hears it not now, but used to notice such things'?   20

6. *dewfall-hawk*: a night-hawk.
7. *wind-warped upland thorn*: cf. Gray's 'aged thorn', 'Elegy', l. 116.
7. *a gazer may* ...] will a gazer ... ? MS, *MV* 1917.
11. Hardy supported the Royal Society for the Prevention of Cruelty to Animals, writing an ode for its centenary ('Compassion') and leaving it money in his will (cf. also 'The Mongrel').
11. *One may* ...] Will they ... ? MS, *MV* 1917.
16. cf. 1 Corinthians 15: 51–2 (see headnote).
17. *bell of quittance*] parting bell MS. Cf. the 'passing-bell' of 'To Shakespeare' (84), l. 16. A quittance is a discharge (from a debt).
18] And a crossing breeze makes a blank in its utterings, MS del.
19. *rise again*: Hardy seems to play against the religious overtones of the phrase (Christ 'rose again from the dead') and thus to deny a literal resurrection.

Late Lyrics and Earlier (1922)

Hardy's sixth volume of poetry was published on 23 May 1922. As the title and 'Apology' suggest, he included a number of poems which seem to have been written up from old drafts (in contrast to the two previous volumes), as well as poems from the period after Emma's death. Twenty-one of the poems had been previously published, six by Florence Hardy in limited edition pamphlets. The holograph prepared for the printer is in the Dorset County Museum.

Reaction to the volume reflected a developing respect for Hardy's poetic achievement, consolidated by the appearance of the first *Collected Poems* in 1919. The *London Mercury*, July 1922, commented 'a powerful music is made out of the most intractable material', and the *Observer* similarly remarked of Hardy's oddities that 'the force of Hardy's sincerity and vision makes one not merely accept them, but like them'. There were still dissenters, however, in this evaluation of Hardy's 'harshness: A. Williams-Ellis, writing in *The Spectator*, 8 July 1922, found 'no depth, no richness' because of a flatness of technique, adding 'he can really descend to extraordinary ineptness'. Perhaps the most perceptive reviewer was Walter de la Mare, writing in the *Westminster Gazette*, 24 June 1922: he commented on the fascination the 'bias of the recorder' held in Hardy's work, suggesting that 'the effect of even the most objective of his poems is that of a tale being told, of an experience being described, of a memory or secret being related, by a man whose face we can see, whose voice we can hear, whose ghostly presence is extraordinarily close to us'.

Apology

Hardy prefaced the volume with the two-and-a-half thousand word 'Apology', his most extended statement of his poetic principles. It was written in early 1922, and Hardy hesitated over its publication, consulting Sydney Carlyle Cockerell before deciding to include it. In the *Life* he noted that 'some of his friends regretted this preface, thinking that it betrayed an oversensitiveness to criticism which it were better the world should not know' (*LY* 225).

About half the verses that follow were written quite lately. The rest are older, having been held over in MS when past volumes were published, on considering that these would contain a sufficient number of pages to offer readers at one time, more especially during the distractions of the war. The unusually far back poems to be found here are, however, but some that were overlooked in gathering previous collections. A freshness in them, now unattainable, seemed to make up for their inexperience and to justify their inclusion. A few are dated; the dates of others are not discoverable.

The launching of a volume of this kind in neo-Georgian days by one who began writing in mid-Victorian, and has published nothing to speak of for some years, may seem to call for a few words of excuse or explanation. Whether or no, readers may feel assured that a new book is submitted to them with great hesitation at so belated a date. Insistent practical reasons, however, among which were requests from some illustrious men of letters who are in sympathy with my productions, the accident that several of the poems have already seen the light, and that dozens of them have been lying about for years, compelled the course adopted, in spite of the natural disinclination of a writer whose works have been so frequently regarded askance by a pragmatic section here and there, to draw attention to them once more.

I do not know that it is necessary to say much on the contents of the book, even in deference to suggestions that will be mentioned presently. I believe that those readers who care for my poems at all – readers to whom no passport is required – will care for this new instalment of them, perhaps the last, as much as for any that have preceded them. Moreover, in the eyes of a less friendly class the pieces, though a very mixed collection indeed, contain, so far as I am able to see, little or nothing in technic or teaching that can be considered a Star-Chamber matter, or so much as agitating to a ladies' school; even though, to use Wordsworth's observation in his Preface to *Lyrical Ballads*, such readers may suppose 'that by the act of writing in verse an author makes a formal engagement that

---

36. *Star-Chamber*: a powerful 'inner cabinet' abolished in 1641.

he will gratify certain known habits of association: that he not only thus apprises the reader that certain classes of ideas and expressions will be found in his book, but that others will be carefully excluded.'

It is true, nevertheless, that some grave, positive, stark, delineations are interspersed among those of the passive, lighter, and traditional sort presumably nearer to stereotyped tastes. For – while I am quite aware that a thinker is not expected, and, indeed, is scarcely allowed, now more than heretofore, to state all that crosses his mind concerning existence in this universe, in his attempts to explain or excuse the presence of evil and the incongruity of penalizing the irresponsible – it must be obvious to open intelligences that, without denying the beauty and faithful service of certain venerable cults, such disallowance of 'obstinate questions' and 'blank misgivings' tends to a paralysed intellectual stalemate. Heine observed nearly a hundred years ago that the soul has her eternal rights; that she will not be darkened by statutes, nor lullabied by the music of bells. And what is to-day, in allusions to the present author's pages, alleged to be 'pessimism' is, in truth, only such 'questionings' in the exploration of reality, and is the first step towards the soul's betterment, and the body's also.

If I may be forgiven for quoting my own old words, let me repeat what I printed in this relation more than twenty years ago, and wrote much earlier, in a poem entitled 'In Tenebris':

If way to the Better there be, it exacts a full look at the Worst:

that is to say, by the exploration of reality, and its frank recognition stage by stage along the survey, with an eye to the best consummation possible: briefly, evolutionary meliorism. But it is called pessimism nevertheless; under which word, expressed with condemnatory emphasis, it is regarded by many as some pernicious new thing (though so

56. *'obstinate questionings' and 'blank misgivings'*: from Wordsworth's 'Intimations' Ode, ll. 143–7:
>But for those obstinate questionings
>Of sense and outward things,
>Fallings from us, vanishings;
>Blank misgivings of a Creature
>Moving about in worlds not realized. . . .

57. *Heine observed*: on Hardy and Heine, see Björk entry 1017n.

old as to underlie the Gospel scheme, and even to permeate the Greek drama); and the subject is charitably left to decent silence, as if further comment were needless.

Happily there are some who feel such Levitical passing-by to be, alas, by no means a permanent dismissal of the matter; that comment on where the world stands is very much the reverse of needless in these disordered years of our prematurely afflicted century: that amendment and not madness lies that way. And looking down the future these few hold fast to the same: that whether the human and kindred animal races survive till the exhaustion or destruction of the globe, or whether these races perish and are succeeded by others before that conclusion comes, pain to all upon it, tongued or dumb, shall be kept down to a minimum by loving-kindness, operating through scientific knowledge, and actuated by the modicum of free will conjecturally possessed by organic life when the mighty necessitating forces – unconscious or other – that have 'the balancings of the clouds,' happen to be in equilibrium, which may or may not be often.

To conclude this question I may add that the argument of the so-called optimists is neatly summarized in a stern pronouncement against me by my friend Mr. Frederic Harrison in a late essay of his, in the words: 'This view of life is not mine.' The solemn declaration does not seem to me to be so annihilating to the said 'view' (really a series of fugitive impressions which I have never tried to co-ordinate) as is complacently assumed. Surely it embodies a too human fallacy quite familiar in logic. Next, a knowing reviewer, apparently a Roman Catholic young man, speaks, with some rather gross instances of the *suggestio falsi* in his whole article, of 'Mr. Hardy refusing consolation,' the 'dark gravity of his ideas,' and so on. When a Positivist and a Romanist agree there must be something wonderful in it,

---

79–80. *Levitical passing-by*: in the parable of the Good Samaritan, Luke 10: 32, a Levite passes by the victim of a robbery.
93–4. *'the balancings of the clouds'*: Job 37: 16, 'Dost thou know the balancings of the clouds, the wondrous works of him which is prefect in knowledge?'
98–9. Harrison's essay is in *The Fortnightly Review*, 2 February 1920, p. 183.
104–5. the 'knowing reviewer' is J.M. Hone (later Yeats's biographer), whose 'The Poetry of Mr Hardy' appeared in the *London Mercury*, February 1922, pp. 399–400.

which should make a poet sit up. But ... O that 'twere 110
possible!

   I would not have alluded in this place or anywhere else
to such casual personal criticism – for casual and
unreflecting they must be – but for the satisfaction of two
or three friends in whose opinion a short answer was 115
deemed desirable, on account of the continual repetition of
these criticisms, or more precisely, quizzings. After all, the
serious and truly literary inquiry in this connection is:
Should a shaper of such stuff as dreams are made on
disregard considerations of what is customary and expected, 120
and apply himself to the real function of poetry, the
application of ideas to life (in Matthew Arnold's familiar
phrase)? This bears more particularly on what has been
called the 'philosophy' of these poems – usually reproved
as 'queer.' Whoever the author may be that undertakes 125
such application of ideas in this 'philosophic' direction –
where it is specially required – glacial judgments must
inevitably fall upon him amid opinion whose arbiters largely
decry individuality, to whom *ideas* are oddities to smile at,
who are moved by a yearning the reverse of that of the 130
Athenian inquirers on Mars Hill; and stiffen their features
not only at sound of a new thing, but at a restatement of
old things in new terms. Hence should anything of this sort
in the following adumbrations seem 'queer' – should any of
them seem to good Panglossians to embody strange and 135
disrespectful conceptions of this best of all possible worlds,
I apologize; but cannot help it.

   Such divergences, which, though piquant for the nonce,
it would be affectation to say are not saddening and
discouraging likewise, may, to be sure, arise sometimes 140
from superficial aspect only, writer and reader seeing the
same thing at different angles. But in palpable cases of
divergence they arise, as already said, whenever a serious
effort is made towards that which the authority I have cited

110–11. O that 'twere possible: as in Tennyson's poem of that title, *Maud* II,
iv.
122–3. Arnold's familiar phrase: in 'The Study of Poetry', in *Essays in
Criticism*, Second Series (see also Björk entry 1148).
131. Athenian inquirers: the open-minded listeners who wish 'to hear some
new thing' when Paul preaches to them (Acts 17: 19–34).
135. Panglossians: Dr Pangloss is the ridiculous optimist in Voltaire's
Candide (1759).

– who would now be called old-fashioned, possibly even parochial – affirmed to be what no good critic could deny as the poet's province, the application of ideas to life. One might shrewdly guess, by the by, that in such recommendation the famous writer may have overlooked the cold-shouldering results upon an enthusiastic disciple that would be pretty certain to follow his putting the high aim in practice, and have forgotten the disconcerting experience of Gil Blas with the Archbishop.

To add a few more words to what has already taken up too many, there is a contingency liable to miscellanies of verse that I have never seen mentioned, so far as I can remember; I mean the chance little shocks that may be caused over a book of various character like the present and its predecessors by the juxtaposition of unrelated, even discordant, effusions; poems perhaps years apart in the making, yet facing each other. An odd result of this has been that dramatic anecdotes of a satirical and humorous intention following verse in graver voice, have been read as misfires because they raise the smile that they were intended to raise, the journalist, deaf to the sudden change of key, being unconscious that he is laughing with the author and not at him. I admit that I did not foresee such contingencies as I ought to have done, and that people might not perceive when the tone altered. But the difficulties of arranging the themes in a graduated kinship of moods would have been so great that irrelation was almost unavoidable with efforts so diverse. I must trust for right note-catching to those finely-touched spirits who can divine without half a whisper, whose intuitiveness is proof against all the accidents of inconsequence. In respect of the less alert, however, should any one's train of thought be thrown out of gear by a consecutive piping of vocal reeds in jarring tonics, without a semiquaver's rest between, and be led thereby to miss the writer's aim and meaning in one out of two contiguous compositions, I shall deeply regret it.

Having at last, I think, finished with the personal points that I was recommended to notice, I will forsake the immediate object of this Preface; and, leaving *Late Lyrics* to

---

153. *Gil Blas with the Archbishop*: in Le Sage's picaresque novel *Gil Blas* (1735) the hero Gil Blas tests the archbishop's sermons, but is rebuffed when he attempts to report back, the archbishop being ill.

whatever fate it deserves, digress for a few moments to
more general considerations. The thoughts of any man of
letters concerned to keep poetry alive cannot but run
uncomfortably on the precarious prospects of English verse
at the present day. Verily the hazards and casualties
surrounding the birth and setting forth of almost every
modern creation in numbers are ominously like those of
one of Shelley's paper-boats on a windy lake. And a
forward conjecture scarcely permits the hope of a better
time, unless men's tendencies should change. So indeed of
all art, literature, and 'high thinking' nowadays. Whether
owing to the barbarizing of taste in the younger minds by
the dark madness of the late war, the unabashed cultivation
of selfishness in all classes, the plethoric growth of
knowledge simultaneously with the stunting of wisdom, 'a
degrading thirst after outrageous stimulation' (to quote
Wordsworth again), or from any other cause, we seem
threatened with a new Dark Age.

I formerly thought, like other much exercised writers,
that so far as literature was concerned a partial cause might
be impotent or mischievous criticism; the satirizing of
individuality, the lack of whole-seeing in contemporary
estimates of poetry and kindred work, the knowingness
affected by junior reviewers, the overgrowth of meticulous-
ness in their peerings for an opinion, as if it were a
cultivated habit in them to scrutinize the tool-marks and be
blind to the building, to hearken for the key-creaks and be
deaf to the diapason, to judge the landscape by a nocturnal
exploration with a flash-lantern. In other words, to carry on
the old game of sampling the poem or drama by quoting
the worst line or worst passage only, in ignorance or not of
Coleridge's proof that a versification of any length neither
can be nor ought to be all poetry; of reading meanings into
a book that its author never dreamt of writing there. I
might go on interminably.

But I do not now think any such temporary obstructions
to be the cause of the hazard, for these negligences and
ignorances, though they may have stifled a few true poets
in the run of generations, disperse like stricken leaves
before the wind of next week, and are no more heard of

198–9. from Wordsworth's Preface to Lyrical Ballads.
215. Coleridge's proof: in *Biographia Literaria*, ch. 14.
222. like stricken leaves: cf. Shelley, 'Ode to the West Wind', ll. 63–70.

again in the region of letters than their writers themselves.
No: we may be convinced that something of the deeper sort
mentioned must be the cause.

In any event poetry, pure literature in general, religion –
I include religion, in its essential and undogmatic sense,
because poetry and religion touch each other, or rather
modulate into each other; are, indeed, often but different
names for the same thing – these, I say, the visible signs of
mental and emotional life, must like all other things keep
moving, becoming; even though at present, when belief in
witches of Endor is displacing the Darwinian theory and
'the truth that shall make you free,' men's minds appear,
as above noted, to be moving backwards rather than on. I
speak somewhat sweepingly, and should except many
thoughtful writers in verse and prose; also men in certain
worthy but small bodies of various denominations, and
perhaps in the homely quarter where advance might have
been the very least expected a few years back – the English
Church – if one reads it rightly as showing evidence of
'removing those things that are shaken,' in accordance with
the wise Epistolary recommendation to the Hebrews. For
since the historic and once august hierarchy of Rome some
generation ago lost its chance of being the religion of the
future by doing otherwise, and throwing over the little band
of New Catholics who were making a struggle for
continuity by applying the principle of evolution to their
own faith, joining hands with modern science, and
outflanking the hesitating English instinct towards liturgical
restatement (a flank march which I at the time quite
expected to witness, with the gathering of many millions of

---

234. witches of Endor: the witch of Endor raises Samuel's spirit in 1 Samuel 28 (see 'Apostrophe to an Old Psalm Tune' (79)).
235. 'the truth that shall make you free': John 8: 32 (cf. 'He Resolves to Say No More' (178), l. 18).
243–4. from Hebrews 12: 27: 'And this word, Yet once more, signifieth the removing of things that are shaken, as of things that are made, that those things which cannot be shaken may remain' – a passage which Hardy cited in the context of 'reconstruction' in the church in *Tess of the D'Urbervilles*, ch. 18 (p. 128), and in a 1915 symposium on 'The War and Literature' (*PW* 247). The 'shaking' of things in this passage seems related to the 'earthquake and fire' of Hardy's favourite passage in 1 Kings 19 (discussed in the Introduction, p. 12), which involves a sense of human fragility and life's trials. On Hardy's hopes for the reform of the church and a more 'rational' Christianity, see also *LY* 121–2, 177.

waiting agnostics into its fold); since then, one may ask, what other purely English establishment than the Church, of sufficient dignity and footing, with such strength of old association, such scope for transmutability, such architectural spell, is left in this country to keep the shreds of morality together?

It may indeed be a forlorn hope, a mere dream, that of an alliance between religion, which must be retained unless the world is to perish, and complete rationality, which must come, unless also the world is to perish, by means of the interfusing effect of poetry – 'the breath and finer spirit of all knowledge; the impassioned expression of science,' as it was defined by an English poet who was quite orthodox in his ideas. But if it be true, as Comte argued, that advance is never in a straight line, but in a looped orbit, we may, in the aforesaid ominous moving backward, be doing it *pour mieux sauter*, drawing back for a spring. I repeat that I forlornly hope so, notwithstanding the supercilious regard of hope by Schopenhauer, von Hartmann, and other philosophers down to Einstein who have my respect. But one dares not prophesy. Physical, chronological, and other contingencies keep me in these days from critical studies and literary circles.

>   Where once we held debate, a band
>   Of youthful friends, on mind and art

258–9. Hardy added a note at the end of this passage in WE 1926: 'However, one must not be too sanguine in reading signs, and since the above was writen evidence that the Church will go far in the removal of "things that are shaken" has not been encouraging.'
264. 'breath and finer spirit ...': adapted from Wordsworth's Preface to *Lyrical Ballads,* 'poetry is the breath and finer spirit of all knowledge; it is the impassioned expression which is the countenance of all Science'. Hardy marked this passage in his copy of Wordsworth's *Poems,* and added a comment: 'briefly = poetry is science become impassioned' (Wright 1967: 86)
267. as Comte argued: in *Social Dynamics, System of Positive Polity,* Vol. III, trans. Edward Spencer Beesley (London, 1876), p. 60 – a passage which Hardy summarized with a diagram of a 'looped orbit' when making extensive notes from Comte in the 1880s: '*Social Progress* – like a "looped orbit", sometimes apparently backwards, but really always forwards' (Björk entry 749; on Comte see 618n).
277–8. from *In Memoriam* 87.

(if one may quote Tennyson in this century). Hence I cannot know how things are going so well as I used to know them, and the aforesaid limitations must quite prevent my knowing henceforward.

I have to thank the editors and owners of *The Times*, *Fortnightly*, *Mercury*, and other periodicals in which a few of the poems have appeared for kindly assenting to their being reclaimed for collected publication.

T.H.

February 1922.

113 Weathers

First published in *Good Housekeeping*, May 1922, 'Weathers' sets the pattern for the opening groups of Hardy's last three volumes: pastoral scenes with bird-song. It was selected by Hardy for *Chosen Poems* (1929).
Metre: $a^4B^2a^4b^2c^4c^4c^4B^2$ dr, modelled on one of Hardy's favourite poems, Thomas Lodge's 'Rosalynd's Madrigal', which he would have found in Palgrave (Taylor 1988: 251). Bailey writes: 'the movement of the poem is that of a folk-dance or country jig, lively with anapests in the first stanza, tired with spondees ("hill-hid tides trob") in the second' (1970: 431). Hardy uses this metre as the basis for other poems: see e.g. 'A Sheep Fair' (139).

I

This is the weather the cuckoo likes,
    And so do I;
When showers betumble the chestnut spikes,
    And nestlings fly:
And the little brown nightingale bills his best,
And they sit outside at 'The Travellers' Rest,'
And maids come forth sprig-muslin drest,
And citizens dream of the south and west,
    And so do I.

II

This is the weather the shepherd shuns,
    And so do I;

---

5. *bills*] sings MS, *Good Housekeeping*.
6. *'The Travellers' Rest'*: inn southeast of Higher Bockhampton.
7. *sprig-muslin*: thin cloth with sprig-like decorations.

When beeches drip in browns and duns,
    And thresh, and ply;
And hill-hid tides throb, throe on throe,
And meadow rivulets overflow,   15
And drops on gate-bars hang in a row,
And rooks in families homeward go,
    And so do I.

114 'According to the Mighty Working'

First published in John Middleton Murray's *Athenaeum*, 4 April 1919; selected by Hardy for *Chosen Poems* (1929). He had been asked for a topical piece, and commented in a letter 'It must have been more of an accident than design I imagine that the lines suited the present date, for I told the editor I had nothing "topical"' (*CL* V, 306–7). However, he later drew the 'topical' conclusion himself: 'In February he signed a declaration of sympathy with the Jews in support of a movement for "the reconstitution of Palestine as a National Home for the Jewish People." ... about the same time there appeared a relevant poem by Hardy in the *Athenaeum* which was much liked, entitled in words from the Burial Service, "According to the Mighty Working"' (*LY* 190). The post-war 'peace', this suggests, covered deeper divisions (on the Palestine, cf. 'Jezreel', which maps Allenby's attack on Jezreel in 1918 onto that described in 2 Kings 9).

Metre: abcbca^3 dr, with other near-rhymes ('cease/stormless', 'mumming/being') which underscore the poem's subject of 'transmutation'.

I

When moiling seems at cease
    In the vague void of night-time,
And heaven's wide roomage stormless
Between the dusk and light-time,
And fear at last is formless,   5
    We call the allurement Peace.

---

14. *hill-hid tides*: i.e. those of the sea beyond the hills. *Good Housekeeping* has 'distant tides'.
Title. from the Anglican Burial Service's description of the resurrection of the body: 'Christ ... shall change our vile body, that it may be like unto his glorious body, according to the mighty working, whereby he is able to subdue all things to himself'. Hardy also considered 'Transmutation' as a title (CPW II, 336).
1. *moiling*: toil.

II

    Peace, this hid riot, Change,
      This revel of quick-cued mumming,
      This never truly being,
      This evermore becoming,   10
      This spinner's wheel onfleeing
    Outside perception's range.
1917.

115 The Contretemps

Another ballad-like piece, with Hardy's common suggestion that forms and contexts determine action: cf. 'At Wynyard's Gap', with its similar situation: 'since we've gone so far, / And what we've acted feel we almost are!' (ll. 92–3).
Metre: $a^4b^3a^4a^4b^5$ dr with variations. The last stanza has an extra line.

    A forward rush by the lamp in the gloom,
      And we clasped, and almost kissed;
    But she was not the woman whom
    I had promised to meet in the thawing brume
On that harbour-bridge; nor was I he of her tryst.   5

    So loosening from me swift she said:
      'O why, why feign to be
    The one I had meant! – to whom I have sped
    To fly with, being so sorrily wed!'
– 'Twas thus and thus that she upbraided me.   10

    My assignation had struck upon
      Some others' like it, I found.
    And her lover rose on the night anon;
    And then her husband entered on
The lamplit, snowflaked, sloppiness around.   15

7. Hardy marked a line in his Dryden, *Absalom and Achitophel* I, l. 752: 'And Peace itself, is war in masquerade.'
8. *quick-cued mumming*: mechanical acting. Hardy often describes human actions in such terms.
11. *spinner's wheel*: cf. 'The Convergence of the Twain' (45), l. 31n.
12. *perception's*] conception's MS del., *Athenaeum*.
4. *brume*: fog.
5. *tryst*: meeting.

'Take her and welcome, man!' he cried:
   'I wash my hands of her.
I'll find me twice as good a bride!'
   – All this to me, whom he had eyed,
'Twas clear, as his wife's planned deliverer.   20

   And next the lover: 'Little I knew,
      Madam, you had a third!
   Kissing here in my very view!'
   – Husband and lover then withdrew.
I let them; and I told them not they erred.   25

   Why not? Well, there faced she and I –
      Two strangers who'd kissed, or near,
   Chancewise. To see stand weeping by
   A woman once embraced, will try
The tension of a man the most austere.   30

   So it began; and I was young,
      She pretty, by the lamp,
   As flakes came waltzing down among
   The waves of her clinging hair, that hung
Heavily on her temples, dark and damp.   35

   And there alone still stood we two;
      She one cast off for me,
   Or so it seemed: while night ondrew,
   Forcing a parley what should do
We twain hearts caught in one catastrophe.   40

   In stranded souls a common strait
      Wakes latencies unknown,
   Whose impulse may precipitate
   A life-long leap. The hour was late,
And there was the Jersey boat with its funnel agroan.   45

   'Is wary walking worth much pother?'
      It grunted, as still it stayed.
   'One pairing is as good as another
   Where all is venture! Take each other,
And scrap the oaths that you have aforetime made.'. . .   50

---

20. *'Twas clear*] Plainly All editions (corrected in Hardy's copy of *CP* 1923, DCM).
26. *Well*: Clements (1980: 152–3) compares a similarly pivotal 'Well' in 'The Convergence of the Twain' (45), l. 16.
46. *pother*: fuss, worry.

> – Of the four involved there walks but one
>   On earth at this late day. ~
> And what of the chapter so begun?
> In that odd complex what was done?
> Well; happiness comes in full to none: 55
> Let peace lie on lulled lips: I will not say.
>
> Weymouth.

116 'And There Was a Great Calm'
(On the signing of the Armistice, Nov. 11, 1918)

Published in a Special Armistice Day Section of *The Times*, 11 November 1920 (the second anniversary of its signing), and privately printed in December 1920 by Florence Hardy. The *Life* records that Hardy at first refused the request to write a poem for the occasion, 'being generally unable to write to order. In the middle of the night, however, an idea seized him, and he was heard moving about the house looking things up' (*LY* 215). Taylor suggests that what Hardy 'looked up' included Tolstoy's essay on war, 'Bethink Yourselves!', *The Times*, 27 June 1904, pp. 4–5 (praised by Hardy, *LY* 107); an article entitled 'What is Militarism?', *TLS*, 27 July 1916, pp. 349–50, and Dean Inge's *Outspoken Essays* (Taylor 1981: 131–5).

Metre: abaab^5 dr. Herbert's 'The World' and Rosamond Watson's 'In a London Garden' (marked by Hardy in her *Poems* of 1912) are possible models (Taylor 1988: 235).

> I
>
> There had been years of Passion – scorching, cold,
> And much Despair, and Anger heaving high,
> Care whitely watching, Sorrows manifold,
> Among the young, among the weak and old,
> And the pensive Spirit of Pity whispered, 'Why?'   5
>
> II
>
> Men had not paused to answer. Foes distraught
> Pierced the thinned peoples in a brute-like blindness,
> Philosophies that sages long had taught,
> And Selflessness, were as an unknown thought,
> And 'Hell!' and 'Shell!' were yapped at Lovingkindness.   10

Weymouth: Hardy was employed there as an architect's assistant, 1869–70.
Title. used in both Matthew 8: 26 and Mark 4: 39 to describe the sudden calming of the seas after Jesus rebukes the winds. A similar calm opens the first of Hardy's longer war poems, 'The Souls of the Slain' (13).
5. *Spirit of Pity*] Spirit of Compassion *Times*. The former is one of the spirits which comments on human affairs in *The Dynasts*.

III

The feeble folk at home had grown full-used
To 'dug-outs,' 'snipers,' 'Huns,' from the war-adept
In the mornings heard, and at evetides perused;
To day-dreamt men in millions, when they mused –
To nightmare-men in millions when they slept.   15

IV

Waking to wish existence timeless, null,
Sirius they watched above where armies fell;
He seemed to check his flapping when, in the lull
Of night a boom came thencewise, like the dull
Plunge of a stone dropped into some deep well.   20

V

So, when old hopes that earth was bettering slowly
Were dead and damned, there sounded 'War is done!'
One morrow. Said the bereft, and meek, and lowly,
'Will men some day be given to grace? yea, wholly,
And in good sooth, as our dreams used to run?'   25

VI

Breathless they paused. Out there men raised their glance
To where had stood those poplars lank and lopped,
As they had raised it through the four years' dance
Of Death in the now familiar flats of France;
And murmured, 'Strange, this! How? All firing stopped?'   30

VII

Aye; all was hushed. The about-to-fire fired not,
The aimed-at moved away in trance-lipped song.
One checkless regiment slung a clinching shot

11–15. Tolstoy comments on the 'general stupefaction and brutalization of men' by war, and writes of the Sino-Russian War: 'Those who remain at home are gladdened by news of the murder of men, and when they learn that many Japanese have been killed they thank some one whom they call God.'
17. Sirius: the dog-star; brightest star in the sky.
20. plunge] echo *Times*. The same image of a stone in a well is used in the previous poem in *Late Lyrics and Earlier*, 'Where Three Roads Join', l. 12.
21. cf. Hardy's comments on the war in his autobiography: 'It was seldom he had felt so heavy at heart as in seeing his old view of the gradual bettering of human nature, as expressed in ["The Sick Battle-God"] of 1901, completely shattered by the events of 1914 and onwards' (*LY* 162).
25. in good sooth: truly.
29. flats] mud *Times*.

And turned. The Spirit of Irony smirked out, 'What?
Spoil peradventures woven of Rage and Wrong?' 35
VIII
Thenceforth no flying fires inflamed the gray,
No hurtlings shook the dewdrop from the thorn,
No moan perplexed the mute bird on the spray;
Worn horses mused: 'We are not whipped to-day';
No weft-winged engines blurred the moon's thin horn. 40
IX
Calm fell. From Heaven distilled a clemency;
There was peace on earth, and silence in the sky;
Some could, some could not, shake off misery:
The Sinister Spirit sneered: 'It had to be!'
And again the Spirit of Pity whispered, 'Why?' 45

117 The Selfsame Song

One of Hardy's series of seasonal bird-poems, echoing Wordsworth, Keats and others: see Introduction, p. 00. Included in *Chosen Poems* (1929).
Metre: $a^3b^3a^3b^2$ dtr.

> A bird sings the selfsame song,
> With never a fault in its flow,
> That we listened to here those long
> Long years ago.

34. *The Spirit of Irony*: another of the Spirits from *The Dynasts*.
35. *peradventures*: chance happenings.
38. *spray*: twigs.
40. *weft-winged engines*: aeroplanes ('weft' suggests the blur of a propellor, but also continues the weaving imagery of l. 35).
42. *peace on earth*: Luke 2: 14, 'Glory to God in the highest, and on earth peace, good will toward men.'
44. *Sinister Spirit*: from *The Dynasts*.
45. *Spirit of Pity*] Spirit of Compassion *Times*.
Title. from Keats's 'Ode to a Nightingale', ll. 63–6:
> The voice I hear this passing night was heard
> In ancient days by emperor and clown:
> Perhaps the self-same song that found a path
> Through the sad heart of Ruth. . . .

Selfsame: cf. 'A Backward Spring' (103), l. 13.
1. *sings*] bills MS, *LL* 1922 (reversing the change in 'Weathers').

> A pleasing marvel is how 5
> A strain of such rapturous rote
> Should have gone on thus till now
>   Unchanged in a note!
>
> – But it's not the selfsame bird. –
> No: perished to dust is he.... 10
> As also are those who heard
>   That song with me.

118 At Lulworth Cove a Century Back

One of Hardy's many poetic tributes to other writers. Earlier in 1920 he had joined a committee set up to acquire what is now the Keats House Museum at Hampstead, and sent a poem, 'At a House in Hampstead', as a contribution to a Centenary celebration. Hardy's note states: 'In September 1820 Keats, on his way to Rome, landed one day on the Dorset coast, and composed the sonnet, "Bright Star! would I were steadfast as thou art." The spot of his landing is judged to have been Lulworth Cove.' In 1914 he had corresponded with Keats's biographer Sidney Colvin on the issue. Modern scholarship, however, suggests that 'Bright Star' was written in 1819, and that Keats's landing was at Holworth Bay.

Metre: abab^5 dr, elegiac stanza (as in Gray's 'Elegy').

> Had I but lived a hundred years ago
> I might have gone, as I have gone this year,
> By Warmwell Cross on to a Cove I know,
> And Time have placed his finger on me there:
>
> '*You see that man?*' – I might have looked, and said, 5
> 'O yes: I see him. One that boat has brought
> Which dropped down Channel round Saint Alban's Head.
> So commonplace a youth calls not my thought.'
>
> '*You see that man?*' – 'Why yes; I told you; yes:
> Of an idling town-sort; thin; hair brown in hue; 10
> And as the evening light scants less and less
> He looks up at a star, as many do.'

9–12. cf. Meredith's 'The Thrush in February': 'Full lasting is the song, though he / The singer passes....'
Title. *Lulworth Cove*: about 10 miles southeast of Dorchester.
3. *Warmwell Cross*: an intersection on the downs above Lulworth Cove.
6. *that boat*: the *Maria Crowther*, which Keats boarded in London, driven up the Dorset coast by bad weather.
7. *Saint Alban's Head*: a promontory eight miles east of Lulworth Cove.
8. *so commonplace*: cf. 'To Shakespeare' (84), l. 2.

'*You see that man?*' – 'Nay, leave me!' then I plead,
'I have fifteen miles to vamp across the lea,
And it grows dark, and I am weary-kneed: 15
I have said the third time; yes, that man I see!'

'Good. That man goes to Rome – to death, despair;
And no one notes him now but you and I:
A hundred years, and the world will follow him there,
And bend with reverence where his ashes lie.'   20

September 1920.

119 The Collector Cleans His Picture

The poem's collector is based on the Reverend William Barnes of Came Rectory (see note to 'The Last Signal' (95)), who restored pictures as a hobby. However, it is also a meditation on a common topic in nineteenth-century writing, the uncovering or covering of truth through a painting (as in Balzac's 'The Unknown Masterpiece' and Wilde's *The Picture of Dorian Gray*).
Metre: irregular pentameter in a generally falling metre. If, as Taylor suggests (1988: 259), some lines are like those in Sapphics, Hardy may be recalling Barnes's discussion of Sapphics in his *Philological Grammar*.

Fili hominis, ecce ego tollo a te desiderabile oculorum tuorum in plaga. – Ezech. xxiv. 16.

How I remember cleaning that strange picture! . . .
I had been deep in duty for my sick neighbour –
His besides my own – over several Sundays,
Often, too, in the week; so with parish pressures,
Baptisms, burials, doctorings, conjugal counsel –   5
All the whatnots asked of a rural parson –
Faith, I was well-nigh broken, should have been fully
Saving for one small secret relaxation,
One that in mounting manhood had grown my hobby.

14. *vamp across the lea*: walk across the hills.
18. the context suggests 'Time' as the speaker; but Keats was accompanied by his friend Joseph Severn.
20. on Keats's burial place, see 'Rome. At the Pyramid of Cestius near the Graves of Shelley and Keats' (15).
Epigraph. from the Vulgate, 'Son of man, behold, I take away from thee the desire of thine eyes with a stroke' (Ezekiel 24: 16).
1] indentation in the MS implies that this line (and perhaps the epigraph) was a late addition.

This was to delve at whiles for easel-lumber, 10
Stowed in the backmost slums of a soon-reached city,
Merely on chance to uncloak some worthy canvas,
Panel, or plaque, blacked blind by uncouth adventure,
Yet under all concealing a precious artfeat.
Such I had found not yet. My latest capture 15
Came from the rooms of a trader in ancient house-gear
Who had no scent of beauty or soul for brushcraft.
Only a tittle cost it – murked with grimefilms,
Gatherings of slow years, thick-varnished over,
Never a feature manifest of man's painting. 20

So, one Saturday, time ticking hard on midnight
Ere an hour subserved, I set me upon it.
Long with coiled-up sleeves I cleaned and yet cleaned,
Till a first fresh spot, a high light, looked forth,
Then another, like fair flesh, and another; 25
Then a curve, a nostril, and next a finger,
Tapering, shapely, significantly pointing slantwise.
'Flemish?' I said. 'Nay, Spanish. . . . But, nay, Italian!'
– Then meseemed it the guise of the ranker Venus,
Named of some Astarte, of some Cotytto. 30
Down I knelt before it and kissed the panel,
Drunk with the lure of love's inhibited dreamings.

Till the dawn I rubbed, when there leered up at me
A hag, that had slowly emerged from under my hands there,
Pointing the slanted finger towards a bosom 35
Eaten away of a rot from the lusts of a lifetime . . .
– I could have ended myself at the lashing lesson!
Stunned I sat till roused by a clear-voiced bell-chime,
Fresh and sweet as the dew-fleece under my luthern.
It was the matin service calling to me 40
From the adjacent steeple.

10. easel-lumber: second-hand paintings. Bailey suggests that the diction reflects Barnes's preference for Anglo-Saxon compounds (1970: 459).
18. tittle: tiny amount.
29–30. i.e. it seemed to me the picture of the goddess whom some people call Astarte, and others Cotytto. Astarte was the Phoenician goddess normally equated with Venus.
33. leered] gazed *LL* 1922.
37. at the lashing lesson!] in heart-shook horror. *LL* 1922.
39. dew-fleece: covering of dew (cf. 'grimefilms', l. 18).
39. luthern: dormer window.

120 On the Tune Called the Old-Hundred-and-Fourth

A variation on the poem structured around the repeated hearing of a biblical passage or song, though here it is the failure to sing together which is the topic. Lines 9–10 are presumably a reference to the situation at Max Gate: Emma Hardy's attic room was some distance from Hardy's, and among the issues separating them in later life was her increasing religious devotion. Cf. the treatment of Psalm 69 in 'Apostrophe to an Old Psalm Tune' (79).

Hardy habitually preferred the old tunes of hymns and psalms: in a 1916 diary entry he contrasts the modern version of Psalm 34 in *Hymns Ancient and Modern* with the way it had been sung at Stinsford, 'in the good old High-and-Dry Church way' (*LY* 173). In a letter of 4 August 1918 Florence Hardy wrote 'We are not going to church today because T.H. says he hates new services and new prayers' (Meynell 1940: 299).

Metre: abCab^3 dr, with each C-line identical.

> We never sang together
>   Ravenscroft's terse old tune
> On Sundays or on weekdays,
> In sharp or summer weather,
>   At night-time or at noon.   5
>
> Why did we never sing it,
>   Why never so incline
> On Sundays or on weekdays,
> Even when soft wafts would wing it
>   From your far floor to mine?   10
>
> Shall we that tune, then, never
>   Stand voicing side by side
> On Sundays or on weekdays? . . .
> Or shall we, when for ever
>   In Sheol we abide,   15
>
> Sing it in desolation,
>   As we might long have done
> On Sundays or on weekdays
> With love and exultation
>   Before our sands had run?   20

Title] Hardy first wrote 'On a Tune by Dr. Gauntlett' then substituted 'On a Tune by Ravenscroft'. Henry Gauntlett (1805–76) composed a number of hymns. Thomas Ravenscroft was the author of the *Whole Book of Psalms* (1621), one of the standard metrical versions in use before the publication of *Hymns Ancient and Modern* (1861).
10. your far floor: i.e. Emma's room at Max Gate.
15. Sheol] Topet Haides MS del. (Sheol is the Hebrew underworld).
20. sands had run: cf. 'Quid Hic Agis?' (85), l. 27.

121 Voices from Things Growing in a Churchyard

First published in the *London Mercury*, December 1921; reprinted as a pamphlet by Florence Hardy, February 1922. Hardy returns here to the mode of 'Friends Beyond' (6), and to the monuments and graves in Stinsford churchyard. He had, in the meantime, copied Emily Dickinson's 'I died for beauty' into his notebooks, with its first-person graveyard soliloquy (Björk entries 2294–5). The idea of the dead being absorbed into the life of trees is also used in Hardy's 'Transformations', though here it is applied more systematically, with plants matching each person.

Metre: $a^4B^2a^4a^4c^4c^4D^2D^2$ dr, the B- and D-lines in falling rhythm – the separateness of the refrain perhaps suggesting the collectivity of the dead. Taylor notes that 'the voice of each ghost is given a distinctive rhythm and a distinctive series of vowel and consonant sounds' (1988: 159).

    These flowers are I, poor Fanny Hurd,
        Sir or Madam,
    A little girl here sepultured.
    Once I flit-fluttered like a bird
    Above the grass, as now I wave   5
    In daisy shapes above my grave,
        All day cheerily,
        All night eerily!

    – I am one Bachelor Bowring, 'Gent,'
        Sir or Madam;   10
    In shingled oak my bones were pent;
    Hence more than a hundred years I spent
    In my feat of change from a coffin-thrall
    To a dancer in green as leaves on a wall,
        All day cheerily,   15
        All night eerily!

    – I, these berries of juice and gloss,
        Sir or Madam,

Title] Voices from Things Growing *Mercury*, Pamphlet.
1. Fanny Hurd: 'Fanny Hurd's real name was Fanny Hurden, and Hardy remembered her as a delicate child who went to school with him. She died when she was about eighteen, and her grave and a head-stone with her name are to be seen in Stinsford Churchyard' (*LY* 223). Her daisies are associated with romance (cf. 'Rain on a Grave' (54)).
9. Bachelor Bowring: the 'Benjamin Bowring, gent.', d. 1837, whose memorial is in Stinsford Church. His change from oak to dancing leaves suggests a release from formality or sexual repression.
11. shingled: made of heavy boards.
13. feat] growth *Mercury*, pamphlet.

Am clean forgotten as Thomas Voss;
Thin-urned, I have burrowed away from the moss 20
That covers my sod, and have entered this yew,
And turned to clusters ruddy of view,
    All day cheerily,
    All night eerily!

– The Lady Gertrude, proud, high-bred, 25
    Sir or Madam,
Am I – this laurel that shades your head;
Into its veins I have stilly sped,
And made them of me; and my leaves now shine,
As did my satins superfine, 30
    All day cheerily,
    All night eerily!

– I, who as innocent withwind climb,
    Sir or Madam,
Am one Eve Greensleeves, in olden time 35
Kissed by men from many a clime,
Beneath sun, stars, in blaze, in breeze,
As now by glowworms and by bees,
    All day cheerily,
    All night eerily! 40

– I'm old Squire Audeley Grey, who grew
    Sir or Madam,
Aweary of life, and in scorn withdrew;
Till anon I clambered up anew
As ivy-green, when my ache was stayed, 45

19] Am he who was known as Thomas Voss; MS del.
19. Thomas Voss: from *Under the Greenwood Tree* I, iv, 'the only real name in the story' (*EL* 122). The yew he inhabits suits his ghoulish hobby: he is described in the *Life* as making casts of the heads of executed criminals (*EL* 280).
25. Lady Gertrude: unidentified. Her laurel suggests aristocratic distinction.
33. withwind: convolvulus or bindweed: cf. 'Dame the Second' in *A Group of Noble Dames* (p. 266): 'those sweet-pea or with-wind natures which require a twig or stouter fibre than its own to hang upon and bloom'.
35. Eve Greensleeves: 'It was said her real name was Eve Trevillian or Trevelyan; and that she was the handsome mother of two or three illegitimate children, *circa* 1784–95' (Hardy's note). Hardy discovered her story in the Stinsford Register in 1921 (*PN* 277).
41. Audeley Grey: commemorated with his family in a monument in Stinsford Church. Perhaps related to Eve Trevelyan (Bailey 1970: 463).
43. in scorn withdrew] its senseless hue MS del.

And in that attire I have longtime gayed
    All day cheerily,
    All night eerily!

– And so these maskers breathe to each
        Sir or Madam   50
Who lingers there, and their lively speech
Affords an interpreter much to teach,
As their murmurous accents seem to come
Thence hitheraround in a radiant hum,
    All day cheerily,   55
    All night eerily!

122 After a Romantic Day

Like 'At Castle Boterel' (66), this poem uses the idea of the mind inscribing its visions on the landscape (see Paulin 1975: 121–2). It echoes (and opposes itself to) a notebook extract from Dean Stanley on the Geologist Lyell: '*The enthusiasm* of Sir Charles Lyell, who when travelling along a cutting gazed out of the railway carriage as if the sides were hung with beautiful pictures' (Björk entry 1078).

Metre: irregular stanzas; the basis is alternating three and four stress lines, $a^3 b^4 a^3 c^4 c^3$ dr etc.

The railway bore him through
An earthen cutting out from a city:
    There was no scope for view,
Though the frail light shed by a slim young moon
    Fell like a friendly tune.   5

    Fell like a liquid ditty,
And the blank lack of any charm
    Of landscape did no harm.
The bald steep cutting, rigid, rough,
    And moon-lit, was enough   10
For poetry of place: its weathered face
Formed a convenient sheet whereon
The visions of his mind were drawn.

49] – And so they breath, these masks (growths, *Mercury*, Pamphlet), to each *LL* 1922.
51. who lingers there: i.e. Hardy, who now seems almost one of the dead. He read the poem with Walter de la Mare in the churchyard on 16 June 1921 (*LY* 223).
Title] MS has a deleted epigraph 'Your young men shall see visions', a reference to Joel 2: 28: 'your old men shall dream dreams, your young men shall see visions' (cf. Acts 2: 17).

123 In the Small Hours

One of a series of poems on Hardy's memories of music in his childhood: cf. 'The Country Wedding', four poems later in *Late Lyrics and Earlier*, 'The Self-Unseeing' (23), and 'Song to an Old Burden' (152). The sudden awakening in the last four lines is similar to that in a number of Hardy's reverie-poems.
Metre: abcbdbeb³ dr (double hymn stanza), with the final stanza resolving the series of link-rhymes on the d-lines and ending more regularly, dbdb.

> I lay in my bed and fiddled
>   With a dreamland viol and bow,
> And the tunes flew back to my fingers
>   I had melodied years ago.
> It was two or three in the morning   5
>   When I fancy-fiddled so
> Long reels and country-dances,
>   And hornpipes swift and slow.
>
> And soon anon came crossing
>   The chamber in the gray   10
> Figures of jigging fieldfolk –
>   Saviours of corn and hay –
> To the air of 'Haste to the Wedding,'
>   As after a wedding-day;
> Yea, up and down the middle   15
>   In windless whirls went they!
>
> There danced the bride and bridegroom,
>   And couples in a train,
> Gay partners time and travail
>   Had longwhiles stilled amain! . . .   20
> It seemed a thing for weeping
>   To find, at slumber's wane
> And morning's sly increeping,
>   That Now, not Then, held reign.

2. *viol*: violin, fiddle.
13–14. in his autobiography Hardy describes how 'little Thomas played sometimes at village weddings' (*EL* 29). 'Haste to the Wedding' is played in the last chapter of *Under the Greenwood Tree*, and may also be linked to 'The Voice' (59).
20. amain: with all their force.
21–4. cf. the final lines of 'The Man Who Forgot' and 'The Dream is – Which?'.

124 Last Words to a Dumb Friend

An animal-lover, Hardy had a pet cemetery at Max Gate, and when S.M. Elias visited in 1913 he was shown the graves of five cats including '"Snowdove", who inspired that beautiful tribute in verse ... written in 1904' (quoted Bailey 1970: 479). Cf. 'Dead "Wessex" the Dog to the Household'.

Metre: tetrameter couplets, aabb[4], etc., often with both an initial and a final stress. Richardson wonders whether 'some nearly imperceptible undertow of mock-heroism allowed Hardy to write in such a broad and assured manner' (1977: 81).

Pet was never mourned as you,
Purrer of the spotless hue,
Plumy tail, and wistful gaze
While you humoured our queer ways,
Or outshrilled your morning call   5
Up the stairs and through the hall –
Foot suspended in its fall –
While, expectant, you would stand
Arched, to meet the stroking hand;
Till your way you chose to wend   10
Yonder, to your tragic end.

Never another pet for me!
Let your place all vacant be;
Better blankness day by day
Than companion torn away.   15
Better bid his memory fade,
Better blot each mark he made,
Selfishly escape distress
By contrived forgetfulness,
Than preserve his prints to make   20
Every morn and eve an ache.

From the chair whereon he sat
Sweep his fur, nor wince thereat;
Rake his little pathways out
Mid the bushes roundabout;   25
Smooth away his talons' mark
From the claw-worn pine-tree bark,
Where he climbed as dusk embrowned,
Waiting us who loitered round.

Strange it is this speechless thing,   30
Subject to our mastering,

14. blankness: see 'Exeunt Omnes' (74), l. 6n.

Subject for his life and food
To our gift, and time, and mood;
Timid pensioner of us Powers,
His existence ruled by ours,   35
Should — by crossing at a breath
Into safe and shielded death,
By the merely taking hence
Of his insignificance —
Loom as largened to the sense,   40
Shape as part, above man's will,
Of the Imperturbable.

As a prisoner, flight debarred,
Exercising in a yard,
Still retain I, troubled, shaken,   45
Mean estate, by him forsaken;
And this home, which scarcely took
Impress from his little look,
By his faring to the Dim
Grows all eloquent of him.   50

Housemate, I can think you still
Bounding to the window-sill,
Over which I vaguely see
Your small mound beneath the tree,
Showing in the autumn shade   55
That you moulder where you played.

    October 2, 1904.

125 A Drizzling Easter Morning

One of Hardy's series of poems of religious scepticism, here focusing on the central Christian doctrines of atonement and resurrection.
   Metre: irregular, abaacc bbbdbd[4] dr with link-rhymes between stanzas on the b-lines.

    And he is risen? Well, be it so. . . .
    And still the pensive lands complain,
    And dead men wait as long ago,
    As if, much doubting, they would know

34. *pensioner of us Powers*: i.e. dependent on humans for his food.
36. *crossing*: cf. the 'crossing breeze' of 'Afterwards' (112), l. 18.
1. *And is he risen?*: the traditional greeting on Easter Mondays is 'Christ is risen' (the expected reply is 'He is risen indeed').

>   What they are ransomed from, before 5
>   They pass again their sheltering door.
>
>   I stand amid them in the rain,
>   While blusters vex the yew and vane;
>   And on the road the weary wain
>   Plods forward, laden heavily; 10
>   And toilers with their aches are fain
>   For endless rest – though risen is he.

126 'I was the midmost'

One of a number of poems on the stages of the human life-cycle: others include 'Quid Hic Agis?' (85) and 'The Five Students' (100).
Metre: $a^4b^3c^4b^3c^4b^3$ dr, with variations on a common a-line.

>   I was the midmost of my world
>   When first I frisked me free,
>   For though within its circuit gleamed
>   But a small company,
>   And I was immature, they seemed 5
>   To bend their looks on me.
>
>   She was the midmost of my world
>   When I went further forth,
>   And hence it was that, whether I turned
>   To south, east, west, or north, 10

5. ransomed: Christ is said to ransom man from sin and the grave (Hosea 13: 14, Matthew 20: 28, Mark 10: 45, cf. Lyte's hymn 'Praise, my soul, the King of Heaven').
6. door: the word has many overtones: Jesus himself (John 10: 9), the door of the grave which Jesus opens in order to rise from the dead (Matthew 27: 60), but also the door of faith (Acts 14: 27). 'Behold, I stand at the door, and knock' (Revelation 3: 20) was a text made famous by Holman Hunt's painting 'The Light of the World'.
7. amid them: i.e. the dead.
8. vane: weather-vane.
9. wain: wagon.
11. fain: longing (cf. the same word in the next poem).
1. as Terri Witek points out, 'the point is made syntactically by the position of "midmost" in the line' (1990: 127).

Beams of an all-day Polestar burned
From that new axe of earth.

Where now is midmost in my world?
I trace it not at all:
No midmost shows it here, or there, 15
When wistful voices call
'We are fain! We are fain!' from everywhere
On Earth's bewildering ball!

127 The Inscription
(A Tale)

Hardy was fascinated by the way in which intentions are 'fixed' and frozen in inscriptions, often with ironic results. 'The Memorial Brass: 186-' (in *Moments of Vision*) involves a similar story about a over-zealous young wife writing her name prematurely on her husband's tomb.
Metre: $a^5b^5a^5b^2$ dtr.

Sir John was entombed, and the crypt was closed, and she,
Like a soul that could meet no more the sight of the sun,
Inclined her in weepings and prayings continually,
    As his widowed one.

And to pleasure her in her sorrow, and fix his name 5
As a memory Time's fierce frost should never kill,
She caused to be richly chased a brass to his fame,
    Which should link them still;

11. Polestar: the fixed star in the North around which the heavens seem to rotate (the poem itself is a series of shifting orbits).
12. axe: axis.
16. wistful] vibrant MS del.
17. fain: can mean either 'glad to' or 'content to', or 'obliged to'.
Title] The Words on the Brass MS del.
1. Sir John: modelled on Sir John Horsey (d. 1531), whose effigy and that of his wife Elizabeth and their accompanying brasses are in the Church of St Andrew at Yetminster, near Yeovil. Hardy would have found the inscription, with the date of Elizabeth's death left empty, in Hutchins's *The History and Antiquities of the County of Dorset* (1861–73) IV, 456.
2. sight of the sun: cf. Nathan's prophecy against David in 2 Samuel 12: 11: 'I will take thy wives before thine eyes, and give them unto thy neighbour, and he shall lie with thy wives in the sight of the sun.'
7. chased: engraved.

For she bonded her name with his own on the brazen page,
As if dead and interred there with him, and cold, and numb, 10
(Omitting the day of her dying and year of her age
    Till her end should come;)

And implored good people to pray 'Of their
    Charytie
For these twaine Soules,' — yea, she
    who did last remain
Forgoing Heaven's bliss if ever with spouse should she 15
    Again have lain.

Even there, as it first was set, you may see it now,
Writ in quaint Church-text, with the date of her death left
    bare,
In the aged Estminster aisle, where the folk yet bow
    Themselves in prayer. 20

Thereafter some years slid, till there came a day
When it slowly began to be marked of the standers-by
That she would regard the brass, and would bend away
    With a drooping sigh.

Now the lady was fair as any the eye might scan 25
Through a summer day of roving — a type at whose lip
Despite her maturing seasons, no meet man
    Would be loth to sip.

And her heart was stirred with a lightning love to its pith
For a newcomer who, while less in years, was one 30
Full eager and able to make her his own forthwith,
    Restrained of none.

But she answered Nay, death-white; and still as he urged
She adversely spake, overmuch as she loved the while,
Till he pressed for why, and she led with the face of one
    scourged 35
    To the neighbouring aisle,

And showed him the words, ever gleaming upon her pew,
Memorizing her there as the knight's eternal wife,
Or falsing such, debarred inheritance due
    Of celestial life. 40

He blenched, and reproached her that one yet undeceased

13–14] the 'gothic' typeface imitates the script on the tomb.
19. Estminster: Yetminster. Characteristically, Hardy returns to early forms of the name: 'Etiminstre' in the Domesday Book, 'Estminstre' in Hutchins's *History*.
41. blenched: flinched.

Should bury her future – that future which none can spell;
And she wept, and purposed anon to inquire of the priest
    If the price were hell
Of her wedding in face of the record. Her lover agreed,   45
And they parted before the brass with a shudderful kiss,
For it seemed to flash out on their impulse of passionate need,
    'Mock ye not this!'

Well, the priest, whom more perceptions moved than one,
Said she erred at the first to have written as if she were dead   50
Her name and adjuration; but since it was done
    Nought could be said
Save that she must abide by the pledge, for the peace of her
    soul,
And so, by her life, maintain the apostrophe good,
If she wished anon to reach the coveted goal   55
    Of beatitude.

To erase from the consecrate text her prayer as there prayed
Would aver that the joys of the earth had so wound her about,
That prayers for her joy above by Jesu's aid
    Could be done without.   60
Moreover she thought of the laughter, the shrug, the jibe
That would rise at her back in the nave when she should pass
As another's avowed by the words she had chosen to inscribe
    On the changeless brass.

And so for months she replied to her Love: 'No, no';   65
While sorrow was gnawing her beauties ever and more,
Till he, long-suffering and weary, grew to show
    Less warmth than before.

And, after an absence, wrote words absolute:
That he gave her till Midsummer morn to make her mind
    clear;   70
And that if, by then, she had not said Yea to his suit,
    He should wed elsewhere.

Thence on, at unwonted times through the lengthening days
She was seen in the church – at dawn, or when the sun dipt
And the moon rose, standing with hands joined, blank of gaze, 75
    Before the script.

43. anon: soon.
54. maintain the apostrophe good: keep faith with the inscription.
58–9] Would aver that, since earth's joys most drew her, past doubt, / Friends'
prayers... All editions (correction in Hardy's copy of *CP* 1923, DCM).
73. unwonted: unaccustomed.

She thinned as he came not; shrank like a creature that cowers
As summer drew nearer; but yet had not promised to wed,
When, just at the zenith of June, in the still night hours,
    She was missed from her bed.   80

'The church!' they whispered with qualms; 'where often she
    sits.'
They found her: facing the brass there, else seeing none,
But feeling the words with the finger, gibbering in fits;
    And she knew them not one.

And so she remained, in her handmaids' charge; late, soon,   85
Tracing words in the air with her finger, as seen that night –
Those incised on the brass – till at length unwatched one
    noon,
    She vanished from sight.

And, as talebearers tell, thence on to her last-taken breath
Was unseen, save as wraith that in front of the brass made
    moan;   90
So that ever the way of her life and the time of her death
    Remained unknown.

And hence, as indited above, you may read even now
The quaint Church-text, with the date of her death left bare,
In the aged Estminster aisle, where folk yet bow   95
    Themselves in prayer.

October 30, 1907.

128 The Whitewashed Wall

Written at the request of John Galsworthy, the editor of *Reveille*, a quarterly for disabled soldiers, and published in the November 1918 issue. Hardy's personal statement of fidelity to what Paulin calls 'eidetic images' like that in this poem is 'The Shadow on the Stone' (106).

Metre: $a^4b^3c^4b^3d^4e^3d^4e^3$ dtr, ballad metre resolving into common metre, with a subtle interplay of internal rhyme in the final stanza (see Introduction, p. 39).

89. talebearers: gossips.
93. indited: written (with legal overtones).
Title. cf. the list of vanished things in Goldsmith's *The Deserted Village*:
    The whitewashed wall, the nicely sanded floor,
    The varnished clock that clicked behind the door. (ll. 227–8)

Why does she turn in that shy soft way
    Whenever she stirs the fire,
And kiss to the chimney-corner wall,
    As if entranced to admire
Its whitewashed bareness more than the sight   5
    Of a rose in richest green?
I have known her long, but this raptured rite
    I never before have seen.

– Well, once when her son cast his shadow there,
    A friend took a pencil and drew him   10
Upon that flame-lit wall. And the lines
    Had a lifelike semblance to him.
And there long stayed his familiar look;
    But one day, ere she knew,
The whitener came to cleanse the nook,   15
    And covered the face from view.

'Yes,' he said: 'My brush goes on with a rush,
    And the draught is buried under;
When you have to whiten old cots and brighten,
    What else can you do, I wonder?'   20
But she knows he's there. And when she yearns
    For him, deep in the labouring night,
She sees him as close at hand, and turns
    To him under his sheet of white.

---

9. *once when her son*] her soldier-son *Reveille*.
10. *drew*] shaped MS del.
14–16. cf. Mrs Martin in *Two in a Tower*, ch. 38, who refuses to cover her son's markings.
18. *draught*: drawing.
19. *cots*: cottages.
22. *labouring*] moaning *Reveille*. 'Labouring' here means restless, distressed (perhaps also suggesting the 'labour' of birth).
24] And kisses him under the white. *Reveille*. The image suggests a shroud, as well as whitewash.

129 After Reading Psalms XXXIX, XL, etc.

The first of the two poems which form the end-group of the volume, structured as a meditation on texts in the Vulgate (Latin) Bible. The assigned date is a puzzle: Hardy purchased a Vulgate in 1902 (*CL* VII, 134), but probably owned a copy earlier, as the epigraphs to the 'In Tenebris' poems imply. However, the metrical experiment of interweaving Latin and English phrases seems more characteristic of the period after 1900, and given the complex nature of the rhymes it is difficult to see him simply reworking an old draft in English.

Metre: $a^4b^3a^4b^3$ dtf (with variations including a final stress on many lines). The use of Latin tags in the final lines of each stanza may be borrowed from a poem in the Egerton manuscript (Taylor 1988: 262). Isobel Grundy contrasts the confident declarative Latin rhymes with the awkward inversions of the English 'tryst, I', etc. (1980: 4) – another way in which the biblical text is played off against the story of Hardy's life.

> Simple was I and was young;
>   Kept no gallant tryst, I;
> Even from good words held my tongue,
>   *Quoniam Tu fecisti!*
>
> Through my youth I stirred me not,   5
>   High adventure missed I,
> Left the shining shrines unsought;
>   Yet – *me deduxisti!*
>
> At my start by Helicon
>   Love-lore little wist I,   10
> Worldly less; but footed on;
>   Why? *Me suscepisti!*

2. *tryst*: meeting.
3. Psalm 39: 3, part of the service for the Burial of the Dead in the *Book of Common Prayer*: 'I held my tongue, and spake nothing: I kept silence, yea, even from good words'. Hardy associated the passage with his sister Mary (*LY* 170).
4. *Quoniam Tu fecisti!*: for it was thy doing! From Psalm 38: 10 in the Vulgate (Latin) Bible, which corresponds to Psalm 39: 10 in the *BCP* (Coverdale's version: translations and line numbers in the Authorized Version differ slightly).
8. *me deduxisti!*: thou hast led me! Psalm 60: 3 in the Vulgate; 61: 3 in the *BCP*.
10. *wist*: know.
12. *Me suscepisti!*: thou upholdest me! Psalm 40: 13 in the Vulgate; 41: 12 in the *BCP*.

When I failed at fervid rhymes,
  'Shall,' I said, 'persist I?'
'*Dies*' (I would add at times) 15
  '*Meos posuisti!*'
So I have fared through many suns;
  Sadly little grist I
Bring my mill, or any one's,
  Domine, Tu scisti! 20
And at dead of night I call:
  'Though to prophets list I,
Which hath understood at all?
  Yea: *Quem elegisti?*'
187–

130 Surview

'Surview' is another typological meditation (see Introduction, pp. 10–14) – here a self-accusing fireside dialogue involving some of Hardy's favourite biblical passages, possibly influenced by Tennyson's 'The Two Voices'. The voice from the fire recalls the 'still small voice' of 1 Kings 19: 12 (see 'Quid Hic Agis?' (85)).

Metre $a^4b^3b^4a^4b^3$ dtr with lines 7, 10, 12, 15, 17 identical (cf. 'Plena Timoris').

  '*Cogitavi vias meas*'
A cry from the green-grained sticks of the fire
  Made me gaze where it seemed to be:
'Twas my own voice talking therefrom to me

15–16. '*Dies*' ... '*Meos posuisti!*': thou hast made my days! Psalm 38: 6 in the Vulgate; 39: 6 in the *BCP*.
18. *grist*: corn for grinding ('to bring grist to the mill' is to profit).
20. *Domine, Tu scisti!*: O Lord, thou knowest. Psalm 39: 10 in the Vulgate; 40: 11 in the *BCP*.
22. *list*: listen.
24. *Quem elegisti?*: whom thou chooseth? Psalm 64: 5 in the Vulgate; 65: 4 in the *BCP*.
Epigraph. '*Cogitavi vias meas*': 'I called mine own ways to remembrance'. Psalm 118: 59 in the Vulgate Bible; 119: 59 in the *BCP*.
1–3. cf. Psalm 39: 4: 'My heart was hot within me, and while I was thus musing the fire kindled: and at the last I spake with my tongue.'

On how I had walked when my sun was higher –
    My heart in its arrogancy.   5

'*You held not to whatsoever was true,*'
    Said my own voice talking to me:
'*Whatsoever was just you were slack to see;*
Kept not things lovely and pure in view,'
    Said my own voice talking to me.   10

'*You slighted her that endureth all,*'
    Said my own voice talking to me;
'*Vaunteth not, trusteth hopefully;*
That suffereth long and is kind withal,'
    Said my own voice talking to me.   15

'*You taught not that which you set about,*'
    Said my own voice talking to me;
'*That the greatest of things is Charity. . . .*'
– And the sticks burnt low, and the fire went out,
    And my voice ceased talking to me.   20

5] My heart where it best could be. MS.
5. *arrogancy*: state of arrogance (cf. Proverbs 8: 13).
6–9. cf. Phillipians 4: 8: 'Finally, brethren, whatsoever things are true, whatsoever things are honest, whatsoever things are just, whatsoever things are pure, whatsoever things are lovely, whatsoever things are of good report . . . think on these things' (also alluded to in 'The Souls of the Slain' (13), l. 82).
11–14. cf. 1 Corinthians 13: 4, 7: 'Charity suffereth long, and is kind; charity envieth not; charity vaunteth not itself, is not puffed up. . . . endureth all things.' The same passage is alluded to in 'The Blinded Bird' (87).
18. cf. 1 Corinthians 13: 13: 'And now abideth faith, hope, charity, these three; but the greatest of these is charity.'

Human Shows, Far Phantasies, Songs and Trifles (1925)

In his mid-80s, Hardy found the task of arranging a new volume difficult, and his literary executor Sydney Cockerell helped him prepare *Human Shows, Far Phantasies, Songs and Trifles*. The original title suggested was 'Poems Imaginative and Incidental: with Songs and Trifles' (*CPW* III, 310). It was published on 20 November 1925; two more impressions following before the end of the year.

Human Shows includes a number of poems from the 1890s and other periods in Hardy's earlier career, including six poems held over from the period of Emma Hardy's death, though the majority were probably written since 1920. Twenty-eight had been previously published, including three privately printed by Florence Hardy. The manuscript is at Yale University. A set of corrected proofs (the only such set of Hardy's proofs) is in the Dorset County Museum. On the flyleaf of the proofs Hardy wrote a typically defensive note analysing the contents (quoted Millgate 1982: 561):

	Total:	*152 poems.*
		– of these there are, roughly,
	60	poems of tragedy, sorrow or grimness
	92	65 of a reflective dispassionate kind
		11 of the nature of comedy
		16 love-songs & pieces, mostly for music
	that is	tragedy or sadness 2/5 of the whole
		Reflection, love, or comedy 3/5 ———

Reviews of the volume generally remarked on Hardy's continued productivity at 85. *The Times Literary Supplement* commented that 'poetry ... is still the art of his old age, saying for him what the prose can no longer say' (*TLS*, 3 December 1925, p. 829). Maurice Amos in the *New Statesman*, 23 January 1926 called Hardy 'the truthfullest of all the poets in the world', adding 'the reader who lays down a volume of Hardy's poetry seems not so much to have read as to have lived and suffered through it'.

131 Waiting Both

First published in the *London Mercury*, November 1924; subsequently included in *Chosen Poems* (1929). *Human Shows*, like *Winter Words*, opens with a poem about the poet living on beyond the closure imposed in the final poem of the previous volume, still waiting for death; in each case this is followed by a 'bird-scene' which suggests the continuity of nature and song.
 Metre: $a^3b^3a^3B^3B^2$ dr.

>A star looks down at me,
>And says: 'Here I and you
>Stand, each in our degree:
>What do you mean to do, –
>   Mean to do?'   5
>
>I say: 'For all I know,
>Wait, and let Time go by,
>Till my change come.' – 'Just so,'
>The star says: 'So mean I: –
>   So mean I.'   10

132 A Bird-Scene at a Rural Dwelling

First published in *Chamber's Journal*, January 1925, commemorating the 60th anniversary of Hardy's first publication, 'How I built myself a house,' in the same journal. Extensively revised in manuscript for *Human Shows* (see *CPW* III, 7). It parallels the bird-scenes in the first poem of *Late Lyrics and Earlier* and the second poem of *Winter Words*.
 Metre: a complex form in the first stanza, followed by a pentameter triplet, $a^5a^5b^3b^3a^4a^4c^5c^5b^3d^3d^5$ $e^5e^5e^5$ dr. The fourteen lines suggest an allusion to sonnet-structure.

>When the inmate stirs, the birds retire discreetly
>From the window-ledge, whereon they whistled sweetly
>   And on the step of the door,
>   In the misty morning hoar;
>But now the dweller is up they flee   5
>To the crooked neighbouring codlin-tree;

8. *Till my change come*: Job 14: 14: 'If a man die, shall he live again? all the days of my appointed time will I wait, till my change come.' Hardy reported reading this passage in 1919, and remembering it as the text of a sermon of 1860 (*LY* 194, cf. 'The Sigh').
4. *hoar*: frost.
6. *codlin-tree*: kind of apple.

And when he comes fully forth they seek the garden,
And call from the lofty costard, as pleading pardon
   For shouting so near before
   In their joy at being alive: –   10
Meanwhile the hammering clock within goes five.

I know a domicile of brown and green,
Where for a hundred summers there have been
Just such enactments, just such daybreaks seen.

133 In a Former Resort after Many Years

'In a Former Resort after Many Years' can be seen as a central poem in terms of Hardy's self-perception, with its depiction of the mind as a space 'scored' by experience and echoing with the faint voices of the dead (see Introduction, p. 20; Paulin 1975: 33). Similar images of internal marking can be found in 'On an Invitation to the United States', 'His Heart' (92), and '"I thought, my Heart"' (105).

Metre: $a^4b^5a^5b^4a^5b^4$ dr.

   Do I know these, slack-shaped and wan,
   Whose substance, one time fresh and furrowless,
      Is now a rag drawn over a skeleton,
         As in El Greco's canvases? –
   Whose cheeks have slipped down, lips become indrawn,   5
      And statures shrunk to dwarfishness?

8. costard: large apple.
12–14. cf. 'The Selfsame Song' (117).
12. domicile: house (one of Hardy's earliest unpublished poems is 'Domicilium').
4. El Greco] Crivelli's MS El Greco is the Spanish Mannerist painter Domenicos Theotocopoulos (*c.* 1540–1614), who often depicts emaciated and elongated bodies (Crivelli was a Venetian active 1457–93, whose work, rich in symbolism, would be less appropriate). Hardy studied paintings at the National Gallery in London in the 1860s.

Do they know me, whose former mind
Was like an open plain where no foot falls,
But now is as a gallery portrait-lined,
And scored with necrologic scrawls,　　　　　　　　　　10
Where feeble voices rise, once full-defined,
From underground in curious calls?

134 A Cathedral Façade at Midnight

A deleted date in the manuscript, 1897, points to Hardy's diary entry for 10 August 1897: '*Salisbury* . . . Went into the Close late at night. The moon was visible through both the north and south clerestory windows to me standing on the turf on the north side. . . . Walked to the west front, and watched the moonlight creep round upon the statuary of the facade – stroking tentatively and then more and more firmly the prophets, the martyrs, the bishops, the kings, and the queens' (*LY* 71). The description of moonlight on Hallam's grave, *In Memoriam* 67, is a possible influence.

Metre: $a^5 b^3 a^5 b^3 c^5 c^5 c^5$ dr. Taylor comments that 'the tentative effect of the trimeter lines with their feminine rhymes changes to the strong confirmation of the concluding pentameter lines with their three climactic rhymes' (1988: 161). Cf. Shelley's 'Mutability'.

　　Along the sculptures of the western wall
　　　　I watched the moonlight creeping:
　　It moved as if it hardly moved at all,
　　　　Inch by inch thinly peeping
　　Round on the pious figures of freestone, brought　　5
　　And poised there when the Universe was wrought
　　To serve its centre, Earth, in mankind's thought.

7–10. cf. Matthew Arnold's 'The Buried Life':
　　　　Yet still, from time to time, vague and forlorn,
　　　　From the soul's subterranean depth upborne
　　　　As from an infinitely distant land,
　　　　Come airs, and floating echoes, and convey
　　　　A melancholy into all our day.
8. open plain: the Lockean 'tabula rasa' or blank slate which is the mind at birth, subsequently inscribed with the record of experience: see Paulin (1975: 33) and cf. 'After a Romantic Day' (122), and *The Well-Beloved*, III, 3 (p. 117).
10. necrologic] autographic MS del. A necrology is an obituary or a list of the dead.
5. freestone: soft stone used for carving.
7. cf. comments on the Copernican revolution in 'Drinking Song' (171), ll. 10–16.

The lunar look skimmed scantly toe, breast, arm,
    Then edged on slowly, slightly,
To shoulder, hand, face; till each austere form   10
    Was blanched its whole length brightly
Of prophet, king, queen, cardinal in state,
That dead men's tools had striven to simulate;
And the stiff images stood irradiate.

A frail moan from the martyred saints there set   15
    Mid others of the erection
Against the breeze, seemed sighings of regret
    At the ancient faith's rejection
Under the sure, unhasting, steady stress
Of Reason's movement, making meaningless   20
The coded creeds of old-time godliness.

135 The Monument-Maker

The poem's date suggests the context of Emma Hardy's monument in St Juniot Church, which Hardy designed, and which he inspected in September 1916 (cf. 'The Marble Tablet'). Like 'The Obliterate Tomb' (72), 'The Statue of Liberty' (88), and other poems, 'The Monument-Maker' questions Hardy's own commemorative procedures. Selected for *Chosen Poems* (1929).

Metre: one of Hardy's later experiments with irregular forms, mixing lines of two, three, and five beats: $a^3a^2b^3b^3c^5d^2d^5d^2$, etc, dr, with double link-rhymes between stanzas ('daytime/Maytime', etc.).

    I chiselled her monument
        To my mind's content,
    Took it to the church by night,
    When her planet was at its height,
And set it where I had figured the place in the daytime.   5
        Having niched it there
    I stepped back, cheered, and thought its outlines fair,
        And its marbles rare.

15. frail moan: the 'shaking' and 'throbbing' of the supplanted Olympian deities is depicted in a similarly cold light in 'Christmas in the Elgin Room' (176; cf. also 'The Graveyard of Dead Creeds').
19–20. the effects of 'Reason' on Religion are described in detail in 'The Respectable Burgher' (22).
4. the reference is astrological, but obscure.

> Then laughed she over my shoulder as in our Maytime:
> > 'It spells not me!' she said: 10
> 'Tells nothing about my beauty, wit, or gay time
> > With all those, quick and dead,
> > Of high or lowlihead,
> > > That hovered near,
> Including you, who carve there your devotion; 15
> > But you felt none, my dear!'
> And then she vanished. Checkless sprang my emotion
> > And forced a tear
> At seeing I'd not been truly known by her,
> And never prized! – that my memorial here, 20
> > To consecrate her sepulchre,
> > > Was scorned, almost,
> > > By her sweet ghost:
> Yet I hoped not quite, in her very innermost!
>
> 1916.

136 The Later Autumn

Published in the *Saturday Review*, 28 October 1922. The manuscript is dated 1921. Taylor suggests that this poem and similar ones like 'A Sheep Fair' (139), written in the period, constitute a late pastoral period in Hardy's career (1981: 139–55).

Metre: $a^4 b^2 b^2 a^4 c^2 c^2 d^2 d^2$ dtr, though with an initial stress on many lines.

> Gone are the lovers, under the bush
> > Stretched at their ease;
> > Gone the bees,
> Tangling themselves in your hair as they rush
> > On the line of your track, 5
> > Leg-laden, back
> > With a dip to their hive
> > In a prepossessed dive.
>
> Toadsmeat is mangy, frosted, and sere;
> > Apples in grass 10

10. *It spells not*] It is not like MS.
12. *quick*: alive.
13. *high or lowlihead*: of 'high' or 'low' birth.
1. *Gone are the lovers*] No more lovers MS del., *Saturday Review*.
3. *Gone the bees*] No more bees MS del., *Saturday Review*.
9. *Toadsmeat*: a toadstool or fungus.
9. *sere*: dried up.

>   Crunch as we pass,
> And rot ere the men who make cyder appear.
>   Couch-fires abound
>   On fallows around,
>   And shades far extend   15
>   Like lives soon to end.
>
>   Spinning leaves join the remains shrunk and brown
>   Of last year's display
>   That lie wasting away,
>   On whose corpses they earlier as scorners gazed down   20
>   From their aery green height:
>   Now in the same plight
>   They huddle; while yon
>   A robin looks on.

137 An East-End Curate

Published in the *London Mercury*, November 1924; selected for *Chosen Poems* (1929). The poem might be a reflection on a sentence in *Jude the Obscure* III, i: 'But to enter the church in such an unscholarly way that he could not in all probability rise to a higher grade through all his career than that of the humble curate wearing his life out in an obscure village or city slum – that might have a touch of goodness and greatness in it; that might be true religion and a purgatorial course worthy of being followed by a remorseful man' (p. 149).

Metre: irregular, $a^5 b^4 b^4 a^7 c^7 c^7$, etc., dr with variations.

>   A small blind street off East Commercial Road;
>   Window, door; window, door;
>   Every house like the one before,
>   Is where the curate, Mr. Dowle, has found a pinched abode.
>   Spectacled, pale, moustache straw-coloured, and with a long
>   thin face,   5

13. *couch-fires*: fires for burning couch-grass. Cf. 'In Time of "The Breaking of Nations"' (109), l. 6n.
14. *fallows*: fields left unused.
15. *shades far*] shadows MS del., *Saturday Review* ('shades' suggests ghosts).
17–24. on leaves as the souls of the dead, see 'During Wind and Rain' (102), l. 7n and cf. 'The Master and the Leaves'.
1. *East Commercial Road*: runs through Whitechapel and Stepney, in Victorian London a focus for charity and mission work.
4. *Dowle*: a similar name to the Howell who was the secretary of a Reform League with offices under Hardy's workplace in 1862 (*EL* 49); more plausibly it suggests 'Do-well' (Pinion 1976: 204).

Day or dark his lodgings' narrow doorstep does he pace.
A bleached pianoforte, with its drawn silk plaitings faded,
Stands in his room, its keys much yellowed, cyphering, and
   abraded,
'Novello's Anthems' lie at hand, and also a few glees,
And 'Laws of Heaven for Earth' in a frame upon the wall one
   sees.   10

He goes through his neighbours' houses as his own, and none
   regards,
And opens their back-doors off-hand, to look for them in their
   yards:
A man is threatening his wife on the other side of the wall,
But the curate lets it pass as knowing the history of it all.

Freely within his hearing the children skip and laugh and say: 15
   'There's Mister Dow-well! There's Mister Dow-well!' in
      their play;
   And the long, pallid, devoted face notes not,
But stoops along abstractedly, for good, or in vain, God wot!

138 Sine Prole
(Mediaeval Latin Sequence-Metre)

Hardy had earlier hoped for children (*EL* 153), and his 1922 will implies he still saw the possibility of his second marriage producing them. But he also considered that he came from 'an old family of spent social energies' which was dying out (*EL* 5). The family pedigree which he drew up after his second marriage has a line drawn across the bottom. On genealogy, cf. 'Heredity' (81), 'The Pedigree' (91), 'Family Portraits' (175).
   Metre: $a^4a^4b^4c^4c^4b^4$ df. Tail-rhyme modelled on Adam of St Victor's 'Heri Mundus Exultavit', which Hardy knew from his copy of *Sequences from the Sarum Missal* (cf. 'Genitrix Laesa'). He reported that in 1900 he

8. *cyphering*: humming because of faulty dampers (a word more commonly used of organs). In 1922 Florence Hardy referred to 'that most pathetic old piano' on which Hardy played (Meynell 1940: 309).
9. *'Novello's Anthems' . . . glees*: popular religious songs published by Vincent Novello; and part-songs for less serious occasions.
10. *'Laws of Heaven for Earth'*: religious maxims, possibly the ten commandments.
15. *skip and laugh and*] not in *Mercury*.
18. *God wot!*: God knows!
Title. *Sine Prole*: L. without offspring.

'spent time ... hunting up Latin hymns at the British Museum' in order to
expand his metrical range (*LY* 85). The use of 'Sequence-Metre' parallels
the 'sequence' of genealogy which is the poem's subject.

> Forth from ages thick in mystery,
> Through the morn and noon of history,
>   To the moment where I stand
> Has my line wound: I the last one –
> Outcome of each spectral past one   5
>   Of that file, so many-manned!
>
> Nothing in its time-trail marred it:
> As one long life I regard it
>   Throughout all the years till now,
> When it fain – the close seen coming –   10
> After annals past all plumbing –
>   Makes to Being its parting bow.
>
> Unlike Jahveh's ancient nation,
> Little in their line's cessation
>   Moderns see for surge of sighs: 15
> They have been schooled by lengthier vision,
> View Life's lottery with misprision,
>   And its dice that fling no prize!

139 A Sheep Fair

Selected by Hardy for *Chosen Poems* (1929). Another poem used by Taylor
to illustrate the hypothesis of a late 'pastoral' period (1981: 139–55) – a
claim which the 'Postscript' would seem to qualify.

    Metre: $a^4b^2a^4b^2c^4c^4c^4c^4d^5b^2$ dr, with a link-rhyme between stanzas on the
d-line and a near-repeat of the first and last b-lines. Close to the stanza-
form of 'Weathers' (113) with the addition of an extra pentameter line.

1–6. cf. the 'tangles' and 'line' of 'The Pedigree' (91).
7. i.e. nothing interrupted the continuity of Hardy's genealogy until now.
13. Javeh's ancient nation: Israel (whose genealogies and 'increase' are
detailed exhaustively in 1 Chronicles and elsewhere).
16. schooled by lengthier vision: by Darwin in particular, who pushed the
origins of the world and humanity back beyond the biblical date of *c.* 4004
BC.
17. misprision: contempt, scorn.
18. dice: cf. 'dicing Time' in 'Hap' (2).

The day arrives of the autumn fair,
    And torrents fall,
Though sheep in throngs are gathered there,
    Ten thousand all,
Sodden, with hurdles round them reared:
And, lot by lot, the pens are cleared,
And the auctioneer wrings out his beard,
And wipes his book, bedrenched and smeared,
And rakes the rain from his face with the edge of his hand,
    As torrents fall.

The wool of the ewes is like a sponge
    With the daylong rain:
Jammed tight, to turn, or lie, or lunge,
    They strive in vain.
Their horns are soft as finger-nails,
Their shepherds reek against the rails,
The tied dogs soak with tucked-in tails,
The buyers' hat-brims fill like pails,
Which spill small cascades when they shift their stand
    In the daylong rain.

Postscript

Time has trailed lengthily since met
    At Pummery Fair
Those panting thousands in their wet
    And woolly wear:
And every flock long since has bled,
And all the dripping buyers have sped,
And the hoarse auctioneer is dead,
Who 'Going – going!' so often said,
As he consigned to doom each meek, mewed band
    At Pummery Fair.

---

5. *hurdles*: movable fences.
Postscript: in 1920 Hardy commented on postscripts in a letter to Eden Phillpotts: 'I am aware that the time-honoured plan of letting the reader know the end of all the personages is quite out of date'; adding that he would like to do so to his own novels, 'as was done in Fielding's time' (*CLB* VI 57–8).
22. *Pummery Fair*: Poundbury Fair, outside Dorchester.
25. Hardy left money in his will for the promotion of humane slaughtering techniques (cf. 'Bags of Meat' and 'Compassion. An Ode', in the same volume).

140 Snow in the Suburbs

Selected by Hardy for *Chosen Poems* (1929). The first of a group of six poems on winter scenes, three of which are included here. Davie compares this poem's precision to that of the Imagist 'equation' (1973: 47), and the manuscript shows a great deal of effort at achieving its effects, with almost line-by-line revision (detailed below).

Metre: irregular and complex, two different stanza-forms concluding with a quatrain, and with five different line-lengths in the second stanza: $a^3a^3b^4b^4c^6c^6d^5d^5$ $a^3a^3b^5b^5c^2c^2d^4d^6$ $a^3a^3b^4b^2$ dr with variations (including double-rhymes on ll. 1–2, 13–14). The descriptive opening has a falling metre and end-stopped line before the narrative moves on in iambics and enjambment at l. 5, and the poem's shape might suggest the covering effects of snow.

> Every branch big with it,
> Bent every twig with it;
> Every fork like a white web-foot;
> Every street and pavement mute:
> Some flakes have lost their way, and grope back upward, when   5
> Meeting those meandering down they turn and descend again.
> The palings are glued together like a wall,
> And there is no waft of wind with the fleecy fall.
>
> A sparrow enters the tree,
> Whereon immediately   10
> A snow-lump thrice his own slight size
> Descends on him and showers his head and eyes.
> And overturns him,
> And near inurns him,
> And lights on a nether twig, when its brush   15
> Starts off a volley of other lodging lumps with a rush.

Title] Snow at Upper Tooting MS del. The Hardys lived in Tooting, London, 1878–81.
5. *grope*] float MS del.
6. *meandering*] coming MS del.
7. *glued*] joined MS del.
8. *there is no waft*] there's not a whiff MS.
11. *thrice his own slight size*] three-times his own size MS del.
14. *inurns*: buries.
15. *lights*] falls MS del.
15. *nether*] lower MS del.
16. *volley*] cascade MS.
16. *lodging*] waiting MS del.

> The steps are a blanched slope,
> Up which, with feeble hope,
> A black cat comes, wide-eyed and thin;
> And we take him in. 20

141 A Light Snow-Fall after Frost

The second poem of the series, and a poem of outlines and visual transitions in 'neutral tones' of green, brown and white which recall other 'etched' effects in Hardy's work (cf. 'Lying Awake' (160)). Taylor uses the poem as a central example of transitions, the passing of time, and Gothic web-patterns in Hardy's work (1981: xi-xiii, 45–6).

Metre: complex, the first and last stanzas match, $a^5a^3b^5b^5c^3$ and $a^5a^3b^5b^5a^3$ dr, while the two middle stanzas are different, $a^3a^5b^5b^5a^3$ and $a^3b^5b^3b^3a^3a^5$ dr.

> On the flat road a man at last appears:
> How much his whitening hairs
> Owe to the settling snow's mute anchorage,
> And how much to a life's rough pilgrimage,
> One cannot certify. 5
>
> The frost is on the wane,
> And cobwebs hanging close outside the pane
> Pose as festoons of thick white worsted there,
> Of their pale presence no eye being aware
> Till the rime made them plain. 10
>
> A second man comes by;
> His ruddy beard brings fire to the pallid scene:
> His coat is faded green;
> Hence seems it that his mien
> Wears something of the dye 15
> Of the berried holm-trees that he passes nigh.

17. blanched] white MS del.
19. wide-eyed] large-eyed MS del.
4. life's rough pilgrimage: cf. '"For Life I had never cared greatly"' (107), l. 30.
6–10. added to MS. Taylor suggests that Hardy may have added it to an early draft after composing *Tess of the D'Urbervilles* (see note below).
8. worsted: thick woolen material. Frost-covered cobwebs as 'white worsted' feature in a passage with a number of parallels to this one in *Tess of the D'Urbervilles*, ch. 43 (pp. 311–12).
10. rime: hoar-frost or frozen dew (a pun on 'rhyme' is possible).
14. mien: bearing.

>   The snow-feathers so gently swoop that though
>   But half an hour ago
>   The road was brown, and now is starkly white,
>   A watcher would have failed defining quite   20
>   When it transformed it so.
>   Near Surbiton.

142 Music in a Snowy Street

The genesis of the poem in a street-scene in Dorchester is described by Hardy in a descriptive sketch in a diary entry for 26 April 1884 (see *EL* 215–16). His note at the end of the entry implies that the poem was produced by his re-reading the diary for his autobiography.
   Metre: irregularly rhymed dimeter, $a^2b^2a^2c^2b^2c^2$ etc. dtr.

>   The weather is sharp,
>   But the girls are unmoved:
>   One wakes from a harp,
>   The next from a viol,
>   A strain that I loved   5
>   When life was no trial.
>
>   The tripletime beat
>   Bounds forth on the snow,
>   But the spry springing feet
>   Of a century ago,   10
>   And the arms that enlaced
>   As the couples embraced,
>   Are silent old bones
>   Under graying gravestones.
>
>   The snow-feathers sail   15
>   Across the harp-strings,
>   Whose throbbing threads wail
>   Like love-satiate things.
>   Each lyre's grimy mien,

20. a watcher: Simon Gatrell comments on the impersonality of this observer after the implicit 'I' of the previous stanzas (1980: 166).
Near Surbiton: in South London, where the Hardys lived in 1874.
4. viol: violin.
7–14. cf. the dancing 'dead feet' of 'The Self-Unseeing' (23) and the 'phantoms' calling the tune in 'Song to an Old Burden' (152).
19. each lyre's grimy mien: each instrument's grimy appearance.

With its rout-raising tune, 20
Against the new white
Of the flake-laden noon,
Is incongruous to sight,
Hinting years they have seen
Of revel at night 25
Ere these damsels became
Possessed of their frame.

O bygone whirls, heys,
Crotchets, quavers, the same
That were danced in the days 30
Of grim Bonaparte's fame,
Or even by the toes
Of the fair Antoinette, –
Yea, old notes like those
Here are living on yet! – 35
But of their fame and fashion
How little these know
Who strum without passion
For pence, in the snow!

143 In Sherborne Abbey
(17—)

One of a series of poems written across the span of Hardy's career which use architecture as their setting or subject. They include 'Heiress and Architect', 'Rome. Building a New Steet in the Ancient Quarter' (14), 'A Man', 'Architectural Masks', 'The Abbey Mason', 'Copying Architecture in an Old Minster' (83), and 'A Cathedral Façade at Midnight' (134), among others (see Taylor 1972: 48ff; Cox 1972; Knoepflmacher 1990). The setting here is the Abbey Church of St Mary Virgin at Sherborne, Dorset, famous for its Perpendicular fan-vaulting. The moonlit meeting in *A Pair of Blue Eyes*, ch. 32, has some similarities.

Metre: irregular 4- and 6-line stanzas, in couplets (with the exception of lines 15–18), aabb, etc., dtr. The basic rhythm is pentameter, but the line-length varies from three- to six-beat: the lovers speak in short lines in stanza 4, suggesting apprehensiveness, while the more 'funereal' passages are hexameter.

28. heys: cries.
33. Antoinette: Marie Antoinette, wife of Louis XVI of France, guillotined 1793.

The moon has passed to the panes of the south-aisle wall,
And brought the mullioned shades and shines to fall
On the cheeks of a woman and man in a pew there, pressed
Together as they pant, and recline for rest.

Forms round them loom, recumbent like their own, 5
  Yet differing; for they are chiselled in frigid stone;
In doublets are some; some mailed, as whilom ahorse they leapt:
And stately husbands and wives, side by side as they anciently
    slept.

'We are not like those,' she murmurs. 'For ever here set!'
'True, Love,' he replies. 'We two are not marble yet.' 10
  'And, worse,' said she; 'not husband and wife!'
  'But we soon shall be' (from him) 'if we've life!'
A silence. A trotting of horses is heard without.
The lovers scarce breathe till its echo has quite died out.

'It was they! They have passed, anyhow!' 15
  'Our horse, slily hid by the conduit,
They've missed, or they'd rushed to impound it!'
  'And they'll not discover us now.'
  'Will not, until 'tis too late,
And we can outface them straight!' 20

'Why did you make me ride in your front?' says she.
'To outwit the law. That was my strategy.
  As I was borne off on the pillion behind you,
  Th'abductor was you, Dearest, let me remind you;
And seizure of me by an heiress is no felony, 25
Whatever to do it with me as the seizer may be.'

Another silence sinks. And a cloud comes over the moon:
The print of the panes upon them enfeebles, as fallen in a
    swoon,

---

1. another moon-and-window image: see Stallworthy (1980).
2. mullioned: rectangular-shaped (windows).
7. whilom: once.
5–10. human forms often merge with funereal monuments in Hardy's work: cf. esp. *Tess of the D'Urbervilles*, in which the Durbeyfield family camp on their own tomb, and Alex is mistaken for a statue by Tess (ch. 52).
16. conduit: fountain.
26. i.e. no matter that I am her lover, it is not a crime if she 'kidnaps' me.
27. sinks] falls MS, *HS* 1925.

Until they are left in darkness unbroke and profound,
As likewise are left their chill and chiselled neighbours
around.   30

A Family tradition.

144 The Mock Wife

The 'dark drama' described in this poem is an extrapolation of the story of Mary Channing, burnt for poisoning her husband Thomas in Dorchester in 1705. Hardy uses it in *The Mayor of Casterbridge*, ch. 11, and in his essay 'Maumbury Ring', *The Times*, 9 October 1908 (*PW* 228–30), and seems to have taken a rather morbid interest in the details of the execution (see Gittings 1978: 205). The 'cheat' here owes something to the biblical story of Jacob, Esau, and the stolen blessing, told in Genesis 27 (Zeitlow 1974: 108–9).

Metre: aabb[7] dtr, an ancient narrative form (cf. 'Wessex Heights' (47)).

It's a dark drama, this; and yet I know the house, and date;
That is to say, the where and when John Channing met his
fate.
The house was one in High Street, seen of burghers still alive,
The year was some two centuries bygone; seventeen-hundred
and five.

And dying was Channing the grocer. All the clocks had struck
eleven,   5
And the watchers saw that ere the dawn his soul would be in
Heaven;
When he said on a sudden: 'I should *like* to kiss her before I
go, –
For one last time!' They looked at each other and murmured,
'Even so.'

She'd just been haled to prison, his wife; yea, charged with
shaping his death:
By poison, 'twas told; and now he was nearing the moment of
his last breath: 10
He, witless that his young housemate was suspect of such a
crime,
Lay thinking that his pangs were but a malady of the time.

A Family tradition: Pinion suggests that the story relates to the elopement of two eighteenth-century ancestors, Joseph Pitcher and a Miss Heller (1976: 215).

11. young housemate: Mary Channing was only 18 when she was executed.

Outside the room they pondered gloomily, wondering what to do,
As still he craved her kiss – the dying man who nothing knew:
'Guilty she may not be,' they said; 'so why should we torture him   15
In these his last few minutes of life? Yet how indulge his whim?'

And as he begged there piteously for what could not be done,
And the murder-charge had flown about the town to every one,
The friends around him in their trouble thought of a hasty plan,
And straightway set about it. Let denounce them all who can.   20

'O will you do a kindly deed – it may be a soul to save;
At least, great misery to a man with one foot in the grave?'
Thus they to the buxom woman not unlike his prisoned wife;
'The difference he's past seeing; it will soothe his sinking life.'

Well, the friendly neighbour did it; and he kissed her; held her fast;   25
Kissed her again and yet again. 'I – knew she'd – come at last! –
Where have you been? – Ah, kept away! – I'm sorry – overtried –
God bless you!' And he loosed her, fell back tiredly, and died.

His wife stood six months after on the scaffold before the crowd,
Ten thousand of them gathered there; fixed, silent, and hard-browed,   30
To see her strangled and burnt to dust, as was the verdict then
On women truly judged or false, of doing to death their men.

Some of them said as they watched her burn: 'I am glad he never knew,
Since a few hold her as innocent – think such she could not do!

31–2. a wife killing her husband was known as 'petty treason', and could entail such punishment up to 1828. As Hardy's phrasing suggests, he regarded her guilt as 'not proven' (*PN* 38).

> Glad, too, that (as they tell) he thought she kissed him ere he
>   died.' 35
> And they seemed to make no question that the cheat was
>   justified.

145 'Not only I'

One of a number of poems on Emma in *Human Shows*, some dating from 1912–13, some more distant meditations presumably written later. Here Hardy dwells on the death of memory and the 'associations' of the dead, as in poems written before Emma's death, like 'His Immortality' (19).

Metre: another highly irregular experiment, with three 10-line stanza types and 4-line types, $a^2a^3b^4c^4c^4d^2e^2b^3d^2e^2$ dr, etc. In the final stanza the short lines sandwiched between longer ones help suggest the 'compression' of the grave (see Ingham 1980: 125–6).

> Not only I
> Am doomed awhile to lie
> In this close bin with earthen sides;
> But the things I thought, and the songs I sang,
> And the hopes I had, and the passioned pang   5
>   For people I knew
>   Who passed before me,
> Whose memory barely abides;
>   And the visions I drew
>   That daily upbore me!   10
>
> And the joyous springs and summers,
> And the jaunts with blithe newcomers,
> And my plans and appearances; drives and rides
> That fanned my face to a lively red;
>   And the grays and blues   15
>   Of the far-off views,
> That nobody else discerned outspread;
> And little achievements for blame or praise;
> Things left undone; things left unsaid;
>   In brief, my days!   20

3. close bin: cf. the description of the grave in 'Lament' (57); a poem in the original elegiac sequence to which this could be a reply.
14–15. Hardy often described the red flush of Emma Hardy's face: see 'After a Journey' (63), l. 8n.

> Compressed here in six feet by two,
>   In secrecy
>   To lie with me
>   Till the Call shall be,
> Are all these things I knew,   25
> Which cannot be handed on;
> Strange happenings quite unrecorded,
> Lost to the world and disregarded,
> That only thinks: 'Here moulders till Doom's-dawn
> A woman's skeleton.'   30

146 Her Haunting-Ground

Like the next poem, 'Her Haunting-Ground' reflects on the distance between Hardy and Emma. It seems to provide a late comment on the contrast between Cornwall (the poem's 'here') and Dorset which had structured the 'Poems of 1912–13'. It may date from Hardy's last visit to Cornwall in 1916.

Metre: iambic tetrameter, abbacdcd[4], four lines of in *In Memoriam* stanza (abba) resolving into 'long' hymn stanza (abab), mirroring the poem's division between memory and reflection.

> Can it be so? It must be so,
> That visions have not ceased to be
> In this the chiefest sanctuary
> Of her whose form we used to know.
> – Nay, but her dust is far away,   5
> And 'where her dust is, shapes her shade,
> If spirit clings to flesh,' they say:
> Yet here her life-parts most were played!
>
> Her voice explored this atmosphere,
> Her foot impressed this turf around,   10
> Her shadow swept this slope and mound,
> Her fingers fondled blossoms here;
> And so, I ask, why, why should she
> Haunt elsewhere, by a slighted tomb,
> When here she flourished sorrow-free,   15
> And, save for others, knew no gloom?

24. the Call: i.e. the Last Trump.
1. Pinion compares the opening of Henry Vaughan's lyric 'And do they so? Have they a sense / Of ought but influence?' (1976: 228).
14. slighted: wrecked.

147 Days to Recollect

This late and rather teasing poem on Emma is comparable to 'Ten Years Since' and 'The Month's Calendar' in its reliance on external reminders, anniversaries, and the conscious guarding of memory.

Metre: $a^2A^2b^4b^4c^3d^4d^4e^4b^4e^4c^3a^2A^2$ dr with c=d in the first stanza and link-rhymes between stanzas on the c-line. The paired a-lines form a refrain within each stanza.

>   Do you recall
>   That day in Fall
> When we walked towards Saint Alban's Head,
> On thistledown that summer had shed,
>   Or must I remind you? 5
> Winged thistle-seeds which hitherto
> Had lain as none were there, or few,
> But rose at the brush of your petticoat-seam
> (As ghosts might rise of the recent dead),
> And sailed on the breeze in a nebulous stream 10
>   Like a comet's tail behind you:
>   You don't recall
>   That day in Fall?
>
>   Then do you remember
>   That sad November 15
> When you left me never to see me more,
> And looked quite other than theretofore,
>   As if it could not *be* you?
> And lay by the window whence you had gazed
> So many times when blamed or praised, 20
> Morning or noon, through years and years,
> Accepting the gifts that Fortune bore,
> Sharing, enduring, joys, hopes, fears!
>   Well: I never more did see you. –
>   Say you remember 25
>   That sad November!

3. *Saint Alban's Head*: below Swanage, where the Hardy's were living in 1875.
6–11. cf. *The Hand of Ethelberta*, ch. 31 (written at Swanage).
15. Emma Hardy died 27 November 1912.

148 This Summer and Last

One of a number of poems in which the seasonal cycle is implicated in Hardy's recognition of his loss: 'Joys of Memory', 'A Backward Spring' (103). 'It Never Looks Like Summer', 'Paths of Former Time', '"If it's ever spring again"'. The series is 'resolved' by 'Proud Songsters' (155), with its serene contemplation.

Metre: $a^3b^2c^4b^4b^2c^3a^3a^2$ mainly dr (unique), with the rhymes of the first stanza repeated exactly in the third (thus a cyclic structure in the poem, mirroring that of the seasons).

> Unhappy summer you,
> Who do not see
> What your yester-summer saw!
> Never, never will you be
> Its match to me,   5
> Never, never draw
> Smiles your forerunner drew,
> Know what it knew!
>
> Divine things done and said
> Illumined it,   10
> Whose rays crept into corn-brown curls,
> Whose breezes heard a humorous wit
> Of fancy flit. –
> Still the alert brook purls,
> Though feet that there would tread   15
> Elsewhere have sped.
>
> So, bran-new summer, you
> Will never see
> All that yester-summer saw!
> Never, never will you be   20
> In memory
> Its rival, never draw
> Smiles your forerunner drew,
> Know what it knew!
>
>   1913?

3. *yester-summer*: the previous summer. Hardy uses many such time-compounds, 'yester-eve', 'yestertide', and even the bare 'yester' (Elliott 1984: 175).
11. *curls*: on hair, see '"I found her out there"' (55), l. 27n.
14. *purls*: twists (used also in 'A Death-Day Recalled' (64)).
15–16. cf. the heavy 'bled/sped/dead' rhymes of 'A Sheep Fair' (139).

149 'Nothing matters much'
(B.F.L.)

One of a pair of elegies for friends dying in 1922–3 (the other is for Frederic Treeves). Judge Benjamin Fossett Lock (B.F.L.) was Hardy's friend and fellow-Dorsetman, secretary of the Positivist Society, d. August 1922.

Metre: $a^4b^4a^4b^2$ dr with variations (a common hymn stanza, and that of Pope's Horatian 'Happy the Man': cf. 'Life Laughs Onward', 'The Gap in the White').

'Nothing matters much,' he said
Of something just befallen unduly:
He, then active, but now dead,
    Truly, truly!

He knew each letter of the law   5
As voiced by those of wig and gown,
Whose slightest syllogistic flaw
    He hammered down.

And often would he shape in word
That nothing needed much lamenting;   10
And she who sat there smiled and heard,
    Sadly assenting.

Facing the North Sea now he lies,
Toward the red altar of the East,
The Flamborough roar his psalmodies,   15
    The wind his priest.

And while I think of his bleak bed,
Of Time that builds, of Time that shatters,
Lost to all thought is he, who said
    'Nothing much matters.'   20

1. 'Nothing matters much': the phrase is used in *The Dynasts* III, v, 4; and in 'In Tenebris II' (25), l. 11.
11. she who sat there: Lock's wife predeceased him by a few years.
13–16. Judge Lock died at Bridlington, Yorkshire, near Flamborough Head.
20. Faurot comments rather cryptically on the reordering of the title-phrase here: 'Hardy shifts the emphasis from action, being, or condition ... to disempowered substance' (1990: 348)

150 Before My Friend Arrived

The 'friend' of the title is Horace Moule, who killed himself in Cambridge on 21 September 1873 and was buried in Fordington, Dorchester, on 26 September (see 'Standing by the Mantelpiece' (169)).
  Metre: irregular stanzas, $a^3b^3a^4b^3c^3c^3d^3d^3d^3 \quad a^3b^3c^3a^3b^3c^4c^4 \quad a^4a^4b^4b^3b^3$ dtr.

> I sat on the eve-lit weir,
>   Which gurgled in sobs and sighs;
> I looked across the meadows near
>   To the towered church on the rise.
>   Overmuch cause had my look! 5
>   I pulled out pencil and book,
>   And drew a white chalk mound,
>   Outthrown on the sepulchred ground.
>
> Why did I pencil that chalk?
>   It was fetched from the waiting grave, 10
>   And would return there soon,
>   Of one who had stilled his walk
>   And sought oblivion's cave.
> He was to come on the morrow noon
> And take a good rest in the bed so hewn. 15
>
> He came, and there he is now, although
> This was a wondrous while ago.
> And the sun still dons a ruddy dye;
>   The weir still gurgles nigh;
>   The tower is dark on the sky. 20

151 The Bird-Catcher's Boy

One of a series of poems which Hardy wrote on caged birds, beginning with 'The Caged Thrush Freed and Home Again' and climaxing with 'The Boy's Dream' (174). Dated 21 November 1912, published in *The Sphere*, 4 January 1913. Gittings sees it as 'perhaps an allegory of Emma's life and death' (1978: 148, 153). Given Hardy's indebtedness to Shelley for his bird-imagery, there are perhaps distant echoes of Shelley's exile and drowning. The poem was revised considerably and expanded when finally collected in *Human Shows* (the earlier version is printed in Appendix I, below).

  1. weir: Ten Hatches Weir, on the Frome east of Dorchester.
  4. towered church: St George's, Fordington.

Metre: $a^2b^2a^2b^2$ tdf or $a^3b^2a^3b^2$ dtf, depending on the stress placed on the final syllables of odd-numbered lines. The even-numbered lines are generally catalectic (with a dropped off-beat), usually comprising a trochee and an iamb, an effect which occasionally suggests a counterpointing iambic rhythm. The earlier version in *The Sphere* alternated rhymed and unrhymed lines.

'Father, I fear your trade:
　Surely it's wrong!
Little birds limed and made
　Captive life-long.

'Larks bruise and bleed in jail,
　Trying to rise;
Every caged nightingale
　Soon pines and dies.'

'Don't be a dolt, my boy!
　Birds must be caught;
My lot is such employ,
　Yours to be taught.

'Soft shallow stuff as that
　Out from your head!
Just learn your lessons pat,
　Then off to bed.'

Lightless, without a word
　Bedwise he fares;
Groping his way is heard
　Seek the dark stairs

Through the long passage, where
　Hang the caged choirs:
Harp-like his fingers there
　Sweep on the wires.

Next day, at dye of dawn,
　Freddy was missed:
Whither the boy had gone
　Nobody wist.

That week, the next one, whiled:
　No news of him:

---

3. *limed*: birds were caught by smearing a sticky lime compound on trees (cf. Shelley, *A Defence of Poetry*: 'Lucretius had limed the wings of his swift spirit in the dregs of the sensible world').
5–6. cf. '"We are getting to the end"' (177), ll. 5–7.
15. *pat*: by heart.
28. *wist*: knew.

>   Weeks up to months were piled:
>   Hope dwindled dim.
>
>   Yet not a single night
>   Locked they the door,
>   Waiting, heart-sick, to sight   35
>   Freddy once more.
>
>   Hopping there long anon
>   Still the birds hung:
>   Like those in Babylon
>   Captive, they sung.   40
>
>   One wintry Christmastide
>   Both lay awake:
>   All cheer within them dried,
>   Each hour an ache.
>
>   Then some one seemed to flit   45
>   Soft in below;
>   'Freddy's come!' Up they sit,
>   Faces aglow.
>
>   Thereat a groping touch
>   Dragged on the wires   50
>   Lightly and softly – much
>   As they were lyres;
>
>   'Just as it used to be
>   When he came in,
>   Feeling in darkness the   55
>   Stairway to win!'
>
>   Waiting a trice or two
>   Yet, in the gloom,
>   Both parents pressed into
>   Freddy's old room.   60
>
>   There on the empty bed
>   White the moon shone,
>   As ever since they'd said,
>   'Freddy is gone!'

37. long anon: much later.
39–40. Psalm 137: 1–3: 'By the waters of Babylon we sat down and wept: when we remembered thee, O Sion. As for our harps, we hanged them up: upon the trees that are therein. For they that lead us away captive required of us then a song'. On the literary associations of this Psalm, see Hollander 1981: 79.
52. lyres: musical instruments like harps (see previous note).

>   That night at Durdle-Door   65
>   Foundered a hoy,
>   And the tide washed ashore
>   One sailor boy.
>   *November* 21, 1912.

152 Song to an Old Burden

This and the poem which follows form the closing group of *Human Shows*. Both were selected by Hardy for *Chosen Poems* (1929). There are comparable descriptions of dancing in 'The Self-Unseeing' (23) and 'Music in a Snowy Street' (142).

    Metre: $a^4b^3a^3b^4c^5b^3$ dr with repetition and linking vowel-rhymes on the c-line (around around around / again again again), suggesting a dance-tune. Hardy uses similar musical effects in 'Lines to a Movement in Mozart's E-Flat Symphony' (90), and in 'A Duettist to Her Pianoforte'.

>   The feet have left the wormholed flooring,
>   That danced to the ancient air,
>   The fiddler, all-ignoring,
>   Sleeps by the gray-grassed 'cello player:
>   Shall I then foot around around around,   5
>   As once I footed there!
>
>   The voice is heard in the room no longer
>   That trilled, none sweetlier,
>   To gentle stops or stronger,
>   Where now the dust-draped cobwebs stir: 10
>   Shall I then sing again again again,
>   As once I sang with her!
>
>   The eyes that beamed out rapid brightness
>   Have longtime found their close,
>   The cheeks have wanned to whiteness   15
>   That used to sort with summer rose:

65. *Durdle-Door*: 'a rock on the south coast' (Hardy's gloss). In *The Sphere* it was 'Portland Race', further west.
66. *hoy*: a small sailing vessel. It is perhaps worth recalling that Shelley's body was washed ashore after his small boat foundered off Leghorn in 1822.
1–6. Hardy's father played the fiddle, his grandfather the cello (bass-viol) in Stinsford Church and at local festivities.
9. stops: notes.
16. sort with summer rose: be like roses in colour.

>   Shall I then joy anew anew anew,
>   As once I joyed in those!
>   O what's to me this tedious Maying,
>   What's to me this June?
>   O why should vials be playing
>   To catch and reel and rigadoon?
>   Shall I sing, dance around around around,
>   When phantoms call the tune!

153 'Why do I?'

Like many of Hardy's end-pieces, '"Why do I?"' is a dialogue of two parts of Hardy's self (or of self and soul), one of which is described as waiting for the other to die (see Jacobus 1982). In part this involves the Horatian idea of the poet of 'double shape' (*biformis*), one aspect of whom remains on earth while the other flies off (Horace, *Odes* 2: 20). Tennyson's 'The Lotos-Eaters' is a possible influence, with its weary race wishing for death:

>   We only toil, who are the first of things,
>   And make perpetual moan,
>   Still from one sorrow to another thrown;
>   Nor ever fold our wings,
>   And cease from wanderings. . . . (ll. 61–5)

Metre: $a^4b^2a^6b^2b^6$ dr, a rhyme-scheme common in Hardy's work, but not in this metrical pattern. The style seems to reflect the 'mechanic repetitions' and sudden release which are the poem's subject (see Paulin 1975: 81–2).

>   Is Why do I go on doing these things?
>   Why not cease?
>   Is it that you are yet in this world of welterings
>   And unease,
>   And that, while so, mechanic repetitions please?
>   When shall I leave off doing these things? –
>   When I hear

---

22. *catch and reel and rigadoon*: a catch is song like a 'round'; reels and rigadoons are dances. Hardy recalled his father performing jigs and other dances 'with all the old movements of leg-crossing and hop' in a 'fast perishing style' superseded by 'the more genteel "country-dance"' (*EL* 16).
24. cf. the 'heavily-haunted harmony' of 'A Duettist to Her Pianoforte'.
2–4. *cease . . . unease*: 'The Lotos-Eaters' uses the same rhyme, ll. 97–8.
3. *welterings*: disorderly movements, tossings (often used of the sea).

You have dropped your dusty cloak and taken you wondrous
        wings
   To another sphere,
Where no pain is: Then shall I hush this dinning gear.   10

8–9. the idea of death as leaving one's earthly 'clothing' is conventional, cf. e.g. Elizabeth Barrett Browning's 'Insufficiency' ('Wait, soul, until thine ashen garments fall'), Robert Browning's 'How It Strikes a Contemporary' ('No further show a need for that old coat'), or Meredith's 'The Question Whither':   When we have thrown off this old suit,
        So much in need of mending,
      To sink among the naked mute,
        Is that, think you, our ending?
8. taken you wondrous wings: i.e. taken [to] you wondrous wings. There is an amusing diary entry on wings in the *Life*:
    February 21 [1881]. A.G. called. Explained to Em about Aerostation, and how long her wings would have to be if she flew, – how light her weight, etc., and the process generally of turning her into a flying person. (*EL* 191)

Winter Words in Various Moods and Metres (1928)

Hardy's final volume was published posthumously on 2 October 1928; it had been intended for publication on his 88th birthday (2 June 1928). A possible source for the title is Robert Lynd's review of Hardy's poetry in *The Nation*, 22 December 1917, p. 412, entitled 'Mr. Hardy in Winter', mentioned by Hardy in a letter to Lynd in 1919 (*CL* V, 318). A draft title-page shows that Hardy considered other versions of the title, including 'Wintry Things Thought in Verse' and 'A Wintry Voice in Various Moods and Metres' (*CPW* III, 323).

The bulk of the 105 poems in *Winter Words* were written after the publication of *Human Shows*, but it also includes poems from earlier periods. Eleven had been released for publication before Hardy's death; the rights of fifty more were sold to *The Daily Telegraph* by his executors, Sydney Carlyle Cockrell and Florence Hardy, appearing between 19 March and 26 September 1928 (Purdy 1954: 262).

The manuscript is in Queen's College, Oxford (it lacks 'Childhood Among the Ferns'; for details of separate manuscripts see Rosenbaum 1990). It was in an incomplete state at Hardy's death, with no table of contents, alternative titles and variant readings left unresolved, and the order not finalized. Florence Hardy wrote to Macmillan on 11 February 1928: 'I wonder whether it would be a good plan if I were to bring you the poems just as they are, without any re-arrangement', adding that 'the first few poems and the last few have been arranged, but I am not sure that the ones in the middle of the book are arranged' (BL Add MS 54926). The proofs were set from a typescript (lost) prepared by Florence Hardy, with advice from Cockrell.

The volume's reception was understandably muted, given the volume of obituaries earlier in the year. Vita Sackville-West in *The Nation and Athenaeum* wrote of the 'stiff, uncomfortable, rheumaticky' diction, but regarded it as intrinsic to the Hardy universe in which 'carpenters are still making coffins; bastards are still born and furtively disposed of; lovers still fail to coincide; the old romance is still evoked and regretted' (13 October 1928, p. 54). A perceptive reviewer in *The Times Literary Supplement* commented on 'A Reflection': '"Neutral-tinted" might stand for the point of departure in his poetic realism'. The same reviewer praised Hardy's sureness of touch: 'somehow the barest of poems seldom – perhaps never in this volume – misses the point' ('Hardy's Last Poems', *TLS*, 4 October 1928, p. 705).

[*"Winter Words," though prepared for the press, would have undergone further revision, had the author lived to issue it on the birthday of which he left the number uninserted below.*]

Introductory Note

So far as I am aware, I happen to be the only English poet who has brought out a new volume of his verse on his . . . birthday, whatever may have been the case with the ancient Greeks, for it must be remembered that poets did not die young in those days.

This, however, is not the point of the present few preliminary words. My last volume of poems was pronounced wholly gloomy and pessimistic by reviewers – even by some of the more able class. My sense of the oddity of this verdict may be imagined when, in selecting them, I had been, as I thought, rather too liberal in admitting flippant, not to say farcical, pieces into the collection. However, I did not suppose that the licensed tasters had wilfully misrepresented the book, and said nothing, knowing well that they could not have read it.

As labels stick, I foresee readily enough that the same perennial inscription will be set on the following pages, and therefore take no trouble to argue on the proceeding, notwithstanding the surprises to which I could treat my critics by uncovering a place here and there to them in the volume.

This being probably my last appearance on the literary stage, I would say, more seriously, that though, alas, it would be idle to pretend that the publication of these poems can have much interest for me, the track having been adventured so many times before to-day, the pieces

Headnote] presumably written by Florence Hardy.
6–12. see Hardy's note on the flyleaf of *Human Shows* proofs, p. 279 above.

themselves have been prepared with reasonable care, if not quite with the zest of a young man new to print.

I also repeat what I have often stated on such occasions, that no harmonious philosophy is attempted in these pages – or in any bygone pages of mine, for that matter.

T.H.

154 The New Dawn's Business

Hardy's choice as the opening poem of *Winter Words*, first published in *The Daily Telegraph*, 20 March 1928. Like *Human Shows*, *Winter Words* opens with a poem about waiting for death, followed by a poem which describes a bird-scene in which nature's continuity is asserted.

Metre: $a^4b^3c^4c^2b^3d^4b^3$ dr, the d-lines more trisyllabic, with double (two-syllable) link-rhymes between stanzas on the d-lines.

What are you doing outside my walls,
    O Dawn of another day?
I have not called you over the edge
    Of the healthy ledge,
So why do you come this way, 5
With your furtive footstep without sound here,
    And your face so deedily gray?

'I show a light for killing the man
    Who lives not far from you,
And for bringing to birth the lady's child, 10
    Nigh domiciled,
And for earthing a corpse or two,

---

29. *often stated ... no harmonious philosophy*: recalls the Prefaces of *Poems of the Past and the Present* ('little cohesion of thought or harmony of colouring') and *Time's Laughingstocks* ('lack of concord').

Title. Dawn: Hardy often associates dawn with pessimism. In an 1871 diary entry he writes: 'Dawn. Lying just after waking. The sad possibilities of the future are more vivid then than at any other time. ... The laughing child may have now a foretaste of his manhood's glooms; the man, of the neglect and contumely which may wait on his old age' (*PN* 7).

7. *deedily*: intently, busily (Hardy glossed 'deedy' as 'brewing mischief'). The moon is described as 'deedily brooding' in 'Honeymoon Time at an Inn'.

8–12. cf. the ghoulish gaze of the moon in '"I looked up from my writing"' (111).

11. *Nigh domiciled*: living close by.

    And for several other such odd jobs round here
        That Time to-day must do.
'But you he leaves alone (although,   15
        As you have often said,
    You are always ready to pay the debt
        You don't forget
    You owe for board and bed):
The truth is, when men willing are found here   20
        He takes those loth instead.'

155 Proud Songsters

First printed in *The Daily Telegraph*, 9 April 1928. For comparable bird-poems, see 'A Backward Spring' (103), 'The Selfsame Song' (117), and 'A Bird-Scene at a Rural Dwelling' (132).
  Metre: $a^4b^4c^4d^1b^4b^3$ dr, with link-rhymes between stanzas on the a-, c-, d-lines.

    The thrushes sing as the sun is going,
        And the finches whistle in ones and pairs,
    And as it gets dark loud nightingales
        In bushes
    Pipe, as they can when April wears,   5
        As if all Time were theirs.

    These are brand-new birds of twelve-months' growing,

15–21. cf. references to being 'riven of all' and thus protected from death in 'Signs and Tokens'.
17. pay the debt: cf. 'quittance' in 'Afterwards' (112), l. 17n. In 1921 Hardy wrote: 'Those who died before 1914 are out of it, thank Heaven – and "have the least to pay" according to the old epitaph' (*CL* VI, 82). Pinion (1976: 237) notes that this is an allusion to a common mortuary verse (attributed to Quarles):
      Our life is but a winter's day:
      Some only breakfast and away;
      Others to dinner stay, and are full fed;
      The oldest only sups and goes to bed.
      Large is his debt who lingers out the day;
      Those who go the soonest have the least to pay.
5. when April wears: late April.
7–12. cf. *Tess*, ch. 20 (p. 156): 'Another year's instalment of flowers, leaves, nightingales, thrushes, finches, and such ephemeral creatures, took up their positions where only a year ago others had stood in their place when these

> Which a year ago, or less than twain,
> No finches were, nor nightingales,
>> Nor thrushes,
> But only particles of grain.
>> And earth, and air, and rain.

156 The Prophetess

Like 'Apostrophe to an Old Psalm Tune' (79) and 'Quid Hic Agis?' (85), this poem has as its scheme the repeated hearing of a text or tune, with a progressive revelation of its meaning.

Metre: a²a²b⁵c²c²b⁵ dr, extended tail-rhyme-scheme perhaps modelled on Keats's 'O Sorrow' (Taylor 1988: 238).

1
> 'Now shall I sing
> That pretty thing
> "The Mocking-Bird"?' – And sing it straight did she.
> I had no cause
> To think it was
> A Mocking-bird in truth that sang to me.

2
> Not even the glance
> She threw askance
> Foretold to me, nor did the tune or rhyme,
> That the words bore
> A meaning more
> Than that they were a ditty of the time.

3
> But after years
> Of hopes and fears,
> And all they bring, and all they take away,
> I found I had heard
> The Mocking-bird
> In person singing there to me that day.

were nothing more than germs and inorganic particles.' Cf. also Shelley's *Adonais* 18 and Meredith's 'The Thrush in February'.
8. *twain*: two.
3. *'The Mocking-Bird'*: a song which Emma Hardy used to sing, cf. the song with the 'mocking note' of stanza three of 'The Change' (89).
7–12] Hardy first wrote the first and last stanzas, and then added the second stanza at the bottom of the MS.

157 A Wish for Unconsciousness

First published in *The Daily Telegraph*, 5 July 1928. One of a range of pessimistic meditations, from the curse on existence: ('Epitaph on a Pessimist', 'Thoughts from Sophocles' (179)) to the wish for death ('Tess's Lament' (27)) and the expression of indifference ('He Never Expected Much' (168), 'A Placid Man's Epitaph').
Metre: trimeter, ababbcbcdd^3 dtr.

> If I could but abide
> As a tablet on a wall,
> Or a hillock daisy-pied,
> Or a picture in a hall,
> And as nothing else at all,   5
> I should feel no doleful achings,
> I should hear no judgment-call,
> Have no evil dreams or wakings,
> No uncouth or grisly care;
> In a word, no cross to bear.   10

158 The Love-Letters
(In Memoriam H.R.)

The sorting and destruction of letters, notebooks, and other documents is always a painful topic for Hardy: he regularly went through his personal papers after Emma's death and while writing his autobiography. In their period of estrangement, Emma also burnt many of his love-letters to her. Comparable poems are 'The Torn Letter' and 'The Photograph' (94).
Metre: a^{4}a^{4}b^{4}c^{4}c^{4}c^{4}b^3 dr in the first two stanzas, concluding with a couplet, a^{4}a^4. The rhyme-scheme is the same as 'The Maid of Keinton Mandeville'.

> I met him quite by accident
> In a bye-path that he'd frequent.
> And, as he neared, the sunset glow
> Warmed up the smile of pleasantry
> Upon his too thin face, while he   5
> Held a square packet up to me,
>   Of what, I did not know.

3. *daisy-pied*: spotted with daisies.
H.R.: obscure – Henry Reeve (1813–95), editor of the *Edinburgh Review*, is one suggestion.

'Well,' said he then; 'they are my old letters.
Perhaps she – rather felt them fetters. ...
You see, I am in a slow decline, 10
And she's broken off with me. Quite right
To send them back, and true foresight;
I'd got too fond of her! To-night
I burn them – stuff of mine!'

He laughed in the sun – an ache in his laughter – 15
And went. I heard of his death soon after.

159 Throwing a Tree
New Forest

First published in *Commerce* (Paris), winter 1928 as 'Felling a Tree', with a translation by Paul Valéry, and the misleading claim that it was the last poem that Hardy wrote. As the original title suggests, the poem closely resembles William Barnes's 'Vellèn the Tree', included in Hardy's selection from Barnes. Barnes's 'The Gre't Woak Tree That's in the Dell' also supplies a background:

> An' oh! mid never ax nor hook
> Be brought to spweil his stately look. ... (Barnes 1908: 7)

Hardy wrote a number of poems about the connections between trees and human lives, beginning with 'The Tree' in *Poems of the Past and the Present* and including 'The Felled Elm and She' in *Winter Words*. The same connection is present in *The Woodlanders*, ch. 14, where old South associates his life with a tree's.

Metre: $a^5b^5a^5b^6$ tdr.

The two executioners stalk along over the knolls,
Bearing two axes with heavy heads shining and wide,
And a long limp two-handled saw toothed for cutting great
    boles,
    And so they approach the proud tree that bears the death-
        mark on its side.

    Jackets doffed they swing axes and chop away just above
        ground, 5
    And the chips fly about and lie white on the moss and fallen
        leaves;

New Forest: in Hampshire (the 'Great Forest' of Hardy's novels).
5–6. cf. *Jude the Obscure* I, 2 (p. 41): 'He could scarcely bear to see trees cut down or lopped, from a fancy that it hurt them.'

> Till a broad deep gash in the bark is hewn all the way round,
> And one of them tries to hook upward a rope, which at last he achieves.
>
> The saw then begins, till the top of the tall giant shivers:
> The shivers are seen to grow greater each cut than before: 10
> They edge out the saw, tug the rope; but the tree only quivers,
> And kneeling and sawing again, they step back to try pulling once more.
>
> Then, lastly, the living mast sways, further sways: with a shout
> Job and Ike rush aside. Reached the end of its long staying powers
> The tree crashes downward: it shakes all its neighbours throughout, 15
> And two hundred years' steady growth has been ended in less than two hours.

160 Lying Awake

First published in the *Saturday Review*, 3 December 1927, 'Lying Awake' is the last and most abstract of Hardy's great series of dawn meditations, beginning with 'Nature's Questioning' (8) and including such poems as 'Four in the Morning' and 'The New Dawn's Business' (154).

Metre: $a^5b^3a^5b^3$ tdr (the long lines mainly trisyllabic). Tom Paulin sees the final line as 5-beat, however, and the anapaestic opening lines as heavily spondaic (1982: 88).

7. *hewn*: the word perhaps suggests Psalm 74: 6–7: 'He that hewed timber afore out of the thick trees: was known to bring it to an excellent work. But now they break down all the carved work thereof: with axes and hammers' – a psalm which Hardy quoted in 1920 as 'a snapshot of the current generation' in its suggestion of a destructive world (*LY* 212).
9–16. cf. the passage from Carlyle's *The French Revolution* which Hardy cited as an example of 'excellence of style' in a 1887 symposium in the *Fortnightly Review*:
> The oak grows silently, in the forest, a thousand years; only in the thousandth year, when the woodman arrives with his axe, is there heard an echoing through the solitudes; and the oak announces itself when, with far-sounding crash, it *falls*. (*PW* 108)

16. *two hundred*] seventy-odd MS del. (i.e. an individual life-span).

You, Morningtide Star, now are steady-eyed, over the east,
  I know it as if I saw you;
You, Beeches, engrave on the sky your thin twigs, even the
    least;
  Had I paper and pencil I'd draw you.
You, Meadow, are white with your counterpane cover of dew,   5
  I see it as if I were there;
You, Churchyard, are lightening faint from the shade of the
    yew,
  The names creeping out everywhere.

161 Childhood Among the Ferns

First published in *The Daily Telegraph*, 29 March 1928. Details are drawn from a boyhood memory described in Hardy's autobiography (significant changes include the poem's rain):

> He was lying on his back in the sun, thinking how useless he was, and covered his face with his straw hat. The sun's rays streamed through the interstices of the straw, the lining having disappeared. Reflecting on his experiences of the world so far as he had got, he came to the conclusion that he did not wish to grow up. . . . he did not want at all to be a man, or to possess things, but to remain as he was, in the same spot, and to know no more people than he already knew. (*EL* 19–20)

Part of the same passage, on Hardy's 'lack of social ambition' (*EL* 20) is alluded to in 'He Never Expected Much' (168). Cf. also *Jude the Obscure* I, 2 (p. 42).

The poem is part of a tradition of bower-poems, including Vaughan's 'The Retreat' (in Palgrave, with a similar emphasis on lost innocence), Coleridge's 'This Lime-Tree Bower My Prison', Arnold's 'Lines Written in Kensington Garden', and Elizabeth Barrett Browning's 'The Deserted Garden'.

Metre: aaa[5] dr.

3. cf. the pattern of engraved images in such poems as 'The Pedigree' (91), 'After a Romantic Day' (122), 'In a Former Resort after Many Years' (133).
4. in 1922 Hardy defensively remarked that Churchyards were common subjects in his poems because he 'used to spend much time in such places sketching, with another pupil, & we had many pleasant times at the work. Probably this explains why churchyards and churches never seem gloomy to me' (*CL* VI, 122).
8. suggests the gradual appearance of an image during the process of engraving.

I sat one sprinkling day upon the lea,
Where tall-stemmed ferns spread out luxuriantly,
And nothing but those tall ferns sheltered me.

The rain gained strength, and damped each lopping frond,
Ran down their stalks beside me and beyond, 5
And shaped slow-creeping rivulets as I conned,

With pride, my spray-roofed house. And though anon
Some drops pierced its green rafters, I sat on,
Making pretence I was not rained upon.

The sun then burst, and brought forth a sweet breath 10
From the limp ferns as they dried underneath:
I said: 'I could live on here thus till death';

And queried in the green rays as I sate:
'Why should I have to grow to man's estate,
And this afar-noised World perambulate?' 15

162 A Poet's Thought

Hardy made a number of assertions of the gap between the poet and his work or readers: others include 'To Shakespeare' (84) and 'Not Known'. His letters, notebooks, and the annotated scrapbooks into which he pasted reviews include recurrent complaints about critical misapprehensions (see Siemens 1984, and the 'Apology' to *Late Lyrics and Earlier*).

Metre: $a^4a^4b^5b^5$ $a^5a^5b^6b^6$ dr with variations. The shift in line-length parallels the process of self-estrangement and 'mangling' described by the poem.

It sprang up out of him in the dark,
And took on the lightness of a lark:
It went from his chamber along the city strand,
Lingered awhile, then leapt all over the land.

It came back maimed and mangled. And the poet 5
When he beheld his offspring did not know it:

1. lea: meadow.
4. lopping: drooping.
6. conned: studied.
15. perambulate: walk; though in the context of 'estate' the more specific meaning of 'surveying the boundaries' is also relevant.
6. offspring: the metaphor of poems as 'children' has a long history; e.g. the address to the reader in Daniel's *Delia*, sonnet 3:

> If it hap this offspring of my care,
> These fatal anthems, lamentable songs,
> Come to their view who like afflicted are. . . .

Yea, verily, since its birth Time's tongue had tossed to him
Such travesties that his old thought was lost to him.

163 'I watched a blackbird'

First published in *The Daily Telegraph*, 2 July 1928. In part a versification of a diary entry for 15 April 1900 included in the draft of *The Later Years*: 'Easter Sunday. Watched a blackbird on a budding sycamore. Was near enough to see his tongue, and crocus-coloured bill parting and closing as he sang. He flew down: picked up a stem of hay, and flew up to where he was building' (*CPW* III, 326, cf. *EL* 149–50). The poem might also seem a response to the first stanza of Robert Browning's 'Misconceptions':

> This is a spray the Bird clung to.
>   Making it blossom with pleasure,
> Ere the high tree-top she sprung to,
>   Fit for her nest and her treasure.
>   Oh, what hope beyond measure
> Was the poor spray's, which the flying feet hung to, –
> So to be singled out, built in, and sung to!

Metre: $a^6a^6b^5b^5c^5c^6c^6$ dr. 'After the Death of a Friend', eight poems earlier in *Winter Words*, has the same rhyme-scheme in tetrameter.

I watched a blackbird on a budding sycamore
One Easter Day, when sap was stirring twigs to the core;
  I saw his tongue, and crocus-coloured bill
  Parting and closing as he turned his trill;
  Then he flew down, seized on a stem of hay,   5
And upped to where his building scheme was under way,
As if so sure a nest were never shaped on spray.

7–8] a MS in the DCM has (del.):
    Since it had taken form, Time's tongue had brought to him
    So many Nays that his old Yea was nought to him.
7. *spray*: twigs.

164 A Nightmare, and the Next Thing

Hardy wrote a number of turn-of-the-year and Christmas poems (often pessimistic), including among others 'The Darkling Thrush' (21), 'New Year's Eve', 'End of the Year 1912', 'A New Year's Eve in War Time' (110), and concluding in this volume with the cynical quatrain 'Christmas: 1924' (173) and 'Christmas in the Elgin Room' (176). For a survey, see Pinion 1990: 307–33.

Metre: irregular stanza-forms and rhyme-schemes, iambic pentameter ab⁴, etc., dr.

>On this decline of Christmas Day
>The empty street is fogged and blurred:
>The house-fronts all seem backwise turned
>As if the outer world were spurned:
>Voices and songs within are heard,   5
>Whence red rays gleam when fires are stirred,
>Upon this nightmare Christmas Day.
>
>The lamps, just lit, begin to outloom
>Like dandelion-globes in the gloom;
>The stonework, shop-signs, doors, look bald;   10
>Curious crude details seem installed,
>And show themselves in their degrees
>As they were personalities
>Never discerned when the street was bustling
>With vehicles, and farmers hustling.   15
>
>Three clammy casuals wend their way
>To the Union House. I hear one say:
>'Jimmy, this is a treat! Hay-hay!'
>
>Six laughing mouths, six rows of teeth,
>Six radiant pairs of eyes, beneath   20
>Six yellow hats, looking out at the back
>Of a waggonette on its slowed-down track
>Up the steep street to some gay dance,
>Suddenly interrupt my glance.

3–4. cf. the façades in 'Architectural Masks' and 'A Cathedral Façade at Midnight' (134).

7. nightmare Christmas Day: the year's end also takes on demonic overtones in 'A New Year's Eve in War Time' (110).

16. casuals: 'casual paupers' admitted to the poor-house for temporary relief (the tramps enter 'the Casual's gate' in 'Christmastide', also in *Winter Words*).

17. Union House: poor-house or workhouse run by a Poor Law Union (in Dorchester, on Damers Road).

>   They do not see a gray nightmare 25
>   Astride the day, or anywhere.

165 So Various

First published in *The Daily Telegraph*, 22 March 1928. Hardy often meditated on that modernist preoccupation which Oscar Wilde called 'the multiplication of personalities'. A diary entry for 4 December 1890 notes: 'I am more than ever convinced that persons are successively various persons, according as each special strand in their characters is brought uppermost by circumstances' (*EL* 301). This line of thought is reflected in a notebook excerpt from a piece by 'Jacques' of the *Daily Chronicle*, 14 September 1901: 'I have invented four systems for playing *trente-et-quarante*. They represent four different temperaments – bold to rashness, bold but wary, moderately cautious, and meanly plodding. In a word, I am a syndicate of four different men' (Björk entry 2085: cf. entries 1393, 1505). Hardy's *The Well-Beloved* also presents what 'The Chosen' calls a 'composite form' of lovers.
Metre: a⁴a⁴b²b²b² dr (cf. 'He Resolves to Say No More' (178)).

> You may have met a man – quite young –
> A brisk-eyed youth, and highly strung:
>   One whose desires
>   And inner fires
>   Moved him as wires. 5
>
> And you may have met one stiff and old,
> If not in years; of manner cold;
>   Who seemed as stone,
>   And never had known
>   Of mirth or moan. 10
>
> And there may have crossed your path a lover,
> In whose clear depths you could discover
>   A stanch, robust,
>   And tender trust,
>   Through storm and gust. 15

25–6. the image recalls the Horseman of the Apocalypse (cf. 'He Resolves to Say No More' (178)), and also Blake's print 'Pity', with its outstretched horse, which Cockrell had compared with 'A New Year's Eve in War Time' in 1917 (110n).
Title. from Dryden's *Absalom and Achitophel*:
>   A man so various, that he seemed to be
>   Not one, but all mankind's epitome. (ll. 545–6)
3–5. cf. the 'puppet-like movements' of 'Family Portraits' (175), l. 21.

And you may have also known one fickle,
Whose fancies changed as the silver sickle
    Of yonder moon,
    Which shapes so soon
    To demilune!

You entertained a person once
Whom you internally deemed a dunce: –
    As he sat in view
    Just facing you
    You saw him through.

You came to know a learned seer
Of whom you read the surface mere:
    Your soul quite sank;
    Brain of such rank
    Dubbed yours a blank.

Anon you quizzed a man of sadness,
Who never could have known true gladness:
    Just for a whim
    You pitied him
    In his sore trim.

You journeyed with a man so glad
You never could conceive him sad:
    He proved to be
    Indubitably
    Good company.

You lit on an unadventurous slow man,
Who, said you, need be feared by no man;
    That his slack deeds
    And sloth must needs
    Produce but weeds.

A man of enterprise, shrewd and swift,
Who never suffered affairs to drift,
    You eyed for a time
    Just in his prime,
    And judged he might climb.

You smoked beside one who forgot
All that you said, or grasped it not.
    Quite a poor thing,
    Not worth a sting
    By satirizing!

20. demilune: a half moon.
35. trim: condition.

Next year you nearly lost for ever
Goodwill from one who forgot slights never;
   And, with unease,
   Felt you must seize
Occasion to please ...   60

Now. ... All these specimens of man,
So various in their pith and plan,
   Curious to say
   Were *one* man. Yea,
I was all they.   65

166 An Evening in Galilee

One of Hardy's many poems on biblical themes, 'An Evening in Galilee' is related to his deliberately controversial poem 'Panthera' (in *Time's Laughingstocks*), which had embellished an apocryphal story about a Roman soldier who believes that he fathered Jesus. In this poem, set early in Christ's ministry, the emphasis on Mary's apprehensions about her son's destiny, and perhaps even her opening pose, recall Holman Hunt's typological painting 'The Shadow of Death', which has Mary staring at the shadow of a cross cast on the wall by a yawning Jesus (cf. 'Near Lanivet, 1872' (82)). Much of the commentary on Hunt's picture had dwelt on the 'humanity' of Mary, explored by Hardy in terms of her disapproval of his friends as well as uncertainty about his future.

Metre: irregular stanzas, aabbcc^6, etc., dr.

She looks far west towards Carmel, shading her eyes with her hand,
And she then looks east to the Jordan, and the smooth Tiberias' strand.
'Is my son mad?' she asks; and never an answer has she,
Save from herself, aghast at the possibility.
'He professes as his firm faiths things far too grotesque to be true,   5
And his vesture is odd – too careless for one of his fair young hue! ...

Title. Galilee: i.e. the Roman province which lay between the Sea of Galilee and the Mediterranean Sea, *c.* 30 AD.
1. Carmel: Mt Carmel, on the edge of the Mediterranean.
2. Tiberias' strand: the beach at Tiberias, on the Sea of Galilee.
5. firm faiths] beliefs MS del.
5. grotesque] flamed MS del.

'He lays down doctrines as if he were old – aye, fifty at least:
In the Temple he terrified me, opposing the very High-Priest!
Why did he say to me, 'Woman, what have I to do with thee?'
O it cuts to the heart that a child of mine thus spoke to me!   10
And he said, too, 'Who is my mother?' – when he knows so
    very well.
He might have said, 'Who is my father?' – and I'd found it
    hard to tell!
That no one knows but Joseph and – one other, nor ever will;
One who'll not see me again. ... How it chanced! – I
    dreaming no ill! ...

'Would he'd not mix with the lowest folk – like those
    fishermen –   15
The while so capable, culling new knowledge, beyond our
    ken! ...
That woman of no good character, ever following him,
Adores him if I mistake not: his wish of her is but a whim
Of his madness, it may be, outmarking his lack of coherency;
After his 'Keep the Commandments!' to smile upon such as
    she!   20
It is just what all those do who are wandering in their wit.
I don't know – dare not say – what harm may grow from it.
O a mad son is a terrible thing; it even may lead
To arrest, and death! ... And how he can preach, expound,
    and read!

'Here comes my husband. Shall I unveil him this tragedy-
    brink?   25
No. He has nightmares enough. I'll pray, and think, and
    think.' ...
She remembers she's never put on any pot for his evening
    meal,
And pondering a plea looks vaguely to south of her – towards
    Jezreel.

9. *'Woman, what have I to do with thee?'*: Jesus's words, John 2: 4.
11. *'Who is my mother?'*: Mark 3: 33.
12–14. cf. the suggestions about Jesus's father in 'Panthera' (see headnote).
13. *Joseph and – one other*] Joseph I told MS del. (i.e. Hardy added the hint of another father as he drafted the poem).
14] So swift a mystery all of it was, and I dreaming no ill! ... MS del.
15. *those fishermen*: i.e. the apostles Simon Peter, Andrew, James, and John.
17. *that woman*: i.e. Mary Magdalene.
19] Or freak, it may be, showing his lack of coherency; MS del.
28. *Jezreel*: south of Nazareth (cf. Hardy's poem 'Jezreel').

167 We Field-women

A poem which draws its materials from the description of the agricultural workers on Flintcomb-Ash Farm, *Tess of the D'Urbervilles*, chs 42–3, where Tess became 'a field-woman pure and simple'. Bailey argues that the speaker must be Marian or Izz Huett, since Tess does not return to Talbothay's Dairy as the poem implies (1970: 600).

Metre: $A^2b^4c^4c^4b^4A^2$ dfr, highly symmetrical, with each initial b-rhyme the same.

    How it rained
When we worked at Flintcomb-Ash,
And could not stand upon the hill
Trimming swedes for the slicing-mill.
The wet washed through us – plash, plash, plash: 5
    How it rained!

    How it snowed
When we crossed from Flintcomb-Ash
To the Great Barn for drawing reed,
Since we could nowise chop a swede. – 10
Flakes in each doorway and casement-sash:
    How it snowed!

    How it shone
When we went from Flintcomb-Ash
To start at dairywork once more 15
In the laughing meads, with cows three-score,
And pails, and songs, and love – too rash:
    How it shone!

9. *drawing reed*: the preparation of reeds for thatching (described in Hardy's short essay on 'The Ancient Cottages of England', pub. 1927, *PW* 234).
10. *nowise*: in no way (i.e. the swedes were frozen hard).

168 He Never Expected Much
[or]
A consideration
[*A reflection*] On My Eighty-Sixth Birthday

First published in *The Daily Telegraph*, 19 March 1928. A late essay in minimalism which Harold Bloom celebrates as 'a chastened return of High Romantic Idealism, but muted onto Hardy's tonality' (1975: 24). Cf. '"For Life I had never cared greatly"' (107), 'A Self-Glamourer' and 'Childhood Among the Ferns' (161), the latter clearly linked to this poem in its return to childhood expectations (or their absence).

Metre: $a^4a^2a^4b^3c^4c^4b^3$ dr, an extended tail-rhyme with a refrain on the second line (see 'Tess's Lament' (27) and 'A Trampwoman's Tragedy' (31) for other examples, and cf. Wordsworth's 'The Green Linnet').

> Well, World, you have kept faith with me,
>   Kept faith with me;
> Upon the whole you have proved to be
>   Much as you said you were.
> Since as a child I used to lie   5
> Upon the leaze and watch the sky,
> Never, I own, expected I
>   That life would all be fair.
>
> 'Twas then you said, and since have said,
>   Times since have said,   10
> In that mysterious voice you shed
>   From clouds and hills around:
> 'Many have loved me desperately,
> Many with smooth serenity,
> While some have shown contempt of me   15
>   Till they dropped underground.
>
> 'I do not promise overmuch,
>   Child; overmuch;

Title] A Reconsideration / On my eighty-sixth birthday MS in British Library. The published title is the result of Hardy's pencilled alternatives in the MS of *Winter Words*, which he left unrevised (*CPW* III, 225, 328).
1. Well: Hardy wrote only three poems beginning 'Well', all of them in *Winter Words*, suggesting perhaps a weariness or a conversational ease. On 'Well' mid-way through poems, see Gittings (1978: 162), Clements (1980: 153), and cf. 'The Going' (51), l. 8, 'Old Furniture' (99), l. 31.
5–6. cf. 'Childhood among the Ferns' (161).
6. leaze: pasture.
17–24. cf. 'Epitaph', and '"For Life I had never cared greatly"' (107). In his diary for 1 January 1902 Hardy wrote 'A Pessimist's apology. Pessimism ... is, in brief, playing the sure game. You cannot lose at it; you may gain.

> Just neutral-tinted haps and such,'
>   You said to minds like mine.   20
> Wise warning for your credit's sake!
> Which I for one failed not to take,
> And hence could stem such strain and ache
>   As each year might assign.

169 Standing by the Mantelpiece
(H.M.M., 1873)

Unlike many poems in *Winter Words*, the manuscript of this poem is 'clean', substantially unrevised. That and the highly personal nature of its contents suggest it was written earlier and held over. The soliloquy is placed in the mouth of Horace Mosley Moule (H.M.M.), Hardy's friend and literary mentor, who killed himself in his rooms at Queen's College, Cambridge, on 21 September 1873. Moule was eight years older than Hardy and of a different class, the son of the vicar of St George's, Fordington. 'Before My Friend Arrived' (150) describes Hardy waiting for Moule's funeral.
    Metre: abab⁵ dr, elegiac stanza.

> This candle-wax is shaping to a shroud
> To-night. (They call it that, as you may know) –
> By touching it the claimant is avowed,
> And hence I press it with my finger – so.
>
> To-night. To me twice night, that should have been   5
> The radiance of the midmost tick of noon,

It is the only view of life in which you can never be disappointed' (*EL* 91).
19. haps: chance happenings (see 'Hap' (2), written sixty years earlier). Bloom comments: 'the "neutral tinted haps", so supremely hard to get into poems, are the staple of Hardy's achievement in verse, and contrast both to Wordsworth's "sober colouring" and Shelley's "deep autumnal tone"' (1975: 23–4).
24] In each year's twist and twine. MS del.
24. might] might would MS, the latter in pencil (neither del.).
1–2. folk-traditions had it that a shroud-shaped column of wax left by a candle burning down forecast a death (Firor 1931: 14–15). Hardy observed the phenomenon at King's College Chapel, Cambridge, in 1880, on a visit in which he must have been reminded of Moule (*EL* 184).
4. so: the terminal '– so' and these lines generally are reminiscent of Browning: see, e.g., the opening of 'The Last Ride Together' and the opening and closing of 'Too Late'.
5–6. perhaps recalls Samson's cry in Milton's *Samson Agonistes*, l. 80: 'O dark, dark, dark, amid the blaze of noon.'

And close around me wintertime is seen
That might have shone the veriest day of June!

But since all's lost, and nothing really lies
Above but shade, and shadier shade below,　　　10
Let me make clear, before one of us dies,
My mind to yours, just now embittered so.

Since you agreed, unurged and full-advised,
And let warmth grow without discouragement,
Why do you bear you now as if surprised,　　　15
When what has come was clearly consequent?

Since you have spoken, and finality
Closes around, and my last movements loom,
I say no more: the rest must wait till we
Are face to face again, yonside the tomb.　　　20

And let the candle-wax thus mould a shape
Whose meaning now, if hid before, you know,
And how by touch one present claims its drape,
And that it's I who press my finger – so.

170 Our Old Friend Dualism

Dualism is the belief that mind (or spirit) and matter are separate (as opposed to Monism, which asserts their unity). In a letter to Caleb Saleeby on 2 February 1915 Hardy wrote of Bergson 'I fear his theory is, the bulk, only our old friend Dualism in a new suit of clothes' (*LY* 168). Hardy rejected Dualism, in part, in making the moving spirit of *The Dynasts* the 'Immanent Will', i.e. a force within creation only gradually coming to consciousness (cf. the notebook entry from a 1906 article in *The Record*: 'It [the first chapter of Genesis] teaches clearly that dualism ... is entirely impossible, & foreign to the whole idea of true religion' (Björk entry 2299)). But as this poem suggests, Hardy remained attracted to Dualistic assumptions.

Metre: aabbcc[7] dr.

7. *wintertime*: cf. the opening of 'In Tenebris I' (24).
11. *one of us*: the addressee is a biographical puzzle. It may have been a woman with whom Moule was involved, but her identity and the nature of Moule's 'embitterment' remain obscure.

All hail to him, the Protean! A tough old chap is he:
Spinoza and the Monists cannot make him cease to be.
We pound him with our 'Truth, Sir, please!' and quite appear
    to still him:
He laughs; holds Bergson up, and James; and swears we
    cannot kill him.
We argue them pragmatic cheats. 'Aye,' says he. 'They're
    deceiving: 5
But I must live; for flamens plead I am all that's worth
    believing!'
1920.

171 Drinking Song

First published in *The Daily Telegraph*, 14 June 1928. One of a number of poems describing the vanishing of established ideas: cf. 'The Respectable Burgher' (22), 'God's Funeral', and 'An Ancient to Ancients'.
Metre: $a^4b^2b^2a^4c^2c^2a^4$ dr, chorus a^4a^4 dr (final chorus $a^4a^4a^4$ dr).

>   Once on a time when thought began
>   Lived Thales: he
>   Was said to see
>   Vast truths that mortals seldom can;
>   It seems without   5
>   A moment's doubt
>   That everything was made for man.

1. *Protean*: Proteus was a Greek sea-god who could change shape at will.
2. *Spinoza*: Baruch Spinonza (1632–77), the Dutch philosopher who attempted to see the world as composed of 'monads' or spiritual atoms. Hardy's relation to Spinoza is hard to assess: he makes the rather ridiculous Fitzpiers in *The Woodlanders* a Spinozan, but elsewhere he comments favourably on Spinoza's emphasis on Necessity (see Björk entry 112–13n).
4. *Bergson*: Henri Bergson (1859–1941), French dualist philosopher. Hardy excerpted material on Bergson's *Creative Evolution* into his notebooks in 1911 (Björk entries 2422–3).
6. *flamens*: (Roman) priests; here theologians generally.
Title] MS has a subtitle or continuation of the title: on Great Thoughts Belittled.
2. *Thales*: Greek philosopher and scientist (640–546 BC), developed an earth-centered view of the cosmos.

Chorus.
Fill full your cups: feel no distress
That thoughts so great should now be less!

Earth mid the sky stood firm and flat,
   He held, till came
   A sage by name
Copernicus, and righted that.
   We trod, he told,
   A globe that rolled
Around a sun it warmed it at.

Chorus.
Fill full your cups: feel no distress;
'Tis only one great thought the less!

But still we held, as Time flew by
   And wit increased,
   Ours was, at least,
The only world whose rank was high:
   Till rumours flew
   From folk who knew
Of globes galore about the sky.

Chorus.
Fill full your cups: feel no distress;
'Tis only one great thought the less!

And that this earth, our one estate,
   Was no prime ball,
   The best of all,
But common, mean; indeed, tenth-rate:
   And men, so proud,
   A feeble crowd,
Unworthy any special fate.

Chorus.
Fill full your cups: feel no distress;
'Tis only one great thought the less!

8–9. Chorus: Hardy copied a number of passages from Cotter Morison's *The Service of Man* (1887) into his notebook, including one on the evolution of beliefs: 'Beliefs more perishable than the temples they wrought. ... Systems of thought, &c, have many of the characteristics of organs, ceasing to be useful they become shrunken & meaningless; also noxious' (Björk entry 1464, cf. 2082).
13. Copernicus: Polish astronomer (1473–1543) developed the theory that the earth and other planets move about the sun, rather than the earth being the centre of the universe (as in the Ptolemaic system).

Then rose one Hume, who could not see,
   If earth were such,
   Required were much
To prove no miracles could be: 40
   'Better believe
   The eyes deceive
Than that God's clockwork jolts,' said he.
        Chorus.
Fill full your cups: feel no distress;
'Tis only one great thought the less! 45

Next this strange message Darwin brings,
   (Though saying his say
   In a quiet way);
We all are one with creeping things;
   And apes and men 50
   Blood-brethren,
And likewise reptile forms with stings.
        Chorus.
Fill full your cups: feel no distress;
'Tis only one great thought the less!

And when this philosoph had done 55
   Came Doctor Cheyne:
   Speaking plain he
Proved no virgin bore a son.
   'Such tale, indeed,
   Helps not our creed,' 60
He said. 'A tale long known to none.'

---

37. Hume: David Hume, Scottish philosopher (1711–76), argued in his essay 'Of Miracles' that a consistent God would not break the laws of nature.
46. Darwin: English biologist and naturalist Charles Darwin (1809–82) who developed the theory of evolution in *On the Origin of Species* (1859), and suggested in *The Descent of Man* (1871) that humans share a common ancestry with the apes.
47–8. Darwin hesitated over publication, and often left it to others to draw out the radical implications of his ideas. His style was famously reticent.
49. creeping things: Genesis 1: 24, 'And God said, Let the earth bring forth the living creature after his kind, cattle, and creeping thing. . . .'
56. Cheyne: Thomas Cheyne, English biblical scholar (1841–1915), followed the German 'Higher Criticism' in applying historical analysis to the Bible. Hardy's notebooks include part of the entry on 'Virgin Birth' in Cheyne's *Encyclopaedia Biblica* (1902) (Björk entry 2368).

Chorus.
Fill full your cups: feel no distress;
'Tis only one great thought the less!

And now comes Einstein with a notion –
   Not yet quite clear
   To many here –
That's there's no time, no space, no motion,
   Nor rathe nor late,
   Nor square nor straight,
But just a sort of bending-ocean.

Chorus.
Fill full your cups: feel no distress;
'Tis only one great thought the less!

So here we are, in piteous case:
   Like butterflies
   Of many dyes
Upon an Alpine glacier's face:
   To fly and cower
   In some warm bower
Our chief concern in such a place.

Chorus.
Fill full your cups: feel no distress
At all our great thoughts shrinking less:
We'll do a good deed nevertheless!

---

64. *Einstein*: Albert Einstein, Swiss physicist (1879–1955). Hardy read a number of articles on his ideas and owned his *Relativity: The Special and the General Theory: A Popular Exposition*, 3rd edn (London, 1920) (Björk entries 2449–51, 2449n). In a letter to the philosopher McTaggart on 31 December 1919, he commented on Einstein: 'Really after what he says the universe seems to be getting too comic for words' (*CL* V, 353).
70. *bending-ocean*] bending-ocean ether-ocean MS (neither del.). Hynes accepts the latter (*CPW* III, 249), but 'bending' is closer to Einstein's theories, since Relativity removed the need to postulate the 'ether' as the medium for electromagnetic radiation.
74–6. cf. the episode on the cliff-face, *A Pair of Blue Eyes*, ch. 22, itself partly based on Leslie Stephen's essay 'A Bad Five Minutes in the Alps', *Frazer's Magazine*, November 1872.

172 The Aged Newspaper Soliloquizes

Written at the request of J.L Garvin, editor of *The Observer*, and published in the expanded format of the 14 March 1926 issue.
Metre: couplets, mostly iambic, aa⁴, etc., dr.

> Yes; yes; I am old. In me appears
> The history of a hundred years;
> Empires', kings', captives', births and deaths,
> Strange faiths, and fleeting shibboleths.
> – Tragedy, comedy, throngs my page   5
> Beyond all mummed on any stage:
> Cold hearts beat hot, hot hearts beat cold,
> And I beat on. Yes; yes; I am old.

173 Christmas: 1924

End-of-year couplets first published with the title 'Peace upon Earth' in *The Daily Telegraph*, 18 June 1928. The poem's pessimism, with its source in the First World War, is comparable to that in the penultimate poem of the volume.
Metre: aabb⁴, couplets in a falling–rising metre.

> 'Peace upon earth!' was said. We sing it,
> And pay a million priests to bring it.
> After two thousand years of mass
> We've got as far as poison-gas.
>   1924.

1] The Newspaper Soliloquizes *Observer*.
2. The Observer was 135 years old.
4. shibboleths: 'shibboleth' was a hard-to-pronounce Hebrew word used to distinguish friends from foes; thus any modes of behaviour, beliefs, words, etc., acting as social markers.
6. mummed: acted ('mumming', the country tradition of short plays, is described in *The Return of the Native*).
1. Peace upon earth: from Luke 2: 14.

174 The Boy's Dream

First published in *The Daily Telegraph*, 12 June 1928, a final variation on Hardy's series of poems on caged birds, including 'The Caged Thrush Freed and Home Again', 'The Blinded Bird' (87), 'The Caged Goldfinch', and 'The Bird-Catcher's Boy' (151). For comment see Introduction, p. 15; Pinion 1977: 136–47.

Metre: abab^4 dr, 'long' hymn stanza.

Provincial town-boy he, – frail, lame,
His face a waning lily-white,
A court the home of his wry, wrenched frame,
Where noontide shed no warmth or light.

Over his temples – flat, and wan,   5
Where bluest veins were patterned keen,
The skin appeared so thinly drawn
The skull beneath was almost seen.

Always a wishful, absent look
Expressed it in his face and eye;   10
At the strong shape this longing took
One guessed what wish must underlie.

But no. That wish was not for strength,
For other boys' agility,
To race with ease the field's far length,   15
Now hopped across so painfully.

He minded not his lameness much,
To shine at feats he did not long,
Nor to be best at goal and touch,
Nor at assaults to stand up strong.   20

But sometimes he would let be known
What the wish was: – to have, next spring,
A real green linnet – his very own –
Like that one he had late heard sing.

And as he breathed the cherished dream   25
To those whose secrecy was sworn,
His face was beautified by the theme,
And wore the radiance of the morn.

3. *court*: confined space around which houses are built, usually in cities (by analogy, a human 'cage').
19. *goal and touch*: games.
23. *green linnet*: the greenfinch. The linnet is a common poetic subject: Hardy probably knew poems by Akenside, Mickle and Wordsworth on the bird, as well as *In Memoriam* 21, 'I do but sing because I must / And pipe but as the linnets sing' (cf. *In Memoriam* 27).

175 Family Portraits

Published in *Nash's and Pall Mall Magazine*, December 1924, and in this revised and expanded form in *The Daily Telegraph*, 6 August 1928 (the earlier version is reproduced in Appendix I, below). One of a number of poems on heredity, including 'Heredity' (81), 'Sine Prole' (138), and 'The Pedigree' (91), which shares with 'Family Portraits' a sense of the horrors of what Freud calls the 'primal scene', the moment of origin. Hardy's notebook entry from Henry Maudsley's *Natural Causes* is representative of his thought: 'The individual brain is virtually the consolidate embodiment of a long series of memories; wherefore everybody, in the main lines of his thoughts, feelings & conduct, really recalls the experiences of his forefathers' (Björk entry 1519).

The poem also reads like a meditation on the personal implications of a passage which Hardy excerpted from J.A. Froude's book on Carlyle, in which Froude writes of the 'gallery of human portraits' in Carlyle's *French Revolution*, a 'spectral' history in which 'actors appear in it without their earthly clothes ... as in some vast phantasmagoria with the supernatural shining through them, working in fancy their own wills or their own imagination; in reality, the mere instruments of a superior power' (Björk entry 1337).

Metre: $a^4b^2a^4a^4a^4b^2$ tr, with the first and fourth line of each stanza using the same rhyme-word. A unique extended tail-rhyme-stanza with few obvious models (possibly derived from Lamb's 'Hester', $aaa^4b^2ccc^4b^2$ dr).

Three picture-drawn people stepped out of their frames –
    The blast, how it blew!
And the white-shrouded candles flapped smoke-headed
    flames;
– Three picture-drawn people came down from their frames,
And dumbly in lippings they told me their names,   5
    Full well though I knew.

The first was a maiden of mild wistful tone,
    Gone silent for years,
The next a dark woman in former time known;
But the first one, the maiden of mild wistful tone,   10

Title. The Portraits *Nash's*.
1. *Three picture-drawn people*: cf. Hazlitt's essay 'Of persons one would wish to have seen', in which various authors step from the frames of their portraits.
3. *white-shrouded candles*: see 'Standing by the Mantlepiece' (169), l. 1n.
5. *lippings*: speeches (often used for ghost-voices: see 'The Going' (51), l. 9n).
5–6. it is difficult to say how distant these ancestors are. While writing his disguised autobiography in the decade from 1917, Hardy did a good deal of research on his family, but even in his grandparents' generation there were 'ancestral mysteries' (see Gittings 1978: 84–5).

So wondering, unpractised, so vague and alone,
    Nigh moved me to tears.

The third was a sad man – a man of much gloom;
    And before me they passed
In the shade of the night, at the back of the room,
The dark and fair woman, the man of much gloom,
Three persons, in far-off years forceful, but whom
    Death now fettered fast.

They set about acting some drama, obscure,
    The women and he,
With puppet-like movements of mute strange allure;
Yea, set about acting some drama, obscure,
Till I saw 'twas their own lifetime's tragic amour,
    Whose course begot me;

Yea – a mystery, ancestral, long hid from my reach
    In the perished years past,
That had mounted to dark doings each against each
In those ancestors' days, and long hid from my reach;
Which their restless enghostings, it seemed, were to teach
    Me in full, at this last.

But fear fell upon me like frost, of some hurt
    If they entered anew
On the orbits they smartly had swept when expert
In the law-lacking passions of life, – of some hurt
To their souls – and thus mine – which I fain would advert;
    So, in sweat cold as dew,

'Why wake up all this?' I cried out. 'Now, so late!
    Let old ghosts be laid!'
And they stiffened, drew back to their frames and numb state,
Gibbering: 'Thus are your own ways to shape, know too late!'
Then I grieved that I'd not had the courage to wait
    And see the play played.

I have grieved ever since: to have balked future pain,

19–30. cf. 'The Pedigree' (91), stanza iv.
24. whose course begot me: echoes the 'Epilogue' to *The Famous Tragedy of the Queen of Cornwall* (182), ll. 14–15. 'Course' perhaps puns on 'corse', corpse. MS has 'Largely bearing on me' (del.).
29. enghostings: hauntings (Hardy's coinage).
34. law-lacking passions] concatenations MS del. (i.e. a linked series).
35. and thus] perhaps MS del.
43. balked] shunned MS del.

My blood's tendance foreknown,
Had been triumph. Nights long stretched awake I have lain 45
Perplexed in endeavours to balk future pain
By uncovering the drift of their drama. In vain,
    Though therein lay my own.

176 Christmas in the Elgin Room
British Museum: Early Last Century

The last poem published in Hardy's lifetime, and the last of his Christmas poems, issued as one of Florence Hardy's occasional privately printed pamplets and published in *The Times* on 24 December 1927. It concerns the Elgin Marbles, the ancient sculptures and friezes of mythological scenes taken from the Acropolis of Athens in 1806 by Thomas Bruce, Earl of Elgin, and sold to the British nation in 1816 (their return to Greece is still, in the 1990s, the subject of controversy). A number of poems deal with the interaction between the Pagan and Christian worlds, and Hardy was particularly interested by statues and sites converted from Pagan to Christian use (see *EL* 249; Björk entries 148, 174; and cf. 'Aquae Sulis' and 'Rome. Building a New Street in the Ancient Quarter' (14)). There are extensive manuscript revisions (see *CPW* III, 272–3).

As well as providing another example of ghosts protesting at their posterity, the poem recycles the idea of southern beauty brought north from Hardy's 'To Flowers from Italy in Winter', in *Poems of the Past and the Present* (1901):

> Frail luckless exiles hither brought!
>   Your dust will not regain
> Old sunny haunts of Classic thought
>   When you shall waste and wane;
>
> But mix with alien earth, be lit
>   With frigid Boreal flame. . . .

Metre: $a^4a^4b^2b^2a^6$ dr, unique (cf. 'Best Times', $a^5a^5b^2b^2a^5$ dr).

'What is the noise that shakes the night,
And seems to soar to the Pole-star height?'
    – 'Christmas bells,

44. *blood's tendance*: hereditary predispositions.
44. *blood's*] line's MS del.
45. *had*: would have.
46. *balk*] shun MS del.
48. *therein lay*] therein lay   therefrom sprung MS (neither del.).
Title. *Elgin Room*: the large room at the British Museum where the Elgin Marbles are kept.

The watchman tells
Who walks this hall that blears us captives with its blight.'   5

'And what, then, mean such clangs, so clear?'
'– 'Tis said to have been a day of cheer,
    And source of grace
    To the human race
Long ere their woven sails winged us to exile here.   10

'We are those whom Christmas overthrew
Some centuries after Pheidias knew
    How to shape us
    And bedrape us
And to set us in Athena's temple for men's view.   15

'O it is sad now we are sold –
We gods! for Borean people's gold,
    And brought to the gloom
    Of this gaunt room
Which sunlight shuns, and sweet Aurore but enters cold.   20

'For all these bells, would I were still
Radiant as on Athenai's Hill.'
    – 'And I, and I!'
    The others sigh,
'Before this Christ was known, and we had men's good will.'   25

Thereat old Helios could but nod,
Throbbed, too, the Ilissus River-god,
    And the torsos there
    Of deities fair,
Whose limbs were shards beneath some Acropolitan clod: 30

11. cf. the description of the supplanting of beliefs in 'Drinking Song' (171).
12. *Pheidias*: (or Phidias) Greek sculptor (*c.*500–*c.*432 BC) said to have been responsible for the decoration of the Acropolis, and famous for a giant statue of Athena, since destroyed.
15. *Athena's temple*: the Parthenon, built 447–432 BC, was a temple to Pallas Athena, goddess of wisdom.
17. *Borean people*: i.e. the British (from Boreas, Greek god of the north wind).
20. *Aurore*: Greek goddess of the dawn.
22. *Athenai's Hill*: the Acropolis.
26. *Helios*: Greek god of the sun.
27. *Ilissus*: a river near Athens.

Demeter too, Poseidon hoar,
Persephone, and many more
    Of Zeus' high breed, –
    All loth to heed
What the bells sang that night which shook them to the core.   35
1905 and 1926.

177 'We are getting to the end'

The two poems which follow form the 'end-piece' of *Winter Words*. We can be fairly certain the placing is Hardy's (see headnote to volume). First published in *The Daily Telegraph*, 28 May 1928. Hardy's pessimism about the progress of history is visible throughout his writings after the First World War, as in the 'Apology' to *Late Lyrics and Earlier*, where he writes of 'the barbarizing of taste in the younger minds by the dark madness of the late war', and adds 'we seem threatened with a new Dark Age'.

Metre: Petrarchan sonnet (cf. 'Thoughts from Sophocles' (179)), abba abba cdecde[5] dr. The use of the sonnet for this nihilistic poem reinforces the contrast between enclosure and apparent freedom ('pleasuring').

We are getting to the end of visioning
The impossible within this universe,
Such as that better whiles may follow worse,
And that our race may mend by reasoning.

We know that even as larks in cages sing   5
Unthoughtful of deliverance from the curse
That holds them lifelong in a latticed hearse,
We ply spasmodically our pleasuring.

31. Demeter: Greek goddess of harvest and fertility.
31. Poseidon: the sea-god.
31. hoar: grey-haired, venerable.
32. Persephone: queen of the underworld (daughter of Demeter).
33. Zeus: father of the Gods in Greek mythology.
Title. perhaps an ironic echo of Daniel 8: 17, 'At the time of end shall be the vision'.
5–8. on bird-poems, see Introduction, p. 15.
7. latticed hearse: cage; but the comparison between the grave and a cage is implicit in other poems: see e.g. '"Not only I"' (145).

And that when nations set them to lay waste
Their neighbours' heritage by foot and horse,   10
And hack their pleasant plains in festering seams,
They may again, – not warely, or from taste,
But tickled mad by some demonic force. –
Yes. We are getting to the end of dreams!

178 He Resolves to Say No More

First published in *The Daily Telegraph*, 18 September 1928. The poem which Hardy intended to stand at the end of his corpus is an extended example of *occupatio*, the rhetorical refusal to speak, as in *LY* 218: 'Knowledge might be terrible' (cf. Iago's 'From this time forth I never will speak word' at the end of *Othello*, and Hamlet's 'The rest is silence'). In again making the Horatian distinction between the poet's dying body and his escaping soul, Hardy withholds his final apocalyptic vision from his audience, insisting that he takes it with him. The draft manuscript in the DCM shows that Hardy took considerable pains over this poem, altering it from four- to five-line stanzas at a late stage, and producing alternative versions of ll. 2–4 and 12–13.

Metre: $a^4a^4b^2b^2b^4$ dr (expanded from a draft in $a^4a^4b^2b^2$ stanza). A unique stanza, though 'So Various', is close ($a^4a^4b^2b^2b^2$) and its stanza is, in a sense, 'completed' by the final tetrameter lines of 'He Resolves to Say No More'.

    O my soul, keep the rest unknown!
    It is too like a sound of moan
        When the charnel-eyed
        Pale Horse has nighed:

9–11. cf. the vision of warring nations at the opening of *The Dynasts*, and the description of the hacking of the earth in 'The Eve of Waterloo' (180).
10. foot and horse: infantry and cavalry.
12. warely: cautiously, watchfully.
13. demonic force: Taylor (1981: 126–38) discusses Hardy's references to the Witch of Endor as a demon of history, spreading discord and destruction.
14. dreams: prophecy traditionally takes two forms, visions while awake, and dreams (Acts 10–12); Hardy refers to both.
1. (One line from Agathias, Greek epigrammatist.) ['O my heart, leave the rest unknown.' Mackail's trans., 218] (Hardy's note in MS).
1. soul] heart MS del.
2–4] It comes too near a sound of moan / At Death's grey glide / To mortal's side MS in DCM del.
4. Pale horse: Revelation 6: 8 (Hardy's note): 'And I looked, and behold a pale horse: and his name that sat on him was Death, and Hell followed with him.'

Yea, none shall gather what I hide! 5
Why load men's minds with more to bear
That bear already ails to spare?
    From now alway
    Till my last day
What I discern I will not say. 10
Let Time roll backward if it will;
(Magians who drive the midnight quill
    With brain aglow
    Can see it so,)
What I have learnt no man shall know. 15

And if my vision range beyond
The blinkered sight of souls in bond,
    – By truth made free –
    I'll let all be,
And show to no man what I see. 20

---

8. alway: always.
11. Let Time roll backward: cf. the 'Apology' to *Late Lyrics and Earlier*: 'men's minds ... appear to be moving backwards rather than on'; echoing a wartime letter to Cockrell, in which Hardy wrote that the war 'made one sit still in apathy, & watch the clock spinning backwards, with a mild wonder if, when it gets back to the Dark Ages, & the Sack of Rome, it will ever move forward again to a new Renascence, & have a new literature' (*CL* V, 45). A number of contemporary speculations on Time may lie behind the idea of reversal: H.G. Wells's *The Time Machine*, Comte (whose theories of cyclic history Hardy mentions in the 'Apology'), even Browning's 'Rabbi Ben Ezra' 27: 'Time's wheel runs back or stops: Potter and clay endure'.
12] And some (del.) Watchers (del.) Magians Sages (neither del.) MS in DCM. Hardy may have had Shelley's sage Ahasuerus in *Hellas* in mind, who 'rolls back' a vision of history.
13] By genius' glow MS in DCM del.
13. brain aglow: cf. the 'spectacle of the inside of a brain at work' (*LY* 117) as a metaphor for the artist's subjectivity (see Armstrong 1988a: 456–60).
16. vision: the word reinforces the poem's thematic links with the previous poem.
17. the two words referring to forms of constraint, 'blinkered' and 'bond', are precisely applied to the two objects, 'sight' and 'soul', which they bracket.
18. John 8: 32, 'And ye shall know the truth, and the truth shall make you free.'

Uncollected Poems

The poems included below were either not published in Hardy's lifetime or not included in the *Collected Poems*. Hardy left some thirty-five such poems, including early poems, poems and prologues written for special occasions, choruses from *The Dynasts* published only in the *Selected Poems*, poems he decided not to publish ('The Sound of Her'), and one or two already published poems that he either did not wish to collect or forgot about. The number, compared to most poets of comparable output, is small; a testament to Hardy's efficiency in handling his manuscripts.

179 Thoughts from Sophocles
(*Oed. Col.* 1200–1250)

This loose translation of the famous chorus from Sophocles's *Oedipus at Colonus*, ll. 1211–48, was written during Hardy's period of disillusion in the 1890s (see the 'In Tenebris' poems (24–26)). It was first published in 1956 (*London Magazine* 3: 39). The manuscript, in the DCM, has a number of undeleted alternative readings.

While he studied Jebb's edition of the Greek text of *Oedipus Tyrannus* in the 1890s, Hardy's version of this chorus is based on the translation in T.A. Buckley's Bohn's Classical Library edition of Sophocles (for Sophoclean allusions in Hardy's work, see Rutland 1938: 39–43; Steele 1980; Björk entry 366n). Hardy may also have been influenced by Tennyson's 'Will', which seems partly a version of the chorus (however, Ricks lists Horace, *Odes* III, iii and *Aeneid* X, 693–6 as Tennyson's sources, suggesting the shared nature of the topos):

> For him nor moves the loud world's random mock,
> Nor all Calamity's hugest waves confound,
> Who seems a promontory of rock,
> That, compassed round with turbulent sound,
> In middle ocean meets the surging shock. . . .

A comparison with W.B. Yeats's very different rendering of the same passage in 'From "Oedipus at Colonus"' is revealing: Hardy emphasizes grim endurance where Yeats celebrates brief pleasures.
Metre: Petrarchan sonnet, abba abba cdecde⁵ dr (cf. '"We are getting to the end"' (177)).

Who would here sojourn for an outstretched spell
Feels senseless promptings, to the thinking gaze,
Since pain comes nigh and nigher with lengthening days,
And nothing shows that joy will ever upwell.

Death is the remedy that cures at call   5
The doubtful jousts of black and white assays.
What are song, laughter, what the footed maze,
Beside the good of knowing no birth at all?

Gaunt age is as some blank upstanding beak
Chafed by the billows of a northern shore   10
And facing friendless cold calamity
That strikes upon its features worn and weak
Where sunshine bird and bloom frequent no more,
And cowls of cloud wrap the stars' radiancy.

1–4. cf. Buckley's translation, pp. 93–4:
CHORUS. Whoever seeks to live for a lengthened term, neglecting the mean, will be proved in my mind to cherish folly; since oft has length of days brought us nearer to pain, and you can no where see aught of joy when any one may meet with more than his wishes require; but death is the aid (of our troubles) that ends with the grave. ...
2. Feels] Has Feels MS (neither del.).
5–8. Hardy referred to this passage in 1904: 'people call me a pessimist; and if it is pessimism to think, with Sophocles, that "not to have been born is best", then I do not reject the designation' (Archer 1904: 46). There are a number of other poems on it being better to be unborn or dead: cf. 'To an Unborn Pauper Child', 'The Unborn', 'A Wish for Unconsciousness'.
5. cures at call] winds up well cures at call MS (neither del.).
6. doubtful] sorry doubtful MS (neither del.). The image here is derived from the mediaeval tournament ('assays' are trials of strength and skill), but seems also to refer to the chess-board.
9–14. Hardy again follows his source closely. Buckley translates:
In which state [old age] this wretched man, not I alone, as some promontory exposed to the north, is beaten on all sides by the dashings of the billows in the winter storm; – thus also dreadful calamities, bursting like waves over his head, ever present beat on him, – some indeed from the setting of the sun, and some from his rise, and some from his mid-day beam, and some from the cloud-dimmed stars of night.
9. blank] gray blank MS (neither del.).
9. beak: a beak-like promontory.
13. the images, not in Buckley, may derive from Shakespeare's Sonnet 73 (Steele 1980: 76).

180 The Eve of Waterloo
(Chorus of Phantoms)

From *The Dynasts*, Part III (1910), act VI, scene viii. It was published separately in *Selected Poems* (1916), where Hardy gave the poem this title and subtitle; in *The Dynasts* it is introduced by a stage-direction, 'Chorus of the Years (aerial music)' and divided into speeches allocated between the 'Chorus of the Pities', the 'Chorus of the Years', and the 'Chorus of Sinister Spirits' (see annotations). The copy-text here is the Mellstock Edition, Vol. XXXIII (1920).

The Battle of Waterloo (1815) is the climax of *The Dynasts*, and is central to Hardy's thinking about the pathos of war (see 'In Time of "The Breaking of Nations"' (109)). The ground-level view of the poem contrasts with the ariel perspective of much of *The Dynasts*, with its 'filmic' visual effects. It may have been suggested by Byron's meditation on the grass at Waterloo in *Childe Harold* III, 27, responding to Byron's use of the 'pathetic fallacy' in depicting the dew as tears.

Metre: tetrameter modification of Dante's *terza rima*, modelled on Browning's 'The Statue and the Bust': aba^4 bcb^4 cdc^4, etc., dtr, ending with a triplet. Used in a number of poems, e.g. 'George Meredith' (40) (Taylor 1988: 218–19).

> The eyelids of eve fall together at last,
> And the forms so foreign to field and tree
> Lie down as though native, and slumber fast!
>
> Sore are the thrills of misgiving we see
> In the artless champaign at this harlequinade,   5
> Distracting a vigil where calm should be!
>
> The green seems opprest, and the Plain afraid
> Of a Something to come, whereof these are the proofs, –
> Neither earthquake, nor storm, nor eclipse's shade!
>
> Yea, the coneys are scared by the thud of hoofs,   10
> And their white scuts flash at their vanishing heels,
> And swallows abandon the hamlet-roofs.
>
> The mole's tunnelled chambers are crushed by wheels,
> The lark's eggs scattered, their owners fled;
> And the hedgehog's household the sapper unseals.   15

1–3] assigned to the Chorus of the Years in *The Dynasts*. The stage-direction preceding these lines in *The Dynasts* describes both armies settling down for the night, the French 'amid the cornfields around La Belle Alliance' and the English around Mont Saint-Jean.
4–9] assigned to the Chorus of the Pities in *The Dynasts*.
5. champaign: can mean 'open country' or 'battlefield' (the poem explores the shift from one to the other: cf. 'The Peasant's Confession' (4), l. 108).
5. harlequinade: pantomine, farce.
10–27] assigned to the Chorus of the Years in *The Dynasts*.
15. sapper: trench-digger.

The snail draws in at the terrible tread,
But in vain; he is crushed by the felloe-rim;
The worm asks what can be overhead,

And wriggles deep from a scene so grim,
And guesses him safe; for he does not know   20
What a foul red flood will be soaking him!

Beaten about by the heel and toe
Are butterflies, sick of the day's long rheum,
To die of a worse than the weather-foe.

Trodden and bruised to a miry tomb   25
Are ears that have greened but will never be gold,
And flowers in the bud that will never bloom.

So the season's intent, ere its fruit unfold,
Is frustrate, and mangled, and made succumb,
Like a youth of promise struck stark and cold! ... 30

And what of these who to-night have come?
The young sleep sound; but the weather awakes
In the veterans, pains from the past that numb;

Old stabs of Ind, old Peninsular aches,
Old Friedland chills, haunt their moist mud bed,   35
Cramps from Austerlitz; till their slumber breaks.

And each soul sighs as he shifts his head
On the loam he's to lease with the other dead
From to-morrow's mist-fall till Time be sped!

---

17. felloe-rim: wheel-rim.
23. rheum: rain (also suggests tears, cf. 'The Pedigree' (91), l. 6).
25–30. the failure of nature to fructify is a common elegaic topos, cf. 'Hap' (2).
28–31] assigned to the Chorus of the Pities in *The Dynasts*.
29. made succumb: overwhelmed, defeated.
32–6] assigned to the Chorus of the Years in *The Dynasts*.
34. Old stabs of Ind: wounds from India.
34. Peninsular aches: the Peninsular War (1808–14) resulted from Napoleon's efforts to control Spain and Portugal.
35. Friedland: the Battle of Friedland (1807) left Napoleon in control of most of Europe.
36. Austerlitz: in Moravia, site of Napoleon's 1805 victory.
37–9] assigned to the Chorus of Sinister Spirits in *The Dynasts*, followed by a final stage direction: 'The fires of the English go out, and silence prevails, save for the soft hiss of the rain that falls impartially on both the sleeping armies.'
37. sighs as he shifts] shivers as sinks   All editions (Hardy made the correction in his copy of SP, DCM).

181 Prologue

The Prologue to Hardy's *The Famous Tragedy of the Queen of Cornwall* (1923), a one-act 'play for mummers'. Hardy's version of the legend of Tristram and Isolde (or Iseult) is closely linked to memories of his own romance in Cornwall. In the *Life* he describes its connection with his courtship:

> His hosts drove him to various picturesque points on the wild and rugged coast near the Rectory, among others to King Arthur's Castle, Tintagel, which he now saw for the first time; and where, owing to their lingering too long among the ruins, they found themselves locked in, only narrowly escaping being imprisoned there for the night by much signalling with their handkerchiefs to cottagers in the valley. The lingering might have been considered prophetic, seeing that, after it had been smouldering in his mind for between forty and fifty years, he constructed *The Famous Tragedy of the Queen of Cornwall* from the legends connected with that romantic spot. Why he did not do it sooner, while she was still living who knew the scene so well, and had frequently painted it, it is impossible to say. (*EL* 103).

The play was substantially revised for the second edition (1924). The copy-text here is the first edition.

Metre: irregular rhymed stanzas, a^4a^4, etc., dr, with some lines three-beat.

Enter MERLIN, *a phantasmal figure with a white wand. The room is darkened: a blue light may be thrown on Merlin.*

MERLIN

I come, at your persuasive call,
To raise up in this modern hall
A tragedy of dire duresse
That vexed the Land of Lyonnesse: –
Scenes, with their passions, hopes, and fears   5
Sunk into shade these thousand years;
To set, in ghostly grave array,
   Their blitheness, blood, and tears,
Feats, ardours, as if rife to-day
   Before men's eyes and ears.   10

The tale has travelled far and wide: –
Yea, that King Mark, to fetch his bride,
Sent Tristram; then that he and she
Quaffed a love-potion witlessly
While homeward bound. Hence that the King   15
   Wedded one heart-aflame
For Tristram! He, in dark despair,

16–17. one heart-aflame / for Tristram!: i.e. Queen Iseult, married to King Mark.

Roved recklessly, and wived elsewhere
   One of his mistress' name.
I saw these times I represent,   20
Watched, gauged them as they came and went,
Being ageless, deathless! And those two
Fair women – namesakes – well I knew!
Judge them not harshly in a love
   Whose hold on them was strong;   25
Sorrow therein they tasted of,
   And deeply, and too long!

                                                Exit.

182 Epilogue

Epilogue from *The Famous Tragedy of the Queen of Cornwall* (see previous poem). There are echoes of this piece in 'Family Portraits' (175), suggesting that Hardy saw the Iseult story as in some ways prefiguring his own.
  Metre: irregular rhymed stanzas, mostly couplets, aa⁴, etc., dr, with some lines three-beat.

            Re-enter MERLIN

   Thus from the past, the throes and themes
   Whereof I spake – now dead as dreams –
      Have been re-shaped and drawn
      In feinted deed and word, as though
   Our shadowy and phantasmal show   5
   Were very movements to and fro
      Of forms so far-off gone.

   These warriors and dear women, whom
   I've called, as bidden, from the tomb,
      May not have failed to raise   10
   An antique spell at moments here?
   – They were, in their long-faded sphere,
      As you are now who muse thereat;
   Their mirth, crimes, fear and love begat
      Your own, though thwart their ways;   15
   And may some pleasant thoughts outshape
   From this my conjuring to undrape
      Such ghosts of distant days!

   Begun 1916: *resumed and finished* 1923.

19. i.e. Iseult the Whitehanded.
15. thwart: across.

183 On One Who Thought No Other Could Write Such English as Himself

One of two epitaphs attacking his reviewers, the last poems Hardy wrote. The envelope containing the manuscript, in the DCM, is signed by Florence Hardy and labelled 'Last lines dicated [sic] by T.H. referring to George Moore and G.K. Chesterton'; an outer envelope is labelled 'Two epitaphs – on George Moore and G.K. Chesterton – dictated by Hardy on his death-bed.' They were first published in Gibson's *Complete Poems* (1976).

George Moore (1852–1933), Anglo-Irish author, had incurred Hardy's wrath by criticizing *Far from the Madding Crowd* as 'one of George Eliot's miscarriages' in *Confessions of a Young Man* (London, 1888); and by describing Hardy's prose as the worst in the nineteenth century and his novels as 'ill-constructed melodramas' in *Conversations in Ebury Street* (London, 1924).

Metre: couplets, aabb⁴ cc⁴ dr.

'No mortal man beneath the sky
Can write such English as can I
They say it holds no thought my own
What then, such beauty is not known.'

Heap dustbins on him: they'll not meet   5
The apex of his self conceit.

---

4. *beauty*] (perfection)   beauty MS (neither del.).

Selections from Hardy's Autobiography

The passages below are designed to illustrate Hardy's views on life, art, writing, religion, and other topics. They are identified as coming from *The Early Life of Thomas Hardy* (1928) or *The Later Years of Thomas Hardy* (1930). The dates given refer to the period of Hardy's life described; where the excerpts are presented with quotation marks Hardy is reporting his diary entries from that period. Appendix II cross-references different editions of the autobiography.

'*May*. How often we see a vital truth flung about carelessly wrapt in a commonplace subject, without the slightest conception on the speaker's part that his words contain an unsmelted treasure.'

'In architecture, men who are clever in details are bunglers in generalities. So it is in everything whatsoever.'

'More conducive to success in life than the desire for much knowledge is the being satisfied with ignorance on irrelevant subjects.'

'The world does not despise us; it only neglects us.'

EL 63 (1865)

However, as yet he did not by any means abandon verse, which he wrote constantly, but kept private, through the years 1866 and most of 1867, resolving to send no more to magazines whose editors probably did not know good poetry from bad, and forming meanwhile the quixotic opinion that, as in verse was concentrated the essence of all imaginative and emotional literature, to read verse and nothing else was the shortest way to the fountain-head of such, for one who had not a great deal of spare time. And in fact for nearly or quite two years he did not read a word of prose except such as came under his eye in the daily newspapers and weekly reviews. Thus his reading naturally covered a fairly large tract of English poetry, and it may be mentioned, as showing that he had some views of his own, that he preferred Scott the poet to Scott the novelist, and never ceased to regret that the author of 'the most Homeric poem in the English language – *Marmion*' – should later have declined on prose fiction.

He was not so keenly anxious to get into print as many young men are; in this indifference, as in some qualities of his verse, curiously resembling Donne. The Horatian exhortation that he had come across in his reading – to keep his own compositions back till the ninth year – had made a deep impression on him. *Nescit vox missa reverti*; and by retaining his poems, and destroying those he thought irremediably bad – though he afterwards fancied he had destroyed too many – he may have been saved from the annoyance of seeing his early crude effusions crop up in later life.

EL 64 (1865)

'*Aug.* 23. The poetry of a scene varies with the minds of the perceivers. Indeed, it does not lie in the scene at all.'

EL 66 (1865)

'Read again Addison, Macaulay, Newman, Sterne, Defoe, Lamb, Gibbon, Burke, *Times* leaders, etc., in a study of style. Am more and more confirmed in an idea I have long held, as a matter of common sense, long before I thought of any old aphorism bearing on the subject: "Ars est celare artem". The whole secret of a living style and the difference between it and a dead style, lies in not having too much style – being, in fact, a little careless, or rather seeming to be, here and there. It brings wonderful life into the writing:

> A sweet disorder in the dress ...
> A careless shoe-string, in whose tie
> I see a wild civility,
> Do more bewitch me than when art
> Is too precise in every part.

'Otherwise your style is like worn half-pence – all the fresh images rounded off by rubbing, and no crispness or movement at all.

'It is, of course, simply a carrying into prose the knowledge I have acquired in poetry – that inexact rhymes and rhythms now and then are far more pleasing than correct ones.'

EL 138 (1875)

'*June* 26. If it be possible to compress into a sentence all that a man learns between 20 and 40, it is that all things merge in one another – good into evil, generosity into justice, religion into politics, the year into the ages, the world into the universe. With this in view the evolution of species seems but a minute and obvious process in the same movement.'

EL 146–7 (1876)

'"All is vanity", saith the Preacher. But if all were only vanity, who would mind? Alas, it is too often worse than vanity; agony, darkness, death also.'

'A man would never laugh were he not to forget his situation, or were he not one who never has learnt it. After risibility from comedy, how often does the thoughtful mind reproach itself for forgetting the truth? Laughter always means blindness – either from defect, choice, or accident.'

EL 148 (1876)

'*April* 22. The method of Boldini, the painter of "The Morning Walk" in the French Gallery two or three years ago (a young lady beside an ugly blank wall on an ugly highway) – of Hobbema, in his view of a road with formal lopped trees and flat tame scenery – is that of infusing emotion into the baldest external objects either by the presence of a human figure among them, or by mark of some human connection with them.

'This accords with my feeling about, say, Heidelberg and Baden *versus* Scheveningen – as I wrote at the beginning of *The Return of the Native* – that the beauty of association is entirely superior to the beauty of aspect, and a beloved relative's old battered tankard to the finest Greek vase. Paradoxically put, it is to see the beauty in ugliness.'

EL 157–8 (1878)

A peculiarity in the local descriptions running through all Hardy's writings may be instanced here – that he never uses the word 'Dorset', never names the county at all (except possibly in an explanatory footnote), but obliterates the names of the six counties, whose area he traverses in his scenes, under the general appellation of 'Wessex' – an old word that became quite popular after the date of *Far from the Madding Crowd*, where he first introduced it. So far did he carry this idea of the unity of Wessex that he used to say he had grown to forget the crossing of county boundaries within the ancient kingdom – in this respect being quite unlike the poet Barnes, who was 'Dorset' emphatically.

EL 160–1 (1878)

'Arnold is wrong about provincialism, if he means anything more than a provincialism of style and manner in exposition. A certain provincialism of feeling is invaluable. It is of the essence of individuality, and is largely made up of that crude enthusiasm without which no great thoughts are thought, no great deeds done.'

Some days later he writes:

'Romanticism will exist in human nature as long as human nature itself exists. The point is (in imaginative literature) to adopt that form of romanticism which is the mood of the age.'

EL 189 (1880)

'*January* 31. Incidents of lying in bed for months. Skin gets fair: corns take their leave: feet and toes grow shapely as those of a Greek statue. Keys get rusty; watch dim, boots mildewed; hat and clothes old-fashioned; umbrella eaten out with rust; children seen through the window are grown taller.'

'*February* 7. Carlyle died last Saturday. Both he and George Eliot have vanished into nescience while I have been lying here.'

'*February* 17. Conservatism is not estimable in itself, nor is Change, or Radicalism. To conserve the existing good, to supplant the existing bad by good, is to act on a true political principle, which is neither Conservative nor Radical.'

EL 190–1 (1881)

'*May* 9. After infinite trying to reconcile a scientific view of life with the emotional and spiritual, so that they may not be interdestructive I come to the following:
'General Principles. Law has produced in man a child who cannot but constantly reproach its parent for doing much and yet not all, and constantly say to such parent that it would have been better never to have begun doing than to have *over*done so indecisively; that is, than to have created so far beyond all apparent first intention (on the emotional side), without mending matters by a second intent and execution, to eliminate the evils of the blunder of overdoing. The emotions have no place in a world of defect, and it is a cruel injustice that they should have developed in it.

'If Law itself had consciousness, how the aspect of its creatures would terrify it, fill it with remorse!'

EL 192 (1881)

'*June* 3. ... As, in looking at a carpet, by following one colour a certain pattern is suggested, by following another colour, another; so in life the seer should watch that pattern among general things which his idiosyncrasy moves him to observe, and describe that alone. This is, quite accurately, a going to Nature; yet the result is no mere photograph, but purely the product of the writer's own mind.'

EL 198 (1881)

'*August*. – An ample theme: the intense interests, passions, and strategy that throb through the commonest lives.

'This month blackbirds and thrushes creep about under fruit-bushes and in other shady places in gardens rather like four-legged animals than birds. ... I notice that a blackbird has eaten nearly a whole pear lying in the garden-path in the course of the day.'

EL 199 (1881)

'Since I discovered, several years ago, that I was living in a world where nothing bears out in practice what it promises incipiently, I have troubled myself very little about theories. ... Where development according to perfect reason is limited to the narrow region of pure mathematics, I am content with tentativeness from day to day.'

EL 201 (1882)

'*October* 20. Query: Is not the present quasi-scientific system of writing history mere charlatanism? Events and tendencies are traced as if they were rivers of voluntary activity, and courses reasoned out from the circumstances in which natures, religions, or what-not, have found themselves. But are they not in the main the outcome of *passivity* – acted upon by unconscious propensity?'

EL 219–20 (1884)

'*Easter Sunday*. Evidences of art in Bible narratives. They are written with a watchful attention (though disguised) as to their effect on their reader. Their so-called simplicity is, in fact, the simplicity of the highest cunning.

And one is led to inquire, when even in these latter days artistic development and arrangement are the qualities least appreciated by readers, who was there likely to appreciate the art in these chronicles at that day?

'Looking round on a well-selected shelf of fiction or history, how few stories of any length does one recognize as well told from beginning to end! The first half of this story, the last half of that, the middle of another.... The modern art of narration is yet in its infancy.

'But in these Bible lives and adventures there is the spherical completeness of perfect art. And our first, and second, feeling that they must be true because they are so impressive, becomes, as a third feeling, modified to, "Are they so very true, after all? Is not the fact of their being so convincing an argument, not for their actuality, but for the actuality of a consummate artist who was no more content with what Nature offered than Sophocles and Pheidias were content?"'

EL 222–3 (1885)

'Cold weather brings out upon the faces of people the written marks of their habits, vices, passions, and memories, as warmth brings out on paper a writing in sympathetic ink. The drunkard looks still more a drunkard when the splotches have their margins made distinct by frost, the hectic blush becomes a stain now, the cadaverous complexion reveals the bone under, the quality of handsomeness is reduced to its lowest terms.'

'*January* 3. My art is to intensify the expression of things, as is done by Crivelli, Bellini, etc., so that the heart and inner meaning is made vividly visible.'

EL 231–2 (1886)

'Everybody is thinking, even amid these art examples from various ages, that this present age is the ultimate climax and upshot of the previous ages, and not a link in a chain of them.

'In a work of art it is the accident which *charms*, not the intention; *that* we only like and admire. Instance the amber tones that pervade the folds of drapery in ancient marbles, the deadened polish of the surfaces, and the cracks and the scratches.'

EL 251 (1887, visit to Italy)

'*January* 5. Be rather curious than anxious about your own career; for whatever result may accrue to its intellectual and social value, it will make little difference to your personal well-being. A naturalist's interest in the hatching of a queer egg or germ is the utmost introspective consideration you should allow yourself.'

EL 267 (1888)

As to the above remark on the value of life, Hardy writes whimsically a day or two later:

'I have attempted many modes [of finding it]. For my part, if there is any way of getting a melancholy satisfaction out of life it lies in dying, so to speak, before one is out of the flesh; by which I mean putting on the manners of ghosts, wandering in their haunts, and taking their views of surrounding things. To think of life as passing away is a sadness; to think of it as past is at least tolerable. Hence even when I enter into a room to pay a simple morning call I have unconsciously the habit of regarding the scene as if I were a spectre not solid enough to influence my environment; only fit to behold and say, as another spectre said: "Peace be unto you!"'

EL 275 (1888)

'*March* 15. What has been written cannot be blotted. Each new style of novel must be the old with added ideas, not an ignoring and avoidance of the old. And so of religion, and a good many other things!'

'*April* 5. London. Four million forlorn hopes!'

'*April* 7. A woeful fact – that the human race is too extremely developed for its corporeal conditions, the nerves being evolved to an activity abnormal in such an environment. Even the higher animals are in excess in this respect. It may be questioned if Nature, or what we call Nature, so far back as when she crossed the line from invertebrates to vertebrates, did not exceed her mission. This planet does not supply the materials for happiness to higher existences. Other planets may, though one can hardly see how.'

EL 286 (1889)

'*August* 5. Reflections on Art. Art is a changing of the actual proportions and order of things, so as to bring out more forcibly than might otherwise be done that feature in them which appeals most strongly to the idiosyncrasy of the artist. The changing, or distortion, may be of two kinds: (1) The kind which increases the sense of vraisemblance: (2) That which diminishes it. (1) is high art: (2) is low art.

'High art may choose to depict evil as well as good, without losing its quality. Its choice of evil, however, must be limited by the sense of worthiness.' A continuation of the same note was made a little later, and can be given here:

'Art is a disproportioning – (*i.e.* distorting, throwing out of proportion) – of realities, to show more clearly the features that matter in those realities, which, if merely copied or reported inventorially, might possibly be observed, but would more probably be overlooked. Hence "realism" is not Art.'

EL 299 (1890)

'Poetry. Perhaps I can express more fully in verse ideas and emotions which run counter to the inert crystallized opinion – hard as a rock – which the vast body of men have vested interests in supporting. To cry out in a passionate poem that (for instance) the Supreme Mover or Movers, the Prime Force or Forces, must be either limited in power, unknowing, or cruel – which is obvious enough, and has been for centuries – will cause them merely a shake of the head; but to put it in argumentative prose will make them sneer, or foam, and set all the literary contortionists jumping upon me, a harmless agnostic, as if I were a clamorous atheist, which in their crass illiteracy they seem to think is the same thing. . . . If Galileo had said in verse that the world moved, the Inquisition might have let him alone.'

LY 57–8 (1896)

'1897. *January* 27. To-day has length, breadth, thickness, colour, smell, voice. As soon as it becomes *yesterday* it is a thin layer among many layers, without substance, colour, or articulate sound.'
. . .

'*February* 10. In spite of myself I cannot help noticing countenances and tempers in objects of scenery, *e.g.* trees, hills, houses.'

LY 58 (1897)

The misrepresentations of the last two or three years affected but little, if at all, the informed appreciation of Hardy's writings, being heeded almost entirely by those who had not read him; and turned out ultimately to be the best thing that could have happened; for they wellnigh compelled him, in his own judgement at any rate, if he wished to retain any shadow of self-respect, to abandon at once a form of literary art he had long intended to abandon at some indefinite time, and resume openly that form of it which had always been more instinctive with him, and which he had just been able to keep alive from his early years, half in secrecy, under the pressure of magazine writing. He abandoned it with all the less reluctance in that the novel was, in his own words, 'gradually losing artistic form, with a beginning, middle, and end, and becoming a spasmodic inventory of items, which has nothing to do with art'.

The change, after all, was not so great as it seemed. It was not as if he had been a writer of novels proper, and as more specifically understood, that is, stories of modern artificial life and manners showing a certain smartness of treatment. He had mostly aimed at keeping his narratives close to natural life and as near to poetry in their subject as the conditions would allow, and had often regretted that those conditions would not let him keep them nearer still.

LY 65 (1897)

He wrote somewhere: 'There is no new poetry; but the new poet – if he carry the flame on further (and if not he is no new poet) – comes with a new note. And that new note it is that troubles the critical waters.

'Poetry is emotion put into measure. The emotion must come by nature, but the measure can be acquired by art.'

In the reception of this and later volumes of Hardy's poems there was, he said, as regards form, the inevitable ascription to ignorance of what was really choice after full knowledge. That the author loved the art of concealing art was undiscerned. For instance, as to rhythm. Years earlier he had decided that too regular a beat was bad art. He had fortified himself in his opinion by thinking of the analogy of architecture, between which art and that of poetry he had discovered, to use his own words, that there existed a close and curious parallel, both arts, unlike some others, having to carry a rational content inside their artisitic form. He knew that in architecture cunning irregularity is of enormous worth, and it is obvious that he carried on into his verse, perhaps in part unconsciously, the Gothic art-principle in which he had been trained – the principle of spontaneity, found in mouldings, tracery, and such like – resulting in the 'unforeseen' (as it has been called) character of his metres and stanzas, that of stress rather than of syllable, poetic texture rather than poetic veneer; the latter kind of thing, under the name of 'constructed ornament', being what he, in common with every Gothic student, had been taught to avoid as the plague. He shaped his poetry accordingly, introducing metrical pauses, and reversed beats; and found for his trouble that some particular line of a poem exemplifying this principle was greeted with a would-be jocular remark that such a line 'did not make for immortality'. The same critic might have gone to one of our cathedrals (to follow up the analogy of architecture), and on discovering that the carved leafage of some capital or spandrel in the best period of Gothic art strayed freakishly out of its bounds over the moulding, where by rule it had no business to be, or that the enrichments of a string-course were not accurately spaced; or that there was a sudden blank in a wall where a window was to be expected from formal measurement, have declared with equally merry conviction, 'This does not make for immortality'.

One case of the kind, in which the poem 'On Sturminster Foot-Bridge' was quoted with the remark that one could make as good music as that out of a milk-cart, betrayed the reviewer's ignorance of any perception that the metre was intended to be onomatopoeic, plainly as it was shown; and another in the same tone disclosed that the reviewer had tried to scan the author's sapphics as heroics.

If any proof were wanted that Hardy was not at this time and later the apprentice at verse that he was supposed to be, it could be found in an examination of his studies over many years. Among his papers were quantities of notes on rhythm and metre: with outlines and experiments in innumerable original measures, some of which he adopted from time to time. These verse skeletons were mostly blank, and only designated by the usual marks for long and short syllables, accentuations, etc., but they were occasionally made up of 'nonsense verses' – such as, he said, were written when he was a boy by students of Latin prosody with the aid of a 'Gradus'.

Lastly, Hardy had a born sense of humour, even a too keen sense occasionally: but his poetry was sometimes placed by editors in the hands of reviewers deficient in that quality. Even if they were accustomed to Dickensian humour they were not to Swiftian. Hence it unfortunately happened that verses of a satirical, dry, caustic, or farcical cast were regarded by them with the deepest seriousness.

LY 78–80 (1899)

Hardy's memoranda on his thoughts and movements – particularly the latter – which never reached the regularity of a diary – had of late grown more and more fitful, and now (1900) that novels were past and done with, nearly ceased altogether, such notes on scenes and functions having been dictated by what he had thought practical necessity; so that it becomes difficult to ascertain what mainly occupied his mind, or what his social doings were. His personal ambition in a worldly sense, which had always been weak, dwindled to nothing, and for some years after 1895 or 1896 he requested that no record of his life should be made. His verses he kept on writing from pleasure in them.

LY 84 (1900)

In a pocket-book of this date appears a diagram illustrating 'the language of verse':

Verse

| Fanciful | Meditative | Sentimental | Passionate |

Language of Common Speech.

Poetic Diction

and the following note thereon:

'The confusion of thought to be observed in Wordsworth's teaching in his essay in the Appendix to *Lyrical Ballads* seems to arise chiefly out of his use of the word "imagination". He should have put the matter somewhat like this: In works of *passion and sentiment* (not "imagination and sentiment") the language of verse is the language of prose. In works of *fancy* (or *imagination*), "poetic diction" (of the real kind) is proper, and even necessary. The diagram illustrates my meaning.'

For some reason he spent time while here in hunting up Latin hymns at the British Museum, and copies that he made of several have been found, of dates ranging from the thirteenth to the seventeenth century, by Thomas of Celano, Adam of S. Victor, John Mombaer, Jacob Balde, etc. That English prosody might be enriched by adapting some of the verse-forms of these is not unlikely to have been his view.

LY 85–6 (1900)

On the last day of the year he makes the following reflection: 'After reading various philosophic systems, and being struck with their contradictions and futilities, I have come to this: *Let every man make a philosophy for himself out of his own experience.* He will not be able to escape using terms and phraseology from earlier philosophers, but let him avoid adopting their theories if he values his own mental life. Let him remember the fate of Coleridge, and save years of labour by working out his own views as given him by his surroundings.'

'*January* 1 (1902). A Pessimist's apology. Pessimism (or rather what is called such) is, in brief, playing the sure game. You cannot lose at it; you may gain. It is the only view of life in which you can never be disappointed. Having reckoned what to do in the worst possible circumstances, when better arise, as they may, life becomes child's play.'

LY 91 (1901–2)

'I prefer late Wagner, as I prefer late Turner, to early (which I suppose is all wrong in taste), the idiosyncrasies of each master being more strongly shown in these strains. When a man not contented with the grounds of his success goes on and on, and tries to achieve the impossible, then he gets profoundly interesting to me. To-day it was early Wagner for the most part: fine music, but not so particularly his – no spectacle of the inside of a brain at work like the inside of a hive.'

LY 117 (1906)

'In a dramatic epic – which I may perhaps assume *The Dynasts* to be – some philosophy of life was necessary, and I went on using that which I had denoted in my previous volumes of verse (and to some extent prose) as being a generalized form of what the thinking world had gradually come to adopt, myself included. That the Unconscious Will of the Universe is growing aware of Itself I believe I may claim as my own idea solely – at which I arrived by reflecting that what has already taken place in a fraction of the whole (*i.e.* so much of the world as has become conscious) is likely to take place in the mass; and there being no Will outside the mass – that is, the Universe – the whole Will becomes conscious thereby: and ultimately, it is to be hoped, sympathetic.

'I believe, too, that the Prime Cause, this Will, has never before been called "It" in any poetical literature, English or foreign.

'The theory, too, seems to me to settle the question of Free-will v. Necessity. The will of a man is, according to it, neither wholly free nor wholly unfree. When swayed by the Universal Will (which he mostly must be as a subservient part of it) he is not individually free; but whenever it happens that all the rest of the Great Will is in equilibrium the minute portion called one person's will is free, just as a performer's fingers are free to go on playing the pianoforte of themselves when he talks or thinks of something else and the head does not rule them.'

LY 124–5 (1907, letter)

In connection with this subject it may be here recalled, in answer to writers who now and later were fond of charging Hardy with postulating a malignant and fiendish God, that he never held any views of the sort, merely surmising an indifferent and unconscious force at the back of things 'that neither good nor evil knows'. His view is shown, in fact, to approximate to Spinoza's – and later Einstein's – that neither Chance nor Purpose governs the universe, but Necessity.

LY 128 (1907)

'And when all has been said on the desirability of preserving as much as can be preserved, our power to preserve is largely an illusion. Where is the Dorchester of my early recollection – I mean the human Dorchester – the kernel – of which the houses were but the shell? Of the shops as I first recall them not a single owner remains; only in two or three instances does even the name remain. As a German author has said, "Nothing is permanent but change". Here in Dorchester, as elsewhere, I see the streets and the turnings not far different from those of my schoolboy time; but the faces that used to be seen at the doors, the inhabitants, where are they? I turn up the Weymouth Road, cross the railway-bridge, enter an iron gate to "a slope of green access", and there they are! There is the Dorchester that I knew best; there are names on white stones one after the other, names that recall the voices, cheerful and sad, anxious and indifferent, that are missing from the dwellings and pavements. Those who are old enough to have had that experience may feel that after all the permanence or otherwise of inanimate Dorchester concerns but the permanence of what is minor and accessory.'

LY 145–6 (1910, speech)

'What should certainly be protested against, in cases where there is no authorization, is the mixing of fact and fiction in unknown proportions. Infinite mischief would lie in that. If any statements in the dress of fiction are covertly hinted to be fact, all must be fact, and nothing else but fact, for obvious reasons. The power of getting lies believed about people through that channel after they are dead, by stirring in a few truths, is a horror to contemplate.'

LY 153 (1912)

It may be added here that the war destroyed all Hardy's belief in the gradual ennoblement of man, a belief he had held for many years, as is shown by poems like 'The Sick Battle-God', and others. He said he would probably not have ended *The Dynasts* as he did end it if he could have foreseen what was going to happen within a few years.

Moreover, the war gave the *coup de grâce* to any conception he may have nourished of a fundamental ultimate Wisdom at the back of things. With his views on necessitation, or at most a very limited free will, events seemed to show him that a fancy he had often held and expressed, that the never-ending push of the Universe was an unpurposive and irresponsible groping in the direction of the least resistance, might possibly be the real truth. 'Whether or no', he would say,

'Desine fata Deûm flecti sperare precando.'

LY 165–6 (1914)

'I hold that the mission of poetry is to record impressions, not convictions. Wordsworth in his later writings fell into the error of recording the latter. So also did Tennyson, and so do many other poets when they grow old. *Absit omen!*

'I fear I have always been considered the Dark Horse of contemporary English literature.

'I was quick to bloom; late to ripen.

'I believe it would be said by people who knew me well that I have a faculty (possibly not uncommon) for burying an emotion in my heart or brain for forty years, and exhuming it at the end of that time as fresh as when interred. For instance, the poem entitled 'The Breaking of Nations' contains a feeling that moved me in 1870, during the Franco-Prussian war, when I chanced to be looking at such an agricultural incident in Cornwall. But I did not write the verses till during the war with Germany of 1914, and onwards. Query: where was that sentiment hiding itself during more than forty years?'

Hardy's mind seems to have been running on himself at this time to a degree quite unusual with him, who often said – and his actions showed it – that he took no interest in himself as a personage.

'*November* 13. I was a child till I was 16; a youth till I was 25; a young man till I was 40 or 50.'

The above note on his being considered a Dark Horse was apt enough, when it is known that none of the society men who met him suspected from his simple manner the potentialities of observation that were in him. This unassertive air, unconsciously worn, served him as an invisible coat almost to uncanniness. At houses and clubs where he encountered other writers and critics and world-practised readers of character, whose bearing towards him was often as towards one who did not reach their altitudes, he was seeing through them as though they were glass. He set down some cutting and satirical notes on their qualities and compass, but destroyed all of them, not wishing to leave behind him anything which could be deemed a gratuitous belittling of others.

LY 178–9 (1917)

'*January* 16. As to reviewing. Apart from a few brilliant exceptions, poetry is not at bottom criticized as such, that is, as a particular man's artistic interpretation of life, but with a secret eye on its theological and political propriety. Swinburne used to say to me that so it would be two thousand years hence; but I doubt it.

'As to pessimism. My motto is, first correctly diagnose the complaint – in this case human ills – and ascertain the cause: then set about finding a remedy if one exists. The motto or practice of the optimists is: Blind the eyes to the real malady, and use empirical panaceas to suppress the symptoms.'

LY 183 (1918)

'*January* 30. English writers who endeavour to appraise poets, and discriminate the sheep from the goats, are apt to consider that all true poets must be of one pattern in their lives and developments. But the glory of poetry lies in its largeness, admitting among its creators men of infinite variety. They must be all impractical in the conduct of their affairs; nay, they must almost, like Shelley or Marlowe, be drowned or done to death, or like Keats, die of consumption. They forget that in the ancient world no such necessity was recognized; that Homer sang as a blind old man, that Aeschylus wrote his best up to his death at nearly seventy, that the best of Sophocles appeared beween his fifty-fifth and ninetieth years, that Euripides wrote up to seventy.

'Among those who accomplished late, the poetic spark must always have been latent; but its outspringing may have been frozen and delayed for half a lifetime.'

LY 184 (1918)

In a United States periodical for March it was stated that 'Thomas Hardy is a realistic novelist who ... has a grim determination to go down to posterity wearing the laurels of a poet'. This writer was a glaring illustration of the danger of reading motives into actions. Of course there was no 'grim determination', no thought of 'laurels'. Thomas Hardy was always a person with an unconscious, or rather unreasoning, *tendency*, and the poetic tendency had been his from the earliest. He would tell that it used to be said to him at Sir Arthur Blomfield's: 'Hardy, there can hardly have been anybody in the world with less ambition than you.' At this time the real state of his mind was, in his own words that 'A sense of the truth of poetry, of its supreme place in literature, had awakened itself in me. At the risk of ruining all my worldly prospects I dabbled in it . . . was forced out of it. . . . It came back upon me. . . . All was of the nature of being led by a mood, without foresight, or regard to whither it led.'

LY 185 (1918)

'*April* 30. By the will of God some men are born poetical. Of these some make themselves practical poets, others are made poets by lapse of time who were hardly recognized as such. Particularly has this been the case with the translators of the Bible. They translated into the language of their age; then the years began to corrupt that language as spoken, and to add grey lichen to the translation; until the moderns who use the corrupted tongue marvel at the poetry of the old words. When new they were not more than half so poetical. So that Coverdale, Tyndale, and the rest of them are as ghosts what they never were in the flesh.'

LY 186 (1918)

Some sense of the neglect of poetry by the modern English may have led him to write at this time:
'The poet is like one who enters and mounts a platform to give an address as announced. He opens his page, looks around, and finds the hall – *empty*.'
A little later he says:
'It bridges over the years to think that Gray might have seen Wordsworth in his cradle, and Wordsworth might have seen me in mine.'

LY 187 (1918)

'In my fancies, or poems of the imagination, I have of course called this Power all sorts of names – never supposing they would be taken for more than fancies. I have even in prefaces warned readers to take them as such – as mere impressions of the moment, exclamations in fact. But it has always been my misfortune to presuppose a too intelligent reading public, and no doubt people will go on thinking that I really believe the Prime Mover to be a malignant old gentleman, a sort of King of Dahomey – and idea which, so far from my holding it, is to me irresistibly comic. "What a fool one must have been to write for such a public!" is the inevitable reflection at the end of one's life.'
. . .
Mr. Noyes in a further interesting letter, after reassuring Hardy that he would correct any errors, gave his own views, one of which was that he had 'never been able to conceive a Cause of Things that could be less in any respect than the things caused'. To which Hardy replied:
'Many thanks for your letter. The Scheme of Things is, indeed, incomprehensible; and there I suppose we must leave it – perhaps for the best. Knowledge might be terrible.'

LY 217–18 (1920, letters)

'*November* 28. Speaking about ambition T. said to-day that he had done all that he meant to do, but he did not know whether it had been worth doing.

'His only ambition, so far as he could remember, was to have some poem or poems in a good anthology like the Golden Treasury.

'The model he had set before him was "Drink to me only", by Ben Jonson.'

LY 263 (1927)

Appendix I: Two Early Versions of Poems by Hardy

The Bird-Catcher's Boy

The Sphere, 4 January 1913, p. 21. Extensively revised for *Human Shows*.

'I don't like your trade, father,
  Surely it's wrong –
Prisoning those little birds
  All their lives long.

'The larks bruise their tender crowns   5
  Trying to rise,
Every year every caged
  Nightingale dies.'

'Don't be a fool, my boy.
  Birds must be caught;   10
My business 'tis to earn,
  Yours to be taught.

'Keep such cursed sentiment
  Out of your head;
Just learn your lessons, then   15
  March off to bed.'

Softly and lightless
  To bed he repairs,
They hear him feel his way
  Toward the dark stairs,   20

Through the long passage where
  Hang the caged choirs;
Groping, his fingers sweep
  Over the wires.

Next day at ruddy dawn 25
   Freddy was missed,
Whither the boy had gone
   No parent wist.

That week and next week,
   And nothing of him; 30
Weeks grew to months and more,
   Hope dwindled dim.

Yet not a single night
   Locked they the door,
Waiting, heartsick, to see 35
   Freddy once more.

One winter midnight
   The twain lay awake,
No cheer within them,
   Their days one long ache. 40

Then someone seemed to be
   Entering below.
'Freddy's come!' Up they sit,
   Faces aglow.

Over the bird-cage wires 45
   Fingers swept light
As when he felt his way
   Stairward at night,

Sounding the wires by touch
   Like a light broom: 50
Both parents rose and sought
   Freddy's old room.

There on the empty bed
   White the moon shone,
All was as ever since 55
   Freddy had gone.

That night at Portland Race
   Foundered a hoy,
And the tide washed ashore
   One sailor boy. 60

The Portraits

Nash's Magazine and Pall Mall, December 1924, p. 27. The poem appeared within a two-page Art Deco frame with an illustration by Harry Clarke, depicting figures and candles. Revised for *Winter Words* as 'Family Portraits'.

Three picture-drawn people stepped out of their frames –
    The blast, how it blew! –
And the white-shrouded candles flapped smoke-headed
    flames;
The picture-drawn past ones came down from their frames,
And dumbly in lippings they told me their names,   5
    So well though I knew!

The first was a maiden of mild wistful tone,
    Gone silent for years,
The next a dark woman aforetime well known:
But the first one, the maiden of mild wistful tone,   10
So wondering, unpractised, so vague and alone,
    Nigh moved me to tears.

The third was a sad man – a man of much gloom;
    And before me they passed
In the shade of the night, at the back of the room,   15
The dark and fair woman, the man of much gloom,
Three persons, in far-off years forceful, but whom
    Death now fettered fast.

They set about acting some drama obscure –
    The women and he,   20
With puppet-like movement of mute, strange allure: –
Yea, set about acting some drama obscure –
Till I saw 'twas their own lifetime's tragic amour,
    Strangely bearing on me.

'Why wake up all this?' I inquired. 'Now, so late!   25
    Let old ghosts be laid!'
And they stiffened, drew back to their frames and numb state,
Gibbering: 'Such your own story will be, know too late!'
Then I grieved that I'd not had the patience to wait,
    And see the play played.   30

For why should it not have been? Could it have hurt,
    Had they paced again through
Those orbits that once they had trod when expert
In the laboursome passions of life – of deep hurt
To them, maybe to me? But I found them inert,   35
    And the blast again blew.

I have grieved ever since; for I fed my own pain
    By the interdict thrown:
Years long night by night stretched awake I have lain
Perplexed in endeavours to heal my own pain   40
By uncovering the drift of their drama. In vain!
    Yet they called it my own.

Appendix II: Page References in Hardy's Autobiography

The following table collates page numbers in the three versions of Hardy's autobiography in common use: the two-volume first edition used in notes above, *The Early Life* (1928) and *The Later Years* (1930); the *Life of Thomas Hardy* (1962), the same text published in one volume; and the 'restored' text as Hardy prepared it before his wife's editing, published as *The Life and Work of Thomas Hardy*, ed. Michael Millgate (1985).

Early Life	*Life*	*Life and Work*	*Later Years*	*Life*	*Life and Work*
10	8	13	1	241	253
20	16	21	10	248	262
30	23	28	20	256	272
40	31	35	30	263	280
50	38	—	40	271	289
60	46	48	50	279	296
70	53	54	60	286	304
80	60	62	70	295	313
90	68	71	80	302	325
100	76	79	90	309	332
110	84	86	100	317	341
120	91	93	110	324	348
130	99	101	120	331	357
140	106	109	130	340	366
150	114	117	140	348	375
160	122	125	150	357	384
170	130	133	160	364	393
180	138	142	170	371	402
190	147	151	180	379	409
200	154	159	190	388	421
210	161	167	200	395	429

Early Life	Life	Life and Work	Later Years	Life	Life and Work
220	169	175	210	403	423
230	176	182	220	411	442
240	183	190			
250	191	199	230	419	452
260	198	206	240	426	460
270	206	215	250	423	468
280	214	223	260	442	476
290	221	232	270	450	488
300	229	240			
310	236	248			

The line above right denotes the end of Hardy's authorship: *The Later Years*, chs 18–19 (*Life*/*Life and Work*, chs 37–8) were written by Florence Hardy.

Bibliography

A Note on Reading

The bibliography below lists all works referred to in the annotations, and gives a number of references on individual poems and issues. This note is designed to help the student beginning to read Hardy's poetry and seeking some sense of the resources available.

In terms of primary resources, the student of Hardy's poetry is now very well served. There are two modern versions of his poetry, James Gibson's *Variorum Edition* (1979), published without apparatus as the Macmillan *Complete Poems*, and Samuel Hynes's authoritative three-volume edition *The Complete Poetical Works of Thomas Hardy* (1982–85). Hardy's letters have now appeared in a seven-volume edition edited by Richard Little Purdy and Michael Millgate; the most critically interesting included in the *Selected Letters*, ed. Michael Millgate (1990). Hardy's critical essays have been edited by Harold Orel as *Thomas Hardy's Personal Writings* (1966), and his autobiography (*The Early Life* and *The Later Years*) has been restored to a putative 'original' state (before editing by his wife and executors) as *The Life and Work of Thomas Hardy*, ed. Michael Millgate (1985). A number of Hardy's various notebooks have been edited, as the *Personal Notebooks*, ed. Richard H. Taylor (1979), and the *Literary Notebooks*, 2 vols, ed. Lennart Björk (1985). The latter is particularly rich in annotation, its index an invaluable guide to Hardy's reading and influences.

There are a number of bibliographical works on Hardy. Richard Little Purdy's *Thomas Hardy: A Bibliographical Study* (1954) is the standard work on Hardy's writings. The most comprehensive listing of manuscripts is that in Barbara Rosenbaum's *Index of English Literary Manuscripts, Vol IV, 1800–1900, Part II, Hardy–Lamb* (1990). For writings about Hardy, see Helmut Gerber and Eugene Davis's *Thomas Hardy: An Annotated Bibliography of Writings About*

Him, 2 vols. (1973, 1983). A recent short work, Ronald Draper and Martin Ray's *An Annotated Critical Bibliography of Thomas Hardy* (1989), summarizes a selection of major books and articles. Some early responses to Hardy's poetry (to 1914) are collected in *Thomas Hardy: The Critical Heritage*, ed. R.G. Cox (1970).

A number of journal issues and collections of essays have represented landmarks in the study of Hardy's poetry. The *Southern Review* Hardy issue in 1940 contained important early appreciations, the *Agenda* Hardy issue in 1972 was closely related to the 1970s revival in Hardy studies (see epecially articles by Davie, Gunn, Peck). The *Victorian Poetry* Hardy double issue in 1979 contained several useful essays, as did the 1980 collection edited by Patricia Clements and J. Grindle, *The Poetry of Thomas Hardy*.

There are many general works on Hardy's poetry, some of which are now rather dated. J.O. Bailey's *The Poetry of Thomas Hardy: A Handbook and Commentary* (1970) is the essential source for poem-by-poem commentary; supplemented by F.B. Pinion's *A Commentary on the Poems of Thomas Hardy* (1976). Samuel Hynes's *The Pattern of Hardy's Poetry* (1961) is useful, as are Paul Zeitlow's *Moments of Vision* (1974) and J. Richardson's *Thomas Hardy: The Poetry of Necessity* (1977). Perhaps the best individual works on Hardy's career and aesthetics are Dennis Taylor's *Hardy's Poetry, 1860–1928* (1981), and Tom Paulin's *Thomas Hardy: The Poetry of Perception* (1975), though J. Hillis Miller's essays on Hardy's poetry, scattered over several volumes, also constitute a powerful reading. For a succinct general introduction to Hardy's poetry see the chapter on Hardy in John Lucas's *Modern English Poetry from Hardy to Hughes* (1986). Hardy's British critics have inevitably oriented themselves with respect to Donald Davie's strong views (positive and negative) in *Thomas Hardy and British Poetry* (1973).

Also recommended on Hardy's preoccupation with time, pattern, memory, and loss are Mary Jacobus's elegant 1982 piece in *Essays in Criticism*, 'Hardy's Magian Retrospect' and the chapter on Hardy in Philip Davis's *Memory and Writing* (1983). Hardy's elegies have been explored brilliantly by Donald Davie in 'Hardy's Virgilian Purples' (*Agenda*, 1972), Rosenthal and Gall in *The Modern Poetic Sequence* (1983), Peter Sacks in *The English Elegy* (1985), by Eric Griffith in *The Printed Voice of Victorian Poetry* (1989), and by David Gewanter and Melanie Sexton in two recent articles in *Victorian Poetry* 29 (1991). On Hardy's philosophy, Walter Wright's *The Shaping of The Dynasts* (1967) is still among the best accounts. On Hardy and religion, Timothy Hands's *Thomas Hardy: Distracted Preacher?* (1989) provides a careful account of the evolution of his religious beliefs. An excellent recent collection on Hardy and gender, *The Sense of Sex* (1993), edited by Margaret Higonnet, focuses mainly on the novels but provides a number of openings into the neglected issue of gender in the poetry.

On Hardy's metrics, the best work has been that of Griffith, Paulin, and Taylor, the latter in his authoritative *Hardy's Metres and Victorian Prosody* (1988). A specific aspect of Hardy's verse-forms often discussed is his use of ballad-forms (discussed by Tom Gunn 1972; Zeitlow 1974; Taylor 1982). The most thorough guide to Hardy's language is Ralph Elliott's *Thomas Hardy's English* (1984), while Isobel Grundy (in Clements and Grindle, above) discusses Hardy's 'roughness' to good effect.

On Hardy and Wessex, the chapter on Hardy in Stan Smith's *Inviolable Voice* (1982) is useful, and George Wotton's *Thomas Hardy: Towards a Materialist Criticism* (1985) provides a stringent account of the material basis of Hardy's area. For topographical reference see Bailey (1970) and Pinion (1976), and Denys Kay-Robinson, *Hardy's Wessex Reappraised* (1972), among other guides. Finally, Pinion's recent *A Hardy Dictionary* (1990) is a good general reference guide to places, character, dialect, etc., in Hardy's work.

Works Cited

Abrams, M.H. (1960), 'The Corresponding Breeze: A Romantic Metaphor', in *English Romantic Poets*, M.H. Abrams ed., New York.

Archer, W. (1904), *Real Conversations with Thomas Hardy*, London. Reprinted from *Critic* (1901) 38: 309–18.

Armstrong, T. (1988a), 'The Latent and the Patent: Hardy and the Subjectivity of Old Age', *Criticism* 30: 455–66.

Armstrong, T. (1988b), 'Supplementarity: Poetry as the Afterlife of Thomas Hardy', *Victorian Poetry* 26: 381–94.

Armstrong T. (1991), 'Hardy's Dantean Purples', *Thomas Hardy Journal* 7(2): 47–54.

Armstrong, T. (1992), 'Hardy, Thaxter, and History as Coincidence in "The Convergence of the Twain"', *Victorian Poetry* 30: 29–42.

Attridge, D. (1982), *The Rhythms of English Poetry*, London.

Auden. W.H. (1960), 'Making, Knowing, and Judging', in *Literature: An Introduction*, eds H. Summers and E. Whan, New York.

Bailey, J.O. (1963), 'Evolutionary Meliorism in the Poetry of Thomas Hardy', *Studies in Philology* 60: 569–87.

Bailey, J.O. (1970), *The Poetry of Thomas Hardy: A Handbook and Commentary*, Chapel Hill.

Barnes, W. (1908), *Select Poems of William Barnes*, ed. Thomas Hardy, London.

Benson, M. (1982), 'Wessex Heights', *Thomas Hardy Society Review* 1(8): 243–6.
Bies, W. (1980), 'A Note on Hardy, W.B. Yeats, and the Brownings', *Thomas Hardy Society Review* 1(6): 193.
Blackmur, R.P. (1940), 'The Shorter Poems of Thomas Hardy', *Southern Review* 6: 20–48. Reprinted in *Language as Gesture*, New York (1952), pp. 51–79.
Bloom, H. (1973), *The Anxiety of Influence*, New York.
Bloom, H. (1975), *A Map of Misreading*, Oxford.
Bloom, H. (1982), *The Breaking of the Vessels*, Chicago.
Blunden, E. (1942), *Thomas Hardy*, London.
Boone, C. (1990), 'Hardy's Poem "Lines to a Movement..." – which Symphony?', *Thomas Hardy Journal* 6(1): 61–9.
Boumelha, P. (1982), *Thomas Hardy and Women: Sexual Ideology and Narrative Form*, Brighton.
Bronfen, E. (1993), 'Pay as you go: Exchange of bodies and signs,' in Higgonet (ed).
Brooks, J. (1971), *Thomas Hardy: The Poetic Structure*, Ithaca.
Buckler, W.E. (1979), 'The Dark Space Illumined: A Reading of Hardy's "Poems of 1912–13"', *Victorian Poetry* 17: 98–107.
Buckler, W.E. (1983a), *The Poetry of Thomas Hardy: A Study in Art and Ideas*, New York.
Buckler, W.E. (1983b), 'Victorian Modernism: The Arnold-Hardy Succession', *Browning Institute Studies* 11: 9–21.
Campbell, M. (1992), 'Tennyson and Hardy's Ghostly Metres', *Essays in Criticism* 42(4): 279–98.
Chapman, R. (1990), *The Language of Thomas Hardy*, London.
Christ, C.T. (1984), *Victorian and Modern Poetics*, Chicago.
Clements, P. (1980), 'Unlawful Beauty: Order and Things in Hardy's Poetry', in Clements and Grindle (eds), pp. 137–54.
Clements, P. and Grindle, J., eds (1980), *The Poetry of Thomas Hardy*, London.
Collins, V.H. (1928), *Talks with Thomas Hardy at Max Gate, 1920–1922*, New York.
Collins, M.J. (1984), 'Comic Technique in the Poems of Thomas Hardy', *Thomas Hardy Year Book* 11: 31–6.
Cook, C. (1980), 'Thomas Hardy and George Meredith', in Clements and Grindle (eds), pp. 83–100.
Cox, D.D. (1972), 'The Poet and the Architect', *Agenda* 10 (2–3): 50–65.
Cox, R.G., ed. (1970), *Thomas Hardy: The Critical Heritage*, London.
Coxon, P. (1982), 'Hardy's Use of the Hair Motif', *Thomas Hardy Annual* 1: 95–114.
Coxon, P. (1983), 'Thomas Hardy: "The Voice" and Horace: Odes II, xiv', *Thomas Hardy Society Review* 1(9): 291–3.

Creighton, T.R.M. (1974), *Poems of Thomas Hardy*, London.
Davie, D. (1972), 'Hardy's Virgilian Purples', *Agenda* 10 (2–3): 138–56.
Davie, D. (1973), *Thomas Hardy and British Poetry*, London.
Davis, P. (1983), *Memory and Writing: From Wordsworth to Lawrence*, Liverpool.
Day-Lewis, C. (1951), 'The Lyrical Poetry of Thomas Hardy', *Proceedings of the British Academy* 37: 155–74. Part reprinted in Gibson (1979).
Doherty, P. and D. Taylor (1974), 'Syntax in "Neutral Tones"', *Victorian Poetry* 12: 285–90.
Draper, R.P. and M.S. Ray (1989), *An Annotated Critical Bibliography of Thomas Hardy*, London.
Ebbaston, R. (1982), *The Evolutionary Self: Hardy, Forster, Lawrence*, Brighton.
Edmond, R. (1981), 'Death Sequences: Hardy, Patmore, and the New Domestic Elegy', *Victorian Poetry* 19: 151–65.
Elliott, R. (1984), *Thomas Hardy's English*, London.
Faurot, M. (1990), *Hardy's Topographical Lexicon and the Canon of Intent*, New York.
Firor, R. (1931), *Folkways in Thomas Hardy*, Philadelphia.
Gatrell, S. (1980), 'Travelling Man', in Clements and Grindle (eds), pp. 155–71.
Gewanter, D. (1991), '"Undervoicings of loss" in Hardy's Elegies to His Wife', *Victorian Poetry* 29: 193–207.
Gibson, J., ed. (1979), *Thomas Hardy: Poems. A Casebook*, London.
Giordano, F.R. (1975), 'Hardy's Farewell to Fiction: The Structure of Wessex Heights', *Thomas Hardy Yearbook* 5: 58–65.
Giordano, F.R. (1979), 'A Reading of Hardy's "A Set of Country Songs"', *Victorian Poetry* 17: 85–97.
Giordano, F.R. Jnr (1984), *'I'd Have My Life Unbe': Thomas Hardy's Self-destructive Characters*, University, Alabama.
Gittings, R. (1975), *Young Thomas Hardy*, London.
Gittings, R. (1978), *The Older Hardy*, London.
Gifford, H. (1972), 'Hardy's Revisions (*Satires of Circumstance*)', *Agenda* 10 (2–3): 126–37.
Green, B. (1990), 'Darkness Visible: Defiance, Derision, and Despair in Hardy's "In Tenebris" Poems', *Thomas Hardy Journal* 6 (2): 126–46.
Griffith, E. (1989), *The Printed Voice of Victorian Poetry*, Oxford.
Griffith, P. (1963), 'The Image of the Trapped Animal in Hardy's *Tess of the D'Urbervilles*', *TSE* 13: 85–94.
Grundy, I. (1980), 'Hardy's Harshness', in Clements and Grindle (eds), pp. 1–17.
Grundy, J. (1979), *Hardy and the Sister Arts*, London.

Gunn, T. (1972), 'Hardy and the Ballads', *Agenda* 10 (2–3): 19–46.
Hands, T. (1989), *Thomas Hardy: Distracted Preacher? Hardy's Religious Biography and its Influence on his Novels*, London.
Hickson, E. (1931), *The Versification of Thomas Hardy*, Philadelphia.
Higonnet, M.R. (1990), 'A Woman's Story: Tess and the Problem of Voice', in *Out of Bounds*, eds L. Claridge and E. Langland, Amhurst. Reprinted in Higonnet 1993.
Higonnet, M.R., ed. (1993), *The Sense of Sex: Feminist Perspectives on Hardy*, De Kalb, Illinois.
Hollander, J. (1975), *Vision and Resonance: Two Senses of Poetic Form*, New York.
Hollander, J. (1981), *The Figure of Echo: A Mode of Illusion in Milton and After*, Berkeley.
Houghton, W.E. (1957), *The Victorian Frame of Mind, 1830–1870*, New Haven.
Howe, I. (1967), *Thomas Hardy*, New York.
Hutchins, J. (1873), *The History and Antiquities of the County of Dorset*, 3rd edn, Westminster.
Hynes, S. (1961), *The Pattern of Hardy's Poetry*, Chapel Hill.
Ingham, P. (1980), "Hardy and the Cell of Time", in Clements and Grindle (eds), pp. 119–36.
Jacobus, M. (1982), 'Hardy's Magian Retrospect', *Essays in Criticism*, 32: 258–82.
Johnson, H.A.T. (1977), '"Despite Time's Derision": Donne, Hardy, and the 1913 Poems', *Thomas Hardy Yearbook* 6: 7–20.
Johnson, T. (1979), '"Pre-Critical Innocence" and the Anthologist's Hardy', *Victorian Poetry* 17: 9–24.
Jones, B. (1981), 'Hardy and the End of the Nineteenth Century', *Thomas Hardy Society Review* 1(7): 224–8.
Jones, L. (1980), 'Leslie Stephen and "Nature's Questioning"', *Thomas Hardy Society Review* 1(6): 190–3.
King, K. and W.W. Morgan (1979), 'Hardy and the Boer War: A Public Poet in Spite of Himself', *Victorian Poetry* 17: 66–83.
Knoepflmacher, U.C. (1990), 'Hardy Ruins: Female Spaces and Male Designs', *PMLA* 105: 1055–70. Reprinted in Higonnet (1993).
Landow, G.P. (1980), *Victorian Types, Victorian Shadows*, London.
Larkin, P. (1966), 'Wanted: Good Hardy Critic', *Critical Quarterly* 8: 174–9. Reprinted in *Required Writing: Miscellanous Pieces 1955–1982*, London (1983).
Leavis, F.R. (1940), 'Hardy the Poet', *Southern Review* 6: 87–98.
Leavis, F.R. (1953), 'Reality and Sincerity', *Scrutiny* 19 (2): 90–8. Reprinted in *The Living Principle* (1975).
Lucas, J. (1986), *Modern English Poetry from Hardy to Hughes*, London.
McCarthy, R. (1980), 'Hardy's Baffled Visionary: A Reading of "A

Sign-Seeker"', *Victorian Poetry* 18: 85–90.
MacDougall, H.A. (1982), *Racial Myth in English History: Trojans, Teutons, and Anglo-Saxons*, Montreal.
Mahar, M. (1978), 'Hardy's Poetry of Renunciation', *ELH* 45: 303–24.
Marsden, K. (1969), *The Poems of Thomas Hardy*, London.
Mason, M. (1988), 'The Burning of *Jude the Obscure*', *Notes and Queries* 233: 332–4.
Meynell, V., ed. (1940), *Friends of a Lifetime: Letters to Sydney Carlyle Cockerell*, London.
Miller, J.H. (1970), *Thomas Hardy: Distance and Desire*, Cambridge, Mass.
Miller, J.H. (1982), *Fiction and Repetition*, Oxford.
Miller, J.H. (1985), *The Linguistic Moment: From Wordsworth to Stevens*, Princeton.
Miller, J.H. (1990), *Tropes, Parables, Performatives: Essays on Twentieth Century Literature*, London (reprints several earlier essays on Hardy).
Millgate, M. (1982), *Thomas Hardy: A Biography*, New York.
Millgate, M. (1992), *Testamentary Acts: Browning, Tennyson, James, Hardy*, Oxford.
Morgan, W.W. (1974), 'Form, Tradition, and Consolation in Hardy's "Poems of 1912–13"', *PMLA* 89: 496–505.
Murfin, R. (1978), *Swinburne, Hardy, Lawrence, and the Burden of Belief*, Chicago.
Murfin, R. (1982), 'Moments of Vision: Hardy's "Poems of 1912–13"', *Victorian Poetry* 20: 73–84.
Neuman, S.C. (1980), '"Emotion Put into Measure": Meaning in Hardy's Poetry', in Clements and Grindle (eds), pp. 33–51.
Orel, H. (1976), *The Final Years of Thomas Hardy, 1912–1928*, London.
Page, N., ed. (1980), *Thomas Hardy: The Writer and His Background*, London.
Paulin, T. (1975), *Thomas Hardy: The Poetry of Perception*, London.
Paulin, T. (1982), 'Words, in all their intimate accents', *Thomas Hardy Annual* 1: 84–9.
Paulin, T. (1987), 'Hardy and the Human Voice', *Thomas Hardy Journal* 3 (1): 30–7.
Peck, J. (1972), 'Hardy and the Figure in the Scene', *Agenda* 10 (2–3): 117–25.
Perkins, D. (1959), 'Hardy and the Poetry of Isolation', *ELH* 26: 253–70.
Perkins, D. (1976), *A History of Modern Poetry: From the 1890s to the High Modernist Mode*, Cambridge, Mass.
Persoon, J. (1986), 'Once More to "The Darkling Thrush": Hardy's Reversals of Milton', *CEA Critic* 4; 76–86.

Pinion, F.B. (1976), *A Commentary on the Poems of Thomas Hardy*, London.
Pinion, F.B. (1977), *Thomas Hardy: Art and Thought*, London.
Pinion, F.B. (1990), *Hardy the Writer*, London.
Pound, E. (1938), *A Guide to Kulchur*, London.
Purdy, R.L. (1954), *Thomas Hardy: A Bibliographical Study*, London.
Ramazani, J. (1991), 'Hardy's Elegies for an Era: "By the Century's Deathbed"', *Victorian Poetry* 29: 131–44.
Richards, I.A. (1979), 'Some Notes on Hardy's Verse Forms', *Victorian Poetry* 17: 1–8.
Richardson, J. (1977), *Thomas Hardy: The Poetry of Necessity*, Chicago.
Robinson, P. (1982), 'In Another's Words: Thomas Hardy's Poetry', *English* 31: 221–46.
Rosenbaum, B. (1990), *Index of English Literary Manuscripts, Vol. IV, 1880–1990, Part II, Hardy-Lamb*, London.
Rosenthal, M.L. and Gall, S.M. (1983), *The Modern Poetic Sequence*, New York.
Rutland, W.R. (1938), *Thomas Hardy: A Study of his Writings and their Background*, Oxford.
Said, E.W. (1975), *Beginnings: Intention and Method*, New York.
Sacks, P. (1985), *The English Elegy*, Baltimore.
Schweik, R.C. (1984), review of Vols I and II of *The Complete Poetical Works of Thomas Hardy*, ed. S. Hynes, *Victorian Poetry* 22: 341–5.
Sexton, M. (1991), 'Phantoms of His Own Figuring: The Movement Toward Recovery in Hardy's "Poems of 1912–13"', *Victorian Poetry* 29: 209–26.
Shaw, W.D. (1987), *The Lucid Veil: Poetic Truth in the Victorian Age*, London.
Simpson, P. (1979), 'Hardy's "The Self-Unseeing" and the Romantic Problem of Consciousness', *Victorian Poetry* 17: 45–50.
Smith, S. (1982), *Inviolable Voice: History and Twentieth Century Poetry*, Dublin.
Snell, K.D.M. (1985), *Annals of the Labouring Poor: Social Change in Agrarian England*, Cambridge.
Southworth, J. (1947), *The Poetry of Thomas Hardy*, New York.
Stallworthy, J. (1980), 'Read by Moonlight', in Clements and Grindle (eds), pp. 172–87.
Steele, J.V. (1980), 'Thoughts from Sophocles: Hardy in the 90s', in Clements and Grindle (eds), pp. 67–82.
Taylor, D. (1981), *Hardy's Poetry, 1860–1928*, London.
Taylor, D. (1986), 'Hardy and Wordsworth', *Victorian Poetry* 24: 441–54.
Taylor, D. (1988), *Hardy's Metres and Victorian Prosody*, Oxford.

Taylor, D. (1990), 'Hardy's Missing Poem and His Copy of Milton', *Thomas Hardy Journal* 6 (1): 50–60.
Thatcher, D. (1970), 'Another Look at Hardy's "Afterwards"', *Victorian Newsletter* 38: 14–18.
Weatherby, H.C. (1983), 'Of Water and the Spirit: Hardy's "The Voice"', *Southern Review* 19: 302–8.
Widdowson, P. (1989), *Hardy in History: A Study in Literary Sociology*, London.
Wilson, K. (1976), 'The Personal Voice in the Poetry of Thomas Hardy', in *Budmouth Essays on Thomas Hardy*, ed. F.B. Pinton, Dorchester, pp. 205–17.
Witek, T. (1990), 'Repetition in a Land of Unlikeness: What "life will not be balked of" in Thomas Hardy's Poetry', *Victorian Poetry* 28: 119–28.
Wotton, G. (1985), *Thomas Hardy: Towards a Materialist Criticism*, Totowa, N.J.
Wright, D. (1972), 'Notes on Hardy', *Agenda* 10 (2–3): 66–74.
Wright, T.R. (1989), *Thomas Hardy and the Erotic*, London.
Wright, W. (1967), *The Shaping of* The Dynasts: *A Study in Thomas Hardy*, Lincoln, Nebraska.
Zeitlow, P. (1967), 'The Tentative Mode of Hardy's Poems', *Victorian Poetry* 5: 113–26.
Zeitlow, P. (1969), 'Thomas Hardy and William Barnes: Two Dorset Poets', *PMLA* 84: 291–303.
Zeitlow, P. (1974), *Moments of Vision: The Poetry of Thomas Hardy*, Cambridge, Mass.

Index of Titles

Poems are identified by poem number.

'According to the Mighty Working' 114
After a Journey 63
After a Romantic Day 122
After Reading Psalms XXXIX, XL, etc. 129
After the Last Breath 38
Afterwards 112
Aged Newspaper Soliloquizes, The 172
'ΑΓΝΩΣΤΩi ΘEVi 29
'And There Was a Great Calm' 116
Apostrophe to an Old Psalm Tune 79
At Castle Boterel 66
At Lulworth Cove a Century Back 118
At the Word 'Farewell' 80

Backward Spring, A 103
Beeny Cliff 65
Before My Friend Arrived 150
Bird-Catcher's Boy, The 151
Bird-Scene at a Rural Dwelling, A 132
Blinded Bird, The 87
Boy's Dream, The 174

Cathedral Facade at Midnight, A 134
Change, The 89
Channel Firing 44
Childhood Among the Ferns 161
Christmas: 1924 173
Christmas in the Elgin Room 176
Circular, A 61
Collector Cleans His Picture, The 119
Commonplace Day, A 16
Contretemps, The 115

Index of Titles

Convergence of the Twain, The 45
Copying Architecture in an Old Minster 83

Darkling Thrush, The 21
Days to Recollect 147
Dead Quire, The 36
Death-Day Recalled, A 64
Dream or No, A 62
Drinking Song 171
Drizzling Easter Morning, A 125
Drummer Hodge 12
During Wind and Rain 102

East-End Curate, An 137
Epilogue 182
Evening in Galilee, An 166
Eve of Waterloo, The 180
Exeunt Omnes 74

Family Portraits 175
Figure in the Scene, The 96
Five Students, The 100
'For Life I had never cared greatly' 107
Friends Beyond 6

George Meredith, 1828–1909 40
Going, The 51

Hap 2
Haunter, The 58
He Abjures Love 33
He Never Expected Much 168
Heredity 81
He Resolves to Say No More 178
He Revisits His First School 104
Her Haunting-Ground 136
Her Reproach 18
His Heart: A Woman's Dream 92
His Immortality 19
His Visitor 60

'I found her out there' 55
'I looked up from my writing' 111
'I look into my glass' 10
In a Eweleaze near Weatherbury 9
In a Former Resort after Many Years 133
In Front of the Landscape 43
Inscription, The 127
In Sherborne Abbey 143

Index of Titles

In Tenebris I   24
In Tenebris II   25
In Tenebris III   26
In the Cemetery   76
In the Mind's Eye   32
In the Small Hours   123
In Time of 'The Breaking of Nations'   109
'I thought, my Heart'   105
'I was the midmost'   126
'I watched a blackbird'   163

Julie-Jane   35

Lament   57
Last Signal, The   95
Last Words to a Dumb Friend   124
Later Autumn, The   136
Let Me Enjoy   34
Light Snow-Fall after Frost, A   141
Lines to a Movement in Mozart's E-Flat Symphony   90
Love-Letters, The   158
Lying Awake   160

Mock Wife, The   144
Moments of Vision   77
Monument-Maker, The   135
Musical Box, The   98
Music in a Snowy Street   142

Nature's Questioning   8
Near Lanivet, 1872   82
Neutral Tones   3
New Dawn's Business, The   154
New Year's Eve in War Time, A   110
Night in the Old Home   37
Nightmare, and the Next Thing, A   164
'Nothing matters much'   149
'Not only I'   145

Obliterate Tomb, The   72
Old Furniture   99
On a Midsummer Eve   86
One We Knew   39
On One Who Thought No Other Could Write Such English as Himself   183
On the Tune Called the Old Hundred-and-Fourth   120
Our Old Friend Dualism   170
Overlooking the River Stour   97
Oxen, The   93

Index of Titles

Peasant's Confession, The 4
Pedigree, The 91
Phantom Horsewoman, The 68
Photograph, The 94
Pity of It, The 108
Places 67
Poet, A 75
Poet's Thought, A 162
Prologue 181
Prophetess, The 156
Proud Songsters 155

Quid Hic Agis 85

Rain on a Grave 54
Respectable Burgher on 'The Higher Criticism', The 22
Revisitation, The 30
Rome: At the Pyramid of Cestius near the Graves of Shelley and Keats 15
Rome: Building a New Street in the Ancient Quarter 14

St. Launce's Revisited 70
Sapphic Fragment 28
Selfsame Song, The 117
Self-Unconscious 49
Self-Unseeing, The 23
Shadow on the Stone, The 106
Sheep Fair, A 139
Sign-Seeker, A 5
Sine Prole 138
Singer Asleep, A 48
Snow in the Suburbs 140
Song to an Old Burden 152
Souls of the Slain, The 13
So Various 165
Spell of the Rose, The 69
Standing by the Mantlepiece 169
Statue of Liberty, The 88
Surview 130

Temporary the All, The 1
Tess's Lament 27
This Summer and Last 148
Thoughts from Sophocles 179
Thoughts of Phena 7
Throwing a Tree 159
To an Unborn Pauper Child 17
To Shakespeare 84
Trampwoman's Tragedy, A 31

Under the Waterfall   50

Voice, The   59
Voice of Things, The   78
Voices from Things Growing in a Churchyard   121
V.R. 1819–1901   11

Waiting Both   131
Walk, The   53
'We are getting to the end'   177
Weathers   113
We Field-Woman   167
Wessex Heights   47
'When I set out for Lyonnesse'   46
Where the Picnic Was   71
Whitewashed Wall, The   128
'Why do I?'   153
Wind's Prophecy, The   101
Winter in Durnover Field   20
Wish for Unconsciousness, A   157
Without Ceremony   56
Workbox, The   73

Yell'ham Wood's Story   41
Young Man's Epigram on Existence   42
Your Last Drive   52

Index of First Lines

Poems are identified by poem number.

A bird sings the self-same song   117
A cry from the green-grained sticks of the fire   130
A forward rush by the lamp in the gloom   115
All hail to him, the Protean! A tough old chap is he   170
Along the sculptures of the western wall   134
Along the way   49
And he is risen? Well, be it so   125
A senseless school, where we must give   42
As I drive to the junction of lane and highway   66
As I lay awake at night-time   30
As 'legal representative'   61
A small blind street off East Commercial Road   137
A star looks down at me   131
At last I put off love   33
At midnight, in the room where he lay dead   92
Attentive eyes, fantastic heed   75

Beeny did not quiver   64
Beside the Mead of Memories   36
Breath not, hid Heart: cease silently   17
Bright baffling Soul, least capturable of themes   84

Can it be so? It must be so   146
Change and chancefulness in my flowering youthtime   1
Christmas Eve, and twelve of the clock   93
Clouds spout upon her   54
Con the dead page as 'twere live love: press on!   18
Coomb-Firtrees say that Life is a moan   41

Dead shalt thou lie; and nought   28
Do I know these, slack-shaped and wan   133
Do you recall   147

Index of First Lines

Everybody else, then, going   74
Every branch big with it   140

'Father, I fear your trade'   151
For life I had never cared greatly   107
Forth from ages thick in mystery   138
Forty Augusts – aye, and several more – ago,   78
Forty years back, when much had place   40
From Wynyard's Gap the livelong day   31

Gone are the lovers, under the bush   136
Good father! ... It was eve in middle June   4

Had I but lived a hundred years ago   118
He does not think that I haunt here nightly   58
Here by the moorway you returned   52
Here is the ancient floor   23
Hereto I come to view a voiceless ghost   63
How I remember cleaning that strange picture!   119
How it rained   167
How she would have loved   57
How smartly the quarters of the hour march by   83

I am the family face   81
I bent in the deep of night   91
I chiselled her monument   135
I come across from Mellstock while the moon wastes weaker   60
I come, at your persuasive call   181
If but some vengeful god could call to me   2
If I could but abide   157
I found her out there   55
I idly cut a parsley stalk   86
I know not how it may be with others   99
I lay in my bed and fiddled   123
I leant upon a coppice gate   21
I looked up from my writing   111
I look into my glass   10
I mark the months in liveries dank and drear   5
'I meant to build a hall anon'   69
I met him quite by accident   158
I met you first – ah, when did I first meet you?   79
In a solitude of the sea   45
In this fair niche above the unslumbering sea   48
I sat one sprinkling day upon the lea   161
I sat on the eve-lit weir   150
I saw a dead man's finer part   19
I should not have shown in the flesh   104
I thought, my Heart, that you had healed   105
It pleased her to step in front and sit   96

I travel on by barren farms   101
It's a dark drama, this; and yet I know the house, and date   144
It sprang up out of him in the dark   162
It was your way, my dear   56
I walked in loamy Wessex lanes, afar   108
I was the midmost of my world   126
I watched a blackbird on a budding sycamore   163
I went by the Druid stone   106
I would that folk forgot me quite   27

Let me enjoy the earth no less   34
Long have I framed weak phantasies of Thee   29
Lifelong to be   98

'More than half my life long'   72

Nobody says: Ah, that is the place   67
'No mortal man beneath the sky'   183
Not a line of her writing have I   7
'Nothing matters much,' he said   149
Not only I   145
'Now shall I sing'   156

O my soul, keep the rest unknown!   178
Once upon a time when thought began   171
Only a man harrowing clods   109
On the flat road a man at last appears   141
On this decline of Christmas Day   164
O the opal and the sapphire of that wandering western sea   65
Out of the past there rises a week   89

'Peace upon earth!' was said. We sing it   173
Pet was never mourned as you   124
Phantasmal fears   110
Plunging and labouring on a tide of visions   43
Provincial town-boy he, – frail, lame   174

Queer are the ways of a man I know   68

'See, here's the workbox, little wife'   73
She looked like a bird from a cloud   80
She looks far west towards Carmel, shading her eyes with her hand   166
She told me how they used to form for the country dances –   39
Show me again the time   90
Silently I footed by an uphill road   95
Simple was I and was young   129
Since Reverend Doctors now declare   22
Sing; how 'a would sing!   35
Sir John was entombed, and the crypt was closed, and she   127

Slip back, Time!   70
So zestfully canst thou sing?   87

That mirror   77
That night your great guns, unawares   44
That was once her casement   32
The day arrives of the autumn fair   139
The day is turning ghost   16
The eyelids of eve fall together at last   180
The feet have left the wormholed flooring   152
The flame crept up the portrait line by line   94
The mightiest moments pass uncalendared   11
The moon has passed to the panes of the south-aisle wall   143
The railway bore him through   122
There are some heights in Wessex, shaped as if by a kindly hand   47
There had been years of Passion – scorching, cold   116
There have been times when I well might have passed and the ending have come –   26
There's no more to be done, or feared, or hoped   38
There was a stunted handpost just on the crest   82
These flowers are I, poor Fanny Hurd   121
These umbered cliffs and gnarls of masonry   14
The sparrow dips in his wheel-rut bath   100
The swallows flew in the curves of an eight   97
The thick lids of Night closed upon me   13
The thrushes sing as the sun is going   155
The trees are afraid to put forth buds   103
The two executioners stalk along over the knolls   159
The years have gathered grayly   9
They sing their dearest songs –   102
They throw in Drummer Hodge, to rest   12
The weather is sharp   142
This candle-wax is shaping to a shroud   169
This is the weather the cuckoo likes   113
This statue of Liberty, busy man   88
Three picture-drawn people stepped out of their frames –   175
Throughout the field I find no grain   20
Thus from the past, the throes and themes   182

Unhappy summer you   148

We are getting to the end of visioning   177
Well, World, you have kept faith with me   168
We never sang together   120
We stood by a pond that winter day   3
What are you doing outside my walls   154
'What is the noise that shakes the night'   176
'Whenever I plunge my arm, like this'   50
When I look forth at a dawning pool   8

When I set off for Lyonnesse   46
When I weekly knew   85
When moiling seems to cease   114
When the clouds' swoln bosoms echo back the shouts of the many and
  strong   25
When the inmate stirs, the birds retire discreetly   132
When the Present has latched its postern behind my tremulous stay   112
When the wasting embers redden the chimney-breast   37
Where we made the fire   71
Who, then, was Cestius   15
Who would here sojourn for an outstretched spell   179
Why did you give no hint that night   51
Why does she turn in that soft way   128
Why do I go on doing these things?   153
Why go to Saint-Juliot? What's Juliot to me?   62
William Dewey, Tranter Reuben, Farmer Ledlow late at plough   6
Wintertime nighs   24
Woman much missed, how you call to me, call to me   59

Yes; yes; I am old. In me appears   172
You did not walk with me   53
You may have met a man – quite young –   165
You, Morningtide Star, now you are steady-eyed, over the east   160
'You see those mothers squabbling there?'   76

Where's Je-rt-sha Timmons? 36
Where's Nicely Nicely? 52
When mother went to sew? 112
Who rides abroad, with a legions of her back, the ghosts of the many, and also, 25
When the mourn-ers turn in to refreshments? 157
Where the People' has landed I's posters behind the frontispiece? 112
What are waving embers radiant the chimney brook? 79
Who were inside the fire? 71
Who then was Ceasar? 13
Who could hear a turn or an unidentified spell? 170
Who did you see no liar that night? 51
Why does she turn till that sod out? 14
Who did you on bring these things? 131
Why so its battle Juliet West is fairly to met? 82
William, Dewey, Bradley, Reuben, Eleanor, bedded late at night at Minecomno valley? 24
Woman much raised how you call it the call it me? 53

Yes sir, I am old to the asperin? 172
You did not walk with me? 52
Yoh me have not I can't quite stamp? 105
Yon Mukonjaki, Sir, now you are see them describe the east? 160
You see the see mothers squabbling there? 98